Connecting the Dots
to the Caliphate

Connecting the Dots to the Caliphate

A Primer for the Thinking Person

Shanbreen

Strategic Book Publishing and Rights Co.

Strategic Book Publishing and Rights Co., LLC
USA | Singapore
www.sbpra.com

For information about special discounts for bulk purchases, please contact Strategic Book Publishing and Rights Co. Special Sales, at bookorder@sbpra.net.

ISBN: 978-1-68181-886-3

"Vers l'Orient compliqué, je volais avec des idées simples." ("Towards the complicated East I was flying with simple ideas.")

— Charles de Gaulle

Translated by Claude Girault, elected representative of France in the United States.

This book is dedicated to the memories of my daughter, Shanbreen; my parents; my sister, Fatima; and my brother, Yusuf.

Contents

Note on Title

The meaning of the words *"caliphate"* and *"caliph"* are often misunderstood by non-Muslims, as well as some Muslims. Contrary to many theories, these words do not connotate a "dark," hidden meaning. The caliphate is, basically, an area ruled under Islamic *Sharia* law, akin to the Vatican in Rome. The caliph, on the other hand, is a religious leader who is regarded in Islam as the successor of the Prophet Muhammad.

There are no known caliphs or caliphates existing in the world today, partly because of the divisiveness of modern Muslim communities; the widespread dissemination of Muslims around the world; and, most importantly, due to a lack of consensus among the many factions and sub-factions of Islam as to who their caliph "should" be. There are, however, some segments of the Muslim world that have made claims to the existence of a caliph without the prescribed format of caliphate, such as the small group of Shi'a Muslims living in India known as Dawoodi Bohras. The term "caliphate" referred to in the title, therefore, is merely a symbolic reference to an area where Muslims live— including places where there are pseudo claims to the existence of a caliph.

James E. Sowerwine, in his contribution to *Oxford Bibliographies*, provides the following meanings for the terms "caliph" and "caliphate": "The term 'caliph' is generally regarded to mean 'successor of the Prophet Muhammad,' while 'calipha' denotes the office of the political leader of the Muslim community or state.[1]

Although the caliph was not considered a spiritual authority akin to Muhammad, he presided over a state governed under Islamic law, whose territories constituted the "abode of Islam." Thus, "the caliph served as the symbol of the supremacy of the Sharia, as commander of the faithful, and as leader of prayers (*Imam*), which clothed the caliphate with religious meaning."

While Sunni Muslims believe the successor of Muhammad should be elected, leaving the decision to the community, Shi'a Muslims reject the, "Sunni notion of rightly guided (*Rashidun*) caliphs, a term used for the first four caliphs." Instead, they acknowledge the rightful succession of Muhammad's cousin and son-in-law, Ali ibn Abi Talib Ali, and his descendants.[2]

The Rashidun Caliphate (632–661) was followed by the Umayyad Caliphate (661–750) established by Mu'awiya in Damascus, Syria. The dynastic succession established by Mu'awiya lasted until a rival clan of the Quraysh tribe, the Abbasids, successfully revolted. The Abbasid Caliphate (750–1258) established a dynasty with its capital in Baghdad, though its control over the state was severely reduced during its last three centuries by rival secular rulers, including the Buyids and Seljuks along with the Fatamid Caliphate (909–1171) in Egypt, and the Umayyad Caliphate (929–1031) of Spain. The Ottoman conquest of the Mamluk state led to the establishment of the Ottoman Caliphate (1517–1924).[3]

While the terrorist group, Al-Qaeda, has made no claim to a caliph or a caliphate, its members subscribe to the creation of an emirate where Muslims can live under a conservative form of Sharia law without cultural and moral influences from the West. In its long-term fight to establish an emirate, Al-Qaeda has resorted, and continues to resort to terrorist activities. On the other hand, the leader of Daesh (ISIS), Abu Bakr al-Baghdadi, living in Raqqa, Syria (his supposed caliphate), has proclaimed himself caliph of all Sunni Muslims. Instead of implementing Sharia law in the governance of his caliphate, he preaches his own perverted, violent ideology, which is not in line with Islamic principles. It should be understood that al-Baghdadi, other than by his followers, was not duly elected by the Sunni Muslim community at large, of which he considers himself the caliph.

---

1. James E. Sowerwine, "Caliph and Caliphate," *Oxford Bibliographies*, December 14, 2009, http://www.oxfordbibliographies.com/view/document/obo-9780195390155/obo-9780195390155-0013.xml.
2. Ibid.
3. Ibid.

Acknowledgments

Books of this proportion and depth, covering a complexity of different interpretations, opinions, cultures, and ethnicities, are seldom written in isolation. This manuscript started off as an essay, but soon morphed into a book due to the numerous topics born from the discussion of a single point on this subject. In this context, I am grateful to a number of people across the world who were generous enough to have discussed their feelings, beliefs, and opinions (both Muslims and non-Muslims). They are too numerous to be acknowledged individually by their names.

Then there are those who provided me their invaluable critiques in the earlier stages of my writing. My dear friend, Claude Girault, whose help in matters of international affairs comes to mind; as does Tom Dingo, who reads everything I write. Even my friend, Michael Brunk, played a hand in "challenging" me with his knowledge of historical Islam.

A thank-you is also in order to my friend John Mason, for introducing me to Thomas Esper, past president of the Arab American Anti-Discrimination Committee, who helped me understand the nuances associated with discrimination, and boosted my confidence in being "on the right track." Many of my thoughts and doubts were also practiced on my friend John Sheppard, who always managed to ask the right questions, and on Halah Young, who instilled in me the importance of making the book read less like a textbook. Of course, it was also good to have my brother, Dr. Akil Taher, on my side. He is forever trumpeting on my behalf, especially when it comes to my writing.

My wife, Fatema, and my daughter, Shazeena, deserve a pat for putting up with me, especially when the proverbial "writer's block" hit, or research was hard to come by. I often wonder if I would have exercised the same patience they have shown if the shoe had been on the other foot.

Preface

The world is in turmoil, with each passing day bringing one more reason to scratch our heads and wonder: what next? In this book, I have tried to provide a logical path, which may not directly answer this question, but hopefully will provide some understanding of what, where, and why this war against the Islamic State of Iraq and Syria (ISIS) and Al-Qaeda is occurring. While a direct prescription of the military strategies required to fight this war lies outside the realm of this book, I sincerely hope the material will assist in the momentous task of understanding these enemies in the context of negating or countering their ideology.

Dr. Simon Cottee, an academic and senior lecturer in criminology at the University of Kent, England, brings to our attention that many Western leaders do not seem to know what ISIS' and Al-Qaeda's intentions are, or where the groups have come from.[1] In December 2014, Major General Michael K. Nagata, the special operations commander for the United States in the Middle East, stated that he had yet to figure out ISIS's appeal to its followers.[2] In his opinion, it was important to defeat the "idea," not just overcome the enemy militarily. However, defeating an idea rooted in lengthy historical consideration is likely not easy for people who have lived their entire lives in the context of the "idea." Not only would it take years of reconditioning to change their minds from such accumulated beliefs, but most importantly it would demand an answer to the question of what, in fact, *is* the "idea"? Confusion with respect to what is happening may have, according to the major general, "contributed to significant strategic errors," which in turn, could have led to further "justification" for extremist groups in carrying out their actions.[3]

This book is written to depict information that may have flown under the radar for many non-Muslims, as well as Muslims. It is my intention to evaluate and analyze popular information that exists in the collective consciousness of the West in order to preserve productive contextual understandings, or find "chinks in the armor" to rebuke such understandings. As a trained research scientist with a PhD in psychometrics, I am the author of various publications in scientific journals. However, I justify writing a book that is outside my scope of expertise on the same basis as Dr. Chris Martenson who has presented his analyses at such institutions as the United Nations (UN), the United Kingdom House of Commons, and the United States' State Legislature. Martenson believes that both his education and training inform and direct his thought processes, guiding him to reject or fail to reject hypotheses he develops.[4] Furthermore, being born in a Muslim family in Bahrain, having many Muslim friends, and having published both papers and books on various subjects, as a technical, fictional, and opinion writer, has been very helpful in my endeavor in writing this book. Such related publications of mine include *I, A Terrorist?*, a fictional book published by America Star Books, which was written several years prior to 9/11, and a fictional story titled "Homeless" from my anthology *Moments in Life*, published by Wild Child Publishing, which deals with profiling in the United States.

This non-fictional book derives much of its material from reports or presentations of scholars, media reports, research studies, journalist views, testimony of experts, and above all, from various Muslims and non-Muslims I have met in my travels to parts of Asia, Europe, the United States, and during my very early years spent as an assistant director of the lower Persian Gulf area at an advertising company.[5] I have, however, been careful about specifying sources in the text when it is an opinion or a point of view that is not mine, or is a direct quote by an author or reporter. Also, at times, there may be a sense of redundancy to a statement or a point made, but in each case, it is done to add to a different idea or concept in the context of the chapter under which it resides.

There are other books by experts on the subjects of terrorists and terrorism, and the manner of war taking place against ISIS and Al-Qaeda. They are all commendable, whether they outline the history of terrorist activities, depict how and why the current war is fought, or provide potential strategies for fighting such a war. In this book, however, I provide some perspectives on what the war means to Muslims, the role of the Israel-Arab conflict in the creation of Al-Qaeda, the causes of the birth of ISIS, and the need for language clarification in the identification of ISIS as "Daesh." I also touch on aspects of religion as it pertains to the various conflicts in the Middle East. But, beside these common denominators, I delve into sensitive issues for Muslims, such as the effect of drawing cartoons featuring Prophet Muhammad, the way religion is understood in the minds of Westerners in comparison to people of the East, the importance of "respect" in the context of relationships between countries – not trying to impose one's will over the other due to a superior military or political standing, and the effects of Western colonization and occupancy of Eastern lands. According to some scholars, the colonization of Eastern lands, likely perpetuated the belief that Westerners have instilled or tried to instill their cultural, ethnic, moral, and political values on Easterners with the inherent belief in their superiority with respect to Eastern mores.

The cause of Islamophobia in the West, which is at an all-time high, is also discussed. In this context, one can understand statements from famous TV personalities, such as Bill Maher in the United States, who states that Islam is violent because most *international* terrorists are Muslims. However, despite an appreciation of why some Westerners may come to his belief, it should be recognized that such violence is directed against the West by only a minute fraction of the 1.6 billion Muslims living in the world, which does not sit well with Maher's insinuations that the entire religion is prone to tendencies of violence. In this context, Christianity has never been accused of being a radicalized religion, even considering the activities of groups like the Ku Klux Klan (KKK) that used to murder Jews and African Americans in the United Sates, and spread terror by burning crosses (a religious symbol) on their front lawns. Such Christian extremists are generally prosecuted for racial intolerance, but never face accusations of Christian radicalization, even though some of them utilize their interpretation of the Bible in their perceived role as race purifiers. To further expound the point, Maher's comments are akin to saying that since most domestic crimes in the United States are committed by Christians, there is something within *all* Christians that encourages such behavior.

While these activities are seldom religiously condoned, "common" men often try to adhere to the lofty demands (whatever they are) of their own "personalized" *interpretative* religious calling. Unless the ultimate task of "forgiveness" for religious infractions is left to the respective god or gods, ideological actions promulgated by a religious body could promote counter actions against it, often inspiring others to illogical and cruel actions, which may fall outside the interpretative understanding of their own religious laws.

On the other hand, Mr. Maher is perhaps correct in expounding the rudiments of misogyny practiced by many Muslims around the world. While a gender divide is evident in the scriptures of most monotheistic, as well as polytheistic, religions, there is an effort — a movement, if you will — by the followers of these religions to close the gender gap. Such progress has also been noticed in Islam, although in Western eyes, it may be lagging way behind the progress made by other religions in terms of gender equality.

However, it is not religion alone, but gender-specific "rules" guided often by historically ingrained cultural beliefs that are the culprits of such prescribed gender roles. It is these cultural beliefs and practices observed within certain regions that often delineate gender-based behaviors, irrespective of the observed religion. For example, some Rajasthani women in India, who are Hindus, cover their faces and practice deference towards males, just like some Muslim women living in the same region.

Generally speaking, however, in some countries of the Middle East, particularly those in the Persian Gulf region, gender roles in the community are well-defined, even when most of us in the West strive for equality between males and females. There also seem to be innuendos in the West that Muslim males view all females as sex objects, and that the slightest contact, even if it is not physical, sparks all sorts of sexual insinuations, at times culminating in "honor" killings. As discussed in this book, there may be some truth to these allegations; however, once again, it should be noted that such behavior is promulgated by a small fraction of the total Muslim population who have a convoluted interpretation of Islamic beliefs, which are likely based on their cultural upbringing, or an *interpretation* of the scriptures to justify their self-serving behavior. For example, some ultra-conservative Muslims vouch for the justification of specific gender roles because it helps "control" women's "behavior." According to them, these gender-based rules contribute to a lower rate of sexual assault and rape crimes against women than in the West. While the veracity of such a statement, except for the opinions of a few Muslim men I have met during my travels, is not referenced, it goes without saying that such demeaning enforcement of laws against women's behavior *may* control criminal activities against them, but it is done at the price of women's freedom and rights, which are increasingly important issues in the Western world.

Muslim assimilation or integration, particularly as it pertains to Europe, also looms large on the horizon as a conduit for Islamophobia in the West. But aside from a reflection on the merits of assimilation and integration in terms of its effects on Islamophobes, the never-ending turmoil in the Middle East may also be a cause that enhances Islamophobia. For example, the recent conflict where Saudi Arabia, Egypt and Bahrain have demanded, among other things, the dissolution of *Al Jazeera Newspaper* operating from Qatar (a clear violation of freedom of speech forced upon a foreign country), and a stop to Qatar's rather cordial relationship with Iran, is likely one more reason that perpetuates a picture of Muslims being hostile and constantly fighting with others and among themselves.

The desire for hegemony in the region between the Iranians and the Saudis, is also an important variable in understanding the geopolitical policies in the Middle East. In this context, history is referenced when necessary, as is the dual role of the Persian Gulf monarchies with respect to their international policies, and the governing of their countries under the umbrella of being Islamic. This type of balancing act is particularly hard in most Islamic countries (especially in the monarchies of the

Persian Gulf), where the separation of state and religion does not exist.

This book further depicts an understanding of the internal and external conflicts within major countries in the Middle East based on their governance, the differences attributed to the different factions of Islam practiced, and the clashes among ethnicities living in the region. The issue of governance is further complicated when the majority Muslim faction is ruled by monarchs who believe in a different denomination of Islam than the belief of the majority in their populations. Furthermore, the perception of the West being unfair and as a creator of tensions in the region is examined from the point of view of Muslims from across the world. This book also contrasts the rise of Daesh and Al-Qaeda, and provides insight into the differential modus operandi of these terrorist groups and their beliefs, as a prelude to figuring out how to annihilate the "idea" based on relatively short-term activity, and the long-term effort that will be required in the creation of a less tremulous world.

As alluded above, in writing this book, I have depended heavily on others for information, particularly through the pinions of experts from world-renowned think tanks in the United States, England, and a few other parts of the world. These groups of experts are what many lawmakers, government officials, and media outlets have long relied on to provide independent policy analysis and scholarship. However, Washington D.C.-based correspondent Eric Lipton and his colleagues, Brooke Williams and Nicholas Confessore, writing in *The New York Times*, provide disturbing information that has emerged in recent years regarding the work of these experts. It seems that more than a dozen prominent research groups, such as the Brookings Institute and the Center of Strategic and International Studies, have received millions of dollars from foreign governments (mainly from the Persian Gulf Arab countries) in trying to persuade United States government officials to adopt policies that often reflect the donors' priorities.[6] While such transfer of money is done rather clandestinely, and seldom reflects the quid pro quo nature of the activity (if there is one), such activities set off troubling questions about intellectual freedom. For example, Amos Jones, a Washington lawyer who has specialized in the Foreign Agents Registration Act, is surprised, "at how explicit the relationship is between money paid, papers published and policy makers and politicians influenced."[7]

With Persian Gulf money pouring into Washington, researchers who express the sentiments of the donors are granted larger platforms, more job security, and more opportunities. Saleem Ali, a former visiting scholar at the Brookings Center in Qatar, was explicitly told not to write critically of the Qatari government.[8] While there is no doubt that most researchers would likely cave in to the demands of their sponsors and reach conclusions that are "friendly," or not detrimental to the governments financing the research, the situation, according to American businessman Max Fisher, who raises money for philanthropic and political endeavors, is not dire to the point of relaying "untrue" information. Although it seems that demands to stay away from publishing anything controversial about the sponsoring government is implicitly adhered to by researchers, there was an indication, according to Fisher's information from Washington's inner circle, and also by Eric Lipton and his colleagues, of an *explicit* quid pro quo between Norway and the United States. With reference to the emails exchanged between the respective parties, Norway was to donate money to the Center for Global Development, which in turn was expected to persuade government officials in the United States to increase funding for global forestry protection efforts by $250 million.[9] While such give-and-take relationships may be considered common in geopolitical affairs, it undermines the idea of democracy when lobbyist are paid to curry favors for foreign governments, as may have been done by Michael Flynn for the Russians, and recently in 2007 by the Saudis, as stated by Terence Cullen in the *New York Daily News*.[10]

To counter any doubts or suspicion of "controlled" or "biased" presentation, I have also included opinions and reports of scholars and researchers from other not-so-well-known institutions, from those who work independently, and even from online "prejudicial" propaganda. In all such references, I have tried to present the profile of the source as a subtle indication to help the reader assess the authenticity of such reporting, based on the principles of fairness and honesty. However, their additions to the discussion are important because they are indicative of the existence and festering of deep-rooted thoughts in both the West and the Islamic world that, as will be shown in the book, may not be well-represented by the mainstream media.

To untangle the differences in terminology among different authors, the media, and for the sake of adapting a uniform language throughout this book, certain liberties have been taken, among which the most important are:

1. Differentiation between domestic and international terrorism in the United States
2. The generic term used in identifying the countries included in the "West"
3. Countries identified as "Islamic" countries
4. The use of the words, "Islamism" and "Islamists"
5. Countries identified as belonging to the Middle East

The Central Intelligence Agency (CIA) in the United States gives detailed technical information as to what constitutes domestic terrorism and what constitutes international terrorism. In this book, however, to simplify the definitions of different types of terror, "international" terror in the United States, will encompass the spreading of terror by individuals based on a belief, an association or by an inspiration derived from a "foreign" group that has a political or a religious agenda in spreading terror. Therefore, all terror activities committed within the United States in the name of groups such as Al-Qaeda, and ISIS, will be deemed *international* terrorism. All other terrorist activities in the country by people who are motivated by hatred for others, based on religion, ethnicity, race, and anti-government views, but with their hatred not prescribed by a belief in an internationally-functioning terror group/s (Al-Qaeda, ISIS, Hezbollah), will be considered *domestic* terrorism. It should be noted that the definitions outlined above are within the detailed definition of international and domestic terror committed in the United States, as specified by the CIA.

In the context of the discussions in this book, "West" is used generically to encompass all countries of western Europe, the United States, Canada, Australia, and New Zealand. Though some people may consider Turkey a part of Europe, I have excluded it from this distinction (only to facilitate my discussions) because it straddles both Asia and Europe, has close proximity to Islamic countries in the Mideast, has *direct* involvement in the current conflict in Syria, and because the majority of its population are Muslims.

The basis for identifying an Islamic country will be the same as the guidelines set out in the membership application of the Organization of Islamic Conference (OIC), which requires the country to have adopted Islam as the official state religion, or that Islam is the country's primary religion, or that the country's majority population is Muslims, or that the country simply declares itself to be an Islamic Republic. By the same token, pluralistic countries such as Malaysia, where Muslims are in the majority, are considered Islamic countries even if they do not entirely adopt Islamic laws.

As explained in Chapter 1, the words "Islamists" and "Islamism" are used with similar meaning as attributed to radicalized Muslims and radicalized Islam respectively, so as not to disturb the familiarity of such terms for most readers. However, these terms are expanded to incorporate the violence associated in the furtherance of extremist ideology outside the country of origin, as practiced by known international terrorist groups, such as Al-Qaeda and Daesh.

There is also some liberty taken in regard to which countries are considered part of the Middle East. Because there is no real understanding of the demarcation between "Middle" and "Near" East in literature, a general rule of thumb used in this book is that besides the common countries of the Middle East, Islamic countries in North Africa (such as Egypt and Libya), and some countries in Asia (such as Pakistan and Afghanistan), are often referenced under the umbrella term, "Middle East."

To make the book read less like a textbook, I have tried to make it accessible by writing in a somewhat colloquial rather than entirely academic style. Despite the precautions taken in my attempt to make the book as reader-friendly as possible, I could not completely eliminate a somewhat academic presentation, simply due to the nature of research and the subject of the book. My apologies for that!

There may be cases, however, when not every source of information is attributed to an author who has quoted from other sources, but instead is attributed to the original source.

While such credit may not be directly given to the author in the main text of the book, it is nonetheless available for the reader in the Notes section provided at the end of the book. These notes may be particularly helpful, not only for relating information to the source of reference, but also for providing meaning and clarification related to some concepts, foreign words, and statements.

With respect to the content, I have tried to refrain from bias towards any one issue or any particular country, although being an American, there may occasionally be shades of prejudice in my writing with respect to my country. If it comes across as such, it is not because I am ethnically or religiously inclined (which I am not), but rather because I have tried, as far as possible, to reserve my opinions based on research-based evidence, the opinions of experts in the field, and the logic involved through verifiable examples or through empirical awareness, which may also include many hours of discussions with Muslims and non-Muslims alike.

In the final analysis, I leave the reader to discern the credibility of various information and nuances referred to in the book. Not all referenced sources may uphold the same lofty ideals of unearthing "untethered" truths as those expected from professional, well-reputed sources, but such sources should nonetheless provide a representation of the opinions and thoughts of some segments of the general public.

Introduction

The ongoing terrorist activities in several countries of the world have not only induced fear in the populations where these activities take place, but have also impacted the lifestyles of the general public in the terrorists' home countries. To a substantial degree, the world population has been affected, primarily with respect to security requirements within and outside their country based boundaries.

On one hand, fear of Al-Qaeda and the Islamic State of Iraq and Syria (ISIS) has precipitated lifestyle changes, such as stricter security checks while travelling by air, and before entering ballparks and other large-event venues in the United States. On the other hand, there seems to be a renewed determination in the heart of the public (particularly in the West) to destroy ISIS.

While such resolve on the part of the public is understandable, destroying ISIS is not an easy task. The enemy is a cruel monster with far reaching tentacles; forcing its ideology on Sunni Muslims, and seducing impressionable citizens of the world (particularly those who reside in the Middle East) to commit horrendous crimes. It kills all those who do not subscribe to its ideology, including those from the second largest denomination in Islam, known as Shi'as (see Chapter 5), who are considered by most Al-Qaeda and ISIS members as apostates.[1]

While there are likely different motives for committing acts of terror among members of such groups, their general motivating factor can be summed up as that which is steeped in a self-serving *interpretative* Islamic ideology. Such an ideology is partly based on a political agenda, promoted under the banner of an interpretative religious righteousness to give legitimacy to a minute number of disgruntled Muslims for their cruel and violent actions. This hateful ideology is further promulgated by calling its followers to martyrdom in the name of Islam, and promising them a heavenly abode for suicidal acts committed against the "non-believers" who are perceived as a threat, not so much to the practices of Islam, but to their perverted ideology.

Many discussions have taken place around the world about how one should protect their countries from the evil of today's terrorist threats. However, for all their resolve in destroying ISIS and Al-Qaeda, there is a simple realization among the countries involved that the military dominance of the United States will be required to lead the effort in eradicating such terrorist groups physically from the Middle East. Due to the atypical problem the West faces in the context of its war with ISIS and Al-Qaeda, particularly with respect to the random nature of the acts of terror occurring in several countries around the world, psychological aspects of the war have also become paramount to understanding ISIS. In this respect, the "labeling" of the enemy as "ISIS" by the media and politicians around the world, the interpretation of Islamic scriptures by terrorist groups, the differences in the ways that the East and the West approach religion, and the effect of religion on politics, are all quite telling.

But, besides understanding the "where," "how," "what," and "why" with respect to terror groups, there is also an interest in how we go about eradicating them. In this context, various insights from experts in the field are presented, such as that of Brookings Institute's Research Director, Professor Daniel Byman's testimony to the House Committee on Homeland Security in the United States. While military strategies for fighting the war against Al-Qaeda and ISIS are, as stated in the Preface, not within the scope of this book, the experiences of analysts and researchers produce a coherent picture of some actions the West has undertaken, or can undertake, in eradicating the idea based on terrorist ideology.

In order to consolidate the different aspects of this book and provide logical directive in its reading, the book is divided into three parts, listed below:

I.   Fundamental Knowledge for Understanding Islamism and Islamist Ideologies (Chapters 1 to 4)

II. The Rise and Spread of Islamists (Chapters 5 to 7)

III. Current Challenges and Strategies for the Future (Chapters 8 to 13)

In Chapter 1, I outline the importance of using precise language, primarily due to its effect on ISIS, the general Muslim population, and Islamophobes living in the West. Reasons are provided why ISIS should be called "Daesh." In addition, the issue of language and terminology also relates to the problem of different interpretive meanings and varying understandings of Islamic dogmas. Chapter 1 also identifies Islamists (Al-Qaeda, Daesh, and their associates) based on their activities as terrorist groups. In this context, the definitions of "Islamists" and "Islamism" are discussed in order to highlight the differences between the beliefs of terrorist groups and the beliefs of those who observe the strictest form of Islamic laws.

Chapter 2 discusses a few anomalies as examples of contradictions in religious scriptures, as well as some examples of similarities between the scriptures of the three major monotheistic religions of the world: Christianity, Islam, and

Judaism. The chapter defines how religion is used interpretatively and selectively by some people who acquire from it what is acceptable in their personal lives, and rejecting that which falls outside the demands of their chosen lifestyle. The chapter also expounds upon the meaning of *jihad*, and ends by comparing differing interpretations of Sharia law by Muslims and Islamists. It discusses how the latter uses these interpretive meanings to justify and compel others to adopt their agendas.

In Chapter 3, the importance of the Palestinian-Israeli conflict on the psyche of the Muslim population, as well as for terrorist groups trying to justify their violent actions, is brought to light. In this context, several topics are examined that personifies the role of Hamas, the role of the Muslim Brotherhood, the hatred between the peoples of Israel and Palestine emerging partly as a religiously based difference, and the factors at play in the Israeli-Palestinian conflict. The effect of profiling Prophet Mohammed through vile cartoons that are hateful for the Muslim population (although well-protected under the freedom of speech laws in the West) is also examined. The chapter ends with a reminder of the importance of respect accorded to countries in geopolitical dealings with them.

Chapter 4 discusses the fusion of religious and national laws in Islamic countries.

In Chapter 5, I outline the major religious factions in Islam, and depict how these factions, together with ethnic and cultural affiliations of the people in the region, have an impact on the governance of Islamic countries in the Middle East. Arabs and Iranians are differentiated not only by ethnicity and culture, but also by the religious faction they practice. Atrocities committed by autocrats against the minority population, based on religious divide, are examined, and the history of warfare between Iraq and Iran is discussed. Foreign intervention in these wars and the overthrow of Saddam Hussein are also examined in the context of instability in the region.

Chapter 6 focusses in detail on the birth, rise, and functioning of Al-Qaeda and Daesh. In this chapter, differences between the two groups are outlined, and their justification for violence, their goals, and their impact on Mideast geopolitics are scrutinized. The chapter also touches on the West's differential efforts in warring with Al-Qaeda, Daesh, and the Taliban in Afghanistan.

Chapter 7 deals primarily with the spread of Islamism — the reason for its spread, and the conditions that allowed for its success. The chapter focuses on Islamic countries' claims of adherence to the Quran and *Hadith* (relating to Prophet Muhammed) when enforcing economic and social values in their countries, but concludes that they fall far behind in actually abiding by the teachings of Islam.

In Chapter 8, some problems with American policies in the Middle East and Afghanistan are examined. The chapter is divided into America's relationship with the Middle East in general, and with Saudi Arabia and Turkey in particular; the Arab Spring's effect on the Middle East; and America's venture into Afghanistan.

Chapter 9 discusses the role of Iran in the Middle East, the status quo that exists with respect to the United States' relationship with its Arab allies, and the justification of a proposed "friendlier" relationship with Iran.

In Chapter 10, I delve into the covert game being played in the region by the United States that occasionally does not work out as expected – as in the case of Al-Qaeda affiliate al-Nusra. In this chapter, the pull of religious fanatics in disrupting the stability of the region on religious grounds is provided, and the Kurds, as a major "fighting" force, are profiled with respect to their location and aspirations in the region. The problem of regime change is examined in the context of the country's population and the difficult role America has to play in the aftermath of the war.

Chapter 11 delves into the reasons for Islamophobia in the West, discusses some potential remedies, and examines the role the media and Muslims need to play, especially with an eye towards the type of Muslim population residing in the United States. Statistics from Pew Research group are also provided, addressing such fundamental issues as the wearing of veils and the obedience of women to their husbands.

In Chapter 12, the special circumstances of the present involvement of the United States and the West in various wars with Islamist terror groups in the Middle East (Iraq, Syria, Libya, and Yemen) are highlighted in terms of the West's reluctance to put its own boots on the ground, and its hesitation in confronting Russia in Syria. The unique nature of these wars is also examined with regards to citizens who enter the West after being radicalized, and Western citizens who are radicalized within the West — the so-called "lone-wolf" or "lone-wolves."

Finally, in Chapter 13, I present some peripheral thoughts on the relationship between the United States and Israel with respect to the Palestinian-Israeli conflict – unearthing Israel's standing in the region with its Muslim neighbors that goes beyond the conflict discussed in Chapter 3. The chapter ends with a summary evaluation of activity in the Middle East, and a projection of the United States' future course of action. This chapter also examines the effects of colonization and Western occupancy of the Middle East, particularly by the Europeans.

Part I:

Fundamental Knowledge for Understanding Islamism and Islamist Ideologies

Chapter 1

It's All in the Semantics

Discussing language implications can be a semantic fog, the lifting of which is important only to those who require a precise understanding of the language in question. However, for the sake of curbing Islamophobia, it is important to label ISIS in a manner that deters from inspiring prejudices against a segment of our population. As a bonus, a delegitimizing or derogatory identifier for ISIS should be an additional reason for using it, because it would be hated by the terrorist group which is at war with us.

It should be noted that acronyms such as ISIS (Islamic State of Iraq and Syria) and IS (Islamic State) are precisely what the so-called "Islamic State" wants everyone to use, primarily because they include the word "Islam," which lends legitimization and justification to ISIS's quest for a separate state for its constituents through the interpretation of religious dictates. In this context, it is important to note that according to journalist and author Fareed Zakaria's special on CNN, titled "Why They Hate Us?", it seems that many of ISIS's members are not educated, and have no accurate knowledge of Islamic scriptures. For ISIS, "ignorant" recruits are perhaps much more favorable because they are likely to be easily manipulated into subscribing to the group's radicalized interpretation of Islam.

Members of ISIS and Al-Qaeda would benefit greatly from an association between their activities and religion, because religion seems to be a great motivating factor for people of the Middle East. Especially vulnerable to recruitment are those who are poor, hopeless, and ignorant, to whom ISIS can sell its ideology in the name of Islam in return for a meal, a place to live and a reason to "belong." It is in ISIS's interest to entice Sunni Muslims (or at least get a sympathetic ear from the Sunnis who are, by far, the largest faction of Islam), by including references to religion into their conversations in formulating familiar and common ground between them. In this context, ISIS would love the inclusion of "Islam" in its name, partly due to its own sectarian ideology, but also because a name tied directly to Islam could far more easily evoke religious sentiments from some conservative religious Sunnis, a few of whom may have "latent" tendencies for transforming their "for-ISIS-sentiments" into action.

While most Sunnis do not subscribe to the ideology of radicalized groups, they may lend a sympathetic ear to them when and if battle lines are drawn based on religion, such as a divide between the Shi'as, Sufis, and Ahmadis on one side, and the Sunnis on the other. Based on ISIS's desire to associate Islam with its ideology, it behooves the West to remove "Islam," "jihad," and any other religious lexicon from the description of such terrorist groups. Removing religious references from the group's name would nullify the "godly" association in religious calls for Muslims to join the group. In other words, by removing the ability to recruit susceptible Muslims and some non-Muslim converts based on face-value religious legality, there may be a reduction in the numbers of recruits (however small) because such recruitments would, at least on the surface, no longer be justifiable as a command from Allah. The elimination of religious connotations from the name of terrorist groups may also be helpful in dissuading lone-wolves from justifying their behavior through the requirements of religious dictates.

Most importantly, however, the crux of the argument for eliminating "Islam" from the name is that such an action would not be appreciated by ISIS. The terrorist group would like to give religious significance to the war in an effort at winning Sunni support through a call of religious dictates, even though their *interpretative* belief in Islam is far removed from what the vast majority of Muslims' belief.

An ideal solution would be to simply refer to the group as "terrorists," but a designation of this sort could be problematic since it is also used for those who commit domestic terror. It also would likely be ineffective on followers of ISIS, who could easily relegate it to a generic term, which to them would be akin to "name-calling" by the non-believers.

However, as luck would have it, a more corrosive name for ISIS has surfaced, which is fortunately hated by them. As referenced by world leaders such as David Cameron of the United Kingdom, Francois Hollande of France, Tony Abbott of Australia, and Barrack Obama of the United States, the word "Daesh" is now often used instead of "ISIS." The name Daesh is an acronym for the Arabic phrase *Al-Dawlah Al-Islamiyah Fe Al-Iraq wa Al-Sham*, which in English means the Islamic State of Iraq and Syria.[1] Often "IS" or "ISIL" is used by the media and politicians, where the "L" stands for "Levant," which refers to Syria and the vaguely defined land around it, likely including Lebanon, Israel, Palestinian territory, and Jordan. However, it could also reach as far as Saudi Arabia and Yemen on one side, and Turkey on the other, depending on Daesh's definition of how many of the surrounding countries around Syria are included in the term "Levant."

Writer, editor, researcher, and Arabic translator, Alice Guthrie, states that the use of the name "Daesh" is important because it delegitimizes the group's activities. According to her, the transliteration of D.A.E.S.H lends itself well to satire and humor, which are essential weapons for those in Syria who are trying to resist the group's advances. For many Syrians, satire is not only an act of defiance but also a coping strategy in their nightmarish fight against the violent extremist group. In satirical Arabic media and conversation, various diminutives of the word that elegantly belittle Daesh have gone viral, patronizing and relegating them to insults, making the name sound silly and powerless, but most importantly implying they are monsters.[2]

As well as being an acronym, Guthrie explains that the word is only one letter different from the word 'Dahesh," or, as social audience editor of *Mirror Online*, Nicola Oakley, and her colleague Suchandrika Chakrabarti state, "those who sow discord."[3] Daesh reportedly hates the label so much that, according to *The Guardian* correspondent Matthew Weaver, it has threatened to cut off the tongue of all those who use the name. They prefer, at the behest of Abu Bakr al-Baghdadi, the leader of Daesh, to be called the "Islamic State" (IS).[4] The use of "IS" (Islamic State) is preferable by al-Baghdadi, perhaps because "ISIL" promotes a restriction on the location of Daesh's caliphate as stated by the area identified within its name – Iraq, Syria and the Levitant, which is not the case in using "IS" as an acronym for its name.

The real utility of the name "Daesh," therefore, lies in the fact that it undermines the group's activities, which could have a powerful psychological advantage, specifically in the Middle East, where importance is given to names that include religious connotations. Most importantly, however, "Daesh" should be the name used to identify ISIS because of the hatred al-Baghdadi and his followers have for it.

Disputing over names may seem rather trivial at this stage of the conflict, especially since the repeated use of the titles

"ISIS," "ISIL", and "IS" by the media and government officials has them well-integrated into the Western lexicon. However, its purpose as a "hateful" name for the terrorist group cannot be understated. Even though the various alternatives are now well-entrenched into Western vocabulary, the word "Daesh" is already being used by some in the United States, and many others around the world. Therefore, its usage can be successfully adopted by the media without major effect on their reporting. Such an effort is definitely not as crucial as it would have been in the early stages of the war, but it is worth using if it causes even an iota of discomfort for the terrorist group in its final days. Most importantly, however, the change in terminology would be useful for restarting the debate within the West about the perceived role of Islam in the war against Daesh.

It should be noted that language nuances can be very telling in formulating opinions in the West, especially for those who suffer from Islamophobia. For example, the promise of 72 virgins in paradise has been a source of embarrassment for most Muslims, despite it seemingly being a source of motivation for members of Daesh and Al-Qaeda. While a number of virgins is not specified in the Quran, it is, according to Ibn Warraq's special report on religions in Britain (also published in *The Guardian*), incorporated into the rewards of heavenly life through a lesser-known hadith (traditions of Islamic life in the times of Prophet Muhammed) collected by al-Tirmidhi in the *Book of Sunan*.[5] Furthermore, according to the *Encyclopedia of Islam (Third Edition)*, even orthodox Muslim theologians such as al-Ghazali and al-Ash'ari have "admitted sensual pleasures in paradise."[6]

Ibn Warraq describes the sensual rewards in paradise from the Quran through various surahs and verses. The author quotes from the celebrated Penguin translation by N.J. Dawood of Surah 56, Ayahs 12–39:

They shall recline on jeweled couches face to face, and there shall wait on them immortal youths with bowls and ewers and a cup of purest wine (that will neither pain their heads nor take away their reason); with fruits of their own choice and flesh of fowls that they relish. And theirs shall be the dark-eyed huris, chaste as hidden pearls: a guerdon for their deeds... We created the huris and made them virgins, loving companions for those on the right hand...."[7]

In Surah 55, Ayahs 72–74, Dawood translates the Arabic word *huris* as "virgins," as did early commentators on this verse. It should be noted that the context in which "huris" is used makes it clear that "virgins" or "maidens" is the appropriate translation because it imparts a human characteristic upon them (being dark-eyed).[8]

In the context of Dawood's translation, many Muslims have downplayed the importance of materialist and sexual rewards in such descriptions of paradise. However, in recent years, sensual references, especially with sexual implications, are negated by German researcher and author, Christoph Luxenberg, in his book *The Syro-Aramaic Reading of the Koran: A Contribution to the Decoding of the Koran*, which, according to many Muslim scholars, is arguably the most important book written on languages in the Quran. Luxenberg shows that many obscurities in the Quran disappear if certain words are read as Syriac and not Arabic. Syriac is an Aramaic dialect and the language of Eastern Christianity — a semitic language closely related to Hebrew and Arabic. In Syriac, the word *hur* is a feminine adjective meaning "white," applying to the noun "raisin," which is understood implicitly. The doe-eyed *huris*, therefore, is translated as "white raisins" of "crystal clarity" rather than doe-eyed and ever-willing virgins. Similarly, the immortal, pearl-like youths mentioned in surahs like 76:19, are, according to Luxenberg, a misreading of a Syriac expression meaning "chilled raisins" (or drinks), which the faithful will have the pleasure of tasting instead of the boiling hot drinks promised to the unfaithful and damned. The author claims that the context makes it clear that it is food and drink being offered and not unsullied maidens.[9] With respect to these new revelations, Ibn Warraq jokingly points out that it would do well for suicide bombers to abandon their culture of death and instead concentrate on getting laid 72 times in *this* world, unless they prefer chilled white raisins as a substitute for virgins in the afterlife.[10]

For non-Muslims and Muslims alike, the use of words from a different language to articulate preconceived expectations may seem to be a tremendous leap in faith. However, keeping in mind that Syriac is very close to Arabic, there is a great likelihood that these words were adopted from one language to another. As an example of this phenomenon, "thank you" has been adapted into Gujarati, a language spoken in India, due to the Indians' exposure to English by the British Raj. This word is even found in the vocabulary of those who speak "pure" Gujarati, not just those with a mixed dialect. Similarly, one can understand that Syriac could have been used for specific words and references, especially in Arabic, which resembles it closely. Furthermore, the words make contextual sense, thus giving the translation further legitimacy. Most importantly, its validity is solidified by the fact that it is what most Muslims interpret it to mean.

If accepted, the Syriac translation offered by Luxenberg would likely pacify Muslims hard-pressed to explain the previously referenced, rather sexual and exploited role played by women in Islam — they would now have a "new" understanding of the surahs through a "justifiable" translation that meets with their expectancy of a non-derogatory role for women in their religion. The new translation could also be an eye-opener for non-Muslims who may have preconceptions about the treatment of women in Islam. Aside from such revelations, the new translation may also have negative consequences for Al-Qaeda, because it nullifies a major motivator used in their recruitment strategies for Muslim men. Such targets are likely to already have an expectation of a full belly in paradise, but the additional bonus of limitless women for their pleasure is completely delegitimized by Luxenberg's translation. For Daesh, however, there is no difference. It can continue to entice the disfranchised uneducated Muslim men with promises of 72 virgins in heaven because most uneducated recruits are not likely to question what they cannot understand or read for themselves.

In the context of the discussions above with respect to the importance of semantics, it is evident that labeling terrorists as "radicalized-Muslims" would also not sit well with most Muslims, who are not radicalized and do not believe in such radicalized forms of Islam. While one can never condone the atrocities performed in the name of any religion, from Daesh and Al-Qaeda's points of view, the formulation of political policies by using the power of religion to gain compliance from religiously motivated populations can be quite tempting. In this context, terms that have an attachment to Islam (such as "radical Muslims" and "radical Islam") could inadvertently appeal to disfranchised Muslims who might, as stated earlier, find justification for their violent acts through the association with a higher authority.

The use of terms like "radicalized Islam" may also have an added side-benefit for Daesh and Al-Qaeda in that the disenfranchised youths in the West would likely be more drawn to radicalized Islam than the more popular, peaceful version of it. In other words, it is likely that impressionable youth, whether in search of adventure, victimized by subtle or explicit forms of racism or Islamophobia, shunned by the society they live in, or suffering from mental health issues, may find that the more radicalized the religion, the greater its lure of violence, adventure, and thus its acceptability to them. It should be noted, however, that this is just an opinion, with no known studies or literature from experts to justify the link between the interpretative radicalization of a religion and the violence committed in its name.

There is yet one more reason why terms like "radicalized Muslims" and "radicalized Islam" may not be the best choices as identifiers for followers of Daesh and Al-Qaeda. While speaking with an old Muslim man in India, who had just a rudimentary knowledge of English, it became apparent that he was upset that Islam was being considered as radicalized. Even after careful explanation that it was not Islam itself that was seen as radicalized, and that not all Muslims were considered radical, but rather it was terrorist groups such as Al-Qaeda and Daesh who were using religion in the "wrong way," he was still not entirely convinced by my explanation. This may be an isolated incident, but it gives us a sense of the impact such associated words and terms can have on people, especially when such words are not a part of their native language.

In retrospect, disassociating Islam from the identification of Daesh and Al-Qaeda members and their ideology would have been relatively easy to do. For example, a word such as *"kafir"* (a derogatory Arabic term for a person who rejects or disbelieves in Islam) to denote members of Daesh and Al-Qaeda, and *"kafirism"* (a made-up word relating to the ideology of a *kafir*) to denote their beliefs would have worked better than calling these international terrorists "radicalized Muslims" and their ideology "radicalized Islam," respectively.

However, terms such as "radicalized Muslims" and "radicalized Islam" have been bandied around for some time in the United States. These words have now come to be used by Americans as a differentiation from their understanding of "regular" Muslims who believe in Islam. Some academicians and others, have taken the liberty to use different identifiers, but have still included religious connotations in their labeling. For example, Dr. Qanta Ahmed, a board-certified British medical doctor, newspaper columnist, and author of the *In the Land of Invisible Women: A Female Doctor's Journey in the Saudi Kingdom*, identifies radicalized Muslims and radicalized Islam as "Islamists" and "Islamism" respectively.[11] The usage of these words has a relatively large acceptance in the United States and elsewhere in the Western world, within Dr. Ahmed's contention that the use of the word "Islamists" does not encompass *all* Muslims in the minds of Americans. Concurring with Dr. Ahmed, and others such as Dr. Daniel Pipes, president of the Middle East Forum (a Philadelphia-based think tank), it seems likely that most Americans have disassociated the violent interpretative form of Islam (Islamism) from the non-violent interpretative of it, and have, as such, learnt that while Islamism and Islamists are synonyms for radicalized Islam and radicalized Muslims respectively, Islamism is not Islam and Islamists are not Muslims.[12]

Using the blanket label of "Muslims" for Islamists, as is used in some countries, is evidence of a lack of understanding of the difference between the two.[13] Such a misunderstanding could lead to unwarranted mass hysteria against Muslims based on the perception that Islam, the religion of billions of Muslims around the world, commits violence and cruelty against "non-believers." However, this type of a belief among peoples around the world can be understandable because, at the present time, no other non-Muslim terrorist groups are fighting a war based on a religious platform. Moreover, these types of religious attributes toward common Muslims are perpetuated by Daesh and Al-Qaeda, because "Islamist" and "Islamism" do not exist in their vocabulary. The followers of these terrorist groups acknowledge their actions as those of Muslims (not Islamists) undertaken in the name of Islam (not Islamism).

At this stage of the conflict, the replacement of well-entrenched terminologies in the identification of terrorist groups seems rather inconsequential, especially since it wouldn't have as significant an impact on terrorist groups as say, calling ISIS "Daesh." Earlier in the war, it would certainly have made some difference for would-be terrorists if derogatory terms had been used instead of identifying Daesh and Al-Qaeda members as radicalized Muslims who practiced radicalized Islam, or as Islamists practicing Islamism. However, because of the familiarity with these well-established terminologies by the general public, and the fact that replacing old lexicons with completely new terminologies is not practical or useful, based on the advanced state of the conflict with Daesh and Al-Qaeda, they will also be used in this book with some modifications -- Islamists will be referenced as those who *violently* enforce their religious ideology (Islamism) on others -- irrespective of where they reside -- and they fight a military jihad without following the basic tenets of Islam that instructs on how and against whom the war would be justified.

In this context, it is important to note that some people may construe "Islamism" with the ideology of ultra-conservative Sunni sects, such as the Wahhabis, and the Salafists. However, while Islamists have the same fundamental reckoning of a very strict form of religious and cultural behavior, they also advocate their own separate diabolic *interpretation* of Islamic scriptures that justifies violence against innocent people (including women and children) who do not believe in Islamism. When ultra-conservative Muslims operate both inside *and* outside the sphere of country-containment, using terrorism against those who they *perceive* to be a threat to Muslims or to Islam, or against those who do not abide by their literal, pedantic interpretation of Islamic laws, then these Muslims are considered to be Islamists, with Islamism as their ideology. In other words, the Wahhabis, Salafists, and other ultra-conservative factions of Islam are not Islamists — they are Muslims who practice an ultra-conservative form of Islam, within the confines of their own countries. It is in this context that the Taliban defined as a terrorist group operating in Afghanistan, is not considered Islamist, even though its members have been known to clandestinely crisscross from Afghanistan into Pakistan and vice versa – generally speaking, not for the purpose of terrorism, although an occasional flare-up has been observed on both sides of the border.

Unless otherwise stated, Islamists, in this book, will be used as an identifier for members belonging to the two major Sunni Muslim terrorist groups, Daesh and Al-Qaeda, and their associates. While Islamists are characterized as those belonging to the Sunni faction of Islam, Shi'a groups, such as those in Iran or backed by Iran, could also have a hostile agenda. However, the Iranian-based terrorist agenda is very different from that of the Islamists, and since it has hardly carried out any violent activities *in* the West, its violent activities are not considered as those of the Islamists. [14]

Chapter 2

Comparing Different Religious Scriptures, and the Sharia Law

Generally speaking, most common Muslims, including those who live in the Persian Gulf region, reject Islamism. If one were to propagate a radicalized form of Islam as a cause for Daesh and Al-Qaeda's ideology, a pseudo veneer of Islamic interpretation could be attributed to the terrorist groups. This ideology could then be seen as the groups' efforts to control the state, run society, forcefully convert or manipulate Sunni Muslims to abide by the dictates of their distorted interpretation of Islamic laws, and give credence to a political agenda that side-steps peaceful Islamic beliefs by killing, enslaving or kidnapping for ransom, those whom it considers as non-Muslims or apostates. Such a definition for Islamist ideology falls in accordance with Daniel Pipes's succinct definition of Islamism as an ideology that demands man's complete adherence to a particular interpretation of the sacred laws of Islam (Sharia).[1] The followers of the ideology are *some* Muslims who have a deep antagonism towards those who do not subscribe to their beliefs, and have a particular hostility towards the West.

In 1998, Pipes claimed that Islamism was a powerful force that ran governments in Iran, Sudan, and Afghanistan, and was an important force of opposition in Algeria, Egypt, Turkey, Lebanon, and for the Palestinian Authority. While it is true that the author's definition of Islamism in 1998 may differ somewhat from that which is used in this book, it is worthwhile to note that Pipes's assertion identifies Islamism as country-based, and therefore not practiced across different denominations of Muslims in different geographical locations. But, while he stated that such a spread of the ideology can lead to economic contraction, to the oppression of women, to the spread of terrible human rights abuses, to the proliferation of arms, to terrorism, and to the spread of a viciously anti-American ideology, he did not include countries such as Saudi Arabia in such targeting. While there may be various differences between the laws of the Islamists and those of the Wahhabis in Saudi Arabia, Rori Donaghy and her colleague, Mary Atkinson, reporting in the *Middle East Eye*, state that according to the founder of the Emirates Centre for Human Rights, most of the punishments dealt out for breaking Islamic laws, especially for punishments for crimes "against the rights of God," are very similar, if not the same, between the Wahhabis and the Islamists.[2]

In attaching a philosophical argument to the derived meaning of Islamism, the movement can be seen as an effort to turn Islam, a religion, into an ideology that would return the power of Islam to its glory days (circa 1000 AC), where health, wealth, literacy, culture, and other indices of success were among the best in comparison to the world of Christianity, Judaism, Hinduism, and other non-monotheistic religions practiced at that time. But, the glories of yesteryears are hard to attain in present times. Other than the few efforts taken by small sheikdoms such as Dubai and Abu Dhabi in the United Arab Emirates (UAE), Muslims are no longer the harbingers of health, wealth, and literacy.

In analyzing the Muslims' fall from the pinnacle of success, the tremendous rise of Western civilization cannot be ignored. But, a more important reason to consider in the analysis of the Muslim empire's demise, which may have nothing to do with the growth of the Western empire, is to decipher its fall through internal factors that would likely include a lack of forward thinking and progression, and the belief that the Islamic empire declined from the height of its pinnacle because of modern religious innovations and an abandoning of the "pure" Islamic teachings of the seventh century. While a part of Muslims' reluctance for not advancing with the Western world's progressive phase could be attributed to complacency and nostalgia for an inexistent past, there are some of the opinion that there was an inherent fear among Muslims that such progress would distance them from their religious ideology.

All religions have their share of "old-school" thought, however, some Muslim factions, mainly in countries of the Middle East, have clung ardently to the belief in an Islamic society of "the past." This is particularly true of those who believe they are persecuted by other Islamic factions, or those who believe their beliefs are subtly undermined by the presence of hedonistic Western influence, as well as those who may be theologically "misguided." These ultra-conservative Muslims believe that the word of God cannot change, even though, according to a survey by the Pew Research Center, many Muslims believe that human beings have evolved over time.[3] According to these literal-minded Muslims, since God is omnipotent and all-knowing, the words related to the Prophet from God must remain unchanged in different circumstances and different times. These people take the scripture very literally, without consideration of historical context.

While this may be seen as a noble undertaking for conservative Muslims, the same literalized belief is not followed as restrictively by the conservative followers of other monotheistic or by polytheistic religions. Other religions seem to have included important historical and circumstantial considerations in the molding of their present-day following. In this context, most of these religious people have evolved to accommodate advances in science and technology, as well as cultural and moral changes that occur in society over time.

While these changes have also been recognized, although with different degrees of acceptance, by large populations of Muslims living in places such as Mali, Russia, Nigeria, Malaysia, Indonesia, Morocco, most parts of India, and even in some parts of the Arab world, such as Dubai, Muslims as general rule, seem to have been careful in not sculpting or molding their religious beliefs to accommodate the impositions introduced by a changing society, for fear that advances in the sciences would be in contradiction to their religious beliefs. The unwillingness to change over time has many ultra-conservative sects of Islam stuck in the past, clinging to their literal understanding of a "pure, unscathed" Islam, founded more on regional culture than actual Islamic doctrine. The outcome of such an intense adherence to the glories of the past, has not only restricted progress, but in abandoning the credible scholarly material developed over different time periods, it has allowed the fermentation and growth of extremist ideology offered by groups like Al-Qaeda and Daesh.

As it stands, Daesh's ideology seems to culminate in an apocalypse, from which a supposed caliphate would emerge as a symbol of the next phase of the Muslim world, which would adhere to an adoption of interpretive, historically-based religious beliefs. However, to understand Islamism, one first needs to examine the interpretative understanding of Islamic scriptures vis-à-vis those of other religions.

Understanding Religious Scriptures

Many Westerners are xenophobic about Islam, with a rigid belief that Islam is incompatible with life in the West because it is rooted in misogyny and violence, and its scriptures are fundamentally different from the Bible. This belief could partially be based on ignorance or close-mindedness, but it is likely worsened by misinformed or biased media coverage. According to Nicholas Kristof, writing in *The New York Times*, even among religiously literate people (of all religions), there is a perceptual problem when it comes to understanding other peoples' religions, specifically due to the fact that all religions are a tangle of contradictory and conflicting teachings (for example, the harshness of Deuteronomy contrasted with the warmth of Isaiah in the Bible).[4]

These paradoxical teachings exist in the scriptures of each of the three Abrahamic religions. It is perhaps this issue which causes "confusion" for some Islamists when interpreting Islamic scriptures. For example, the Quran (Surah 2:256) explicitly states that "there is no compulsion in religion," yet later, in Surahs 4:89 and 9:11–12, it prescribes death for apostasy (as does the Bible in the Book of Deuteronomy). As mentioned, these paradoxical teachings are also prominent in Christianity, when St. Paul, writing to the Corinthians, emphasizes the prominence of love in the hearts of mankind, while in the Gospel of Matthew 10:34, Jesus is interpreted by some to have told the religious leaders that he came to bring "not peace but the sword."

To emphasize the interpretive and selective aspect of understanding monotheistic religions' scriptures like the Bible and the Quran, it should be noted that there are plenty of similarities between most major religions of the world. For example, most monotheistic religions do not tolerate gays and lesbians. Furthermore, both the Gospels of Matthew and Luke, together with the Quran, attribute Jesus' birth to a virgin. While most non-Muslims profess a subjugated role for women in Islam, the same is also true for other major monotheistic and polytheistic religions in the world. For example, in Leviticus 12:2–5, the Bible states that "...if a woman has conceived seed, and born a man child: then she shall be unclean seven days ... but if she bears a maid child, then she shall be unclean two weeks...."

However, one thing that stands out as especially degrading for women in Islam, is Surah 4:34 in the Quran, which according to its English translation states: "... as for those from whom you fear disobedience, admonish them and send them to beds apart and beat them. Then if they obey you, take no further action against them." According to some sources on the internet, this surah in the Quran explicitly allows the beating of women.[5] But, other sources assert that a plausible contextual explanation is given, specifically regarding the historical time period that the verse was written.

According to an explanation on the British-based Islamic site *Nour*, the fundamental rule of Quranic exegesis is that the explanation of the scriptures in the Quran also occur within the Quran itself. In other words, different parts of the Quran explain one another, and unqualified statements should be interpreted in light of qualified ones. Since the implied intensity of the "beating" mentioned in Surah 4:34, according to the site, has not been qualified in the Quran explicitly, it is to be interpreted with regard to the qualified statement made through the only other verse in the Quran that categorically refers to what people have labeled as "wife beating."

The verse in question focusses on the story of Job, who found himself in a dilemma, having taken an oath to beat his wife for blasphemy. Since this oath was in contradiction with

Prophet Muhammad's teachings — believers should not engage in "violent" and "unworthy" behavior towards their wives — Job was said to have asked for advice from the Prophet on how he should proceed. Because the oath made to God by Job could not be broken, Muhammad asked that Job "beat" his wife with soft grass or palm leaves instead. This non-violent behavior towards women is also exemplified in the Farewell Pilgrimage, a lengthy hadith on the final sermon the Prophet gave prior to his pilgrimage to Mecca for Haj. This hadith is included in *Sahih Muslim*, *Sunan Abi Dawud*, and *Sunan ibn Majah*, in which Muhammad stated:

> My last recommendation to you is that you should treat women well. Truly they are your helpmates, and you have no right over them beyond that — except if they commit a manifest indecency [*fahisha mubina*]. If they do, then refuse to share their beds and hit them without indecent violence [*fadribuhunna darban ghayra mubarrih*]. Then, if they desist, do not show them hostility any longer.[6]

The site, *Nour*, further explains the problems that come with translating the Arabic language to English, whereby "to beat" has very different connotations in English than in Arabic. In this respect, the connotation of violence is removed from "beating" in the Arabic context, relegating it to nothing more than a symbolic gesture provoked by a woman being unfaithful.

In the same vein, while Islam is considered violent by non-Muslims because of passages in the Quran stating that unrepentant idolaters should be sentenced to death, Christianity has shown itself to be equally as intolerant. For example, the Biblical leader Joshua (The Book of Joshua 6:21) massacred an entire city, including domesticated animals, saving only one

21

prostitute and her family. Furthermore, Christian abbot Arnaud Amalric, under the auspices of Saint Barnard, ordered a massacre of heretics and innocents alike with the explanation, "Kill them all. God will know his own."[7]

While it is not in the interest of these discussions to count the number of contradictions or similarities in the Quran, the Bible, the Torah, and the scriptures of other monotheistic and non-monotheistic religions, it is important to note that these scriptures were written through the interpretation of different human beings, often many years after the fact, who had their own understandings of the panorama unfolding before them. In this context, the differential interpretation of religious text and dogmas is true of every religion because the word of God through scholars and prophets is not written in absolute terms. These words are written not by God Himself, but by those who were close to the prophets (Moses, Jesus or Muhammad, for example) or by those who had been given the authority to write on such matters by the religious clergy or had a religious following (based on their interpretative understanding of the religion) to write on the subject at a particular period in history. It is, therefore, likely that these scriptures could have been interpreted differently depending on the writer's own religious understanding for the purpose of describing a particular meaning, or perhaps as an ulterior motive to fulfill a particular personal or denominational desire.

It is perhaps this particular interpretive nature of the scriptures which is responsible for the conviction of some Jews who believe that the land of Israel (including where the Palestinians dwell) is God's given gift to the people of Israel to build the Third Temple. A similar understanding is subscribed to by some Christians and Muslims who believe that the same land must be in *their* respective ownership prior to the coming of the Christian Messiah and the Muslim Mahdi.

Changes in cultural attitudes and beliefs also influence supposedly "divine" writings, specifically those that are written or revised over time. Importantly, it is the interpretation and context in which the text is written that is responsible for different understandings of the *same* words in the scriptures. In the fifteenth century, the Crusaders directly violated Jesus's prescription to "turn the other cheek" in favor of the entrenchment and spread of Christianity, stopping the spread of the Ottoman Empire with swords in their hands.

Even in today's world, the interpretative meaning of scriptures is often hard to decipher. As an example, a part of Surah 2:190–194 in the Quran is translated as:

> Fight in the cause of God those who fight you, but do not transgress limits; for God loves not transgressors. And kill them wherever ye catch them, and turn them out from where they have turned you out; for persecution and oppression are worse than slaughter; but fight them not at the Sacred Mosque, unless they (first) fight you there; but if they fight you, kill them.[8]

In the context of the surah outlined above (as well as similar ones, like Surahs 8.36, 8:39, 9:29, 9:33), Gregory Davis, who believes Islam to be religion of hate, states that, "the Quran's commandments to Muslims to wage war in the name of Allah against non-Muslims are unmistakable. They are, furthermore, absolutely authoritative, as they were revealed late in the Prophet's career, and so cancel and replace earlier instructions to act peaceably."[9]

While some non-Muslims, and even some Muslims, may find it hard to dispute Mr. Davis's understanding of the Islamic scripture, Muslim scholar Hasan al-Banna explains the underlying context in Surahs 2:190–194, stating that:

These verses were revealed at a time when Muslims of Madinah were under constant attack from the Makkans. An example would be when the Makkans conducted the public crucifixion of the companion of the Prophet Muhammad (peace and blessings be upon him), Khubaib bin Adi. These would be classified as 'terrorist activities' according to the modern usage of the term. So, what does this verse say in this context? 'Fight in the cause of God those who fight you, unless they (first) fight you there' — the context of this verse applies to those who initiate the attack against Muslims.[10]

To further expound the difficulty of how interpretative meanings and selective quotes are used by practitioners, or by those outside of the religion, the issue of the word and concept of jihad is a good example of that which is often viewed differently by Muslims and non-Muslims. The word "jihad," like some other words and statements in Islamic scriptures, has often been applied with a selective meaning, depending on the purpose and views of the applicator. This is true not only for Islamic scriptures, but also for other faiths and religions. However, in this book, to reach common acceptance of the meanings of words in the scripture, a consensus of the majority of Muslims is often relied upon when deciphering most-plausible meanings. Majority consensus is usually considered that which is espoused by authoritative bodies that have a majority or substantial following, such as the Islamic Supreme Council of America.

The meaning of jihad. According to the Islamic Supreme Council, the Arabic word "jihad" is often translated as "holy war," but in a purely linguistic sense, it means "struggling" or "surviving." In a religious sense, jihad has many meanings. It can refer to internal or external efforts to be good Muslims, as well as simple efforts to inform people about Islam. Jihad can be performed using anything from legal, diplomatic, economic, political, or military means. Military action is therefore only one means of jihad, and according to Sheikh Muhammad Hisham Kabbani (Chairman of the Islamic Supreme Council of America) and Sheikh Seraj Hendricks (Head Mufti, Capetown, South Africa), is very rare in the history of Islam. Some examples of sanctioned military jihad include the Muslims' battle against the Byzantine and Persian Empires during the early part of the establishment of Islam, and against the Crusaders during the Medieval period. According to the sheikhs, the concept of jihad has been utilized by many political and religious groups over the ages in a bid to justify various forms of violence. In most of these cases, Islamic splinter groups invoked violent jihad to fight against the established Islamic order.

In case military action is necessary, the religious military campaign must be declared by a proper authority, advised by scholars who verify that Islam or Muslims are under threat and violence is imperative to defend them.[11] With all due respect to Kabbani and Hendricks, their understanding of jihad does not alleviate the interpretative and selective nature of such discourse. Who, for example, is considered a proper authority to declare war? Similarly, what is considered to be a legitimate "threat" to Islam? Once again, such questions are susceptible to threats of interpretation and selective arguments. For example, Imam Shafi'i states that Surahs 9:5 and 9:29 support the condition of jihad as a continual war against non-Muslims until they repent and accept Islam or pay *jizya* (a form of taxation). However, most scholars argue against this position, citing the succeeding verses as evidence: "and if any one of the polytheists seeks your protection then grant him protection...." (Surah 9:6).

Other scholars have also argued that as long as the non-believers are willing to live peacefully among the believers, the Quran obligates them to be treated peacefully. Surah 9:7 provides instruction about the meticulous keeping of treaties that are signed with the non-believers, and urges Muslims not to break them unless the unbelievers break them first. The treaty command is reiterated in Surah 9:8, in which God orders Muslims not to make a treaty with unbelieving enemies who break their oaths and whose intention is to overpower the Muslims.[12] In this context, Kabbani's and Hendricks's assertion that military jihad in Islam has been a rarity, is worth acknowledging — if jihad's objective had been to fight all non-believers, then there would have been no need for treaties, and no differentiation between polytheists, Christians, Jews and others who remained loyal and faithful to their word, and those who were deceitful.

In the context of majority Islamic belief, one can rightly state that warring jihad is valid only if Muslims are directly attacked and persecuted. Even then, if force must be used, it is only to be used if there is no "peaceful" alternative. In addition, it should be enforced with strict rules of non-engagement against women, children, and the physically or mentally challenged. Furthermore, any peaceful overtures from the so-called enemy must be accepted. In other words, war is to be undertaken as a last resort, with strict adherence to the dictum of no-harm towards bystanders, and within the concept of a "just" war, without which there would be a major threat to the existence of Islam.[13]

Muslim scholars like Dr. Jamal Badawi explain that justification for military jihad becomes much easier for Islamists when they remove the context.[14] Likewise, according to David Rodier from the American University in Washington D.C., an expert on world religions, "if people are intent on using religion to motivate terror or violence, they'll find an excuse there no matter what the actual text says." He further acknowledges that, like the Quran, most holy scriptures are filled with stories of war and warriors, and these images have been used throughout history by some members to justify their own violent actions.[15] As Muslim scholar Imam Sulayman S. Nyang of Howard University in Washington, D.C. states, it is okay to fight back, "if you are attacked by your persecutors, but don't fight back indiscriminately. Follow the rules of engagement." According to mainstream Muslim clerics, the "rules of engagement" are explicit: women, children, and innocent civilians are off-limits.[16]

But contrary to most people's impression about jihad, the role of jihad has another meaning that has less to do with a political- or religious-based action against an opposing party, and more towards a spiritual struggle within one's self. Prophet Muhammad called this the "greater" jihad. As explained by Michael G. Knapp, a Middle East and Africa analyst writing for the United States Army War College's *Parameters*, many Muslims (especially the Sufi faction of Islam) understand the "greater" jihad to be an inner struggle against the base instincts of the body and the corruption of the soul – a necessary step toward spiritual insight.[17]

The Nature of Religious Beliefs

One could, in a final analysis, identify issues relating to interpretation, lack of context, and selective understanding of scriptures in all three major monotheistic religions as reasons for religious-based disparity among different peoples in the world. If the scripture is *interpreted* as being hateful and violent by a Muslim imam, or if a Christian clergy harbors hatred for a certain group, they may justify their own self-fulfilling meaning of the scriptures through an interpretation that presents a selection of segmented text as an absolute truth. Some could argue that this, in fact, is one reason why different denominations exist in all three major monotheistic religions in the world, as well as in some polytheistic religions, such as Hinduism and Buddhism.

While most people in any religion are inclined to contextualize their existence within the context of religion, some try hard to subscribe to an interpretative religious belief that promotes what they would like to follow in their quest for attaining nirvana. In the interpretation of religious doctrines, most "progressive" people subscribe to religious beliefs that are "necessary" for their particular lifestyle, and shun those which they find hard to accept in the following of their objectives -- often through the justification that their religion does not consider it mandatory or by finding an interpretative "loop-hole" that justifies their behavior as "sanctioned" by their religion. In this respect, it should be noted that for most Muslims, eating pork is a major violation of their religious teachings. By the same token, while drinking alcohol is also a taboo, it is not as strictly followed by "progressive" Muslims. As one Muslim explained: this could partly be because a substitute for pork is available in the form of other meats, such as chicken, beef, and lamb, but there is nothing that can give Muslims a buzz like alcohol, short of using drugs, which to many would be much worse than alcohol.

However, a more scholarly view on the subject of drinking alcohol stems from N.J. Dawood's translation of Surah 56, Ayahs 12–39 from the Quran, which depicts heaven where wine, that "will neither pain their heads nor take away their reason," is available.[18] In other words, one interpretive meaning in the scripture is that Islam allows the drinking of alcohol without *khamr* (getting intoxicated). Therefore, drinking alcohol and using tobacco, according to this interpretative understanding, is not forbidden as long as one does not get drunk or "high" by its consumption.

Similarly, in Christianity, scriptures are often interpreted by people in a way that still allows them to fulfill their desired lifestyle, whether that involves drinking alcohol, sexual freedom, or accumulation of wealth. For example, the basic tenets of most religions state that a better life is in store for people who are religiously motivated, either as a higher form of a reincarnate to strengthen the whole of society, or to earn a place in paradise. While belief in a "heavenly" afterlife is also a major aspect of Christianity (the major religion of the West), the pursuance of wealth, for example, is tempered by selective interpretation of the scripture, which for some, not only allows but seems to promote their quest for material ecstasy.

Scott Bothic Rae, a theologian, scholar, and professor of Christian ethics, writing for the *Acton Institute* in the study of religion and liberty, states that the Bible appears to condemn the accumulation of wealth. Classic verses in the Bible, such as, "it is easier for a camel to go through the eye of a needle than for a rich man to enter the kingdom of heaven" (Lk 18:25 NT) and "blessed are the poor" (Lk 6:20 NT), suggest that possession of wealth is not a favored virtue. However, in other passages, Paul acknowledges that God gives liberally to his people for their enjoyment (1 Tim. 6:17 NT).[19] According to Rae, the Bible only condemns the *love* for wealth, not its accumulation (1 Tim. 6:10 NT). As evident from passages in the Bible, Jesus appears to have lived a modest middle-class lifestyle as a carpenter, in contrast to some portrayals of him residing in poverty. It appears that possession of wealth is not problematic per se in interpretative Christian scriptures, but the wealthy are condemned for their callousness when they hoard wealth and do not attend to the needs of the poor (Am 4:1-4 OT; James 2:1-7 NT).

The Interpretative Nature of Sharia Law in Islam

To differentiate Islamists' contradictive understanding of Sharia (Islamic law), from that of other Muslims, it is necessary to outline what Sharia actually means to the general Muslim population and how it is compiled and practiced in contemporary Muslim societies around the world.

The etymology of "Sharia" in Islamic literature refers to the divine law of Islam formulated through three primary sources: the precepts set forth in the Quranic *ayats* (verses), the *Sunnah*, and the Hadith of Prophet Muhammad. The Sunnah, according to Muslim scholar Farhad Shafti, is very important to Muslims because it contains the religious practices that were established by the Prophet, who is believed to have been sent by God as an example on how Muslims should live their lives. As an extension of this belief, his companions' lives — those who lived close to him — are also be observed by Muslims in the understanding of how Muhammad conducted his daily affairs (such as what he ate, how he slept, and how he treated other people). In many such contexts, the Quran only provides a command, say, to pray, but how to pray and how many times to pray is provided by the Prophet. These practices have mostly originated from the religion of Ibrahim, to which the Prophet made revisions or additions where appropriate, as commanded by God.[20]

The Hadith, on the other hand, is seen as something "new," or outside of what is outlined in the Quran, although much of the text in the Sunnah is in the Hadith. Hadiths can be anything from a remark made by the Prophet or his companions, to narrations about a s story told by him. It could also be an observer's comment with respect to the views and statements of the Prophet with respect to Muslim life and practice, or of those who were close to him. The Hadith, which began as a verbal transmitted record of the teachings, deeds, and sayings, and silent permissions (or disapprovals) of Prophet Muhammad, as well as various reports about his companions, was related for Muslims through witness accounts in every generation.

According to Islamic teachings, the Quran was recited to Muhammad by the angel Gabriel. Muhammad, who was illiterate, then recited it to his companions, instructing them to write it down. The Quran is thus viewed as the unalterable word of God (through His prophet), and is considered an infallible source in the creation of the Sharia. Since the Sunnah is based on the history of the Prophet, and in many cases, he directly helped modify it for future use, it, together with the Quran, remain the primary sources for understanding Islam, even though they may be susceptible to interpretation. While the Hadith remains a rich source for understanding the life of the Prophet and his *sira* (way of living), and is revered as a model for Muslim life, it is not considered as reliable as the Quran and the established Sunnah. It is, thus, vulnerable to different interpretative meanings. For the Twelver Shi'as (the largest Shi'a denomination), the Hadith, in addition to representing the life of the Prophet, also depicts the exemplary life of the twelve imams who they believe followed Muhammad as the caretakers of the religion.

While there are a few different versions of the Quran and Sunnah, there are no *major* differences between them. However, there are many "differential" compilations of Hadith. It is, therefore, the Hadith that is most likely to be the source of interpretative and selective meanings employed through Sharia law. Due to the subjective aspect of hadiths, a system is set up to establish its reliability based on, among other things, the number of sources that can be traced back to the original occurrence, and how far removed those sources are from the original speaker (whether the Prophet himself, or his companions). Although such classifications are not always rightfully acknowledged by Muslims, they are meant to help everyday Muslims in judging whether a hadith is sound, good, weak, fabricated, or forged.[21]

Most Islamic countries enforce some aspect of Sharia law, which covers a wide range of topics, from personal and community laws, to acceptable behaviors for Muslims when associating with non-Muslims and apostates, to laws on finance, morals, eschatology, and the commitment to jihad in a holy war. However, Jan Michiel Otto, professor of law and governance in developing countries at Leiden University, Netherlands, in an anthropological research paper commissioned by the Netherlands Ministry of Foreign Affairs, states that Muslims do not often distinguish clearly between norms and practices that are based on local traditions (regional culture) and those that are based on religion. Those who interpret Sharia as confrontational tend to ascribe many undesirable practices to the religion, overlooking custom and culture, even if high-ranking religious authorities have stated otherwise.[22]

It seems that in this hodge-podge interpretation of Sharia law, the ultimate form of belief is far removed from the preaching of the cleric and instead left to the understanding of the individual. As Daniel Pipes points out, this leaves Islam to personal interpretation by followers, wherever they live.[23] In other words, regional governments, sheikhs, and kings could, through an interpretation of religious dogmas, dictate overall public policy, and formulate rules for the governance of the country utilizing the guiding hand of religion, while the public follow their own interpretation of the Quran within the confines of their homes and personal lives. This laissez-faire attitude of countries towards their citizens with regard to religious matters would relegate Islam as the religion of the individuals (as it was meant to be, according to most scholars, based on Surah 2:256 that states, "there is no compulsion in religion"), thus reducing its role in the political sphere to that which is practiced differentially by ordinary people in many Eastern and Western countries around the world.

However, there is potential for individuals — possibly informed by cultural or social influences, or media inspired — to further their own perceived religious doctrines, which might be at odds with those beliefs preached by say, a non-confrontational local clergy who does not have the ability to placate individual "misunderstandings" with his interpretation of the Hadith (which is written in Arabic). In places where Arabic is not spoken (which is substantial in terms of the number of Muslims in the world), the interpretation of the clergy is the only understanding of the text available to the individual.

Because the Quran is written in Arabic, possibly including some words from the Syro-Aramaic language, another layer of interpretation is added for the significant number of non-Arabic speaking Muslims in the world. Thus, though there is a desire by Muslims to reinforce Islam as a religion of the individuals, in reality it is the interpretation of the local clergy or a collective force of clergies, particularly in non-Arabic-speaking Islamic countries such as Indonesia, Pakistan, and Bangladesh, that is responsible for deciphering tenets of Islamic belief. The situation poses an even further setback when clergies themselves have a very rudimentary understanding of Arabic. Many of these clergies would have no means of deciphering the meaning of the text in the Quran, and likely depend on what has been taught to them from other non-Arabic speaking clergy, or through translations, which often include the biases of the translator. To take this issue one step further, we can easily picture the danger of a scenario in which a confrontational cleric with his own selective and interpretative understanding of the scriptures, preaches to highly "charged" individuals.

While individual or group interpretations of Islam can be seen as working models for understanding Sharia, its practice is generally dictated by the laws of the Muslim countries in which they reside. Such national laws are in turn likely influenced by a religious body's interpretation of Sharia law. Most individuals likely take a holistic approach in incorporating Sharia into their daily lives, fusing the preaching of the clergy with their own cultural and religious beliefs – within the confines of the religious based state laws.

In a sense, Sharia law is very similar to the Jewish law known as Halacha. As Professor Marshall Berger from the Catholic University's Columbus School of Law states, both laws purport to instruct the "believers" on how to attend to every aspect of one's life, including such everyday activities as getting up and going out, having sex, and the way business practices are conducted. For some adherents of the two religions, "the law also dictates political life, such as for whom to vote."[24]

However, Rabbi Jon Hausman differentiates between Sharia and the Halacha by stating that in Judaism, the law of the state, unlike Islam, "is the law (in Aramaic, *dina d'malchuta dina*)," and, therefore, it is devoid of religious "imperialism."[25] Berger, on the other hand, argues that "the reach of *dina d'malchuta dina* is debated among rabbinic commentators." Thus, while some limit the application of the Jewish legal system to property issues, others extend it to apply to all secular law that does not violate Jewish law, which is very similar to how Muslims apply Sharia law in civil matters.

Berger further states that Hausman's depiction of the Halacha as a personal legal system that is not relevant to civic life and politics, neglects both Jewish history and Halacha itself. For example, "in Baghdad during the Middle Ages and in Poland during the time of the Council of the Four Lands, from the 16th to the 18th centuries," Jews had their own courts, and "Jewish law was enforced by secular authorities. And even today, thousands of Jews in both the United States and Israel look to rabbinic courts and halacha to resolve all manner of civil disputes."[26]

By the same token, David Yerushalmi, a New York lawyer and anti-Muslim activist, who is adamant in modeling a law banning Sharia, argues that the one major difference between the Sharia and the Halacha is that the Sharia "requires faithful Muslims to impose Islamic law on the world 'violently.'"[27] Yerushalmi's view is true in the view of Islamists, but not in that of the billions of Muslims living around the world. While some so-called Muslims (the Islamists) and their followers do view Sharia as a "hegemonic political force," according to Berger, the vast majority of Muslims view Sharia no differently from the way Jews view the Halachic system — "as an overarching guide to ordering one's life." Muslim jurists have always drawn on Sharia to mandate that fellow Muslims obey the laws of the land in matters that Sharia does not prohibit. As an example, Surah 5:11 states that Muslims have to "honor their contracts" and thus to honor the "social contract" of the land where they reside. In this context, the Islamic School of Jurisprudence (*fiqh*) of North America, the leading interpreter of Islamic law in the United States, ruled on September 2011, that "there is no inherent conflict between the normative values of Islam and the U.S. Constitution, and the Bill of Rights."[28]

However, the interpretations by the various Islamic Schools of Jurisprudence of both the Shi'a and Sunni denominations contain stark differences from one another — ranging from extremely conservative, to moderate, to liberal views (within the definition of "liberalism" in the context of Sharia law). It is the misunderstanding of this multifaceted nature of interpretation that often causes confusion for the West when engaging in dialogue concerning

Sharia law. Knowledge of these existing schools of thought is essential for understanding the internal Islamic laws within a country. For example, the Sharia in Iran (whether influenced by actual Sharia or culture) is interpreted in such a way that gives women the right to drive, but this was not so in Saudi Arabia where women were not allowed to drive until late September, 2017.

This deeper understanding of Sharia stands in stark contrast to the dialogue initiated by people like former presidential candidate Dr. Ben Carson in the United States. The good doctor stated an across-the-board "dislike" for all forms of Sharia, not realizing that Youssoupha Sarr, known as the Green Imam, enforced jihad in Senegal (dictated by the Sharia law) not as an aggressive action against non-believers, but instead in an attempt to save his country from its mountainous piles of trash.[29] Obviously, jihad in this context is not violent. Rather, it is akin to any security position a country takes (violent or non-violent), as a measure to protect the interests of its people. Such action could easily be compared to sanctions imposed by the West on other countries that do not do their bidding, or who are considered "rogue" nations. In other words, there are many aspects of jihad that are beneficial for practitioners in their countries, keeping in mind that the charitable aspect of Sharia is significantly important in countries where economic development has left the poor behind.

Through non-Muslim eyes, Sharia's "do's" and "don'ts" for every aspect of life are often perceived as a curtailment of individuality, and perhaps rightly so. However, it should be noted that in most countries, other than the very few that practice a rather "austere," factional following of Islam, most Muslims practice moderate or liberal interpretations of Sharia. Of course, even in its "milder" form, Sharia may still seem restrictive through Western eyes.

The Islamists' understanding of the Sharia. The Islamists' adherence to Sharia is unique in the sense that it is based on a self-fulfilling concept, which they justify for conducting a military jihad, through an interpretative understanding of the Sharia. In understanding the reasons why Islamists have taken to military jihad, and the manner in which the war is fought, answers to three basic questions might be helpful:

1. What are the reasons for their jihad?
2. Why military jihad?
3. How is this military jihad fought?

As stated earlier, there are various reasons for jihad, all of which must pose a *threat* to Muslims or their religion, Islam. Al-Qaeda and Daesh likely believe that the West, in cahoots with Middle Eastern leaders, have extorted their precious oil, and disrespected their religion. This belief, as explained in Chapter 6, is likely based on a lingering view that the West has, and continues to demonstrate, blatant disregard for their cultural and religious values, thus destroying their pious way of life. Notwithstanding the fact that the relationship between the Middle East and the West has been one of beneficial reciprocation, the pervasive belief for the Islamists seems to be that the relationship has been one-sided in which not enough compensation was paid to the Muslim countries —and what little was paid was not distributed to the common people.

In analyzing why Islamists choose to fight a military jihad against the West, most would argue that negotiations, or some other sort of retaliation (other modes of jihad), would be a more effective route. However, there are likely two reasons for their military undertaking:

1) Al-Qaeda did not have the wherewithal to undertake an alternative jihadist endeavor — they had no faith in their autocrats in driving Western influence out of the area, believing them to be lackeys of the West. By the same token, they had no authority or standing to negotiate on behalf of their followers with their rulers, or the governments of the West, who they believed had desecrated their lands (particularly in Saudi Arabia) with their disrespectful behavior against Islamic beliefs, and plundering their land for oil. The only "plausible" utility available to them was the use of "hit and run" tactics, and, later on, suicide bombers who operated under the guise of martyrdom. It is this very simple lack of options that most likely caused the group to resort to terroristic jihad against the West, as well as against their own autocrats.

2) From Daesh's perspective, the catalyst for violent actions was similar to the reasons outlined for Al-Qaeda. However, their operative violent actions found great support from disgruntled fellow Sunni Arabs (many of whom were displaced from the job they had in Saddam's Iraqi army) for the unjustified invasion of Iraq by the United States and Britain. This provided the already volatile Islamist group with an unquestionable justification to retaliate against the invasion of their land and their lives with military jihad.

While analyzing such justifications by the Islamists in their commitment to military jihad is useful for philosophical discourse, it is important to note that the process used in the administration of Islamist jihad does not even remotely fall within the military jihad sanctioned by Islam. In this context, the Islamists have violated the concept of a "just" military jihad with their cruelty and violence against innocent civilians (including women and children), which is a blatant contradiction to all fundamental Islamic beliefs of past and present.

A gruesome aspect of Daesh's ideology in corralling innocent Sunni Muslims in areas where there is concentrated bombing by the West, might be based on their belief that they are helping the common Sunni Muslim attain martyrdom. By the same token, those who are not Sunnis are considered disposable, while the Shi'as are considered to be apostates which in the perverted minds of Islamists, is enough justification for having them killed. However, there is no clear prescription for how apostates are supposed to be handled in Islam. According to Islamic scholar Dr. Ahmad Shafaat, the Quran and the Hadith do *not* prescribe the punishment of death for apostates, although Islamists likely interpret the issue differently.[30]

The use of suicide bombers, which the Islamists use in their fight against "non-believers," is also carefully orated as an act of martyrdom. According to most scholars of Islam, the religion strictly forbids committing suicide. However, Islamists have circumvented the issue by calling suicide-bombers "martyrs" who die for the cause of protecting the faith. In this context, all suicide-bombers initiated by the Islamists are believed to be destined for eternal happiness in paradise. Thus, the Islamists in their quest for creating a self-styled religious-based euphoric Muslim society has manipulated some extremely conservative beliefs of seventh-century Islam to promote its own brand of senseless cruelty and violence by a misguided, interpretative understanding of Sharia.

Ironically, in spreading their construed interpretation of violent jihad, the Islamists fail to acknowledge that there are some countries in Asia, Africa, and Europe, which are not Muslim-majority countries, but still allow a limited form of Sharia for rules of divorce, inheritance, and other personal affairs with respect to their Islamic population. For example, in Britain, the Muslim Arbitration Tribunal makes use of Sharia family law to settle disputes among and within Muslim families. A similar system exists for Muslims in India. Such legalistic freedoms allowed by non-Islamic countries in appeasing a segment of their populations are commendable, even though such practices are not new — the United States allows the same for Amish and Native American populations, who have certain liberties in handling their community and personal affairs, as long it does not conflict with state or federal laws.

Chapter 3

An Eastern Mind Shaped by Western Policies

For many Muslims (both Shi'as and Sunnis) in the Persian Gulf, a fundamental dislike for the West is based on its supposedly "hedonistic" behavior in the region, its perceived "unfair" exploitation of Arab resources, and its undue political influence on their leaders. Ironically, however, even though many Muslims enjoy Western pop culture (Western music, TV programs and movies), a clear majority of Muslims in most countries surveyed by the Pew Research Center think that Western entertainment has a negative effect on morality in their country. In four of the six regions surveyed, at least half of those who said they enjoy this type of entertainment also said Western cultural imports undermine morality — keeping in mind that according to the same survey, belief in God, for Muslims, is essential for a person to be considered "moral." In nearly every country surveyed in South Asia, Southeast Asia, the Middle East, North Africa, and sub-Saharan Africa, most Muslims believe that Western entertainment has a negative influence on their society, including around nine-in-ten Muslims in Pakistan, and around eight-in-ten people in the Palestinian territories, Tanzania, and Uganda.[1]

But, aside from the grievances outlined above, one of the major causes of disgruntlement among Muslims is that the United States plays favorites in the Israeli-Palestinian conflict.

According to Bruce Riedel at the Brookings Institution, the single most important factor in the rise of Al-Qaeda was the Israeli-Palestinian conflict.[2]

The Israeli-Palestinian Conflict

The Israeli-Palestinian conflict was a central theme in the rhetoric of both Osama bin Laden, the deceased founder of Al-Qaeda, and Ayman al-Zawahiri (the current leader of Al-Qaeda). Of Osama's eight major speeches before 9/11, seven of them highlighted the Israeli-Palestinian conflict as a central motivator for his ideology. In most of his speeches between the later part of 2001 and 2008, he continued to focus on the Israeli-Palestinian conflict. For example, as Riedel quotes from a speech given by Osama in May 2008, on the sixtieth anniversary of the creation of Israel, where he justified 9/11 with the following:

> The main root of the conflict between our civilization and your civilization is the Palestine question. I stress that the Palestine question is my country's central issue. Since childhood it has provided me and the free 19 [a reference to the hijackers of September 11] with an overwhelming feeling of the need to punish the Jews and those supporting them. This is why the events of September 11 took place.

Similarly, virtually every statement al-Zawahiri has given on behalf of Al-Qaeda, focuses on the Israeli-Palestinian conflict. Furthermore, the 9/11 Commission, focusing on Khalid Sheikh Muhammed, the so-called mastermind of 9/11, stated that "... his animosity towards the Americans stems from his violent disagreement with the United States' foreign policy favoring Israel."[3]

Riedel highlights an important reason for the West to push for a just, fair, and lasting peace between Israelis and Palestinians. Interestingly, as he states, this is not to appease Al-Qaeda, but rather to conciliate extremism so that the West can isolate Al-Qaeda and its allies in the Islamic world, expose them as the extremists and murderers they are, and to strengthen the moderates who are fighting for the soul of Islam today — for peace and for a two-state solution.

As Riedel theorizes in his essay for the Middle East Policy Council, the Israeli-Palestinian conflict is a national security threat to America. A peace agreement is key to achieving most of the United States' goals in the greater Middle East, and in saving American lives. While it is not a panacea for all problems between the West and the Muslim world, according to Riedel, that is a "stupid reason not to try to move ahead and solve it." The conflict creates anger, frustration, and humiliation for Palestinians, for Arabs, and for Muslims in general. It also alienates and weakens Western allies — the moderates of the Islamic world — who are trying to fight the United States' enemies.[4]

In this respect, it should be noted that the problems of Palestinians are, in extension, problems for most Muslims across the world (indeed, Islam prescribes that a trial for one Muslim is a trial for all Muslims). Even Saudi Arabia (America's ally) has never come to terms with America's non-committal governmental policies with respect to Israel. According to Christopher Dickey, a veteran foreign correspondent and editor of *The Daily Beast World News*, Saudi Arabia, which did not want to see the Jewish state recognized in 1948, had supported wars against it, funded terrorists who attacked it, and imposed an oil embargo in 1973 to try to keep Washington from re-arming it. In short, over the last seventy years or so, American support for Israel has been opposed by Saudi Arabia either directly, indirectly, or silently.[5]

Bruce Riedel explains that in addition to Saudi Arabian leaders, Egyptian, Jordanian, Moroccan, and other Arabian Gulf leaders have also continued to raise the issue of the Israeli-Palestinian conflict with the United States, and pleaded with it for intervention. For example, the late King Hussein of Jordan, close to his deathbed in 1998, implored President Clinton to push Bibi Netanyahu and Yasser Arafat to conclude the Wye River agreement for the children of Jordan as well as the children of Israel and Palestine.[6]

The Muslim Brotherhood's role in the Israeli-Palestinian conflict. To complicate matters in the Israeli-Palestinian conflict, the Palestinian region is infiltrated by the Muslim Brotherhood through the radical group known as Hamas. The Muslim Brotherhood is a religious based political group that originated from Egypt in 1928 (See Chapter 5 for an explanation of the Brotherhood as a religious movement) but is now hated by the Egyptian government. According to a report by Khaled Abu Toameh, an Israeli-Arab journalist, lecturer, documentary filmmaker, and a distinguished fellow for the New York-based Gatestone Institute, Egyptian President Sisi has not forgiven Hamas for its alliance with the Brotherhood, and its involvement – according to Sisi – in terrorist attacks against Egyptian civilians and soldiers during the Arab uprising.[7]

Sisi's hatred for the Muslim Brotherhood, based on a political and personal dislike, is personified with rhetoric that accuses the Brotherhood of links to extremist groups like Daesh. According to an interview by Dieter Bednarz and Klaus Brinkbäumer, for the German online site *Spiegel*, Sisi justified the overthrow of a democratically elected Muslim Brotherhood in Egypt by stating that, "had the army not intervened, hundreds of thousands if not millions would have died."[8]

It is debatable whether there is truth in Sisi's claim that the Muslim Brotherhood is a progenitor of modern Islamic extremism, and would have committed genocide against the people of Egypt if it had remained in power. In a bid to win Muslims to his cause, Sisi makes invalid claims that Hamas, Daesh, and all Islamic extremist groups are descendants of the Brotherhood. As a means to invalidate the Brotherhood's religious calling, he asks all Muslims to distance themselves from the Brotherhood, and for "true" Muslims to take action against such purposed extremists, who are both hurting the cause of Muslims and insulting Allah.[9]

By the same token, Saudi Arabia's support for Israel in their fight against Hamas could also be a case where politics has overruled religious affiliation. Saudi Arabia's hatred for the Brotherhood seems to stem from the fact that the Muslim Brotherhood believes in the absolute amalgamation of church and state. This belief implies that members of the House of Al-Saud are illegitimate rulers of Saudi Arabia because their political decisions are officially separated from the beliefs of the central religious body, known as the *Ulama*. It is in this context that one can understand the interest of the Saudi Ruling Party in helping perpetuate the Muslim Brotherhood's demise from power, despite their common interest in driving out the Shi'a Houthis from Yemen, Assad from Syria, and a stance against Israel in their conflict with the Palestinians. According to Robert Baer, an American author and former CIA case officer who worked primarily in the Middle East, the Brotherhood is one of the most serious threats to the Saudi Royal Family, especially considering the its influence on the two-million relatively poor Egyptians living in Saudi Arabia.[10]

There is, however, great affinity between the Saudi ruling family and the Egyptian ruling party. Not only do both parties hate the Brotherhood, but the Saudi ruling family has a personal reason for its close attachment with Egyptian army generals: In 2003, it was Egyptian President Hosni Mubarak (an ex-air chief marshal) who helped foil Libya's Muammar Qaddafi's plan to assassinate the then Saudi crown prince and de facto king, Abdullah.[11]

While there is call to the international community by Egypt and Saudi Arabia to label the Brotherhood as a terrorist group, such a request has not been actualized by the United States. Past American administrations have not agreed with this designation, although there has been some talk in Washington of revisiting the subject. Part of the reason for the United States' concerns against classifying the Brotherhood as a terrorist organization could be because the Brotherhood has not carried out terrorist activities against the West. More importantly, however, there could be a concern that labelling the Brotherhood as a terrorist organization would alienate one of America's staunchest ally, the pro-Brotherhood Qatar (where the United States has one of its largest military base), and its other strategic ally in the region, Turkey, whose president, Recep Tayyip Erdoğan, and his political party have ideological ties to the Muslim Brotherhood.[12]

The role of Hamas in the Israeli-Palestinian conflict. But, while the hatred for the Muslim Brotherhood continues to percolate among some powerful Islamic countries, Hamas, as a fundamentalist, militant Islamic organization, operating in the West Bank and Gaza in Palestine, continues its governance in parts of Palestine, based on Islamic laws. Its manifesto, like most Palestinian factions and political parties, purports to liberate the Palestinians from their occupying power. In 2006, Hamas won legislative support in Palestinian territories, ending the secular

Fatah party's hold on the Palestinian authority and challenging Fatah's leadership of the Palestinian national movement. In contrast to Hamas, Fatah, the other major political party in the region, has kept up with Palestinian cultural norms, and has taken a secular stance in establishing a Palestinian state based on universal human rights rather than religious dogmas.

It should be noted that while many Palestinians have shifted their support in favor of Hamas over Fatah, this shift is not indicative of an abandonment of non-religious movements. Instead, as pointed out by author Graham Usher, support for Hamas is based on three basic factors: (1) the Palestinian peoples' disillusion regarding the Fatah-led Palestinian Authority's negotiations with Israel, (2) appreciation for Hamas' civic role in providing services to the Palestinian community, and (3) Fatah's perceived misrule of the Palestinian Authority (an extension of the Palestinian Liberation Organization [PLO]). Just prior to the First Intifada (Palestinian uprising against the Israelis) in 1987, the creation of Hamas embodied a new wave of thinking, which still retains elements of the original charter of the PLO.[13]

In many Palestinian minds, Fatah ceased to promote the right to return (the settlement issue) for the Palestinian refugees, and rarely challenged Israel's military prowess, establishing a trend of compromise that robbed it of its constituents' trust. On the other hand, Hamas has maintained a strong position on the refugees' right to return to their homes. Its fiery rhetoric challenges rivals, and while it cooperated with the Palestinian Authority's recognition of Israel (the joint agreement was signed in 2007), it has not been accepted as one of the negotiators by the Israelis who have it designated a terrorist group. The group is also labelled as a terrorist organization by the United States, the European Union (EU), and some Arab states that does not include Turkey.

As a provider of social services, Hamas offers hope of restored dignity to Palestinians, who are tired of constant oppression and inept leadership. Author Jeroen Gunning's in-depth analysis, based on his theoretical acuity and prolonged field work, relates that Hamas, unlike Fatah, does not denounce the use of arms against Israel, believing that negotiations without the backing of a military agenda would be ineffective. The reason for this belief, according to Gunning, stems from Hamas' assertion that there is a lack of a powerful neutral arbitrator who could force the Israelis to live up to their commitments.[14]

If Hamas continues to play an important role in the regional conflict, little support is likely to be given to them by key players such as Saudi Arabia and Egypt. With the shift in the current balance of power in the region, the future of peace is increasingly reliant upon a softening of the Palestinian Authority's and Israel's rigid stances. According to the Palestinian Authority's constituents, the legitimacy Hamas could provide would likely bolster a joint-government of the West Bank and Gaza, should reconciliation come into full effect. Rather than continuing the cycle of a struggle for hegemony, the evidence examined by Gunning suggests that Hamas is a vital asset for the future of Palestine, that can lay a foundation for a stronger, cohesive Palestinian government.[15]

On the other hand, Samantha Borders, as part of her dissertation, succinctly points out that the possibility of the Palestinian Authority holding talks with Israel behind Hamas's back, as a plot to dispose of the group, is a constant threat.[16] However, Ahmad Melhem, a Palestinian journalist, reports that Palestinian President Mahmoud Abbas, on August 13, 2016, approved the initiative of the High Follow-Up Committee for Arab Citizens of Israel to achieve reconciliation between Fatah and Hamas. To-date (June 2017), no such reconciliation has been achieved. If the initiative results in a reconciliation, there is hope for moderation in Hamas' attitude towards the pursuance of peace with Israel.[17]

The differential expectations of Hamas and Fatah for the Palestine people create yet one more hindrance to the singular, majority voice for Palestinians in the peace process. Though many Palestinians have sided with Hamas, there is still a dissident attitude of defiance from hardcore Fatah members, which adds an extra level of difficulty for the progress of peace between the Palestinians and the Israelis. Perhaps, the fruition of Hamas and Fatah's reconciliation efforts will be the catalyst for singling out a strong voice from the Palestinian side in their negotiations with the Israelis.

The religiously based factional hatred in the Israeli-Palestinian war. In understanding the consequences of the Palestinian-Israeli conflict, it should be noted that in spite of the recent laissez-faire attitude by the Saudis and some other Islamic countries, sectorial hatred based on the Sunni-Shi'a divide has sometimes been used by commoners, to justify actions for or against the Palestinian people. For example, Hawraa Zakery, a social justice and civil advocate, most known for her research on minority rights and advocacy for Shi'a Muslims, a Wahhabi Egyptian cleric, Tala'al Zahran, who, according to Zakery. is also the representative for Daesh, believes that Egyptians should not support Palestinians against Israel because "most Gazans are Shi'as, and are communists."[18]

However, BBC News: Middle East (December 2013), and many other internet sites, point out that most Palestinians are Sunnis, although there has been a large insurgence of Shi'as through the Palestinian borders with Syria and Lebanon. While Zahran and others are factually incorrect about Palestinians being Shi'a, one thing stands out: the Saudis prefer to defend

Israel over Shi'as or the Brotherhood. To this end, it should be noted that while such incidences may be isolated, perpetuated by blind hatred for a particular Muslim denomination, it underlines a persistent demarcation within Muslim communities, which has far more significant consequences than obvious at first reckoning.

Some factors at play in the Israeli-Palestinian negotiations. As words of caution, the cordial support given to Israel by some Islamic countries does not imply that the Palestinian issue is "swept under the rug" by the general Muslim population. While they realize that the United States is Israel's strongest supporter, and always will be, they echo Jewish-American Senator Bernie Sanders's sentiments that there needs to be a give-and-take on both sides of the conflict, with an underlying understanding that the status quo is not to anyone's advantage.

The Israeli-Palestinian issue needs to be resolved, but it has a much better chance if the United States, in Muslim minds, is more aggressive with the Israelis and less biased in the pursuance of a two-state solution. However, according to Yashwant Raj, a correspondent for the *Hindustan Times*, Prime Minister Netanyahu believes that the issue of settlements is "not the core of the conflict nor does it drive the conflict."[19] However, the recent declaration in 2017, that permits the expansion of Jewish settlements in Israeli-occupied Palestinian land is not only unacceptable to most Muslims, but is also considered unacceptable by most world leaders — including those of the EU.

The problem is accentuated in Arab minds by the fact that Saudi Arabia's 2002 proposed comprehensive peace plan was signed by all 22 Arab countries, but was rejected by the Israelis. Hassan Yassin, a former spokesman for the Saudis in Washington, wrote that even in 2016, "the United States did not lean enough on Israel to even respond to a peace initiative that offered full peace and diplomatic relations along the lines accepted by the international community. It is a regret that pursues us until this day."[20]

The closest the two parties have come to entering a peace agreement was under former Israeli President Peres and former PLO leader Yasser Arafat, brokered by American President Bill Clinton, which came to be known as the Oslo Accord. However, in this case, it was the Palestinians under Arafat who backed out at the last moment, much to the surprise of both the Israelis and the Americans. The 2000, United States brokered Camp David negotiations was yet one other proposal that was agreed upon by the two parties, but failed to materialize. The proposal which placed the custody of Muslim and Christian sites in East Jerusalem in the hands of the Palestinians, was later rejected because of Israel's opposition leader Ariel Sharon's vehement opposition to the agreement. Discord on this issue was cited as a key reason by journalist Ehab Zahriveh, for the failure of the negotiations between the PLO and Israel.[21]

For Muslims across the globe, the Palestinian dilemma is often seen as that of a cornered population that has very little to lose and nowhere to go, save for the sacrifice of their lives in creating as much hurt as possible to their occupiers — those with sophisticated modern arsenals of war. In the Muslim mind, most people in the world would behave in a similar manner as the Palestinians, if faced with the same situation.

The perceived "unfairness" in any solution to the Israeli-Palestinian conflict (whether attributed to the Israelis or the Palestinians) is not easy to decipher. While the Palestinians are looking for a separate state, the Israelis need assurances that no further terrorist activities will take place. To this end, it must be realized that in the minds of many Palestinians, the building of Israeli settlement on captured Palestinian lands is not acceptable because it conflicts with the issue of resettling displaced Palestinians to their homes prior to the six-day war. On the other hand, in the minds of the Israelis, any concession given to the Palestinians need to be assessed not only as a precondition that all violent activities be stopped, but also in terms of control over key areas, such as divvying up of Jerusalem, a city of great religious importance for each of the world's three great monotheistic religions — Islam, Judaism, and Christianity.

For Israelis, Jerusalem is its "eternal, undivided capital," but the international community, including the United States, continues to regard East Jerusalem as occupied territory, rejecting Israel's decision to settle its citizens there. In the same context, the international community does not recognize Israel's claim that Jerusalem is its capital city. Most foreign nations, including the United States, continue to maintain their embassies in Tel Aviv and not in Jerusalem. The status of Jerusalem has proved to be a major stumbling block in the negotiating efforts to forge a two-state solution that envisages an independent State of Palestine alongside the State of Israel, west of the Jordan River.[22] However, the scenario outlined above, should provide cognizance to Muslim skepticisms that the United States has not blindly sided with Israel on every issue – suggesting also that Israel dances to its own drumbeat, just as some American Muslim allies have done in recent years.

In spite of the independence Israel has shown in attending to its own agenda that is contrary to the expectations of the United States, there is an overall expectation by Muslim nations for the United States to be more forceful in accounting for Israel's "wrong-doings." In this respect, much to the surprise of the Muslim world, the United States, on December 23, 2016, abstained from voting on a UN Security Council resolution, demanding an end to Israeli settlement building, which is a major reversal of United States' usual practice of siding with Israel, irrespective of the wishes of the majority in the Security Council. However, under the new administration in the United States, there has not been any outward rhetoric to stop the Israelis from building settlements in Palestinian territories that were captured by Israel.

But even if the United States were to go to the extreme and threatened to withhold its support through the cutting of its ties with Israel – an unconceivable scenario - pride and/or a firm belief in the adverse effects of the solution, may make Israel reject the proposal advocated by the Muslims. While such a scenario is never likely to happen in the foreseeable future (partly because the Jewish lobby in the United States would never let it happen), it should make Muslims across the world understand the limitations under which the United States functions – the best it can do is abstain from voting or not committing to a particular call by the Israelis, such as making Jerusalem its capital.

While the framework of the solution for the status of Jerusalem is set out in UN resolutions, the establishing of boundaries between Israel and Palestine is still subject to disputes and negotiations, perpetuated by a disagreement on security issues, the refugee (those who are displaced by wars between the two countries) dilemma, and the control of Jerusalem. The solutions to these problems are further handicapped by a deep sense of mistrust between the two nations.

The psychological impact of the conflict on the populations of Israel and Palestine. While negotiations are likely to start again (hopefully) between the two countries, with dogmatic demands from each side on key issues, it is hoped that eventually more flexible expectations by the two sides will make room for peace to prevail in the region. But, while a geopolitical solution in the region rests on the wishes of the political parties involved, the conflict has made a deep impression on civilians, which is likely to have lasting psychological consequences. Oakland Ross, a feature writer and former Middle East correspondent for the *Toronto Star*, expounds these psychological factors, which identify the Israelis as rabid settlers or rampaging soldiers in Palestinian eyes, while the Palestinians are seen as ruthless terrorists by the Israelis. The ingrained hatred between the two groups is so strong that they do not even acknowledge each other as human beings.[23]

Such hatred is further exemplified by views like that of Yossi Alpher, co-editor of the internet site *bitterlemons.org*, who finds that the Jews are "dehumanized" as descendants of pigs and monkeys in the Muslim narrative.[24] On the other hand, Yehuda Shaul states that widespread vandalism and at least some cases of unprovoked killing of civilians by Israeli soldiers are consistent with the war stories he has so far collected as director of *Breaking the Silence*, an organization that publishes accounts of Israeli soldiers' occasional brutal behavior in Palestinian territories.[25]

The Israeli-Palestinian narrative, however, is now made into a Jews versus Muslims conflict, which unfortunately makes an already deadly situation even worse. According to Gabriel Ben-Dor, who heads the School of Politics at the University of Haifa, religion is very important in the Middle East, and thus is an influential factor in the hatred between these two groups.[26]

The worst part, however, is that the children of both Israelis and Palestinians grow up in this hateful environment, subject to propaganda that teaches hatred for each other. As an example, the homepage for the Hamas published show *Al-Fateh* (*The Conqueror*), provides seemingly innocent illustrations, games, and stories, but the site, according to Benjamin Weinthal, a correspondent for *The Palestinian Post*, is far from harmless because it encourages terrorism and heaps praise on suicide bombers.[27] However, Ahmed Abu Tawahina, Director-General of the Gaza Community Mental Health Program, claims that media programs have nothing to do with the opinions of children because their attitudes are formed as a result of their "experiences on the ground." Meanwhile, the conflict grinds on, the hatred deepens, and the death toll climbs relentlessly higher. As Abu Tawahina muses, "the next generation of Palestinians and Israelis will be more fundamentalist and extremist."[28]

Egypt's role in the Israeli-Palestinian conflict. Egypt is a major player in the Israel-Palestine conflict. Its importance to Israel is evident because it is a large influential Arab country on one side of its border who has a hatred for their common enemy Hamas. Because it has a rather forceful stance in halting the flow of Palestinians into Egypt (presumably for concerns of its own safety), it has been instrumental in curtailing terrorist activities by sympathetic Egyptians and Palestinians who would find it easy to move from the Gaza strip into Egypt and vice-a-versa.

However, while the hatred for Hamas by Egypt is acknowledged, it does not imply that Egypt has no concerns for its Palestinian brethren. Egyptian President Sisi, for example, states that the Israeli-Palestinian negotiations are not between equals but rather between the conqueror and the conquered. On the site *Alchetron*, Sisi cautions Israel to adopt self-restraint and to keep in mind that, as an "occupation force," it has a legal and moral duty to protect civilian lives.[29] In this context, a bargaining chip for Palestinians may seem inexistent to Muslims since, according to them, the Palestinians are people who "want" while the Israelis are the people who hold the power to "give." Though the price of "giving" for the Palestinians is a promise of peace for the Israelis, a re-evaluation of when and what constitutes *"want"* is the real defining problem in bargaining for a solution that includes a separate state for the Palestinians.

Because Egypt is an American ally and has peaceful relations with Israel, its involvement in the Israeli-Palestinian conflict can be seen as promising, especially because of Sisi's desire for a resolution to the conflict. *The Economist* hails Sisi as the "the most pro-Israeli Egyptian leader ever."[30] While *The Economist*'s statement has yet to be actualized, according to some observers of the Middle East, the Sisi administration supports a two-state solution in which the Palestinian State would be established on lands that were occupied by the Israelis in 1967, with Eastern Jerusalem as its capital. While the truth of the above statement is not verifiable by any reliable sources, it should be understood that Egypt's as well as Saudi Arabia's involvement as mediators in the peace talks cannot be considered entirely sympathetic to the desires of the Palestinian people, likely because of both countries' hatred for Hamas, which is seen as "working behind the scenes" in negotiating for the Palestinian peoples.

It might be misconstrued by some people that the tacit siding with Israel by some Persian Gulf countries is *entirely* due to their dislike for Hamas. In reality, however, because the United States has maintained hegemony over much of the Middle East through a system of alliances with Arab states, these states, in keeping with American interests, have been reliably pro-American – covertly siding with the United States on the issues of Israel, and fighting Islamist terrorists.

However, as a side note, besides the Israelis', Egyptians', Saudis', and some other Persian Gulf countries' pre-mentioned hatred for Hamas and the Brotherhood, there is also a hatred for Iran, which is deemed to be the greatest enemy of such powerful nations in the Middle East as Israel, Egypt and Saudi Arabia. Therefore, although there has been a pact of "understanding" between Israel on one side, and Saudis, Jordanians and Egyptians on the other, it may have nothing to do with concern for the plight of the Palestinians, but rather for the fear of Iran claiming a dominant position in the area. In fact, according to Christopher Dickey, the hatred between Riyadh and Tehran is so strong that the Saudis gave implicit diplomatic support to Israel in its 2006 war against Hezbollah in Lebanon.[31]

The Freedom of Speech Issue

Aside from Muslims' discontent regarding the Israeli-Palestinian conflict, one other subject that often creates hatred for the Muslims against the West is the freedom of speech issue, which, when applied to religion, becomes a major bone of contention for Muslims. Visual images of Muhammad have been depicted in the past, and in recent years have occurred sporadically throughout the West. According to Hussein Rashid, a professor of Islamic studies at Hofstra University in New York, although satirical representations of Muhammad are not new, derogatory depictions of Muhammad, revered not only as a prophet but also as a moral exemplar, are no laughing matter for Muslims.[32] Sheikh Yasir Qadhi, a Muslim scholar who lives in Tennessee, states that Islamic law draws a distinction between creating images (a statute in the perceived likeness of Muhammed, for example), and portraying Mohammed in a vulgar or disrespectful manner (which is considered blasphemous).[33] In the context of European countries, Hussein Rashid points out that Muslims feel they are besieged because, according to them, these images are used as bullying tactics or racist, xenophobic slurs against them, in the name of free speech.[34] For some Muslims, therefore, retaliating with violence is not so much about religious anger as it is about revenge. But, even in the United States, where Muslims are relatively acclimated, CNN religious editor Daniel Burke states that extremists do oppose the portrayal of Muhammad on *South Park*, the satirical cartoon TV show.[35] These depictions encounter a backlash from Muslims, and in the age of the internet, a recent handful of vile caricature depictions of the Prophet printed in the European press have caused global protests, controversy, and retaliatory violence.

For those who can remember, perhaps the most obvious and publicized tell-tale sign of Islamism in the recent past, is evident in the fatwa issued by previous Ayatollah of Iran, Ruhollah Khomeini, in 1989, which called for the death of author Salman Rushdie on a particular understanding of the Sharia. Contrary to some people's beliefs, the issue in 1989 was not that of Muslims versus non-Muslims, but rather the reach of freedom of speech rights, which was brought to question regarding Rushdie's ridiculing of the Prophet that resulted in his being labelled as an apostate by the Ayatollah.

As is well appreciated in the West, democratic values influence country-specific laws, resulting in a legal system based on the desires of the population and not on the ideology of a single group or groups of believers. In this respect, the repressive nature of Islamism against non-Islamists cannot be tolerated by those who value a voice in their governance, even though, in the process, minority rights may often *seem* to be trampled by majority beliefs. In the West, such "trampling" of beliefs have, or at least proclaim to have, a justifiable reason. For example, the ban on covering Muslim women's faces in France, where many recent violent activities have been promoted by Islamists, is claimed to have been done for security reasons.

Overall, however, aside from some proprieties of bias underlying laws concerning certain groups, the West generally is tolerant toward personal freedoms and rights, intruding only when potential harm could come to an individual or certain group of individuals, such as in the case of those who incite or support the anti-Semitic movement in Europe. However, many people fail to realize that freedom of speech in most Western countries is not an invitation to say whatever they want without consequence. In fact, freedom of speech was championed and attained by those who were the victims of such verbal hatred and discrimination, and is restricted in order to protect people from untrue, damaging statements like, say, the interpretation by the French Judiciary of the 1881 freedom of speech law in France. According to Aurelien Hamelle, a Paris-based attorney, the law provides for a broad principle of freedom of speech, with several exceptions to it.[36] The same is true in the United States' Supreme Court's interpretation of First Amendment rights. The restrictions provide important recourse for people whose careers, reputations, finances, or health are damaged by harmful statements that are *not true* (the operative words being "not true"). For example, the mayor of Paris threatened to sue Fox News in the United States for its portrayal of "no-go" zones (Muslim-ruled enclaves in Paris) because, according to the mayor, the portrayal was not true and was damaging to the city's reputation as promoting equality for its citizens.[37]

But, besides grounds for defamation brought about by freedom of speech, in a Research Service Report prepared for Congress, Kathleen Anne Ruane, legislative attorney in the United States, cites some other examples, such as obscenity, child pornography, or speech constituting words that provoke hostility, colloquially known as "fighting words," which are not protected under the rights of the First Amendment. Even the most extensive First Amendment protections, such as a person's right to express an opinion, can be subjected to regulations of time, place, and the manner of expression, even if such expressions are based on content-neutral material. This is particularly true regarding matters of public concern.[38] And yet, it beguiles the minds of all practicing Muslims that the French and the Danes did nothing to prohibit idolatry and derogatory representations of the Prophet. In other words, to the non-Westerner, there can be some confusion as to the legitimacy of freedom of speech as it is practiced by most countries in the West.

To debate the issue from a Western point of view, political cartoons are meant to be critical of the subjects they depict, but they are considered opinions that are intended to be humorous, with the understanding that the writer or artist did not mean to express a literal fact. According to Hamelle, who specializes in libel and privacy cases, one of the main criteria in past court rulings involving the *Charlie Hebdo* magazine, was that satirical magazines often publish what may at face-value be perceived as offensive, but being *satirical* magazines, their communication through caricatures would not be taken seriously by most reasonable people.[39]

In other words, from the West's point of view, free speech is conditional on the context and manner in which it is applied. In America, for example, in the case of *Gaston versus Sun Services*, the District Court of Connecticut decided that a single use of the "N-word" in an employee's presence, along with a single instance of being called "boy," was not enough to designate a hostile work environment. While "offensive," the court emphasized that isolated instances are typically not enough to prove a hostile work environment.[40] While Hamelle concedes that there is significant leeway for judges and courts in interpreting the law, he explains that legal interpretations have been consistent in France for over 150 years.[41] However, in Muslim minds, this subjectivity in the interpretation of what is allowable and what is not by the judicial system can create suspicion of prejudice and bias against marginalized or unpopular groups within the population, based by a change of heart in the judicial system. In their minds, deep-seated disrespect and animosity, which reek of personal beliefs, can often camouflage hateful messages under the guise of humor. For example, due to a new French law passed in November 2014, internet content considered to be "advocating terrorism" can now be punished by several years in prison and large fines, even if it was intended humorously. The situation is so serious that not only are adults being caught up in the rigorous application of the law, but several children as young as fourteen years old have also been persecuted for the same reason. In voicing his opinion, author and co-founder of the *Electronic Intifada*, Ali Abunimah, states that in France, mocking and denigrating Islam and Muslims is venerated as courageous free speech. Anything criticizing those who engage in such denigration, even if it is through precisely the same techniques used by *Charlie Hebdo*, can get you locked up.[42] By the same token even the *burqini*, a modest swimsuit for women that covers the entire body (except for the face, feet, and hands), was considered unacceptable by French authorities until an outcry by Muslims around the world caused the law to be overturned.

In fighting fire with fire, the only non-violent alternative for Muslims would be to counter *Charlie Hebdo's* and Lars Vilks's derogatory depictions of the Prophet with unflattering or "humorous" portrayals of the prophets of other monotheistic religions. The irony, however, is that Muslims believe in the Bible, and in Jesus as a prophet born of the Virgin Mary, and therefore cannot levy blasphemous insults against the prophets of Judaism (Moses, for example) and Christianity. Besides, such an endeavor would invite grounds for a very "dangerous" humoristic war if undertaken by Muslims, who believe that all other prophets of Judaism and Christianity, although secondary to Muhammad, are very much a part of Islam. Insulting prophets who are central to other religions in a manner similar to the offensive caricature of Muhammad, would, according to some Muslims, likely create a "humoristic war" that could be just as deadly as, say, the abhorrent words used against Jews that incited cruel atrocities towards them in Europe.

In this respect, it should be noted that Muslims are not the only people who believe in the non-application of freedom of speech rights when it comes to preserving religious harmony. Pope Francis' comments on the limitations of freedom of speech (not insulting other people's religions) ring true in this respect. His religious annotations may hold weight when analyzed in terms of what religious beliefs mean to Muslims, or, for that matter, to many religious people living in non-Western areas of the world.

The practice of religions in the East and the West, examined within the context of freedom of speech. As is obvious, there are more Christians in the West, and more Muslims, Jews, Hindus, and Buddhists in the East. However, it is not religion, per se, that differentiates these regions, but what religions mean to the people who practice them, and how that practice is carried out.

To understand what the differential practice of religion means across the world, one needs to understand the perception of religion in different parts of the world, particularly as it is practiced at the present time in the West and the East. In many parts of the East, religion is not only a way of life but it *is* life. It is a part of everything they do, and leaders in Asian countries often take this into consideration in their political dealings, even in countries where politics is separated from religion.

This view is true not only for Muslims but even for those of different religions, including Christians who live in these countries. In India, for example, most taxi drivers keep a picture or a figurine of one of their gods in their taxis, which they kiss or gesticulate to, prior to beginning work. Muslims, too, have the word "Allah" in Arabic, stuck to their car's dashboard or have prayer beads hanging from their rear-view mirror. Many people start their day with a prayer, and many celebratory functions are laced with religiously-based cultural practices. The same devotion to religion is observed in muslin countries where the call to prayers from the minarets of the mosques is a constant reminder of the role Islam plays in a Muslim's life.

Keeping this in mind, it is important to note that activities that disrespect religions, such as burning the Quran, or belittling any religion's deity, or prophets, or sages, is looked upon a bit more tolerantly by people in the West than those in the East. While the burning of a Bible or a Torah may evoke a retaliatory gesture from those of the Christian or Jewish faith, comedians still make fun of religious figures in the West without most of the population raising an eyebrow.

However, it should be noted that an understanding of how religion is perceived in different parts of the world cannot be expected to redefine what "respect" should mean to Western countries. Short of changing its laws, which is almost impossible due to constitutional dictates, there is nothing more the West can do to universally deter religious criticism.

But then, this may not be a simple matter of right and wrong from the East's point of view. According to some laypersons (not only Muslims), freedom of speech rulings in the West should be scrutinized in the same manner as issues like the prohibition of child pornography. In other words, an exception to the freedom of speech rule with respect to "bad-mouthing" religions or religious prophets would likely produce the desired results of respect for others' religions and, in extension, a feeling of goodwill among people of the East. The downside, of course, is that such an action could set precedence for succumbing to the demands of others who have different grievances, and from "foreigners" in other parts of the world, which would have to be managed on a case-by-case basis, once again creating an impractical solution to the problem. Enacting amendments to Western laws in order to pacify people living in other countries would also be unacceptable because no country should succumb to outside interests in the governance of its internal affairs. However, if an internal minority population is affected adversely, then the issue may have to be addressed under moral or other justifiable legal criterion, keeping in mind the natural drawbacks of many "unenlightened" democratic societies with respect to minority is

Muslims' view regarding the freedom of communications. The crux of the argument for Muslims, however, does not entirely rest on the freedom of speech issue, but rather on aspects of culture that are often overlooked in cases relating to freedom of speech. Making fun of religious figures or figurines of religious deities is simply not done in the East. In the West, however, where making fun of religion, families, friends, and loved ones is not sheltered under the label of "disrespect," people subscribe to the rule of freedom of speech, and as such accept lighthearted criticism as falling within acceptable social norms. Comedians often make fun of their mothers and dish out crude sexual jokes, even regarding their loved ones. Everything is "fair game" as long as no kids are involved in sexual situations, no one's economic or social downfall takes place, no one's character is threatened in a detrimental way, and no incitement to terrorism takes place as a result of the jokes. While some of the topics outlined above would be forbidden in the eyes of *most* Muslims (as well as others of different faiths residing in the East), the vulgarity of intentional comedic or satirical portrayals, such as the Prophet depicted without clothes, is simply not acceptable to any and *all* Muslims.

But, besides the personal likes and dislikes of Muslims with respect to visual depictions of the Prophet, a more rigorous examination of the issue brings to light some important religious norms. Oral and written descriptions of religious figures are readily accepted by all traditions of Islam, but there is strong disagreement over visual depictions. It is agreed upon by the global Muslim community that there is no existing, authentic visual record of the appearance of Muhammad, although there are early accounts of portraits of him, and written physical descriptions that can be used as authenticate representation of the prophet.

Like most other monotheistic religions, for Muslims, God is not a person, but an entity that cannot be fully conceived of by the human mind and, therefore, cannot be portrayed visually, verbally, or in any other manner. But even with respect to the prophets of Islam, including those from the Judeo-Christian realm, such as Jesus and Moses, visual depictions remain a point of contention for Muslims, more so for Sunnis than for Shi'as. According to Omid Safi, a religious studies professor at Duke University in the United States, there have been historical instances of Muslims depicting the Prophet in the form of miniatures and pictures in Iran, Turkey, and central Asia. According to Safi, "the one significant context where depictions of the Prophet have not been image-related has been in the Arab context," where pictorial displays of religious figures are normally frowned upon, and, in certain Sunni schools of thought, are completely forbidden.[43]

The prohibition against illustrating Prophet Muhammad's image probably began as an attempt to ward off idol worship, which was widespread in Islam's Arabian birthplace. A central tenet of Islam is that Muhammad was a mortal man, not a god, and that portraying him could lead to revering him in lieu of Allah. In addition, there is fear among many Muslim scholars that the Prophet could be deified in much the same manner as Jesus, who has been, according to them, "deified" as the Son of God in Christianity. In other words, depictions of Muhammad are forbidden to deter Muslims from revering the Prophet to the extent that prayers would be made to him through his "statues" or "pictures" placed in homes or mosques. Beside these major reasons, there is also a respect for and sacredness surrounding the Prophet, which makes physical portrayals of him in plays or movies, or drawing his likeness, blasphemous.

While the Quran does not explicitly forbid images of Muhammad, there are a few interpretations of hadiths which have prohibited Muslims from creating visual depictions of prophets. For example, Akbar Ahmed, who chairs the Islamic studies department at American University, stated in an interview with Daniel Burke, that the Prophet was aware of what his image would mean for Muslims, and was afraid that if people saw his face portrayed, they would start worshiping him. Therefore, he spoke against such images, saying "I'm just a man."[44]

Some scholars have argued that Islamic art could be considered within the realm of religious art, because Muslim artists creating images of Muhammad, and the public who behold them, understand that these images are not created for the purpose of idol worship. However, there are other scholars who are hesitant in using prophets' images because of past rituals that have provided proof of glorifying Muhammed to a spirituality akin to that reserved for God. According to these scholars, such images have an inherently "spiritual element," and were occasionally used historically in informal religiously devoted celebrations, such as on the day of Isra and Mi'raj, two significant events in Islam that occurred on the same day.[45]

Considering the discussions above, it seems that it is not only the visual depiction of the Prophet but the *way* he is depicted that has angered the general Muslim population. In the age of globalization, non-Muslims and critics of Islam have felt free to depict Muhammad, sometimes in offensive manners. In 2006, for example, a Danish cartoonist's depiction of the Prophet wearing a bomb as a turban with a lit fuse, sparked political demonstrations from Muslims across the world.

Laws with respect to freedom of communications. As alluded to earlier, freedom of communication issues in the West, including visual portrayals, can sometime end up as litigation issues determined by the courts. In the United States, for example, a particular political party's appointed judges can have "party-biases," which may unconsciously influence their rulings. This is natural, because judges are human, and have personal likes and dislikes that can sway their opinions on complex matters. This issue is also precisely the reason why the Republican and Democratic parties in the United States were at loggerheads in selecting a Supreme Court Judge to take the place of Justice Scalia, who passed away prior to the 2016 election.

The issue of differential interpretations of the law may seem biased to those living in non-democratically ruled countries, but in fact the same issues exist in monarchical governments like Saudi Arabia's. In Saudi Arabia, for example, *excessively* cruel laws may be perceived differently, depending on the perceiver's definition of "excessive" in contrast to that of the Saudis'. In other words, understanding the legalization of laws are subjective at best, and in the case of Islamism, completely void of objectivity.

But, while mainstream Muslims may make such differential understanding a policy issue in their dealings with the West, for Islamists it becomes an unfair and prejudicial issue. To the Islamists, depicting the Prophet in a derogatory manner is a taboo that easily riles them to the point of killing or dying to defend their honor and beliefs. The West, according to them, has taken advantage of Muslims for too long, spreading its own idea of equity and justice in the world, especially in the oil-rich countries of the Middle East. In their mind, the West has a latent disrespect for Muslims, and when that disrespect manifests in blatant actions against their religion (for example, burning the Quran), it becomes a justification for Islamists to undo a wrong, even if that means an early retirement to their perverted view of heaven.

The Role of "Respect" in Geopolitical Policy Negotiations

While the above-mentioned verbal discourse may seem marginally irrelevant in "shaping" Eastern thoughts, the virtues of respect and "perceived" fairness are, according to Muslims, often overlooked by the West during negotiations with them. In this context, it is possible that the use of things like "respect" played a role in the signing of the non-nuclear proliferation treaty with Iran. This could also have been a factor in the freeing of ten Americans who ventured into Iranian waters. To substantiate the importance of respect for Iran and other Middle Eastern countries, it is important to note that after the quick release of the Americans, Iranian Foreign Minister Javad Zarif stated that he was "happy to see dialogue and respect, not threats and impetuousness, swiftly resolved the sailors' episode." He later tweeted: "let us learn from this latest example."[46]

The fact that negotiations were held based on mutual acceptance of directives rather than ultimatums, was likely one of the factors leading to Iran signing the non-nuclear proliferation treaty with the United States and some other countries in the West. Although United States Senate Armed Services Committee Chairman, Senator John McCain, stated that Iran's detention of the sailors was a violation of international law, it should be noted that the 1982 Law of the Sea Convention, authorizing coastal states to exempt so-called "innocent" vessels from arrest and seizure, was never ratified between the United States and Iran.

Though the issue of respect is important to note for the United States in its global dealings, particularly with respect to countries in the Middle East and Asia, there is little doubt that holding more than $100 billion of Iranian money and placing trade embargoes on Iran, played a very significant part in Iran signing the non-nuclear treaty. However, one can only speculate whether the Iranians would have succumbed to the wishes of the West just to get their money back if the terms of agreement were not mutually acceptable to both countries. If money was the only motivator for the Iranians in signing the treaty, would it have taken two long years for the negotiations to conclude? By the same token, perhaps it would have taken much longer if money was not involved. In this context, it may behoove the reader to also reflect on why Saddam Hussein, who had nothing to hide with respect to weapons of mass destruction, disallowed the inspectors from entering Iraq to search for the "supposedly" hidden weapons even though he would likely have known that the consequences of such an action was not going to be to his advantage. Some might conclude that he tried to save face – unwilling to let a foreign country dictate terms to him (especially when he had done nothing wrong), while others may consider him a "mad dog" who had completely misjudged American and British intentions, much like Kim Jong Yun of North Korea. In either case, he was willing to face the consequences of the West's the United States' anger, since they were blaming him for what he had not done, but what they *thought* he had done.

Chapter 4

The Marriage of Religion and State Laws

Unlike most major religions, Islam is a rule-based system with defined guidelines for every aspect of Muslim life. Because the law explicitly defines good governance with respect to Muslims and non-Muslims, state laws in a Muslim country are established on religious beliefs. On the other hand, Western countries have, to differing degrees, advocated for and adopted the principle of separation between church and state to promote social justice and religious freedom, which is not entirely possible for Islamic countries. Even for those countries that advocate "freedom of choice" within the context of religious factional practices, the "freedom" for Muslims is restricted to the following of civil laws. However, state laws are always observed within the confines of the majority faction's officially-sponsored Islamic code of laws provided by the Sharia.

Since Islam gives its followers much more detailed rules of conduct in the creation of religious based state laws, separating religion from state laws is somewhat problematic as compared to countries that embrace, say Hinduism, Christianity or countries that are religiously neutral. However, even with the following of prescribed laws to follow, a source of indecisiveness exists in Islamic countries because of the interpretative nature of Sharia (explained in Chapter 3), which complicates a uniform application of the law across all Islamic countries.

For those who practice a rigid understanding of Sharia law, such as the Wahhabis and the Salafists, little has changed for them since the earliest form of Islamic practice. Therefore, although the Salafist movement is an ideology that functions under the banner of incorporating science and technology in religion, in reality it has only used science to reinforce its preconceived understanding of the earliest interpretation of the scriptures. While the followers of Sunni Islamic factions like the Wahhabis and the Salafists, clearly define their beliefs within the strictest form of Sharia law, they have tried to do so through an interpretation that balances the dictates of seventh-century Islamic teachings with their population's expectations. This type of balancing act is enforced in most parts of the Persian Gulf and some other Islamic countries where the mixing of religious-demands in the creation of state laws is necessary for pacifying religious conservatives who have a very strong influence on the rules espoused by their autocrats. However, such a mix, which has worked well within most of these countries (although sometimes erratically) could agitate a rather tenuous relationship between these countries and their dealings with other non-Muslim countries, particularly those of the West.

To clarify the underlying problems associated with the inclusion of religious dogmas in the political arena, it should be noted that while it is easy to profess a need for secularism, it is not so easy for the majority religious faction to practice non-interference within pluralistic Islamic societies. This is especially true when aspects of the scriptures from opposing religions, or opposing factions of Islam, are deemed "unbearable" for the majority. In such cases, the majority's demands will always be the norm in national laws, irrespective of how fair or unfair they are to minorities.

Even in non-Islamic democratic countries, such actions are seldom fair in the strictest sense of equality for the minorities. Thus, while most Hindus tolerate the eating of chicken, fish, and lamb by Muslims and Christians in India, the world's largest democracy, it becomes a problem when a religiously-endorsed animal, the cow, is consumed by those who are not of the Hindu faith. This could perhaps explain the lynching of Mohammed Akhlaq, on September 28, 2015, by some villagers in India who believed the man's family had consumed and stored beef at their home. Lack of tolerance for minority beliefs (sanctioned, encouraged, or overlooked) by the religiously promoted laws of the land, can often create a volatile mental imprint on the minds of minorities, even if it is not displayed verbally or denounced with a show of physical force.

In understanding the rules surrounding the preaching of Muslim clerics or imams, it is helpful to draw parallels between the psyche of Islamic fanatics and the psyche of fanatical clergies from other religions. To start with, it should be remembered that extremely conservative Muslim preachers, preaching to crowds that are primarily educated through theologically conservative madrassas, can inspire the same overwhelming hate and prejudicial beliefs as Christian preachers like Pastor Rick Scarborough in the United States, who is vehemently opposed to homosexuality.[1] Scarborough blames AIDs and other calamities on an angry God, who sent them to punish mankind for having, among other things, children out of wedlock.[2] While the West has checks and balances in place for keeping religion separate from politics, such a scenario is much more severe in many Persian Gulf countries, where the interpreted "law of God" controls the law of the land.

While the majority of Muslims around the world have no interest in countering the spread of Western lifestyle and ideology, being quite content to learn from some of the successes of the West, there are others who do not view the awesome scientific advances of the West to be a positive learning model for Muslims. To these Muslims, the advances brought about by the spread of Western culture are a shock to their beliefs that likely stress a gradual transformation from the past, void of any external influences. However, as Daniel Pipes points out, these Muslims overtly take from the West what is essential to their needs. This is particularly noticeable in matters of health, medical, and military technology.[3] In essence, the Salafi, Wahhabi, and other similar movements, accept state-based ideology when it comes to issues like health and education, and advancements in technology and sciences, but try to justify these "borrowings" from the West within the context of their religious ideology. In other words, these movements do not completely separate religion from state laws because religious dictates are used to reinforce political directives in Islamic countries.

This mixing of politics and religion makes it easier to effectively govern populations that strictly live within the guidelines of their religious laws. In so doing, Islamic countries morph a once-religious law into a Western-style national law that is applied to all people living within their respective jurisdiction. These national, religiously-inspired laws are expected to be acknowledged by citizens, irrespective of their diversified cultural and religious beliefs. For example, based on their interpretation of Islamic dictates, there are laws prohibiting the sale of alcohol in countries like Sudan and Saudi Arabia, even though there are significant Christian populations within those countries whose religion does not forbid such activity.

To Westerners, the use of religious dictates to govern Islamic countries likely signifies government interference into the rights of its citizens. However, such an argument does not hold water, because Islamic countries are defined as "Islamic," based on their majority population being Muslims. In this context, the religious homogeneity of the population helps sustain Islamic laws as part of their country laws. Actually, for many Muslims, some form of Sharia is favorable, and not considered an intrusion into their civil or political rights. In a sense, the religiously-based constitutional rules, which may seem to the West to be abjurations of basic human rights, have worked well within the vicinity of individual country boundaries in the region, because in such countries, more often than not, religiously inspired state laws are the will of the majority. For example, in a country such as Saudi Arabia, Wahhabism is the state-sponsored religion that, together with Salafism (another extremely conservative form of Islam), is used to formulate country laws, perhaps because Wahhabism is the religious following of the ruling party, and these two factions of Islam — Wahhabism and Salafism — form the majority of the Saudi Arabian population.

For members of the Human Rights Watch group, however, there is some concern for minority rights with respect to state laws based on the religious preference of the majority. In many such cases, minorities are forced into unification by state laws that are laced with rules which may not be entirely in sync with their own religious practices.

On the other hand, in countries where there is a distinctly heterogeneous population that is factionalized on denominational beliefs (Sunni and Shi'a, for example), as in Syria, Iraq, and Bahrain, the story is very different. The "rights" of the population of these countries, as is the practice across all autocratic Muslim countries, are subjugated under the religious dictates of the ruling party. However, when the ruling party is from the minority population, and state laws are enforced through religious dictates, there is a likelihood of the governing body acting contrary to the will of the majority religious faction. This is precisely what has happened in say, Syria, where the Sunni Arab majority is ruled by Assad, who is considered a Shi'a. In such cases the larger number of people who follow a particular faction have no choice but to live in an uneasy adherence to the laws of their country enforced by the minority group, even though they are in the majority. However, a volatile situation emerges when radical religious rules, which are contrary to the religious beliefs of the *majority*, are propagated through minority political authorities. In this case, the *majority* population is *forcefully* subjected to submit to religiously inspired state laws which may be contrary to their religious beliefs.

It is important to note that religious teachings, and interpretative modifications to them, are often used as a subterfuge to camouflage a latent controversial law. These selective teachings often arise to fulfill a need, whether political, social, or otherwise, usually brought on to control or appease a strong anti-societal demand arising at the time. In this respect, a state-based religious body in conservative Islamic countries has the power to infer religious significances through its own self-fulfilling interpretation of the scriptures in order to create or sustain state laws that otherwise would not be acceptable to its citizens. When one thinks about this phenomenon with regards to the "workings" of Daesh and Al-Qaeda, it becomes clear that the influence of an *interpretive* ideology (Islamism) is the governing factor, and not Islam the religion.

The use of religion in politics also plays a rather dubious role in the supposedly beneficial agreements between the Middle East and Western countries. For example, since the eighteenth century, Saudi rulers have shared power with their religious contemporaries in the country. While the monarch is technically the country's supreme religious leader and custodian of Islam's two holiest mosques at Mecca and Medina, in truth, he shares authority with a powerful group of spiritual leaders. For nearly three hundred years, the House of Al Saud has controlled the state, while the Al ash-Sheikh, the descendants of Sheikh Muhammad ibn 'Abd al-Wahhab (1703–1792) have controlled religious institutions, such as the Ulama.[4] The Saudi ruling family has a non-negotiable agreement with the Wahhabi-dominated religious faction, which allows the Ulama the control of mosques, cultural behavior, and education in the country, as long as they do not interfere in core political issues, such as royal succession, foreign policy, or the control of the armed forces. While this deal has been respected over many years, it underlines the fact that the Saudi royal family cannot completely deny religious implications in its foreign policy decisions. Because the Ulama's dictates are supported by the will of the people (the Wahhabis and the Salafist), the options available to the monarch when it comes to aligning the country's political agenda with the desires of its Western allies can sometimes be limited. The question then arises as to how much leeway does the royal family have when faced with politically problematic rules if, indeed, there is a conflict between the desires of the people and that of the government? In the case of the Saudi government officially siding with Daesh in the initial stages of Daesh's violent activities, it is likely that the Ulama had the same desire as its rulers to drive the hated Shi'a monarch out of the area. Or perhaps it was the Saudi government that was abiding by the demands of the Ulama in its desire to side with the Islamists on religious interpretations.

The way the Saudi ruling party governs its population has hardly, if ever, crossed the minds of average Americans. However, the perception lingers that because the 9/11 attackers were mainly Saudi nationals, the Saudi government must have been involved, despite a twenty-eight-page U.S. government report stating otherwise. On the other hand, this problem does highlight difficulties for the ruling party when attempting to balance the wishes of the people with those regarding its political agenda.

While many Muslims may be reluctant to separate religion from state laws, their expectations are very different from one another because, as stated earlier, Sharia has been interpreted differently by different Muslims. Although secularists in the Muslim world believe that the laws of the state should be devoid of Islamic dictates, there are traditionalists who feel strongly that the laws of the state should be adopted from religiously-based schools. This division persists in the Islamic community to this day. While not quite at par with Western definitions and examples of "progression," Islamic countries such as Malaysia and Turkey (to name a few) could be considered progressive in the context of their being based on Islamic theories that promote the modernization of Islamic laws in areas that include women's rights, and in the non-compulsion format in the practice of the religion.

Regardless of the personal, interpretative aspects of most religions, the majority of people in non-Islamic countries (including Muslims) generally abide by the laws and customs of their countries even if there is a separation of religion and state. In these countries, state rules and regulations, trump religious considerations. That being said, there are occurrences where aspects of religion still seep into political decisions, even when the country promotes secularism as its governing policy. For example, in once again citing the example of India, in most states of the country, the cow (being a religious symbol of motherhood for Hindus) is banned from slaughter for *all* citizens, including Muslims and Christians.

Even in Western countries, the influence of religion, albeit used mainly as a tool to gain political hold, is nothing new.

While the separation of religion and state is a cornerstone of the constitutional rights of the American people, as is evident in presidential elections in the United States, one can take religion out of politics, but it cannot take the power of religious influence from politicians who draw like-minded people to their side with implied promises of religious leanings that could supposedly influence their political policies. However, unlike Islamic monarchies, politicians in the West, because of constitutional demands, can run for office on religious aspirations, but they simply cannot run on a platform that promises the legislation of laws based on religious preferences. As an example, rolling back reproductive funding in the United States is seldom discussed by politicians (except by a few religious extremists) as a religious issue, but is rather made out to be an argument over the fundamental right to life, or on some other political issue.

Part II:

The Rise and Spread of Islamists

Chapter 5

Prominent Islamic Factions in the Middle East

Islam is a religion centered on five basic principles, known as the "pillars" of Islam. These pillars are: (1) the affirmation that "there is no god but Allah, and Mohammed is his prophet;" (2) the five daily prayers that a Muslim must offer to God while facing Mecca, Saudi Arabia (some Shi'a factions allow three daily prayers, perhaps because of the demands of modern life); (3) the obligatory percentage of a Muslim's income that is to be given to charity on an annual basis (similar to tithes, a tax in Christianity for the support of the church and clergy); (4) fasting during Ramadan, the ninth month of the Muslim calendar year; and (5) at least one pilgrimage to Mecca, if financially and physically able.

As has been alluded earlier, similar to other major religions, Islam too has different denominations, such as the Shi'as, the Sunnis, and the Sufis, with further sub-denominations within each sect. To draw parallels, these Muslim denominations can be compared to the divisions of Protestants and Catholics in Christianity. By the same token, sub-denominations, such as the "Twelvers," "Fivers" (Zaydis), and "Seveners" (Ismailis) within the Shi'a denomination, and the various schools of thought (the fiqhs) such as the Hanafi and Hanbali traditions within the Sunni denomination, can be likened to the Baptist and Methodist factions in Protestantism.

Some Prominent Sunni Factions in Islam

Generally speaking, Sunnis do not like being classified into denominations, instead calling themselves just "Sunnis" or "Muslims." Sub-factions in Sunni Muslims are primarily based on the following of a particular school of Sunni jurisprudence – Hanafi, Maliki, Shafi'i, and Hanbali. However, over the years different sub-groups based on cultural and political following have occurred. These groups have all been wrapped in their interpretative religious following of a particular school of jurisprudence or a mixture of the various thoughts provided by the four schools. Some of these movements have a distinct following, and are often considered as separate factions within the following of Sunni Muslims. According to Stephen Schwartz and Irfan Al-Alawi, reporting in the *Millat Times* in India, the Wahhabis in Saudi Arabia, for example, by-passed three of the four recognized schools of Sunni jurisprudence and replaced them with their own form of law, derived mainly from the Hanbali school of jurisprudence.[1]

The Wahhabis and the Salafist. Wahhabism, which is the official fiqh in Saudi Arabia and Qatar, came into being in the eighteenth century in Saudi Arabia, and is based on the beliefs of its founder, Muhammed ibn Abd al-Wahhab. It was Abd al-Wahhab's belief that Sunni Islam was centered on the Ottoman caliphate that gave credibility to Shi'a Islam and spiritual Sufism, which was not acceptable to him. According to al-Wahhab, the Muslim religion of his time represented a return to pre-Muslim polytheism, which had to be eradicated. He also believed that the decline of the Muslim world was not only caused by insidious foreign innovations that included European modernism, but also because the elements of traditional Islam had become unfamiliar to the isolated Bedouins in Saudi Arabia. It should be noted that

Wahhabism gives jihad an unusual prominence in its teachings. It also places an overriding emphasis on *tawhid* (monotheism), condemning many traditional Muslim practices such as praying to "saints" (allowing prayers only to Allah) and considering the veneration of loved ones' graves (as is done by the Shi'as) as *shirk* (polytheism).

However, even within the sect of Wahhabism, there are differences. For example, according to James M. Dorsey (senior fellow at the S. Rajaratnam School of International Studies at Singapore's Nanyang Technological University), Qatar, part of whose native population is also Wahhabi, does not appear to follow Saudi Arabia's rather repressive and restrictive form of Wahhabism.[2]

For Westerners, and for many Muslims, even those who are not progressives, the state-sponsored religion of the Wahhabis in Saudi Arabia can be cruel and misogynic in its establishment of Islamic law for its state. Punishments, such as stoning a married person to death for infidelity and amputating hands for stealing, bolster beliefs that Islam is a violent religion. However, the practices of the Wahhabis and the Salafists (another extremely conservative following of Sunni Islam), represent, as stated in Chapter 4, an extremely small percentage of the total Muslim population. While stats on the total number of Wahhabis in the world vary, estimates in July 2016 by Michael Lipka from the Pew Research Centre, place them at fewer than 5 million (about 0.30 percent of the total population of around 1.6 billion Muslims).[3] In most other parts of the world where the majority of Muslims live, such as Malaysia, Turkey, Iran, India, and even in many parts of Pakistan, the practice of Islam may seem conservative to Westerners, but it is not nearly as extreme as that practiced in Saudi Arabia and a few other parts of the Middle East..

On the other hand, Salafism originated on the broad foundation of an intellectual movement in the nineteenth century, which sought gradual social reform through education. Unlike the Wahhabis, who essentially arose from the Hanbali School of Jurisprudence, the Salafists encompass all four of the Sunni fiqhs: Maliki, Shafi'i, Hanbali, and Hanafi. According to Canadian investigative journalist Bruce Livesey, Salafists constitute about 0.5 percent of the world's Muslims (less than 10 million), with the majority living in Egypt and in some Arab countries in the Persian Gulf.[4] The Salafists believe that early Muslims understood and practiced Islam "correctly," but that true understanding of Islam has gradually drifted, just as the "people" of previous prophets have strayed from the original message of God, preached by Moses and Jesus. The Salafists' goal is to rationally reinterpret early Islam with the expectation of rediscovering a more "modern" religion. As Trevor Stanley points out, most Salafists — the purists who avoid politics, and the activists who get involved in politics — depend on a nonviolent, educational understanding of the religion to change society through preaching, or evangelizing. However, there are a few jihadists within Salafism who prefer to inspire change through violence.[5]

According to a report to the United States Congress by Middle Eastern Affairs, Defense, and Trade Division's Christopher M. Blanchard, the Salafi movement is an ultra-conservative reform movement within Sunni Islam whose doctrine is based on a fundamentalist approach, emulating Prophet Muhammad and his earliest followers. For those who practice Salafism, an Islamic revival can only happen if present-day Muslims emulate early generations of the faith, and purge foreign influences from their lives. This understanding, however, is based not only on the fundamental belief of the Salafist movement, but is also one of the basic tenets of Wahhabism.

While Wahhabism is seen as a pared-down Islam that rejects modern influences, Salafism is understood as a reconciliation of "by-gone" Islam with modernism. What they have in common is that both favor direct, literal reinterpretations of Islam, as understood by very early Muslims. The two movements, Wahhabism and Salafism, therefore, are often considered as the same by many Muslims and non-Muslims alike. Their espoused beliefs in Islamic laws and practices are based on interpretative understandings of their founding fathers and are considered to be among the strictest and most conservative forms of Islamic following, even though Salafists purport to place emphasis on reconciling Islamic principles with modernism.[6]

Based on the definition outlined by Blanchard, Wahhabism is considered a conservative Islamic creed, centered around and emanating from Saudi Arabia. On the other hand, Salafism can be seen as a more general "purist" Islamic movement, which has developed independently in various places around the world.

Mark Durie, reporting in the *Middle East Forum*, states that Salafism is not a single sect based on a unified movement. However, Salafi interpretations of Islam, appeal to many Muslims worldwide who seek religious renewal in the face of modern challenges. Durie points out that according to several scholars, the waging of violent jihad is not inherently associated with puritanical Islamic beliefs, and the ascendancy of militancy within the wider Salafi community was relegated to the war of resistance against the Soviet occupation of Afghanistan during the 1980s. However, violent Salafist-inspired groups, such as Al-Qaeda, continue to advocate the overthrowing of states that do not sustain their breed of puritanical Islam, enforced under a strict application of Islamic law. Although most Salafists do not advocate the violence enshrined in Bin Laden's message, violent Salafist ideology has nevertheless attracted some followers throughout the Muslim world."[7]

The Muslim Brotherhood. The other important movement of interest in the Middle East, which was referenced in Chapter 3, is that of the Muslim Brotherhood. The Brotherhood is a reform movement that like the Salafists, believes in strict adherence to the examples and teachings provided by Prophet Muhammad. The Muslim Brotherhood, while following the Salafist movement, has adopted a strategy for reform that strategically engages with the modern world, and develops policies that engage with modernity in every dimension of life. Consistent with its goal of "penetration and transformation," the Brotherhood ideology takes a positive approach to modern science, and has developed ideological positions on challenges posed by contemporary economic and political realities. Such ideology has strong appeal for Muslim professionals and intellectuals, including doctors and scientists — many of them Western-educated. The founder of the Brotherhood, Hassan Al Banna, outlined his vision through a series of epistles, including one titled "On Jihad." The World Alamac of Islamism, states that:

> ...Al-Banna believed that *jihad* was not restricted to the struggle against *kuffar* (apostates), but was in fact a more comprehensive awakening of Muslim hearts and minds. In the 1930s, Al-Banna's opposition to British rule and influence found expression as his organization began to recruit followers who saw the appeal in its ideology on issues ranging from poverty and education to nationalism and, during his time, the nascent Israeli-Palestinian conflict.[8]

Initially, the reason for the founding of this group of Sunni Muslims was mainly to oust the British from Egypt, and to rid the country of what the Brotherhood saw was "corrupting"

Western influences. In a study for Harvard International Review, the deputy chairman of the Muslim Brotherhood, Mohammad Ma'mun El-Hudaibi, identified two aspects of the group's goals: (1) the extremely conservative use of Sharia in controlling the affairs of state and society, and (2) the unification of all Islamic countries, particularly the Middle East states, in freeing them from foreign imperialism.[9] Because of the Brotherhood's embracement of physical force in achieving its second goal stated above, the organization has lost favor among some countries in the Middle East. However, as stated in Chapter 3, the real reason it being divorced from favor of countries like Egypt and Saudi Arabia, is likely not so much because it has advocated violence for its goal, but because of personal reasons that has more to do with the group's religious beliefs and its desire for political power in Egypt. But in keeping with the desire of a non-violent reputation, the Brotherhood, according to Peter Baker, writing for *The New York Times*, officially renounced violence in 1970 and embraced democracy as its primary source in achieving its goals.[10]

The Deobandi. Besides the Wahhabi, Salafi, and Muslim Brotherhood movements, there are other conservative factions in Sunni Islam, such as the Barelvi and the Deobandi movements, which started in India. Most such subsets would be irrelevant to the current issues in the Muslim world because of their relatively small numbers and subdued existence. However, the Deobandi movement is of interest because of its following in Pakistan's Pashtun region, which is the home of many of the Taliban members in Afghanistan.

The Deobandi movement is rooted within the Hanafi School of Jurisprudence. Besides being represented on the Indian subcontinent, it also has a following among some South Asian Muslims living abroad. The fundamentalist Deobandi Muslim sect, like the Wahhabi and Salafi movements, started with a claim to "reform" Islam. However, in contrast to Wahhabism, which emerged as a violent phenomenon in Nejd, Saudi Arabia, three quarters of a century earlier, the Deobandi movement arose in the nineteenth century as a nonviolent, peaceful revivalism based on the principle that uniting Indian Muslims would assist in the resistance of British colonial rulers, especially after the failure of the 1857 Indian rebellion against the British.[11]

However, once the Pakistani-trained Taliban came into power in Afghanistan, the Wahhabi influence from Saudi Arabia and the influence of militant Islamism based on the Salafi warring jihadism practiced by Osama bin Laden (who was in Afghanistan at that time), were enough to lure the Deobandi into Pakistan and Afghanistan, away from their nonviolent past.

The Taliban originally imposed its brutal, repressive regime in Kandahar, Afghanistan. Culturally, the group followed the societal norms of the Pashtun society, since most members of the Taliban are of that ethnicity. Similar to the Muslim Brotherhood, the Salafists, and the Wahhabis, the Taliban Deobandi movement believes that because Islamic societies have been seduced by the amoral and material accoutrements of Westernization, they have been enslaved by the West in all their endeavors. Their ideology holds that Muslims' primary obligations and principle loyalties are to their religion, and then to their country. Even though the Taliban Deobandi have not committed terrorist activities outside their region, their teachings stress the right and obligation to wage military jihad for the purpose of protecting Muslims residing in any country. The group also does not consider Shi'as to be Muslims, and are extremely misogynistic and cruel. Their ideology is mirrored by that of the Pakistani Deobandi.

Though the Pakistani and the Afghani Deobandi had become increasingly violent over time, it was not until the 2001

Afghanistan War that the Indian Deobandi became radicalized and adopted the Islamist theology of ultra-conservatism and hate. However, in 2008, the Indian Deobandi had a change of heart. Like the Qataris, who follow a milder version of Saudi Wahhabism and are, generally speaking, "neutral" with respect to the Shi'as, *The Times of India* reported that the Islamic seminary Darul-Uloom Deoband in India, issued a fatwa against terrorism, stating that Islam had come to spread the message of global peace and eradicate terrorism.[12]

Similar to the Salafists and the Wahhabis, the Taliban's Deobandi-influenced ideology preaches a distorted utopia of a "pure," literal Islam — one that is disrespectful of other faiths and condemns all Islamic interpretations it disagrees with. However, while both Taliban Deobandi and Wahhabis share common traits in their ideologies, such as their intense hatred for Shi'a Muslims, they also have some differences. For example, the Taliban Deobandi disagree discretely with the Wahhabi practice of creating its own fiqh, which, as stated earlier, shares many similarities with the Hanbali School of Islamic jurisprudence. Similarly, while Deobandi agree with the Wahhabi prohibition of many Sufi practices, such as *milad-an-nabi* (celebration of Muhammad's birthday) and musical performances, the Deobandi, unlike the Wahhabis, do not outright denounce Sufism (a small sect in Islam).

Stephen Schwartz and Irfan al-Alawi point out that one major commonality between the Wahhabis and Deobandi is their "dedication to the gratuitous issuance of weird and illogical fatwas, or religious opinions." One such example they cite is the Saudi-Wahhabi fatwas forbidding gender mixing. According to the authors, the application of the fatwa against causal mixing of sexes seems "strange" when it does not condemn such mixing, if the man in question "drinks the breastmilk of a woman," allegedly making him a member of the woman's family.[13]

While such a pronouncement by Schwartz and al-Alawi may be well-intentioned in their identification of "ridiculous" fatwas, they seem to have missed its underlying significance. While there is no doubt that many ridiculous fatwas exist, this particular one merits some contextual understanding. In many cultures in the world, being nursed by a woman effectively results in that woman being regarded as a member of the family, and thus would deserve the same respect from that child as his or her natural mother.

For many experts, the motives behind fatwas, whether by the Deobandi, the Salafists, or the Wahhabis, are identical, regardless of whether they originate in religious madrassas or from websites. These groups seek absolute control over the lives of Muslims, and, by extension, over all Muslim relations with their non-Muslim neighbors. As Schwartz and al-Alawi rightly point out, "the aim of 'fatwa fanatics' is not religious; it is political and totalitarian."[14]

The Shi'a Faction in Islam

Besides the Sunni sub-factions outlined above, the other major faction in the Muslim religion is Shi'ism, which has a majority following in Iran, Azerbaijan, Bahrain, and Iraq, and as a minority group in countries such as Syria, Yemen, Pakistan, India, and Lebanon. Shi'as take up only about 11 to 15 percent of the worldwide population of Muslims, with the majority (about 30 percent) living in Iran. Generally, the Shi'as, as evaluated through Western eyes, seem much less restrictive in their religious beliefs (especially where females are considered) than the Sunnis who follow Wahhabi or Salafi traditions. It should be remembered, however, that just as Saudi Arabia and Qatar are primarily Wahhabis and Salafists, most of the Twelvers of the

Shi'a denomination of Islam reside in Iran, making it the largest Shi'a populated country in the world with Azerbaijan in second place. Therefore, even though the number of Shi'as around the world is very small with respect to the total Muslim population, the concentration of them in Iran makes it not only the largest populated country in the Persian Gulf by a wide margin, but it also makes its population one of the largest among Middle Eastern countries as well.

The conflict between the Shi'as and the Sunnis began due to a disagreement regarding succession claims after the Prophet's death. According to Shi'as, the successor had to be a blood relation of the Prophet, while the Sunnis believed that the successor should be an individual selected by those who were learned and scholarly in the teachings of Islam (including the Hadith of the Prophet). The hatred between these two groups has been an on-going conflict since the Prophet's death, and has, to this day, played a vital role in the struggle between the Shi'a and Sunni-dominated countries of the Middle East. The hatred between the two groups is so strong that some Sunnis actually believe that Shi'as are apostates and should not be considered Muslims, just as some Shi'as believe that Sunnis are not real Muslims.

As mentioned earlier, there are many sub factions in Shi'a Islam that include the Twelvers, the Seveners, the Jafri, the Tayyibi, and others. A tree diagram depicting the different branches of Islam, including their respective sub-factions and schools of jurisprudence, is provided in Appendix A: Table 1.

The Sufi Faction in Islam

Among the minority factions in Islam, Sufism deserves further exploration because, as Andrew G. Bostom states, "Sufism has attracted favorable attention and converts from all sorts of Westerners, from new agers in Marin County, California, to East Coast intellectuals."[15] While Bostom has some interesting and well-written arguments proving military jihad has been committed by some Sufis, most Sufi mystics believe in jihad as a purely spiritual quest based on the concept of "greater" jihad. In this context, physical actions taken in defense of the religion (although very important), as explained by Knapp, are considered the "lesser" jihad. To this day, according to Michael Knapp, Sufis see jihad as a personal rather than a political struggle.[16]

Though early Sufism concentrated almost primarily on the relation between God and the soul; from 900 onward, a strong Muhammad-mysticism developed. Many practices originally applied to God, in later times were also used in veneration of the Prophet, who was said to be like the "dawn between the darkness of the material world and the sun of Reality."[17] This, perhaps, is one reason why many Muslims who consider Muhammad to be "just a man" find Sufism unacceptable.

The Impact of Religious Factions in the Middle East

While many may suspect that the hatred between the Iranians and the Arabs is based entirely on religious grounds, Iranian intellectual and political scientist Sadek Zibakalam states that the relationship between Arabs and Persians has always been a source of controversy, not only as a struggle for contemporary power in the region, but also because of historical rivalry, which played an integral part in the formation of the national psyche of both peoples. Persians will, according to Zibakalam, never forget their defeat at the hands of Arabs in the Battle of Qadisiya, even though it was fought 1,400 years ago.[18]

While nobody would seriously suggest that all Iranians harbor feelings of hostility over a war fought thousands of years ago, it may have been catalyst for the continuing rift between the Persians and Arabs. In identifying the reasons behind the hostility between the two parties, according to reporter Saud al-Zahed, there is an understanding by scholars such as Zibakalam that Iran's attempts to gain power in the region are triggered by racism. The innate belief that they are racially "better" than their Arab neighbors pushes Iranians to prove their superiority by "standing up" to the West, to which, according to the Iranians, Saudi Arabia and other Arab countries in the Persian Gulf have succumbed. This feeling of superiority is sometimes enforced for the Iranians through religious annotations by the clergy. Thus, religious Iranians, and some others of the Shi'a sect, are likely to express their resentment of Arabs in the form of "curses" directed at Sunnis during preachment time.[19] In this respect, it should be noted that even if religion is not seen as the "real" reason for the animosity between the Arabs and the Persians, it becomes an additional weapon for hatred perpetuated by ethnic, racial, and political divide.

Zibakalam also identifies a connection between racism and lack of education across the world. While this may not be a claim that has been scientifically quantified, the correlation between education and racism in Europe (and recently in the United States against Muslims, and other "undesirable foreigners") may, according to some experts, largely be perpetuated by those who are "uneducated." However, it would be a fallacy to imply that such prejudices are entirely attributed to those who lack an educational background. In Iran, for example, hatred of Arabs is also quite common among intellectuals. In this respect, the desire of the Persian Language Institute to remove Arabic words from great literary works that have been in the Persian language for more than one hundred years, exemplifies the "intellectual barbarism" practiced by elitist groups in Iran. Zibakalam also admits that this "racism" is not only aimed at Arabs, but also at other non-Persian ethnicities inside Iran, such as the Kurds, the Baluchi, the Turks, and the Lur.[20] In light of Zibakalam's revelation, it is likely the Iranians are irked to find the United States dealing "respectfully" with Arabs when they do not convey the same respect to Persians.

But besides the Persian-Arab divide, based partly on religion and partly on cultural differences, various dormant anomalies of conflict in the Middle East have also come to the forefront in the region. In Iraq, until 2003, the Sunni Ba'ath party, led by Saddam Hussein, ran the country, despite the majority population being Shi'ite. The same is true in Bahrain, where despite the majority population being Shi'ite, the ruling Al-Khalifa party is Sunni. On the other hand, in Syria, the ruling party members of President Bashar al-Assad are Alawites (Shi'ite), while most of the population is Sunni.

In this context, it is worthwhile to reflect upon the fact that while Assad has been vilified as a tormentor of the Sunnis and Kurds within his country, the same could be said for the ruling party in Bahrain, which brutally quelled the uprising of the majority Shi'a population, with Saudi Arabian and United Arab Emirate military forces, during the 2011 Arab Spring.[21] While the Shi'a uprising may or may not have been justifiable, the crux of the argument remains that atrocities against the Shi'a population were committed on the island. This, according to *Bahrain Watch*, is exemplified by the fact that the Bahraini regime hid it from the world by systematically shutting out journalists and foreign observers from the area.[22] However, the event was largely ignored by Western media, perhaps because, according to Assistant Professor of Sociology, Dr. Amy Austin Holmes, at

94

the American University in Cairo, the world, at that time, was more interested in the annexation of Crimea in Ukraine by the Russians, than the atrocities committed in a small country like Bahrain.[23]

The undemocratic misrepresentation between those that are governed and those who govern in the Middle East has created an additional chasm and deep-seated hatred between some ruling parties and their populations. This hatred is instrumental in understanding and identifying the Shi'a-Sunni divide as one aspect of the conflict in the Middle East. In the not-too-distant -past, open warfare started on September 22, 1980, when Iraq invaded Iran. According to the editors of *Encyclopaedia Britannica*, the root causes of the war were multiple territorial and political disputes between the two countries. Iraq wanted to seize control of the rich oil-producing Iranian border-region, Khuzestan — a territory inhabited largely by Arabs, over which Iraq sought to extend some form of suzerainty. By attacking when it did, Iraq took advantage of the apparent disorder and isolation of Iran's new government, then at loggerheads with the United States over the seizure of the American Embassy in Tehran by Iranian militants. In addition, at about that time, the Iranian army was demoralized because of the dissolution of Iran's regular armed forces by its new anti-Shah government. For many in the Muslim world, the conflict between the two countries, arising from a tussle for geopolitical advantage was (and even now for many), considered to be a religiously induced denominational conflict (although there is no substantiating evidence for it).

Iraq's aspirations to attack Iran received a boost from fellow Persian Gulf States such as Saudi Arabia and Kuwait, who, despite being hostile over Iraq's leadership ambitions, encouraged Saddam Hussein to attack Iran because they feared that the Islamic revolution in Iran (after the overthrow of the Shah in 1979) would spill over into their own borders. The Arab nations, according to the editors of *Encyclopaedia Britannica*, openly financed Iraq in its war efforts, starting in 1980. By 1982, Iraq was tacitly supported by the United States and directly by the Soviet Union, which was angered over the destruction of Iran's National Communist Party known as the Tudeh Party.[24]

Although the Arabs financed Iraq's war with Iran, Hussein soon lost favor among Sunni-Arab countries in the Middle East because of his ambitions for hegemony in the Muslim world. He was eventually overthrown in 2003, not by the Iranians, but by the Americans and the British, through the erroneous belief that he was hoarding weapons of mass destruction.

In the events leading to the overthrow of Saddam Hussein, it is important to note that a ruler's Sunni identification does not guarantee his acceptance by other Sunni-Arab leaders in the Persian Gulf. Qatar, for example, is disliked by many Arab and some non-Arab countries in the Middle East because of differences in its ideologies and geopolitical standing, particularly with respect to Iran. By the same token, Saddam Hussein, an Arabian Sunni, was not liked by his Sunni neighbors because of his ambition to become a power force in the Arabian world and to take over oil wells in Sunni Kuwait. There was, therefore, a likely nod of approval from the powerful Saudis for the Americans to invade Iraq in the first Gulf War in 1990, when Sunni-governed Iraq invaded Sunni Kuwait. Similarly, in controlling Saddam's desire for hegemony in the region, Arab countries likely gave their approval in 2003 for the American-British invasion to confiscate his weapons of mass destruction. However, it was never expected by Arab countries in the Persian Gulf that Saddam's government would be replaced by democratic rule, which placed the majority Iraqi Shi'as in power, and perhaps made it easier for

Iran to expand its own influence in the region, as was actualized by the first elected democratic party in Iraq under Malaki.

To understand the environment of status quo in the region during that time, it should be noted that Sunni Muslims were quite content living under Sunni monarchs, where they enjoyed an elevated status compared to those who practiced other religions or factions of Islam. However, after the invasion of Iraq by the West, the Sunnis no longer held their coveted superiority, which had benefited them despite Shi'a Arabs being the majority in Iraq. Thus, according to some analysts, what had once been an internal conflict between different regions of the Middle East, now resulted in the Sunnis raising their heads against the West that had tilted the balance from the favor of Iraqi-Arab Sunnis to their arch rivals, the Iraqi-Arab Shi'as.

In the context of the Iraqi war, some in the United States may argue that the removal of Saddam was not in American interest, especially considering the realization that he did not have weapons of mass destruction. But, for whatever consolation one gets in the post mortem of the United States' and Britain's unwarranted invasion of Iraq, dismantling Saddam's armed forces after he was overthrown, as explained later in Chapter 8, has been identified as one of the major causes for Daesh's expansion as the leading terrorist organization in the world. While the West may justify this colossal mistake as having been done in good faith, the terror, ruin, and death caused by Daesh's rise to power — whether attributed partly or wholly as a result of the overthrow of Saddam Hussein — is nothing short of devastating.

Chapter 6

The Rise of Islamists

Generally speaking, most Persian Gulf countries have retained their particular forms of Sharia within their borders. However, there have been, and continue to be some extremists within these countries, such as Saudi national Osama bin Laden (killed by the United States Special Forces), who are so angered by the West that they have stepped outside their country's borders to fight against it. Their anger against the West, among other things, is based mainly on what they perceive as the extortion of exorbitant profits from *their* oil fields; being unfair to their brethren, the Palestinians; disrespecting their religious and cultural norms; and forming alliances with the sheikhs, kings, and dictators in the Persian Gulf who have treated Westerners preferentially over their own people. For example, *The Guardian* correspondent and author, Geraldine Bedell, who spent time in some Persian Gulf countries, points out the hedonistic and racist behavior of some sheikhs who coddled the West. She draws the example of the ruling party in Bahrain, that allowed bikini-clad Western expatriates on Sheikh Isa bin Salman al-Khalifa's beach, but had until very recently, banned locals and non-Western expats from entering it. While the super-affluent locals had no problem accessing the Sheikh's beach, most local population looked from afar, seemingly despising the Westerners who, together with their monarch and his entourage, desecrated their land by flaunting a religiously unacceptable culture in their country. But aside from such moral infractions, Bahrain, in particular, is also guilty of extreme human rights violations from 1975 to 2001, when the fearsome Scotsman Ian Henderson was employed by the ruling party to stamp out all forms of dissidents in the nation. Henderson was seen as the de facto ruler of Bahrain, creating an extremely fearful environment during his strict, sadistic rule. The irony is that while reforms were put in place by the Sheikh's successor Hamad bin Isa al-Khalifa, according to Amnesty International, they deteriorated quickly by the end of 2007.[1]

Even in 2016, according to a report by the Human Rights Watch, there was a marked deterioration in human rights in Bahrain (See Chapter 5) when authorities dissolved the main political opposition group, Al-Wifaq; jailed the country's leading human rights activist, and harassed and prosecuted Shi'a clerics who peacefully protested the arbitrary revocation of the citizenship of Al-Wifaq's spiritual leader, Sheikh Isa Qasim. In 2016, Human Rights Watch stated that the Bahraini authorities stripped 133 individuals of their citizenship, bringing the total to 341 since the beginning of 2015. Bahraini authorities also deported several people and instituted travel bans on a Shi'a cleric, an academic, and a human rights lawyer, as well as tens of individuals who were critical of the country's human rights abuses. In September 2016, an arbitrary travel ban prevented human rights activist Nedal al-Salman from attending a UN' Human Rights Council meeting in Geneva.[2]

The Birth of Al-Qaeda

It was in such an environment that Al-Qaeda, the cause of the 9/11 calamity which culminated in the death of almost 3,000 innocent people in the United States, was born. The beginning of Al-Qaeda, however, has no conclusive starting point, though it is thought to have been largely influenced by an event pointed out by Fareed Zakaria, who links the roots of this organization to a fanatically religious Egyptian student, Sayed Qutb on his visit in 1949 to a local dance hall in Colorado, United States. Qutb reportedly could not bear to see men and women dancing with their "lips meeting lips," and their "chests meeting chests." He was aghast to see women's breasts outlined underneath their clothes, and espoused a deep-seated hatred for everything American from then on. He wrote some 24 books, personifying his disdain for a Western lifestyle that, according to him, had penetrated the Middle East. Osama bin Laden — as well as the present leader of Al-Qaeda, Ayman al-Zawahiri — held Qutb in high esteem and revered his writings about Islam.[3]

It's likely that the cumulative effect of Bin Laden's own experiences, and Qutb's critical writings against the West, which he believed had taken advantage of Muslim resources and strategic locations, disrespected their religious and cultural beliefs, and, above all, had been unfair to Muslims in their dealings with the Israelis, could all be, to some degree or the other, possible reasons for the rise of Al-Qaeda. More importantly, many in the Persian Gulf saw their own monarchs as puppets of the West, catering to its needs, some at the expense of the locals, especially if many local beliefs were not in sync with those of the rulers. Dr. David Vine, associate professor of anthropology at American University in Washington, D.C., identifies part of the reason for the rise of Al-Qaeda as the complete disregard of local wishes by the rulers in the region. Vine cites the example of foreign troops in Muslim holy lands as one major factor in Osama bin Laden's professed motivation for the 9/11 attacks.[4] According to Dr. Michael Ryan, a senior fellow at the Jamestown Foundation and an independent consultant and researcher on Middle East security issues, it was in a festering hatred for regional leaders and for the United States, that al-Zawahiri crafted his vision to establish defensible Islamic countries, free of Western influence, in the heart of the Middle East.

By the same token, it was hatred of Western interference that caused the extremely violent Jordanian, Abu Mus'ab al-Zarqawi, to move into Iraq from Afghanistan, not long after the United States invaded Afghanistan in 2001. Al-Zarqawi formed an independent Salafist-based warring jihadist movement known as the Jama'at al-Tawhid wal-Jihad. By the summer of 2003, Jama'at al-Tawhid wal-Jihad was one of the groups fighting the United States and British forces after they toppled Saddam Hussein from power. At this time, al-Zarqawi's group consisted of a smattering of Iraqis and some foreign fighters, but he made up for his small numbers by using military tactics that differed considerably from other Iraqi insurgent groups. Rather than relying on guerrilla tactics such as ambushes, raids, and hit-and-run attacks against the United States forces, Jama'at al-Tawhid wal-Jihad relied heavily on the use of suicide bombers.[5]

In late 2004, according to Dr. Ahmed Salah Hashim, associate professor in the military studies program at the Institute of Defense and Strategic Studies, Rajaratnam School of International Studies (RSIS) in Singapore, al-Zarqawi brought his group under the control of Osama bin Laden, the head of Al-Qaeda at that time, forming a new organization, *Tanzim Qaidat al-Jihad fi Bilad al-Rafidayn*, also known as Al-Qaeda in Iraq (AQ). The affiliation with Al-Qaeda gave prestige to al-Zarqawi's loosely knit group. It now not only had the backing of Al-Qaeda, but it also inherited their logistical and financial support, which allowed al-Zarqawi to recruit a greater number of people to his cause. By the same token, al-Zarqawi provided

Al-Qaeda with a ready-made base from which to strike the United States in Iraq.[6]

Once al-Zarqawi's group became affiliated with the main body of Al-Qaeda, its objectives, according to Michael Ryan, became the same as those envisioned by al-Zawahiri — stopping American influence within the Middle East region, particularly with respect to the Israeli-Palestinian conflict, and challenging the established world order with an ultimate goal of Muslim world domination. According to some observers, al-Zarqawi's troops not only fought against the insurgency of American and British troops in Iraq, but also fought a denominational war against the Shi'as, and the ethnically different Kurds. After American forces killed al-Zarqawi in 2006, he was succeeded by Abu Omar al-Baghdadi. Abu Bakr al-Baghdadi replaced Abu Omar al-Baghdadi after the United States killed the latter in 2010.[7]

Although al-Zawahiri's goal is to free the Middle East of Western influence, Al-Qaeda differs significantly from other traditional terrorist and in-conflict organizations. For one, it does not depend on the sponsorship of a political state and is not defined by a particular conflict. Instead, Al-Qaeda operates as a franchise, providing logistic support, but most importantly, it provides legitimacy through name-recognition to terrorist groups operating in such diverse places as the Philippines, Algeria, Eritrea, Afghanistan, Pakistan, Chechnya, Tajikistan, Sudan, Somalia, Yemen, and India. However, many local groups often act in the name of Al-Qaeda to bolster their own reputation, even if they do not receive intentional support from the organization.

The Birth of Daesh

In its base form, Daesh started off as an offshoot of Al-Qaeda in Iraq. In 2011, Abu Mohamed al-Julani, a Syrian national under Abu Bakr al-Baghdadi, split with several other Syrians to form the Jabhat al-Nusra Front in Syria (now known by some as Jabhat Fath al-Sham), which had direct affiliation and loyalty to Al-Qaeda. Al-Nusra, considered a terrorist group by the United States and the West for its affiliation with Al-Qaeda, joined other Syrian opposition groups in the ongoing conflict against the regime of President Assad of Syria. On the other hand, Abu-Bakr al-Baghdadi, together with most of his cronies, according to Daniel Byman's testimony to the United States Congress, galvanized and reformed the remnants of Jama'at al-Tawhid wal-Jihad to create ISIL on April 8, 2013. An effort to merge Daesh with the al-Nusra Front by Abu Bakr al-Baghdadi was rejected by al-Nusra's leader al-Julani, with consensus from Al-Qaeda leader al-Zawahiri, who subsequently cut all ties with Daesh in February 2014.[8] However, according to unverified sources, some of al-Julani's men later joined al-Baghdadi, paving the way for Daesh to expand into Syria.

In the context of Daesh's desire for Muslim world dominance, Michael Ryan highlights the connection between the concept of "faith-based loyalty" and the group's activities. This concept originated with Al-Qaeda's chief theoretician, Sheik Abu-Bakar Naji, who substituted Muslims' loyalty based on faith for the commonly held "tribal loyalty" practiced by Arabs. Faith-based loyalty requires the involvement of communities that transcend borders, nationalities, and ethnic groups. Because Daesh requires the creation of international militarized communities, faith-based loyalty seems to work well for its members. The goal of these communities is to challenge the established world order, with the ultimate goal of graduating the centralized global jihadist movement controlled by al-Zawahiri to a decentralized global one promoted by Daesh from its caliphate in Raqqa, Syria, or wherever Abu Bakr al-Baghdadi would reside as the caliph.[9]

It is likely that the initial goal of Daesh was to remain within the confines of the Middle East and build its caliphate within that region. Because its primary focus was on consolidating and expanding its state, it had not actively targeted the West. Except for relatively few Islamists who have operated in the West, such as those involved in the Paris and Brussels attacks, most terrorist activities had been committed by lone-wolves, many of whom had no real religious or party affiliations, save for the use of the Islamist organizations' names as a justification for their evil acts.

However, it seems that Daesh has also reverted to Al-Qaeda's tactics of sending its recruits to perform violence acts in other countries, and remotely recruiting susceptible youth online through social media and message boards to commit terrorist acts on their own soil. In this respect, Daesh seems to have not only re-evaluated its strategy after considering its losses against Kurdish Iraqis, Western-trained Sunni-Iraqis, and Western air assaults in the Middle East, but it has taken full advantage of the Internet in spreading its propaganda, communicating with potential recruits and other Islamists, and procuring new recruits. In this context, the Internet has been very useful to Islamists using platforms like Twitter and Facebook, and through online gaming forums, where they find easy targets in young isolated males playing first-person "shooter" video games.

Daesh now recruits "foreign fighters" not only to fight in the Middle East, but also requires many of them to go back and fight in their own lands. Although the reasons for such a reversal of action are arguable, it's likely an effort by Daesh to force the West's attention from its territories in the Middle East to other parts of the world. In addition, it could also be an effort to fall back on Al-Qaeda's successful guerrilla warfare strategy, and create havoc and fear among Westerners to force their withdrawal from the region. In this context, Michael Weiss, and Nancy Youssef, writing for *The Daily Beast*, state that during Daesh's advancement in the Middle East, thousands of Islamists from abroad entered Manbij in Syria each month from Turkey, and then spread out to other parts of the combat areas. However, due to the successes of the West (including Russia) and its non-Islamist Muslim partners in Iraq and Syria, the number of foreign fighters arriving to fight in the Middle East has, in 2016, dwindled to about five hundred per month.[10]

Daesh's new strategy is substantiated by its increasing guerrilla warfare and suicide bombings around the world, as was evident by the rise in attacks starting in the early part of 2016, such as those in Bangladesh and France in July 2016, in Yemen in June 2016, and in Manchester and London, England, in May and June 2017. The increase in global terrorism by Daesh is further substantiated by Rukmini Callimachi, a Romanian-American journalist writing for *The New York Times*. Rukmini conducted an interview with Harry Sarfo, a German national who had a "change of heart" after being recruited by Daesh. Harry Sarfo and his German girlfriend were told by Daesh that they did not want Europeans to come to Syria. The recruits' services were needed in their own countries to help carry out the group's plan of waging terrorism worldwide. As Mr. Sarfo recalled:

And they always said they wanted to have something that is occurring in the same time: They want to have loads of attacks at the same time in England and Germany and France.[11]

According to the interview, "taking the war to foreign shores" has become a priority for Daesh. In its quest for spreading terror abroad, a special unit that includes an internal police force and an external operations branch, known in Arabic as *Emni*, has emerged. Reinforcing the idea that Emni is a core part of Daesh's operations, the unit has *carte blanche* power to recruit and reroute operatives from all parts of the organization — from new arrivals to seasoned battlefield fighters, to special forces, and Daesh's elite commando units. Mr. Sarfo, along with other captured recruits, describe Emni as a multilevel secret service under the overall command of Daesh's most senior Syrian operative, Abu Muhammad al-Adnani. Below al-Adnani is a tier of lieutenants empowered to plan attacks in different regions of the world, including secret services for sections dealing with European, Asian, and Arab affairs.[12]

A Comparative Analysis of Al-Qaeda and Daesh

According to Dr. Michael Ryan, while Daesh and Al-Qaeda share a relatively similar ideology and a few of the same funding sources, the two organizations disagree on certain tactics, leadership, and organizational concepts when it comes to running their ruthless organizations. Al-Qaeda, as mentioned earlier, has, unlike Daesh, no claims to territory. With headquarters in Afghanistan and/or Pakistan, it functions in a supportive capacity, with its affiliates and partners in Iraq and elsewhere. However, while its ideology can be seen as somewhat similar to Daesh, its process for achieving these goals is quite different.

Although Al-Qaeda considers Shi'a Muslims to be apostates, the killing of Shi'as is not a *primary* objective for them at this stage of the game. For the present, the group sees "Shi'a-killing" as a waste of resources.[13] However, while Al-Qaeda's focus may not currently be concentrated on the destruction of the Shi'a population in the region, the war in Syria, where Assad (whose beliefs are similar to those of the Shi'as) is seen as a champion of sectarian slaughter in the Syrian civil war, propels al-Zawahiri to condone killing Shi'as whenever the chance arises. With that in mind, it is understandable why Al-Qaeda has carried out sporadic terrorist activities against the Shi'as. For example, on August 29, 2003, Al-Qaeda bombed the Shi'a Imam Ali mosque in Najaf, Iraq, and again, in 2005, it bombed two Shi'a mosques in Khanaqin, Iraq.

The spread of Al-Qaeda's ideology, however, came about not through coercion, but through a policy of "persuasion" as it pertains to Sunni Muslims. Although Al-Qaeda favors a "softer" form of persuading the Sunni Islamic population to its cause, it has no scruples in ruthlessly killing innocent Westerners or perpetuating violence against any "non-believers" in an effort at forcing the West to stay out of the "business of the Muslims."[14] In this context, Al-Qaeda's interest is killing "non-believers" in their own countries or abroad through planned terrorist activities with its affiliates, such as the bombing of a German bakery in India on June 15, 2010; the killings of seven CIA agents and one Jordanian official in the Camp Chapman attack on December 30, 2009 in Khost, Afghanistan; and an array of less spectacular terrorist attacks on Western and Jewish targets. As a general observation, however, Al-Qaeda is prone to using more lurid tactics, such as that of the 9/11 attacks on the World Trade Center and the Pentagon in the United States. In these types of attacks, Al-Qaeda may be inspired by the Shi'ite Hezbollah group that bombed the United States marine barracks in Beirut in 1984, killing 241 American military personnel. About three and a half months after the bombing, the United States ordered the withdrawal of all United States troops from Lebanon, which, as pointed out by Micah Zenco, writing for *Foreign Policy Guide*, was perceived as a sign of American weakness by Osama bin Laden.[15]

Besides training insurgents to fight American forces in places like Afghanistan, and planning activities for its affiliates to carry out against Westerners across the globe, Al-Qaeda has also published propaganda with the hope of convincing Muslims to follow its ideology. Such Internet propaganda is comparable to that of Daesh, with one major difference: generally speaking, Al-Qaeda does not deliberately display violence on the internet as a source of recruitment or as glorification of its achievement. Furthermore, it does not use force against those whom it perceives as friends, or against Sunni Muslims, unless threatened by them.

According to Dr. Byman, al-Zawahiri believes that violence against the Sunni Muslim population will eventually turn them against his group and alienate the broader Muslim community. In this context, Byman's testimony points out that a decade ago, al-Zawahiri chastised Iraqi military jihadists for their brutality. Similarly, Al-Qaeda affiliate in Syria, Jabhat al-Nusra, vainly argued with Daesh for the lives of British citizen Alan Henning and American Peter Kassig, who were innocent aid workers. According to the Al-Qaeda affiliate group, they had risked their lives to help ease the suffering of Muslims in Syria, and kidnapping and executing them was "counter-productive" and wrong under Islamic law.[16]

Jabhat al-Nusra seems to be quite confident in spreading its ideology in the region through a "less cruel" approach, particularly in converting Sunni Arabs to its cause. Even though many people believe that Al-Qaeda and its affiliates have no claims to territory, there are others who opine that Al-Qaeda wants to create emirates, much like the caliphate, but within the countries of the autocrats that already exist in the region.

Based on its sporadic activities, Al-Qaeda likely believes the achievement of its goal hinges on a long, drawn-out process, depending mainly on suicidal and guerrilla-type terrorist activities within the United States and the West, or in locations around the world where Westerners and others of different faiths are present.

Al-Qaeda's recruitment of suicide bombers and others to its cause can be summed up as follows:

1. Through the fusing of its religious ideology with a political agenda, which can be appealing to those who believe in Islamism, introduced to them through interpretative teachings of radicalized madrassas they might have attended. It can also act as an inducement for the disfranchised who may find the lure of a heavenly afterlife enticing.
2. Through an ingenious psychological use of social media, whereby disenfranchised or susceptible young men and women in the West are bombarded with messages containing an underlying promise of adventure, either for the purpose of having them join their cause, or better yet, create havoc in their own countries.

On the other hand, Daesh considers itself a worldwide community with a self-declared caliph, who is supposedly the leader of all Muslims across the world, living in a so-called caliphate, governed by an interpretative form of strict Sharia law. Daesh, according to Michael Ryan, claims to have fulfilled al-Zawahiri's vision of a global violent jihadist movement, and now considers itself in the next phase of creating Muslim communities around the world, with a defensible caliphate in the Middle East.[17]

Because of Daesh's land-acquiring agenda in the Middle East, it has had to fight with boots on the ground to preserve its hold on conquered territories, and to protect its caliph, al-Baghdadi. However, besides its land-acquiring strategies, Daesh also creates its own affiliates around the world, perhaps because it has seen the benefits of such, through the observation of Al-Qaeda. It has, for example, gained support from many active military jihadist groups like Boko Haram in Nigeria and Ansar Bayt al-Maqdis in Egypt, both of whom have formally pledged allegiance to Daesh.

However, unlike Al-Qaeda, Daesh seems to be in a tremendous hurry to achieve its goal. This race with time appears to be one of the reasons that might have prompted Abu Bakr al-Baghdadi's decision to spread Daesh's efforts into the chaos of Syria's civil war, without first consolidating its hold in Iraq. The result of this decision has allowed Daesh to seize the large, politically important city of Raqqa that has loosely been declared by Daesh as its caliphate – although the control of the city by the Islamists seems very shaky, with the United States' backed Arab and Kurdish army at its doorstep. While Daesh's caliphate seems to be on the verge of collapsing, the group has found an additional source in Libya for acquiring provinces and recruiting "aimless" Libyans to its cause, after a coalition of NATO forces overthrew Qaddafi and left the country in disarray without any plans for its governance.

Although Daesh's recruitment efforts are somewhat similar to Al-Qaeda's, it has the additional accoutrement of violence and cruelty on its side, exemplified by its habit of abducting young Sunni boys and men to fight for its ideology or commit suicide in the name of Islamism. Daesh's gruesome recordings of beheadings and other atrocities have led to a horrific "fascination" for some Muslim youths. Violence is choreographed by Daesh to mesmerize impressionable, disenfranchised, or troubled Sunni youths, which often culminates in a "make-believe" sense of purpose and bravado for the new recruits. It has, in the past, enhanced its power of recruitment with incentives, such as finding eligible girls for young Sunni males to marry.

110

In the case of Sunni female recruits, Daesh uses them as marriageable commodities for their men. In an article by Iranian-American journalist Azadeh Moaveni, in *The New York Times*, it comes to light that the young Sunni women who join Daesh are often forced into marriage with Daesh males. To iterate the rather subjugated lives of these women, the author relates the information provided by Dua, a former resident of Raqqa in Syria, who belonged to the Khansaa Brigade (Daesh's female morality police), stating that while women are provided with comforts befitting their husbands' status, they generally are bored or scared to death because most times they have very little freedom to do anything without the tacit or explicit approval of Daesh.[18] The women's husbands are seldom home, and they are beaten for such infractions as applying make-up, or listening to music. Their husbands have no time to build relationships with them (in the Western sense), or form emotional family bonds, often using them as mere sex-partners.[19] On the other hand, women of non-Sunni origin or non-Arab ethnicity, such as the Yazidis, the Christians, the Kurds, and the Shi'as, are raped, enslaved, used as ransom, and often killed by Daesh.

As alluded earlier, a fringe benefit for Daesh – and also Al-Qaeda – is the seduction of lone-wolves to their cause through propaganda messages and images published on their social media accounts. According to British actor Riz Ahmed, Daesh's propaganda videos on the internet often "look like action movies," which is likely very engrossing for young people.[20] These type of recruitment efforts often attracts even those who are not of the Muslim faith. For example, Christianne Boudreau's son, Damian Clairmont, from Canada, died for Daesh's cause in Syria.[21]

Lone-wolf targets are the hardest for the West to monitor because they often act on an impulse or personal agenda (that may have nothing to do with their belief in the Islamists' ideology), and are seldom on the West's radar of suspected terrorists. The lack of effort on the part of the Islamists in seducing violent support from people with whom they have no contact, speaks volumes about the Islamists' psychological effectiveness in promoting terrorist activities (whether consciously, subconsciously, directly or indirectly) through their propaganda machines.

Daesh, like Al-Qaeda, also has animosity toward the monarchs in the region, although its motives for creating havoc in Arabian countries seems mainly to grab more lands for its caliphate, and not so much to drive out the monarchs for ideological reasons. In a sense, one can perceive Al-Qaeda as trying to "better" the state of the existing Muslim countries in the region through an overthrow of the monarchies and introducing its own strict form of Sharia. In this context, since it has no desire for personal involvement in the governance of a country, Al-Qaeda *might* accept current autocrats in the region to make modifications in their state laws based on the dictates of its interpretative Sharia law, and force all others of a different faith to follow these laws if they desire to stay in their emirate. An emirate would be less ambitious than Daesh's caliphate in that it would not claim to be a governing body for all the world's Sunni Muslims – only for those who live within its territory, following its strict form of ultra-conservative Sharia laws.[22]

Daesh, on the other hand, would likely not welcome Westerners or anyone who does not believe in its ideology in their caliphate. Based on what it has done so far, it seems to want to acquire lands in the hope of creating "new" regions for the Sunnis that would have a unique "Islamist-identity" ruled by a caliph or an emir (in case al-Baghdadi is killed, and another caliph is not found).

Because Al-Qaeda tries to spread its ideology within existing countries, it has come to rely much more on its affiliates to spread its ideology through warring jihadism, than is done by Daesh who is in the business of acquiring land for its caliphate. For example, Bruce Riedel, senior fellow and director of Brookings Intelligence Project, states in an article in *Lawfare,* that al-Zawahiri formed a new Al-Qaeda branch on the Indian subcontinent on September 4, 2014, with the purpose of intensifying military jihadist activity in India, Pakistan, Bangladesh, Burma, and the Maldives. Al-Zawahiri has promised that this new group will restore Islamic rule in South Asia to the times of the Muslim-based Mughal Empire.[23] In recent years, as stated earlier, Daesh has also followed suit, and is now actively dependent on creating its own affiliates, perhaps because it provides an alternative to its crumbling hopes of a caliphate brought about by the onslaught from opposition military powers supported by Western (including Russian) airpower.

But perhaps the most telling difference between the two groups that is likely to have long-term repercussions, is their ability to generate revenue for their organization. In this context, Daesh has had immense financial successes based on criminal operations over several years, which include human trafficking, ransoms, bank robberies, and profiting from illegal sales of antiquities and petroleum products. Furthermore, an article in *Newsweek* magazine by Janine Giovanni, Leah McGrath Goodman, and Damien Sharkov, states that Daesh holds claims to farm lands outside of towns and cities, and taxes all imports and exports in areas it occupies.[24]

Since Daesh's advances into Syria from Iraq in 2013, the borderline between Syria and Iraq has broken down, and the northeastern Syrian corridor had become an additional entry point for Daesh to launder its currency of cash, crude oil from captured oil fields, and contraband. The article by Giovanni, Goodman, and Sharkov states that Daesh grossed as much as

$40 million, if not more, in just two years of its operations.[25] Matthew Levitt, in his testimony on November 13, 2014, submitted to the House Committee on Financial Services in the United States, estimated Daesh's earnings to be in the vicinity of $3 million dollars a day, with total assets estimated to be between $1.3 billion and $2 billion, making it the most well-funded terrorist group in history.[26]

Initially, the support for Daesh was advanced by the governments of Persian Gulf countries such as Saudi Arabia, Kuwait and Qatar. These countries, according to Daniel Wagner and Alex Stout, writing in the *Huffington Post*, had for many years funded anti-Shi'a political and military movements in the Middle East without any substantial resistance from the international community. The funding to Daesh by these nations was intended to help it fight the Shi'as in Iraq and the Assad regime in Syria, which, with the exception of Iran, is hated by most Sunni countries in the Middle East. This hatred for Assad stems from a variety of reasons that is based not only on religious, ethnic, and cultural divide, but also for the atrocities Assad has committed against the majority Sunnis within the Syrian population. However, Wagner and Stout state that after Daesh "morphed into a monster" that was condemned by governments around the world, and threatened the Persian Gulf countries' *own* survival, that these Arab nations either stopped or substantially reduced their official funding of the organization. Yet, wealthy individuals in these countries picked up where the governments left off, and Daesh continued to be funded unabated from sources within these countries."[27] It was not until 2013, that Saudi Arabia, according to Giovanni, Goodman, and Sharkov, finally passed legislation, criminalizing financial support of the Islamists.[28]

On the other hand, Kuwait and Qatar do not seem to have followed in Saudi footsteps, perhaps because of the functional aspects of their financial system, and the possibility of a political fallout in their countries from such a move. These countries' relatively open banking systems, unlike Saudi banks, do not tag those who siphon off money for the Islamists' cause. Besides, most funds allocated for terrorist groups in Syria and Iraq follow a circuitous route through Kuwait, which is very hard to track by both local and foreign observers. In all likelihood, it becomes impossible for these countries to limit the activities of highly influential Daesh donors. For example, the *Newsweek* article cited above, reports that Kuwaiti Member of Parliament Muhammad Hayef al-Mutairi had raised funds for violent jihadist groups with direct ties to Daesh. However, no actions were brought against him, perhaps because of al-Mutairi's political clout in the country.[29]

It should be noted that as of this writing, the West has been quite successful in chocking some of Daesh's funding, and has seriously hampered the group's revenue-collecting activities. As an example, sources of money earned through black-marketing activities (such as selling antiques) has been tracked and stopped from taking place. The recent advances made by the West in reclaiming Daesh held lands has further limited Daesh's funding; the *coup de grace* being the recent demands against Qatar by neighboring Arab countries to stop the few Qataris who may still be funding the terrorist groups. However, contrary to Saudi Arabia and Egypt's accusations that Daesh is still being funded by Qatar, research by the International Centre for the Study of Radicalization and Political Violence (ICSR) at King's College, London, found no evidence that rumored donations from foreign supporters and governments "continue to be significant," as a revenue source for Daesh.[30]

One of Daesh's important uses of wealth in the promotion of its activities in the past has been based on Abu Bakr Naji's argument that ordinary Muslims, like most peaceful people of different faiths, are resistant to being drawn into battle. Therefore, in order to attract ordinary Sunni Muslims to its community, Daesh had initially used polarization techniques such as liberally using money as an incentive to promote its brand of violence against those who do not believe in its ideology. In this context, it must be remembered that most people living in the war-torn areas of Syria and Iraq are desperate for such basic necessities as food and shelter – the direct result of an inhumane and brutal war. Daesh believes that the local Sunni Muslims may be more cooperative if offered resources for their financial well-being in return for their demands. In this context, some local Sunni Muslims find a good source of income through support activities such as smuggling and spying for Daesh, or by joining the local Daesh police forces.[31]

However, Lizzie Dearden in the *Independent*, provides a different picture of Daesh's new attitude in using financial rewards, now that it has lost most of its holdings in Iraq, and some in Syria, with the reality of losing Raqqa in the near future. Instead of using money as an inducement for Sunni recruits, Daesh now taxes its residents in Raqqa and elsewhere heavily to recuperate a part of its falling revenues. In quoting from the research by ICSR, Dearden found that Daesh's "revenue streams are starting to dry up as the group loses territory and international air strikes target its oil fields," [32] Most of Daesh's revenue now come mainly in the form of punitive taxation, confiscation, fines, ransoms from kidnapping which has substantially reduced its revenues from a maximum of around $1.7 billion in 2015 to $870 million in 2016. Although oil remains the group's second-largest money-maker, Daesh's trade has declined rapidly since the start of a targeted air campaign by the United States-led coalition. Estimated earnings from the looting and confiscation of artefacts from historical sites and abandoned homes across Daesh's territory is also on the decline.[33]

But while $870 million may still seem a substantial amount for any terrorist group, Peter Neumann, director of ICSR explains that while the exploitation of vast territories has been lucrative for Daesh, it incurs massive expenses in running its "bureaucratic operations, such as paying teachers, fixing roads, and maintaining health services" of its own troops as well as that of its population. Neumann compared Daesh's funding strategy as a "pyramid scheme" requiring constant expansion, which has now been brought to a halt. Losing almost all of its territories in Iraq, and much ground in Syria (with the coalition forces close to its doorsteps in Raqqa), leaves Daesh with fewer civilians and businesses to tax, and less control over natural resources.[34]

While Daesh needs large revenues to sustain its operations, Al-Qaeda's requirements to run its operations are not quite as large. Al-Qaeda, because of its major dependency on franchising agreement with its affiliates, does not have to worry about financing constant expansion or protecting acquired properties, that Daesh needs to undertake.

The Conflict Between Al-Qaeda and Daesh

Many of Daesh's recruits could be considered disenfranchised, rough-necked, or mentally disturbed, whose motivations have little, if anything, to do with religion. However, this is not quite the case with Al-Qaeda recruits, whose motivation for fighting the West and other non-believers can be seen as somewhat religiously motivated. While Daesh also likes to project religion as a central theme to its cause, it does not seem to care whether its jihadists have any understanding of Islamism, as long as the terrorist acts to achieve its political goal of acquiring a caliphate, are done in its name.

Much of the rivalry between Al-Qaeda and Daesh now involves competition for affiliates, with both groups trying to spread their operative models, and in Al-Qaeda's case, ensure its operational relevance. After 9/11, Al-Qaeda began to create affiliates and forge alliances in earnest with existing groups to expand its range of operation. As part of its competition with Daesh, Al-Qaeda has stepped up its "affiliation acquiring" activities, establishing relationships with groups, such as those in the Caucasus, and, as stated above, in India. Daesh, too, is playing the same game, in which Afghanistan, Bangladesh, Sudan, Turkey, Algeria, Libya, Pakistan, Sinai, Yemen, and other Muslim countries become targets of destruction in its competition with Al-Qaeda. Thus, as stated by Paul Cruickshank (a terrorism analyst in the United States), a power struggle has erupted between these two groups, their rivalry aggravated by geographical distance, disagreement over jihadist doctrine, and personal ambitions with respect to the war against the West. This struggle was evident in the aftermath of the violent *Charlie Hebdo* attack in Paris, France.[35]

According to Charlie Winter, a researcher and program officer at the London-based think tank, Quilliam Foundation, the first global reaction was that the attack in Paris was probably directed by Daesh or was at least Daesh-linked. However, one of the two gunmen, identified as the Kouachi brother, was heard by an eyewitness as stating: "tell the media it is Al-Qaeda in Yemen." The very next day, when Amedy Coulibaly shot a police officer and four others, a video was circulated by Daesh supporters, in which Coulibaly pledged allegiance to the leader of Daesh and confirmed that he had "coordinated" his attack with that of the Kouachi brothers. The video that Coulibaly produced, however, seemed like the work of an amateur in comparison to Daesh's usual style, which caused some experts to believe that Coulibaly had no direct connection to the organization's main propaganda unit, and likely did not have a direct line to its leadership.[36]

The confusion was evident even on Islamist forums, where supporters of both Al-Qaeda and Daesh seemed reluctant to claim responsibility. It was a few days later before a senior Al-Qaeda ideologue congratulated the attackers and ambiguously hinted that Al-Qaeda was responsible. A form of closure was achieved when Nasr ibn Ali al-Ansi, another senior Al-Qaeda leader, appeared in a video claiming that the attack on *Charlie Hebdo* was his group's "vengeance for the Messenger of Allah," and clarified that Al-Qaeda, and no other, was the responsible group.[37]

To simplify matters, considering the Kouachi brothers specifically named their affiliate group, they could be seen as being inspired by Al-Qaeda, while Coulibaly may have been inspired and supported by Daesh. However, the bifurcation of responsibility by the two Islamist groups raises further questions as to whether this could even have been a joint effort, given that relations between the leadership of Al-Qaeda and Daesh are at an all-time low. Adam Withnall, writing for the *Independent*, states that relations between Al-Qaeda and Daesh "have never been worse."[38]

Essays in *Dabiq* (the Daesh propaganda magazine) published prior to the Paris attack, directly denounced Al-Qaeda's capability as an Islamist organization. And those essays, according to Charlie Winter, came in response to statements from Al-Qaeda scholars who stated that the "caliphate" is illegitimate and that Daesh's leader, al-Baghdadi, is not religiously motivated, merely inciting people to rebel against the authority of a state or monarch. Considering the exchanges between the two groups, it seems highly unlikely (although possible) that they worked, or could likely work together.[39]

Even if one was to accept Al-Qaeda's claim that it was responsible for the attacks, it is a bit perplexing why it hesitated in announcing to the world what it had done. While some believe that Al-Qaeda propagandists timed the video to come out in conjunction with the latest issue of *Charlie Hebdo*, it is much more likely that Al-Qaeda's role was smaller than what is believed. It seems that the events were carried out at the hands of radicalized individuals who were only distantly affiliated to any one of the groups. The attackers may have spent time abroad, and met some important Islamist leaders, but the fact that there was so much ambiguity in the response from both groups suggests that they were playing it safe. As Winter points out, "after all, it would be an almighty gaffe if one were to claim responsibility for an attack carried out by the much hated other."[40]

The hatred between Daesh and Al-Qaeda may prove to be of interest to the West, whereby the United States and its allies could use the increasing dissent between the two groups to their advantage. In this context, al-Baghdadi, according to Michael Ryan, expects the cleansing of military jihadists in Iraq, Syria, and other central Arab-Muslim countries, willing them to swear allegiance only to him, thereby deepening the chasm between his group and Al-Qaeda. As the author states, this goal was clearly articulated in 2010, when strategic planning documents were written by Daesh in anticipation of the withdrawal of American forces from Iraq. Ideological cleansing, according to al-Baghdadi, seems to entail degrading other violent jihadist groups' capabilities, and persuading them to swear allegiance to him. In an audio statement, after his reported wounding in a coalition attack, al-Baghdadi made it known that he valued the assimilation of other jihadist groups under his leadership, and he welcomed the allegiances proffered by groups in Yemen, Sinai, Libya, and Algeria. This kind of assimilation, desired by al-Baghdadi, seems to imply that he would like for Al-Qaeda members to succumb to his leadership.[41]

While the detestation between these two groups has not resulted in their openly fighting each other, it remains for the West to play a hand in furthering the two groups' distrust and hatred of one another as they tussle for power in the region. As Daniel Byman points out, by exploiting the fight between Al-Qaeda and Daesh, the West could weaken the Islamists' movement as a whole.[42]

The differences between Al-Qaeda and Daesh outlined above may seem minor to the Western mind, but they are quite substantial for the two Islamist groups, which in turn makes their agendas at cross-purposes with each other. The infighting between these two groups goes against what either organization would likely claim to want. More importantly, however, it diminishes the appeal of "military jihad" if each of their volunteers believe they are fighting other Sunni military jihadists instead of fighting Assad, the Western forces, the Shi'as, and other non-believers in their ideology. With this in mind, it behooves the West to concentrate on furthering the rift in an effort to create an all-out conflict between these two groups, with the understanding that such a rift would likely weaken both parties in their quest for accomplishing their respective goals.

While it is advantageous for the United States and its allies to fight a divided adversary, a part of whose efforts will hopefully be consumed by their internal conflict, it should be noted that a divided adversary may also have an adverse effect on Western security in the short term, as the two radicalized groups collect notoriety trying to outdo each other in terms of violence committed against the West. Byman, however, concludes optimistically, that even though spikes in violence may occur against the West, the infighting between Al-Qaeda and Daesh will undermine their ability to shape regional politics, thus diminishing both movements' overall influence, and will eventually be discredited not only by the general populace they control, but also by the Islamist themselves.[43]

Although Al-Qaeda and Daesh are not entirely at "military" war with each other, the division between these two groups does have profound implications for the West. In Yemen, Daesh is in direct competition with Al-Qaeda, and recently bombed Shi'a Houthi mosques, playing on the sectarian war narrative it has long emphasized. Al-Qaeda, on the other hand, has sought not to highlight such narratives, and issued a statement publicly disavowing any involvement in the Shi'a mosque bombings.

While Daesh ostensibly seems to be much more successful than Al-Qaeda in carrying forth its goals, Daniel Byman adds a hopeful note that Daesh's ascendance may be transitory. Since its fate is tied to its "holdings" in Iraq and Syria, Byman predicts that reversals in the battlefield (which seem to be coming true in light of the recent territorial gains by non-Islamist forces in the region) would reduce its appeal for potential supporters, and diminish its luster as a successful ruthless force.[44]

For the time being, Al-Qaeda may seem to be playing second fiddle in the world of global terrorism, pushed away from the limelight by Daesh's constant attempts to flood the international media with evidence of its myriad atrocities. The Western media, too, seldom reports on some of Al-Qaeda's activities, such as the role it plays in the civil war racking Yemen. However, even though Daesh has become the household word for terrorism for the vast majority who do not follow international terrorism minutiae, the threat from Al-Qaeda is never forgotten among expert analysts who study such activities.

Different Wars with Different Agendas – Daesh and Al-Qaeda

The West's war with Daesh is more in the limelight than the fight against Al-Qaeda, due to the grander scale and the "concentrated" area in which it is fought. Besides, since Daesh has been more assertive and open in its violence against non-believers, its activities provide tangible physical evidence of towns being captured or lost, captives being beheaded, civilians on the run, houses being destroyed, and prisoners being taken.

Daesh's tactics are not only concentrated through its efforts in Syria, Iraq, and Libya, but also in Saudi Arabia, where, according to Zaina Konbaz, writing in The Jamestown Foundation's *Terrorism Monitor*, it has made every effort to inspire and support sectarian conflict that has surfaced via attacks on Shi'a citizens in the kingdom's eastern region. With the Sunni-Shi'a regional struggle already ablaze, further polarization within Saudi Arabia could be the basis for insurgency from potential Sunni Islamists that oppose the Al-Saud dynasty.[45] As articulated by Dr. Ryan, the Shi'a issue will likely give Daesh the local arousal that Al-Qaeda could never find in its 2003–2006 terrorist insurrection in the country.

Predictions of denominational religiously-based mayhem, according to Ryan, seem to be on the up-swing in Saudi Arabia — the bombing of a Shi'a mosque in the eastern part of the kingdom on January 29, 2016, being just one example. The author further believes there is a possibility that Daesh could create an internal challenge to the Jordanian monarchy to strengthen its own brand in that country. Besides, it is also likely that Daesh would make inroads into Palestinian areas in the West Bank and Gaza once it stabilizes its hold in Syria and has a strong foothold in Libya.[46] However, there does not seem to be much faith in these endeavors coming to fruition because according to most Western experts, Daesh will be defeated in the near future, prior to it having a chance to make inroads in Jordon or Palestine. Furthermore, if push came to shove, there is nothing that would stop the West in putting forth greater effort (with boots on the ground) toward defeating Daesh. Furthermore, consistent defeat in the form of lost territory in Syria and Iraq is, according to some experts, providing enough tangible proof for Daesh's "fans" that the group was vulnerable, and likely shatters its image of perceived indestructibility. The net effect of such failures could be the diminishment of Daesh's luster and propaganda appeal for further recruitment, including the activities of lone-wolves.[47]

On the other hand, there is some fear that if Daesh was indeed defeated on the ground, it would disseminate in a similar manner to Al-Qaeda, furthering its terrorist activities in the Middle East and the West through terrorist activities. However, a dependency on guerrilla or suicidal warfare *alone*, as is Al-Qaeda's modus operandi, may not be very likely for Daesh, primarily because it goes against its core ideology, which demands the appointment of a caliph and the creation of a caliphate.

It took Daesh more than a year of careful arguments to establish al-Baghdadi's credibility as the caliph of the current age. In this context, al-Baghdadi is believed by his followers to be not only the "commander of the faithful" within the self-proclaimed caliphate in Raqqa, and all the conquered territories in Syria and Iraq, but also the descendent of Prophet Muhammad, and, therefore, the caliph for all Muslims. This audacious claim has proven advantageous in recruiting fighters to the jihadist cause because Daesh follows a tradition that allows for only one living caliph at any time. The rule of one caliph is substantiated by *GlobalSecurity.org's* writing on Islam, where it states that "theoretically there can only be one; for the caliph is the person whom God has charged with the interests of His servants in East and West, on sea and land, country and town, plain and mountain."[48]

In this context, Dr. Ryan makes an important point that the group, theoretically speaking, cannot groom a successor caliph while the current one reigns, and there cannot be a "second" caliph in the shadows that would take over in case al-Baghdadi dies.[49] However, theory, in these matters, does not always accord with practice. Religious dictates have often been broken to achieve a desired political goal (especially by Daesh, whose religious dictates seem to be motivated by the political desire for a caliphate). In this context, Islam does not explicitly define the number of caliphs that can exist at any one time. For example, the Ottoman caliph had an Indian caliph reigning beside him in the East and an African caliph reigning to the West of his dominions.[50] In the context of the war with Daesh, it should be noted that the terrorist organization is a springboard for the next stage of the global "Islamic State" movement. Continuity of some kind would, therefore, be needed to carry the concept of a new caliphate-inspired community forward.

But, the survival of Daesh is also complicated by the fact that even if another leader took over, he would have a hard time matching al-Baghdadi's skills as a strategic thinker and manager who gave new life to a moribund group, and inspired confidence and belief from his followers, to the point that they bestowed the coveted title of "caliph" on him. However, there are others who believe that once his successor is found (even if he is not bestowed the title of "caliph"), Daesh would likely survive the current leader's death.

However, there are some experts who believe that killing al-Baghdadi may not be enough to annihilate Daesh. There are two possible scenarios (or a mix of the scenarios) that could take place upon al-Baghdadi's death. In the first place, as explained by Middle East correspondent Alessandria Masi, writing for the *International Business Times*, while al-Baghdadi's death would have a significant impact on the group's morale, a new leader would be appointed "without operational delay," mainly because al-Baghdadi is known to have planned for such a contingency. According to the reporter, Daesh's ground operations would likely continue without a hitch under al-Baghdadi's successor, who would likely be someone high up within the terrorist group's leadership structure.[51]

In this context, skeptics have argued that there is likely an over-emphasis placed on Daesh's continuation after the loss of its caliphate, Raqqa, and/or the killing of its caliph, al-Baghdadi. Daesh would likely continue with a new emir (if not a caliph) because evidence from killing Al-Qaeda leaders such as Osama bin Laden and al-Zarqawi, has not produced an end of these Islamists. It may have slowed down Al-Qaeda activities a bit, but it is far from cutting off the dragon's head. However, contrary to Daesh, Al-Qaeda's "losses," as stated earlier, are not tied to a tangible reward for the West, such as the reclamation of land. Perhaps it is this very reason that keeps Al-Qaeda alive, despite losing some of its key members in recent years. In this context, it is likely that Al-Qaeda, in the long run, could prove to be a greater threat to the West than Daesh, especially when one evaluates the spread of its ideology by the manipulation of Sunni Muslims' psyche, wherever they reside across the globe.

Others, however, have argued that the removal of al-Baghdadi is different because he is known as a caliph to his followers, and, according to Michael Ryan, has been the most successful operational leader to emerge from the terrorist movement.[52] As it stands, however, even with a "God-sent" religious leader in charge, Daesh's atrocities against "moderate" Sunni Muslims will eventually, according to Daniel Byman, discredit the group against its own Sunni Islamists.[53] While such a leap of faith from Byman is hard to accept (although it might prove to be true), for the present, the distinction of having Daesh's followers being acknowledged as a "worldwide Islamic community" makes a great difference to Daesh's near and intermediate goals. As a result, there is a subtle difference in the threat they pose to the West compared to that posed by Al-Qaeda.

The United States fights Al-Qaeda via drones in Afghanistan where the Taliban is also targeted. Killing core and affiliated Al-Qaeda leaders seems to be the stated objective of unmanned American drone strikes, which have resulted in the deaths of many top terrorist leaders. In late 2012, according to a paper by political scientists Patrick Johnston and Anoop Sarbahi, the United States claims to have eliminated at least two-thirds of the top thirty Al-Qaeda leaders in Pakistan and Afghanistan.[54] By November 13, 2016, estimates compiled by New America Foundation stated that drone strikes in Pakistan under President Obama accounted for the killing of thousands of militants.[55] According to Johnston and Sarbahi's study, "drone strikes are associated with decreases in the incidence and lethality of terrorist attacks..." While the authors do not indicate that "these effects are long-term, the results do lend some credence to the argument that drone strikes, while unpopular" with the local population who believe substantial numbers of civilians are killed by these activities, "have bolstered U.S. counterterrorism efforts in Pakistan."[56]

However, drone strikes by the United States near the Federally Administered Tribal Areas (FATA), often described as Pakistan's "lawless frontier" in the northwestern corner of the country bordering Afghanistan and northwest Pakistan, have opened up traffic between the FATA and the Kunar district of Afghanistan. This movement by Al-Qaeda operatives from Pakistan to Afghanistan is, according to Patrick Johnston and Anoop Sarbahi, the result of Osama bin Laden's advice to accommodate hundreds of Al-Qaeda members in a more fortified area with rougher terrain, mountains, rivers, and trees that would make it hard for them to be spotted.[57]

According to some internet sources, the Pakistanis cheer the United States in its fight against Al-Qaeda and the Taliban on Afghani soil. However, they are not as happy when these activities are mistakenly directed by Americans on their soil.

Whether fighting the Taliban, Al-Qaeda, or Daesh, it is never easy for the West to employ target-specific strategies because, as stated earlier, often there is no distinct knowledge signifying the identity of the responsible party for the actions committed. In this context, it may be useful to heed Charlie Winter's warning when he states that it would be helpful for the international media to make an effort of verifying who is responsible for certain terrorist acts, so as to avoid playing into Islamist propaganda of the West bombing their targets indiscriminately – accusations that often tend to exaggerate and intimidate.[58]

It is prophesized, however, that once Daesh is destroyed, Al-Qaeda may rise and once again become a leading force of Islamist activities around the world. There is a likelihood that if al-Baghdadi is killed, its members may disperse in the absence of its leader, or they may join Al-Qaeda, which has vastly greater experience in guerrilla and violent warfare. On the bright side, however, it seems that for the present there is a slight lull in Al-Qaeda activities compared to the past. This could be because Al-Qaeda believes in taking its time to achieve lurid goals. However, there is also a belief that al-Zawahiri has been stifled because of the constant drone operations by the United States in Afghanistan. In this context, Al-Qaeda affiliates too are somewhat incapacitated in carrying out their offensive against the West on their own, since they depend mainly on the central body of Al-Qaeda in Afghanistan, of which al-Zawahiri is the present boss. Because of the rather "scattered" physical nature of the group, killing al-Zawahiri would not likely eradicate the group completely. However, it would certainly weaken it, as al-Zawahiri is the last of the original Al-Qaeda operatives with an international reckoning, especially as it pertains to planning and coordinating "spectacular hits" against the West.

While there is no doubt that the West, for the present, needs to concentrate on destroying Daesh, its strategy for defeating Al-Qaeda would not only involve the removal of al-Zawahiri from his "throne" but an embarking on "non-direct," prolonged efforts at changing Muslim views of the West. In this respect, as stated earlier, it is important to note that unlike Daesh, many of whose members, according to Daniel Byman, are the "most foolish" or mentally low-functioning people recruited through its propaganda machine, Al-Qaeda members are not entirely low-functioning with respect to their understanding of the interpretative aspects of the Al-Qaeda ideology. Therefore, while it may be easier to manipulate the minds of Daesh recruits who try to follow their leader, al-Baghdadi's supposed road to victory, changing the minds of Al-Qaeda followers may be harder to accomplish.[59]

Chapter 7

The Spread of Islamism

The spread of Islamism can be traced to several different philosophical theories, especially with respect to our understanding of the degree to which religion plays a role in the followers' adherence to Islamist ideology. Dr. Simon Cottee argues that the acceptance of such an ideology is essentially a debate between idealists and materialists.[1] Some historians, such as Sir Lewis Namier, believed that high moral principles give an *ex post facto* rationalization for actions that may not even be remotely associated with the actual motives of the activist. In fact, Namier saw the ideals invoked by the perpetuators as mere epiphenomenon, deployed to conceal intentions that may not otherwise be acceptable by their audience. There are others, however, who believe that it is quite possible for people to internalize the contradictory views offered by a person (particularly if he is in "charge"), thus justifying their actions as not only permissible, but necessary.[2] However, for Christopher Browning, an American historian, the actions of Islamist individuals are based mainly on factors such as the desire to conform to a group, or peer pressure, which has nothing to do with ideology.[3]

In the context of the Islamists, British journalist Mehdi Hasan, following in Namier's footsteps, believes that religion does not play an important part in the radicalization process. In other words, the use of Islamism as a radically defined religious ideology acts as a curtain, under which the Islamists conceal their real intention, which is to create a kingdom in the Middle East.[4] By the same token, Ishaan Tharoor of the *Washington Post* argues that "radicalization is driven less by religious fervor than by more local factors, and it is shaped also by ties to gangs and other criminal activity." Far more importantly, in quoting Cas Mudde, an associate professor at the School of Public and International Affairs at the University of Georgia, Ishaan Tharoor zeroes in on the spread of terrorism in Europe not through Islamist ideology, but the fact that Europe has created "the conditions for the resentment that drives the terrorists."[5]

On the other hand, former Muslim, Ayaan Hirsi Ali, a Somali-born Dutch-American activist, author, and former Dutch politician, who is now among Islam's prominent critics, strongly endorses the role of religion in the spread of Daesh-inspired terrorism. The author contends that the reason for Islamist-born terrorism lies in the ideology of radical Islam (Islamism). She also writes contemptuously of the view that religion "is a mere smokescreen for underlying 'real' motivations, such as socio-economic grievances."[6]

While Ayaan Hirsi Ali may not distance religion from every aspect of Muslims' lives, including their socio-economic well-being, George Washington University professors Scheherazade S. Rehman and Hossein Askari's 2010 research portrays a different picture.[7] The authors compared countries that were members of the Organization of Islamic Countries (OIC) with several developed and non-developed countries in order to ascertain how "Islamic" the self-proclaimed Islamic countries actually were with respect to their socio-economic policies. In so doing, Rehman and Askari first determined a common denominator for how "Islamic" would be defined for both Muslim and non-Muslim countries.

In this context, their definition of the word "Islamic" was established based on the dictates of the Quran and the Hadith, which are two of the basic road maps for Muslims in practicing Islam. Rehman and Askari point out that hard work on the part of any individual, and by society as a whole, is considered by Islam to be one of the most critical drivers of economic development and social progress. Islamic laws seek to foster labor, production, and commerce while prohibiting corruption, freeloading, routine beggary, and any vocations that may promote social instability or political, economic, or social oppression. However, like the concept of social security in the United States, Prophet Muhammad also advocated the use of a public treasury to alleviate destitution and poverty, *if* such poverty was not born out of laziness and reliance on handouts by the able-bodied. To enhance productivity, the Prophet encouraged risk-reward sharing in production and trade projects. Fusing the material and spiritual sides of life, according to the Hadith, infuses all "honest" material pursuits with spirituality. It is in this sense that earning one's living through honest means is also regarded by Muslims as a form of worshipping God.

As explained in Chapter 4, most Islamic countries do not separate or "completely" separate religion from state laws. However, one of the questions relevant to scholarly thinking relates to the cause-effect relationship between religion and Islamic countries' socio-economic well-being. In this context, scholars often wonder whether religion produced laws for socio-economic development or whether economic development fostered religious adherence. The question of whether it is religiously specified laws that drive the socio-economic structure of Islamic countries, or vice versa, is debatable. Setting this intriguing question aside, Professors Rehman and Askari, in their research, examine how well religious dictates have served

Islamic countries in comparison to other Islamic and non-Islamic countries. The authors question whether self-declared Islamic countries, as attested by their membership in the OIC, embrace policies that are founded on Islamic teachings.

To ascertain a common denominator for comparing countries with respect to how "Islamic" they are, it was first important to compare Islamic laws with the current socio-economic policies in Western countries. In this respect, the authors point out that Islamic principles are conducive to (a) free markets and strong economic performance; (b) good governance and rule of law; (c) societies with well-formed human rights, civil rights, and equality; and (d) cordial relations and meaningful contributions to the global community. They are in fact quite similar to the aspirations of developed countries in the West. Moreover, the authors' examination of Islamic teachings shows that Islam's guidelines for economic, social, legal, and political practices are in line with today's best practices and recommended institutional structures. If non-Islamic countries, such as the United States, Germany, or Japan, have performed well under laws, regulations, and practices that are in conformity with the Islamic framework, then logic would dictate that Islam is not counter to good economic, political, legal, and social development.

However, according to the authors' results, Islamic countries are not as "Islamic" in their practice as one might expect, in comparison to most developed countries. In fact, in their "Overall Islamicity Index Rank," the highest performing Muslim country, Malaysia, ranked 38 from a total of 208 countries. Kuwait was the next highest, with a ranking of 48, while Turkey was ranked 103. Saudi Arabia was ranked 131, while Iran was 163. Somalia was the last Muslim county on the list, with a ranking of 206. By the same token, the 10 highest-ranking countries with respect to how well they performed on Islamic principles in a socio-economic context, were New Zealand, Luxembourg, Ireland, Iceland, Finland, Denmark, Canada, the United Kingdom, Australia, and Netherlands. The United States was ranked lower, at 25.

The research concludes that contrary to many people's beliefs, Islamic countries do not practice good values for economic and social well-being, as outlined in the Quran and the Hadith. The authors surmise that it is the shortcomings of the governments and their respective policies, not religion, that account for the dismal economic, financial, political, legal, and social developments and progress in the Middle East (even for those countries blessed with oil).[8]

While Rehman and Askari provide some insight into the behavior of Islamic countries with respect to Islamic laws in governing their countries, the question of whether religion precedes politics or politics proceeds religion in the spread of Islamism continues. In this context, authors such as Mehdi Hasan and Graeme Wood can prolong the debate over which came first, but Simon Cottee succinctly surmises that "people who engage in jihadist violence may have mixed motives for doing so; and these may be both secular and religious in character."[9] As the author muses, demarcating Islamists' motives on ideological (religious) or material (secular) grounds is artificial. Even if military jihadists are initially motivated by worldly goals, like fame or retribution for political grievances, there is a transcendent fulfillment for them when their violence is justified by religious ideology. Within such an understanding, the incestuous nature of Daesh's political aspirations within the facade of religious legality provides a good example of the mixed motive theory suggested by Cottee.

American author, think tank executive and security analyst, Peter Bergen, concurs with this line of reasoning in stating that military jihadist activities in the United States since September 11, 2001, have generally been motivated by a variety of factors, which could include a dislike of American foreign policy in the Muslim world, a need to embrace an organization for achieving a sense of purpose, and a search for a "cognitive opening" that allows radical ideas (Islamism) to fulfill a void precipitated by personal disappointments.[10] While the debate over the role religion plays in Islamist behavior is likely to remain inconclusive, the most reasonable and "safe" argument seems to be the mixed motives theory, which places the onus on both secular and religious influences. In this context, it may be wise to paraphrase historian Quentin Skinner's argument that religious ideology may not be the sole cause for an action, but it does *legitimize* the facilitating of a such action.[11]

Skinner's assertion rings especially true when one considers the issues of ethnic and religious divide that plagued Iraq during – what may be a temporary solution – the creation of a democratic government. Only through trial-and-error efforts in forming a parliamentary government that provides for political solidarity based on a religious/ethnic divide, that Sunnis and Kurds have been involved in the governance of the country dominated by Shi'as. By the same token, Islamists have instilled seeds of discontent by using the volatile religious and ethical divide to recruit Sunnis to their cause.

In line with Namier's contention, for some Sunnis who have no meaningful understanding of Islamic scriptures, save for the blind acceptance of their Islamist preachers' interpretations; the injection of religion, and an appeal to cultural hatred is often an alluring incentive to join Daesh. As noted earlier, the Sunnis in Iraq blame the United States and the British for their displacement as the privileged class under Saddam Hussein. In this respect, there may be some truth to religion playing a part in the spread of Islamism, likely due to the strength of the ideology of Islamist leader al-Baghdadi, who is purported to be a fervent religious man with a Ph.D. in Islamic studies. In al-Baghdadi's view, the "non-believers" must be destroyed; for one, because they are seen as having exploited their sacred lands for oil, but also because of the belief that these people infringe on their religious-based political demands that calls for the creation of a caliphate.

If one were to accept the mix of factors at play in the spread of Islamism, it is evident by the sheer lack of the percentage of Sunnis across the world who do not practice Islamism, that most Sunni Muslims do not believe in the perverted ideology of the Islamists. However, it is also possible for some Sunnis to side with the Islamists "in heart," if not physically, because many Muslims believe the Islamists' war to be sectarian, and thus based, among other things, on the Sunnis' hatred for the Shi'as, and vice versa. It is this rivalry that has the potential to sway some mainstream Sunnis to side mentally with Daesh and Al-Qaeda, even though most of them do not approve of the land-grabbing and indiscriminate killings undertaken by their radicalized Sunni brethren, the Islamists. In this respect, as stated in Chapter 6, the fact that Saudi Arabia, Kuwait and Qatar, initially funded Daesh, hoping for their success against Assad's Alawite (Shi'ite) regime, can be seen as an example of some Sunnis' secretive hopes.

In this context, the "group-loyalty" espoused by Christopher Browning fits well with the clandestine behavior of some Sunnis, even if they may not approve of Islamism.[12] Thus, the Islamists' persuasive or forceful tactics can be seen as an effort at re-grouping Sunnis with the pull towards "Sunni loyalty" (group identification), irrespective of their radicalized interpretation of Sunni Islam, which is at odds with most Sunnis' views. Thus, their use of religion, whether as a tool to recruit those who are disfranchised or to appeal to loyalty on the basis of faction-similarity (being Sunnis), becomes a powerful factor in expanding the Islamists' base under the guise of "approval from God."

Some Sunnis are likely to understand Daesh's success (though almost all of them do not condone it) as largely due to the group's appeal in taking up the cause of rectifying historical atrocities supposedly committed against Muslims. For example, some Sunnis attribute the proliferation of Daesh's ideology to a possible atonement for the atrocities committed by Christians in the past. As an example, Ojibwa, writing in the *Daily KOS*, states that South African Theologian J.H. Kritzinger warned Christians not to make light of racial apartheid because God had willed it via the Holy scriptures.[13] It may be for this reason, coupled with a variety of other Western atrocities (perceived or factual) committed in the past, that the present-day West (particularly the United States) is also perceived by Muslims as guilty of unfair and prejudicial treatment against them, in the interest of its own agenda. In other words, while the United States sleeps in the same bed with Saudi Arabia, with its vast oil reserves, strategic location in the Middle East, and dominance of the region, it does not give the same attention to the plight of the Palestinians.

In light of the discussions above, the new religion, Islamism, seems to have disseminated partly by force and the threat of terror, and partly by an appeal to the collective religious reasoning of the ultra-conservative Sunni Muslims in the Middle East and Northern Africa, who consider groups such as Shi'as and Yazidis as apostates. The apostates, together with the Kurds and Westerners, among others, are likely seen by Islamists as obstructions to their cultural and religious beliefs. In overcoming these obstructions, the Islamists rely on manipulative efforts (preaching their interpretive meaning of military jihad) for recruiting "down-on-their-luck" Muslims. However, part of the spread of Islamism could also be attributed to technological advancement, whereby (as stated in Chapter 6) impressionable youths from the West are recruited directly from their own countries via the internet through a promise of motivating factors that would justify their need for excitement, belonging, and adventure.

It should be noted that Daesh is quite dependent on its success on the internet, substantiated by the fact that its experts in media design and usage, according to Azadeh Moaveni, are highly revered and well-paid members of their organization. Besides, the way "cruelty" is exemplified by Daesh on social media, further enhances its appeal to potentially susceptible recruitment targets. For example, Moaveni states that Eleftheriou-Smith, one of the three, former female Daesh members, now living in Turkey, explains the justification given by Daesh men for their savagery. To them, it is a necessity to minimize casualties later, especially when they have conquered a new town. Besides, the men also rationalize their brutal actions as a retaliation against the brutality that they as Sunnis have to face from Alawite Assad's army in Syria.[14] Daesh, therefore, seems to substantiate its actions by blaming the "other" party, passing the buck, stating they are "forced" to commit horrific actions because they have "no choice."

While martyrdom as a recruitment tool is incomprehensible to the Western mind, it should be noted that such power over mankind is no different than the control people like Charles Manson exhibited over the "Manson Family" (a quasi-commune), which killed several people in the United States; and Jim Jones who, in 1978, "hypnotized" 909 people to commit suicide (most of them by taking cyanide) in a remote commune at Port Kaituma, close to Georgetown, Guyana's capital city. Even at a less violent level, where suicide and murder are not committed, examples still exist where persons are manipulated to behave in socially unacceptable ways.[15] For example, the former president of the Fundamentalist Church of Jesus Christ of Latter-Day Saints, Warren Jeffs, lured children into sexual activities (including incest) through his interpretations of Biblical scriptures.[16]

But, as should be evident, such extreme beliefs and ideologies largely flourish in places where majorities or "large" minorities of religious followers have the political clout to assert their beliefs over all people in the community, as is done in countries like Saudi Arabia. However, not all geographical locations where Muslims reside follow the same religious interpretations that are prevalent in parts of the Middle East and Northern Africa. By reducing Islam to a religion that spreads terror, one fails to account for some of the largest populaces of Muslims, such as those in Indonesia and Malaysia (two Islamic countries), and in pluralistic India, who do not interpret or practice a harsh and cruel understanding of their religion.

Some pundits specify the lack of "education" in the Muslim world as the cause for the spread of Islamism. There could be some truth to this claim, since many poor people in the Muslim world, such as those residing in certain parts of the Muslim world such as in Africa, do not have the resources to send their kids to school. However, one major problem in providing education for Muslim children is the issue of gender, which, by decree of terrorist groups such as the Taliban in Afghanistan, and Boko Haram in Nigeria (that have pledged allegiance to Daesh), forbids girls from being educated. Some of these groups not only prohibit girls from attending school, but delegate them to the role of sex-slaves and child-bearers. By the same token, many male children are forced to become soldiers (suicide bombers and guerilla fighters), and are not provided with education. But, even among the boys who are "lucky" to be educated, it is likely that most are sent to radicalized madrassas rather than the more secular schools that many non-Islamist children attend around the world.

It should be understood, that even when there are resources available to send children to the madrassas, there is still the problem of creating an educational curriculum that is void of the personal influence and ideology of the local imam. Such concerns can be similar to those of other religious schools like those in Judaism, Hinduism, and the Protestant sect of Christianity, where one independent interpretation of the word of God does not exist as it does in, say, the practice of Catholicism (see Note 1 in Chapter 4). While some may relate such madrassas (even if they are taught a very conservative understanding of Islam) to Sunday schools at Christian churches, it should be remembered that radicalized madrassas, run by the Islamists, are vehicles for teaching Islamism rather than the mainstream religion of Islam.

Furthermore, in teasing out the differences between the Islamist madrassas and Christian Sunday schools, it should be noted that Sunday schools in the United States, for example, are attended in addition to regular schools, which provide education on all subjects. By the same token, the reliance on discussions and questions, valued so highly in Western schools, likely does not exist in most radicalized madrassas where Islamists' dogmas are meant to infiltrate young minds. Sadly, this type of schooling under Islamist control, might be the only education students receive, ensuring that the hateful ideology (Islamism), is passed on through Sunni children who are unfortunately caught in the web spread by the Islamists.

In the analysis on the spread of Islamism, it should be noted that a perceivably weak government with a large Muslim

140

population works largely in the favor of Islamists, as exemplified by the recent expansion of Daesh's operations in Libya, after the chaos created during and following the overthrowing of its leader, Qaddafi. Furthermore, it is also worthwhile noting that the percolation of Islamism is likely to occur in areas where, according to the Islamists, an injustice seems to have occurred, or a perceived injustice has taken place. In this respect, Syria has proved fertile for the spread of Islamism, where Assad's forceful and unfair handling of the majority Sunni population can be seen as likely justification for the hostility felt towards him from the Islamists. But, aside from the injustices of the ruler over the ruled, the war by the Islamists in Syria and Iraq, likely contains cultural and religiously based factional biases, whereby Assad's Alawite heritage (a close form of Shi'ism), and the displacement of Sunni control in Iraq by the Shi'as, can be seen as one of the reasons for Islamists' infiltration in these countries.

Part III:

Current Challenges and Strategies for the Future

Chapter 8

United States' Uncharted Policies
in the Muslim World

For many dissident Muslim populations around the world, the Arab world's dependency on the West is a troublesome problem, perhaps not realizing that countries in the Persian Gulf, such as Saudi Arabia and Qatar, have a symbiotic relationship with the United States. This symbiotic relationship is meant to prevent upheavals in the global financial markets by reducing or increasing the flow of oil (although in recent years it is not much adhered to), and preserving the United States' hegemony in the region, while the Americans' are expected to provide stability, particularly with respect to the Iranians. For this reason, the United States has, for more than 36 years, built a constellation of military bases that stretch from Southern Europe and the Middle East to Africa and Southwest Asia.[1]

In the Persian Gulf, the United States holds bases in every country except Iran and Yemen. For example, the United States Navy has stationed its Fifth Fleet in Bahrain, while in Qatar, it has Al Udeid, the largest military base in the Middle East. The United States has also expanded operations into the UAE and Oman. Even in Saudi Arabia, where the Americans had to officially withdraw in 2003 because of the Saudi peoples' widespread anger at American military presence in the country, there are still, according to David Vine, small American military contingents and a secret drone base. Vine also claims that there are also some secret American bases in Israel.[2]

Aside from Vine's assertion about the difficulty of verifying exact locations of secret American drone bases (for reasons of secrecy), there are other military bases in Egypt, Jordan, Turkey, Pakistan, Bulgaria, Romania, and Kosovo that are easy to verify. The United States also operates Djibouti's Camp Lemonnier in Africa. Elsewhere on the continent, the United States military has quietly built a collection of small bases and sites for drones, surveillance flights, and special operations forces, from Ethiopia and Kenya, to Burkina, Faso, and Senegal.[3]

According to the report by David Vine, *The New York Times* reported that the United States is further considering a Pentagon proposal to create a "new" and "enduring" system of military bases, the largest of which would permanently host five hundred to five thousand American personnel. The system would include "four 'hubs' — existing bases in Afghanistan, Iraq, Djibouti, and Spain — and smaller 'spokes' in locations like Niger and Cameroon."[4]

American Base-Building Strategies Gone Astray

While the relationship between the United States and some Islamic countries has been symbiotic in nature, American base-building activities in the Greater Middle East has failed as a strategy for controlling turmoil in the region, no less defeating terrorist organizations there. Base-building and its maintenance has cost American tax payers billions of dollars.

Most importantly, however, as David Vine points out, these base-building activities have provided support for a long list of repressive, undemocratic regimes, such as those in Saudi Arabia, Bahrain, and Qatar, which in turn have fostered anti-American anger in the region. For example, in 2011, the United States (as stated in Chapter 5) — perhaps because of its strategic naval base in Bahrain — offered only tepid criticism of the Bahraini government for violently cracking down on pro-democracy protesters with the help of troops from Saudi Arabia and the United Arab Emirates. Furthermore, the United States' bases offer the legitimacy required for nations to be included in the Economist Democracy Index, even if these nations represent non-democratic regimes, such as those in Cameroon, Central African Republic, Chad, Djibouti, Egypt, Ethiopia, Jordan, Kuwait, Oman, Qatar, Saudi Arabia, and the United Arab Emirates. Such an about-face by the United States on one of its most cherished values — the practice of democracy — as Vine states, effectively assists in blocking democracies in these countries.[5]

As the Saudi Arabian case illustrates, contrary to the United States' intentions of providing stability in the region, the bases have fueled radicalism, anti-Americanism, and the growth of the very terrorist organizations now targeted by the West. Dr. Vine substantiates the adverse effects of base-building by quoting former West Point Professor Bradley Bowman's assertions that American bases and troops in the Middle East have been a "major catalyst for anti-Americanism and radicalization" since a suicide bomber killed 241 Marines in Lebanon in 1983.[6] In Africa too, research published by the Army's *Military Review* and the Oxford Research Group identifies the growing presence of American bases and troops as a reason for violent insurgents to operate in the countries.[7]

The Arab Spring Dilemma

Identifying American military bases as the cause that has curtailed the spread of democracy may be a bit of a stretch for some Americans. A more direct example of the United States' inconsistency in its supposed championing of democracy, however, is evident in its complacency during the overthrow of a democratically elected party in Egypt — the Muslim Brotherhood — after the Arab Spring. While the West had hoped for the spread of democracy in the area, or, at the very least, the planting of seeds leading to an eventual democratic rule in the aftermath of the Arab Spring; in actuality the uprising, in part through military action, has further curbed any aspirations of promoting civilian rights in the region. In this context, other than Tunisia, no ideological reform in the creation of democratic governments came about from the Arab Spring.

According to some observers, in the context of its foreign policy regarding the Middle East, the United States has compounded the problem by its recent "least-interference" policy. As Shadi Hamid, senior fellow in the Project on United States Relations with the Islamic World at the Center for Middle East Policy, succinctly points out in his award-winning book, that the "notion of neutrality, for a country as powerful as the United States, is illusory." Doing nothing means "maintaining or reverting to the status quo, which in the Middle East is never neutral, due to America's longstanding relationships with regional actors."[8]

The Syrian civil war serves as an example. The conditions in Syria since early 2012 have progressively worsened to the point of unimaginable chaos and brutality, in part because the United States continued to play a partially-engaged role, debating whether to enact safe zones and no-fly zones in the country. If decisive actions had been taken when the so-called "red line" drawn by the United States was crossed, the Americans would have taken the driver's seat in the conflict, strong-arming the officially latecomer Russians into abiding by pre-established military strategies, unless they chose to enter into an outright confrontation with the United States.[9] In reality, however, although successful in eliminating a large number of chemical weapons with verbal threats, the United States found itself in the midst of a chaotic situation that did not lend well to the enforcement of no-fly zones, since the Russians and Assad's army had already enforced their own military strategies.

As should be evident by now, every action or inaction by the United States has consequences. If the United States opts to remain disengaged, others are likely to move in and fill the void. Even in cases where the United States does engage, it often enters the conflict at a late stage, when others have already established their positions in the war zone.

International players, for better or worse, have been partly responsible in influencing the outcome of the Arab Spring. Although the United States insisted it was not taking sides before, during, and after the Arab Spring, it quickly changed its tune, expressing its support for the revolution in Tunisia after its president, Zine al-Abidine Ben Ali, took refuge in Saudi Arabia on January 14, 2011. While the support of the Tunisian revolution was not of major consequence to the United States, the Egyptian revolution was a different story. Egypt's Hosni Mubarak, a dogged opponent of Iran and a stalwart supporter of the Arab-Israeli peace process, was America's staunch ally. However, America did nothing in preserving his rule, instead preferring its stance of non-involvement. As Shadi Hamid states, although the United States insisted that this was not an American issue, in reality, "it was partly about America, not just because of the past United States role in backing Arab dictatorships, but because of the critical role it would continue to play in the region."[9]

Perhaps it was due to its desire to accommodate the wishes of the population in Egypt that the United States decided not to intervene and prevent Mubarak's overthrow in January 2011, when he stepped down during a popular uprising that was part of the broader Arab Spring movement. In this context, Hamid, who was in Cairo's Tahrir Square during the time of the uprising, observed that the Egyptians overwhelmingly despised Mubarak's pro-Western policies and chanted for his ouster with accusations that he was a lackey of the United States and Israel.[10] In such a case, the United States' non-interference policy could be considered commendable from a moral point of view because it upheld its belief in the power of the people, even though Mubarak had been its very strong ally.

In June 2012, after the overthrow of Mubarak, Mohamed Morsi of the Muslim Brotherhood became the first democratically elected president of Egypt. However, his rule lasted for just one year when he was ousted in a major *coup d'état* led by Field Marshal Abdul Fatah al-Sisi, the head of the Supreme Council of the Armed Forces (SCAF), and the current head of the country. A month later, under the guise of restoring democracy, Sisi's military, according to Human Rights Watch, was responsible for massacring supporters of Mohamed Morsi in one of the worst mass killings in modern Egyptian history.

The SCAF had grown increasingly autocratic in the two and a half years leading to the removal of the Muslim Brotherhood, but the United States failed to put any significant pressure on the army, perhaps believing that a military-led transition would facilitate and manage the democratization process while safeguarding American interests. According to Hamid, its unwillingness to pressure the undemocratically elected SCAF will likely make it even more difficult for the United States to hold future Islamic-led governments, such as Morsi's, to democratic standards.[11]

But while we can commend the United States' non-interference policy in keeping with the demands of Egypt's population in the overthrow of its ally Mubarak, and forgive its naiveté in assuming that the SCAF would eventually transition to a democratic rule, what is hard for some in the Muslim world to understand is America's failure to preserve the rule of the democratically elected Morsi, who was forcefully removed from power by President Sisi.

The removal of Morsi, however, may not have been a primary case of "democracy being tampered with" for the Americans. In this context, many Egyptians, according to Hamid, believe that human rights and democracy are tertiary concerns for the United States.[12] Perhaps it was the Brotherhood's history of vehemently anti-Israel position, or its classification as a terrorist group by some Middle Eastern countries, such as Egypt and Saudi Arabia, that worried the American government enough to overlook "democracy" for the sake of stability.

But, what Morsi allegedly believed and what he actually did or would likely do while in power, are according to some scholars, two different things. For example, although the Brotherhood's general guide, Mahdi Akef, stated outwardly to author Shadi Hamid that the Brotherhood would cancel Egypt's peace treaty with Israel if it ever had the chance, pragmatic members of the Brotherhood adopted a resigned tone regarding the acceptance of Western constraints.[13] A senior Brotherhood figure in Jordan stated: "if we must, we will always, at the very least, believe and long for the liberation of Palestine in our own hearts" — presumably even if that meant abiding by the peace treaty signed with Israel. Radicalized parties in power, according to Hamid, cannot always actualize their idealized desires, because the structure of regional and international order will not allow it. As long as Arab countries are dependent on Western powers for economic and political survival, there will be limits to how far their elected or forcibly attained governments can go.[14]

Classifying pragmatism over dissonance in the realm of foreign policy is understandable, but most Western populations likely do not have the understanding to decipher palatable meanings from the outward orotundity of unacceptable threats and demands from supposedly "errant" countries. In this context, they could be at a loss as to why some countries in the Middle East use different rhetoric when addressing their populations, while simultaneously adopting a political agenda that is more cohesive with Western geopolitical expectations in the region. Western governments, generally speaking, seem to overlook the differential behavior of their Middle East allies toward their populace and the world at large, perhaps because the West has come to realize the necessity for countries like Saudi Arabia and Kuwait in pursuing a two-faced strategy.

On the other hand, Western populations seem unaware of the quandary faced by non-allies of the West, such as Iran, where a large segment of the population does not agree with their government's anti-Western policies. In such cases, it is likely that the "misunderstood" population will change sides and support its governments' policies simply out of frustration at not being able to change the world's opinion of them. The important thing to note here is that once Middle Eastern countries are less reliant on the West, there may be a greater likelihood of some rogue nations' anti-government populations to accept their government-sponsored radical ideologies.

While America's relative silence during the overthrow of Morsi could be attributed to the Muslim Brotherhood's terrorist group classification by some Muslim countries, a more plausible reason could be the current United States policy of leading from behind, consulting, and occasionally using airpower in lieu of direct intervention. As it stands, the murders of Morsi's supporters should have elicited a response from the United States, but they did not, presumably because Morsi was believed to have ties with Hamas (considered a terrorist organization) in Palestine, and because a strong, coherent response to the killings would have been contrary to the United States' limited-involvement policy. In fact, the shift in American policy is defined by what foreign-policy analysts Nina Hachigian and David Shorr call the "Responsibility Doctrine" — a strategy of "prodding other influential nations ... to help shoulder the burdens of fostering a stable, peaceful world order" while America leads from behind.[15]

But the supposedly neutral stance of the United States in protecting human rights and democracy seems to have left a vacuum and struggle for power within and among countries in the Middle East, which bring to light a major reason for the demise of Morsi's rule in Egypt. During Morsi's one-year tenure, Qatar and Turkey (both Muslim Brotherhood supporters) donated $5 billion and $2 billion respectively to Egypt. On the other hand, Saudi Arabia, the United Arab Emirates, and Kuwait provided a massive $12 billion in aid to the Egyptian army at the most "opportune time," which, according to some observers, such as Robert Baer, was a tacit "go-ahead" to the Egyptian army for the brutal extermination of many members of the Brotherhood.[16]

The likely reasons for the United States' allowing such contradictory actions by its allies is examined by author Max Fisher. Through his investigative reporting, Fisher finds that America's tolerance of such behavior can be attributed to its fervent desire to retain the status quo with Arab nations, which promotes American hegemony in the region and a distrust of Iran. In this context, Washington policies in the near past have always favored Saudi Arabia and its interests, with the implicit understanding that the United States, Israel, and the Persian Gulf countries would form an alliance to contain Iran, fight terrorism, keep the oil flowing, and keep Russia out of the region.[17]

Beyond Egypt, the United States' involvement, or lack thereof, continues to matter well after the initial Arab uprisings. For example, its decision to disengage from Libya after a successful military intervention by NATO and the Americans in dislodging Libya's Qaddafi from power (stated in Chapter 7), has now resulted in a safe-haven for Islamists (Al-Qaeda and Daesh), which has forced Americans to re-engage with the purpose of driving them out of the region.

Western Involvement in the Functioning of the Middle East

The relationship between the United States and its Middle Eastern allies was very tenuous prior to President Trump's new attitude in dealing with the Middle East. It was, however, the symbiotic nature of the relationship that had prevented a complete shut-down of the pre-existing alliances between the United States and the Middle East countries. The populations of these countries, on the other hand, in reflecting their own perceptions of the United States, have distanced themselves even further from Western ideologies, voicing their strong anti-American sentiments and disillusionment with the West.

Though the opinions of a few cannot be generalized across the entire Muslim population of the world, in talking to some Muslims in India, it seems that the United States is no longer seen as a strong purveyor of justice, equity, and fairness — a country that purported to uphold the basic values of morality and human rights. But most moderates in the Muslim world also realize that the alternatives for the Middle East are not that promising either. If not the Americans, it would be the Russians, or perhaps the Chinese, who, for the time being, do not seem interested in entering the fray in the Middle East. While Russian President Vladimir Putin may have won a few Shi'a hearts in Assad's Syria, most of the world, it seems, does not hold him in high regards. For the present, then, America remains the de facto global champion in the promulgation of human rights and fairness, however misplaced their policies may seem.

There is, however, another reason for most of the free-world's desire for American leadership and intervention, particularly regarding the defeat of Islamists. According to Max Fisher, the world firmly believed that American involvement is a force for "good." For the Persian Gulf countries, this belief was fortified by President Trump's visit to Saudi Arabia in May 2017, where he iterated that the United States was firmly committed to their safety in the region.

The Arab states' view of the underlying "goodness" of American actions, rests on a belief that United States' policies in the Middle East have historically produced a more stable, welcoming, and durable environment. These policies are, therefore, considered synonymous with the intrinsic goodness that they believe is within America. Such sentiments are easily captured by the governing bodies in the region, who believe that American hegemony in their area is not only useful to them, but perhaps necessary for safe-guarding their own autocratic regimes, which gives their small nations an "out-of-proportion" world-reckoning that they would not otherwise have. However, while the governing bodies of the Persian Gulf may have some adulation for the Americans, it seems that the United States needs to do much more in using this favorable view to its advantage. For example, building bases in the Middle East is one thing, but they should also make an effort at building relationships with the locals — something that America has not been very good at in the past.

Assessing human rights violations pertaining to American geopolitical policies. Aside from direct American intervention through their role as the world's military leader, there is yet one more issue with respect to the United States' moral leadership that needs to be addressed. There is a growing suspicion among others in the East (not only among Muslims) that the West is very selective in voicing its displeasure. Even in cases of universal consensus on issues that are deemed to be in violation of human rights, the United States is not always committed or consistent in its criticism. For example, the United States vehemently opposed human rights violations in China, but at the same time paid little or no attention to the violations of human rights by its Persian Gulf allies. The West, according to the East, simply cannot tout a "universally" condemned human rights violation in one country, and turn a blind eye in the case of another. While there is an intrinsic appeal to ballyhoo the West's supposedly "superior" morality and human rights laws on others, it should be noted that nothing is done when American-allied countries such as Kuwait, Bahrain, and some countries of the United Arab Emirates, turn a blind eye from the atrocities committed by its citizens against legal laborers from Pakistan, Sri Lanka, Philippines, South Korea, and India. These people are physically and mentally abused, and treated with complete disdain. Often their passports are confiscated, and they are forced to work unusually long hours, particularly during Ramadan, while many of them, together with their bosses, fast from sunrise to sunset.

However, under the new administration in the United States, internal country-based atrocities regarding human right issues are not deemed very important, leaving each country to its own definitions of right and wrong. But such a policy is not practiced under the banner of "fairness," because in the case of Syria, the Trump administration did bomb a Syrian airfield in response to Assad using chemical weapons on his own people. The obvious question then is whether such an action was undertaken because these atrocities were too cruel to be bearable, or the action was actualized based on who was committing the atrocities. Perhaps, the action was just a grandiose performance for the rest of the world – to let them know that the United States is still in the driver's seat.

In spite of the "leave-alone" policy promulgated by proponents in some Western countries with respect to the application of human rights law, there is, as discussed above, selective following of moral law, which is completely at conflict with the promotion of equanimity and fair policy for all. In this context, moral "incorrectness" on the battlefield is often justified by the West, chalking it up simply as an act of war.

In preserving moral values during military actions, the argument that dismisses collateral damage as unimportant or "necessary" can be seen by some as a *carte blanche* excuse for the West to do whatever it wants; the indication being that morality from a Western point of view is conditional on its own agenda. Furthermore, there is also an argument by some in the Muslim world that the tacit expectation of collateral damage as a necessary part of war provides a cushioning for rather reckless military actions by the West against civilians in the pursuance of their enemies. On the other hand, as stated earlier, there are others who argue that morality from Western point of view is conditional, depending on which country is violating human rights laws.

However, in concurrence with Dr. Chris Martenson's argument, "either innocent deaths are always unconscionable, or they are not." In other words, civilian deaths cannot be morally unacceptable in one place and "subservient to political realities in another." Under the laws of fairness, the United States cannot weep over the massacre of the children of Sandy Hook one day, but side with the Saudis (as explained later in this chapter) in their supposedly *intentional* killing of Houthi civilians (including children) in Yemen on another, under the guise of collateral damage.[18]

According to Chris Martenson, when the United States hangs a label of "violation" on countries based on human rights and morality issues, it is, in fact, personifying the very things it hates about itself. Using psychological terminology, the United States *projects* traits on other countries that it also has but does not like. Generally speaking, all countries play particular roles as they pertain to their political purpose. Accusations against others for atrocities that may also have been committed by the accusing nation is just a part of the blame equation, and is used by everyone in an effort to fulfill their own political imperatives. Often, the reason for calling out a country for human rights violations is a propaganda game by the accuser in an attempt to evoke global anger against the accused country, or for justifying warring actions against it. Morality issues, in all such cases, will always be secondary.[19] The problem, therefore, is not that the United States does what every other country tries to do, but it does it under the guise of being a champion against such violations.

While Martenson's accusations may call for some Americans to reevaluate their own nations' global actions more critically, there is also a prevalent view that the United States is guilty of human rights violations in its own country. For example, Lilit

Marcus, writing for *Condo Naste Traveler*, states that countries such as Bahrain, Bahamas, and the United Arab Emirates have advised their citizens to avoid crowds, to not be too conspicuous by wearing traditional dress, and use great caution when traveling to America.[20] It is important to note this shift in global perception — the country that "watched" is now being watched. While there may have been some concerns in the past about violence in the United States, such travel warnings, it seems, have seldom been so flagrantly stated.

The issue of fairness in the administration of American global policies that affect the Middle East. As is the case around the world, government policies are, by their nature, self-driven for self-interest. However, in the case of the United States, which is supposed to carry the insignia of a "fair" world leader, its behavior is often likened by some, to bullying tactics used against countries that do not have a quid pro quo with the United States, or do not have the military arsenal to fight back. For these countries, the behavior of the United States towards countries that have nuclear capability is not equivalent to its behavior against countries that do not. In other words, bully those who can be bullied.

To some countries, a possible deterrent for what they posit to be "unwarranted" American aggression might be to build their military capabilities (including nuclear power) in the hope that they would be respected as a major military force. They would likely point to the example of America's "tepid" response to nuclear-powered Russia when it annexed a foreign country's territory, and interfered in other countries' political process. When one compares this docile response to the Russians with the Iraqi invasion of Kuwait in 1990, American bullying tactics, personified by an invasion bent on driving out the Iraqis (Operation Desert Storm), becomes very clear. Even with China, which has a history of human rights violations (according to the West), America pays "lip service," not only because it is one of its largest trading partners, but also because it remains a major military power in Asia. To some non-nuclear possessing countries, the selective aggression of the United States is a typical Catch-22 situation — countries that are militarily weak are doomed if they do not tow the American line, and yet they face an equally undesirable fate of sanctions from the West and threats of war if they try to expand their weaponry — weapons that the United States and some "others" already possess.

It is likely that Middle Easterners consider countries like India, Pakistan, and Israel quite "lucky" because they all have nuclear arsenals despite never having signed the Non-Proliferation Treaty. North Korea, considered a rogue nation by almost every country in the world, withdrew from the agreement in January 2003. Israel, however, manufactures its nuclear warheads in pseudo-secrecy, with no interference from any country regarding its right to possess such weapons. While Israel neither denies nor accepts being a nuclear power, it has, according to Kelsey Davenport, director of non-proliferation policy, assured the world that it would not be the first to deploy nuclear warheads in the Middle East.[21]

However, this fair-treatment issue, in particular for Muslims in the Middle East, becomes blatantly apparent in the context of the West's nonchalance over Israel's nuclear undertakings when, by the same token, it takes military action against Middle Eastern countries it believes to possess weapons of mass destruction or nuclear armaments. While nothing much can be done about Israel's nuclear prowess, Muslims in the Middle East and elsewhere have reason to be cautious in "allowing" Middle Eastern countries to build nuclear arsenals, if, for nothing else, as a means to preserve their own security in light of the extreme volatility in the region. In this context, allowing any country to acquire nuclear weaponry could be dangerous, considering differing geopolitical interests of different countries in the world. In this context, there is a general consensus among peoples of the world that nuclear power is not the answer to world safety, exacerbated by the fact that the United States and Russia could single-handedly annihilate the entire world with the number of nuclear warheads they have in their possession.

The Iraqi war – a show of unthoughtful military extravagance that backfired. To rehash the mangled Middle Eastern policies of the United States in the Middle East, one needs to realize that irrespective of how Mr. Cheney (former vice president of the United States) and some others in the West rationalize their actions in Iraq, it is now clear that there was no justification for engaging in that war. Chris Martenson reasserts the fact that prior to Iraq being attacked, the country had never threatened the United States, was not involved in 9/11, and had allowed the UN access to its country's military bases (albeit on a conditional basis), during which no evidence was ever found that the country was manufacturing weapons of mass destruction. And furthermore, even if the Iraqis had been producing these so-called weapons of mass destruction, there was still no legal case for an attack by the United States, because pre-emptive attacks are never justifiable.[22]

Craig Murray, former British ambassador to Uzbekistan, now a human rights activist, also notes that there was no evidence of Saddam Hussein *ever* having weapons of mass destruction. Mr. Murray, who was, at one time, head of the Foreign Commonwealth Unit (FCO) in charge of the oversight of Saddam's weapons of mass destruction, bluntly states in a video presentation that both Britain and the United States were aware the invasion would never have been upheld by the UN

Security Council, and therefore bypassed it, knowing full well that not only the accusations, but even the suspicion of Saddam having such weapons, was false.[23]

There is some confusion in the West as to how Daesh gained such a strong hold in the region shortly after the overthrow of Saddam Hussein's army. There are some who cite the early withdrawal of the United States from Iraq as the reason. However, a more plausible explanation is given by Dexter Filkins who writes in *The New Yorker* that after Saddam's government was thrown out of office, the Americans under George W. Bush, dissolved the Iraqi army which put around 250,000 Iraqi men who were humiliated, armed, angry and with military training, out of work. According to the Filkins, this was "probably the single most catastrophic decision of the American venture in Iraq. In a stroke, the Administration helped enable the creation of the Iraqi insurgency." While Bush administration officials like Paul Bremer and Walter Slocombe, argued that they were effectively endorsing the reality of disintegration of the Iraqi Army, Filkins states that according to American military commanders he had talked to,

> leaders of entire Iraqi divisions (a division has roughly ten thousand troops) had come to them for instructions and expressed a willingness to cooperate. In fact, many American commanders argued vehemently at the time that the Iraqi military should be kept intact—that disbanding it would turn too many angry young men against the United States. But the Bush White House went ahead.

While there is no count of the number of Iraqi soldiers who joined up with Daesh, many of these unemployed Iraqi soldiers took up arms against the United States and helped consolidate Daesh's reputation as one of the worst terror groups in history.[24]

According to former prime minister of England, Tony Blair, Daesh would not exist if Saddam Hussein was still in power. Even though it freed the Shi'a Iraqis and the Kurds from the hold of a tyrant, the large population of Sunni Arabs in the region have no gratitude for the United States and Britain, due to the part they played in their demise as the ruling ethnicity in Iraq. They had irrevocably voiced concerns over the hateful partiality of Malaki, who was elected as the first Shi'a head of Iraq with American help.

On the other hand, as some have argued, the turn of events in the Middle East was also the result of the quick withdrawal of the United States' army from the region, without first ensuring its stability. The reason for this supposed "early" withdrawal was no doubt an internal political move rather than a strategically devised plan; perhaps for the simple reason that Americans were tired of grieving for lost lives in foreign wars.

However, the "quick" withdrawal from Iraq by the United States, according to former United States' Ambassador to Iraq, Christopher Hill, could also be partly attributed to the fact that the Iraqis themselves did not want the Americans to remain in their country indefinitely.[25] Even the Shi'ite population, although happy with the toppling of the Sunni regime, did not prefer the presence of the West any longer than was absolutely necessary. Ironically, the presence of Daesh has stretched the definition of "absolutely necessary," and American help is once again desired in order to assist the Iraqis in defeating the Islamists.

Eventually, it is hoped that the actualization of democracy will "open" the eyes of all Iraqis to the benefits of democratic rule. But, until then, their path to "true" democracy will be overshadowed by the knowledge that a "say" in their governance came only as an offshoot of an unjust war. While the war worked out to the advantage of the Shi'as and the Kurds, who comprise the majority population of Iraq, it will remain in their collective memories that the United States' intervention had nothing to do with the belief in human rights and justice.

It is perhaps understandable that in the arena of international affairs, a public apology by the United States or Britain for attacking the sovereign state of Iraq with erroneous intelligence is not likely to ever happen. For example, even though Tony Blair takes full responsibility for the unwarranted invasion of Iraq, he is also known to have stated that he would do the same thing again, under similar circumstances.

However, the unwarranted attack on Iraq, the subsequent "flip-flopping" of the United States' government in crossing the "red line" drawn by President Obama in the Syrian war, and the unplanned aftermath of the Libyan war, leaves Americans with no choice but to admit that the world has a harder time trusting the United States than it did prior to its invasion of Iraq. Therefore, it may be useful for Americans to do some self-evaluation regarding their place in the world before undertaking future courses of action. More importantly, a careful evaluation of American agendas must take place. Does the United States want to continue playing the role of world leader? Are they willing to share this role with others who are coming to power? How much are they willing to sacrifice in order to play the leadership role? These are just a few questions that must be raised in forming a coherent (albeit flexible) strategy that matches the dynamic nature of events around the world, with particular focus on the Middle East, the Russians, North Korea, and China.

The Love-Hate Relationship Between Saudi Arabia and the United States

Both within and outside the context of the Arab Spring, Saudi Arabia's relationship with the United States is constantly tested because of the changing dynamics in the battle for hegemony in the Middle East, particularly as it pertains to the Persian Gulf. To analyze the seemingly tenuous relationship that existed between these two countries prior to President Trump's visit to Saudi Arabia, one needs to first understand their relationship as it existed in the past.

Over the years, the relationship between the Persian Gulf countries and the United States has been taken for granted in the sense that both parties had no significant reasons for derailing their alliances. The United States has preferred the status quo, which it has always desired in its relationship with Saudi Arabia, and others in the region. In spite of the status quo, also desired by the Saudis, Saudi Arabia and several other countries in the Persian Gulf, according to Seyed Hossein Mousavian, have had some grievances against the United States. For example, the Saudis have not been happy about the developments in Afghanistan after the downfall of the Taliban regime. Similarly, the Persian Gulf countries are angry about the consequences of the American invasion of Iraq in 2003 and the overthrow of Saddam Hussein's regime.[26] However, in 2010, at the time of the Arab Spring, the rather stoic relationship between Saudi Arabia and the United States exposed a very turbulent side to their alliance, which has never really been acknowledged by the media in either country.

This rather awkward relationship between the two countries became all the more stressful when a defiant Saudi Arabia, together with coalition forces from Morocco, Egypt,

Sudan, and Jordan, attacked the Shi'a Houthis' non-military targets in Yemen in March 2015. In the Yemeni war, the Saudis, according to a report in the *Wall Street Journal* by Maria Abi-Habib and Adam Entous, did not bomb military or strategic targets controlled by Shi'a Houthis, but instead *knowingly* bombed civilian targets, including hospitals, schools, a refugee camp, and Shi'a neighborhoods.[27] The accusation that the Saudis deliberately bombed civilian targets (if true), according to Max Fisher's investigative reporting, becomes even more disturbing when coupled with the troubling fact that the United States had prior information of the targets. While the Americans reportedly warned the Saudis not to follow through with the attacks, they finally gave in, and granted their support, supposedly in return for the Saudis' acquiescence in the nuclear agreement with Iran.[28]

According to The *New York Times Editorial Report*, the Yemeni war is a monumental disaster, with around 6,500 civilians (including children) killed, and resulting in Al-Qaeda and Daesh becoming more entrenched than ever in Yemen.[29] Instead of ending the war, Saudi Arabia has exacerbated the violence in Yemen, and the United States, in the words of Fisher, "has helped Saudi Arabia to accelerate the implosion of another Mideast state, with unknown but surely far-reaching implications."[30]

The revelation above is just one attitude of defiance levied by Saudi Arabia against the United States. The Arabian monarchy also proved itself quite resilient to American request when it refused to stop the execution of a dissident Shi'ite clergy, living in Saudi Arabia, for his grievances against the ruling party. Furthermore, in April 2016, Saudi Arabia threatened to withdraw its investments in the United States, worth billions of dollars, if the report purported to tie the Saudi government to the 9/11 attack, was made public.

The problem with Saudi Arabia's threat was that it was predicated on an inherent fear that something untoward may be included in the report. If the Saudis were confident that they were not involved, why would they presume that the report might state otherwise? While such an indication of a Saudi tie to 9/11 was never proven, according to Washington correspondent for *The New York Times*, Binyamin Appelbaum, withdrawing Saudi investments could have been as detrimental to the Saudis as it would have been for the Americans.[31] However, aside from what may have happened to the world economic structure, the interesting point is that the United States now had a situation where a foreign power was trying to force the United States' hand by blackmailing it in the functioning of its internal affairs.

However, in light of the Arab Spring, which gave rise to populist politics and furthered opportunity for the rise of Islamists, the "much-desired" status quo between the United States and Arab countries would likely have been less stable and less predictable. For a while, the fears of Arab states, many of whom are dictatorial monarchies, were likely exacerbated as the old order began to dissipate under President Obama. However, the United States, perhaps because of concern for stability in the region, seems to have deemphasized its usual role in supporting the rights of democracy. Despite these uncertain developments, the United States later defined "stability" in the region as a reflective product of its relationship with Saudi Arabia. In other words, stability was likely to be preserved if the status quo in the United States' relationship with Saudi Arabia was not disturbed.

On the other hand, from the Saudis' point of view, the desire to maintain the status quo may not have been enough to provide such stability within the context of the changing dynamics post-Arab Spring. In this respect, Saudi Arabia seemed to be looking after its own interests (such as in Yemen), even if those interests were not strictly in accordance with the expectations of the United States.

But, besides the slight distrust between the United States and Saudi Arabia in the past, there are significant reasons for maintaining friendly ties between the two nations. For the Saudis, controlling the Islamists and maintaining its hegemony role in the region requires American presence. This dependency on the United States is not without reason. For example, there is a definite reason to believe that the Islamists have cells in Saudi Arabia that could create havoc within the country, as they did on July 4, 2016, when bombs went off near mosques in Medina and Qatif, and near the American consulate in Jeddah. Keeping in mind that the Wahhabis and Salafis in Saudi Arabia follow a very strict Islamic ideology, such actions could be more than worrisome for the Saudi Royal Family, as they could promote a false message to some susceptible Saudis with respect to the Islamists' agenda. For the Royal Family, this is a burden it has to carry in balancing the desires of its population with its political agenda. One can, therefore, appreciate their fear of Daesh's advancement within their borders, which has the potential to entice a revolt within the country.

It is in this context that the Saudis' dependency on the Americans can be really understood, despite their occasional "foray" against the wishes of Washington. As Max Fisher points out, the Saudis and other Persian Gulf countries explicitly desire American hegemony over their region because it serves their interests in helping maintain their rule at home, their security assurances against their more populous enemy, Iran, and their outsized influence abroad. This confidence in the United States' ability to protect their nations, according to the author, is built on the knowledge that the United States has enormously large monetary and military resources for a military war in comparison to other countries in the world.[32]

Considering the mutual dependency between Washington and Riyadh, there seems to be a visceral understanding that Washington will defend Saudi Arabia irrespective of how contrary its behavior is to the values and goals of the United States. It is as if, at a subconscious level, the United States understands the need for Saudi Arabia to take controversial actions in preserving its sovereignty in the region, even if those actions are not in keeping with American expectations. These actions by the Saudis are likely seen as a necessity for the stability that Washington desires in the region, without seriously jeopardizing the status quo it seems to crave. On the other hand, according to some scholars, it could also be that the United States' strong support of Saudi Arabia, even when it violates American expectations, might in fact be the cause of the derailment of "stability" in the Persian Gulf, such as in places like Yemen, and the recent turmoil in some of the Middle East countries' relationship with Qatar.

Saudi Arabia's relationship with Qatar. The shaky relationship between Qatar and Saudi Arabia has been defined by Max Fisher as a "cold war" between the two countries.[33] In June 2017, however, the conflict did not remain "cold," when Egypt and most of the Gulf Cooperation Council (GCC) countries (Bahrain, Saudi Arabia, UAE, and Oman), broke their diplomatic relationship with Qatar, and imposed sanctions on it. The anger against Qatar is based, according to *The Guardian* report by Patrick Wintour, on various reasons that can be attributed to three major factors: Qatar's support of terrorists and sectarian groups aimed at destabilizing the region, its "antagonistic approach" towards Egypt, and its creation of chaos in Bahrain by funding Iranian groups in the tiny nation. Some other groups, such as Yemen's internationally backed government, the government in control of Eastern Libya, and the Maldives, also joined the move to break relations with Qatar.[34]

The accusation against Qatar for their officially backing terrorist groups, likely stems from the country's support of the Muslim Brotherhood, which the others – Egypt and some countries of the GCC – consider a terrorist organization. It is, therefore, quite possible that the real reason for the anti-Qatar provocative stance by Saudi Arabia and Egypt – both of which hate the Brotherhood – may be personal and not entirely politically motivated. Their provocative actions against Qatar may have less to do with the help, a few Qatari citizens may still be providing clandestinely to the Islamists – almost insignificant as reported by ICSR (see Chapter 6) – and more with the official support of the Qatari government for the Brotherhood, which is not designated a terrorist group at this writing by most countries in the West, including the United States.

The Qatari-Brotherhood association that may be driving the hostility against Qatar is further exemplified by the fact that Kuwait, which as stated earlier, is also known to have had its citizens support Daesh clandestinely, has not been on Egypt's and other GCC countries' radar as a "defaulting" country. Could it be because Kuwait has no known association with the Brotherhood?

The other provocative issue between the Qataris and the others is its relationship with Iran. Contrary to most people's belief, Qatar, unlike Saudi Arabia, Bahrain and Kuwait, is not anti-Iran, presumably because both countries share the world's largest gas field known as the North Dome – the Iranian share of the North Dome is known as the South Pars field.[35] It is in this context that Qatar, even though it has a strict Sunni Islamic following and traditions, has cordial relationship with Shi'ite Iran. On the other hand, the Saudis and the Bahrainis have vehemently opposed this relationship and have accused Qatar of supporting Iran in creating instability in Bahrain where the Shi'as, the majority population in Bahrain, is ruled by a Sunni king. While the veracity of this statement is not researched, this accusation against Qatar is likely the other major reason for the animosity that has surfaced between Qatar and its neighbors.

In this context, it is important to note that Bahrain has been the protected child of Saudi Arabia – amply proven when Saudi Arabia and the UAE sent their armies to quell the Shi'a insurgence in the tiny island country during the Arab Spring. While some may idolize Qatar's actions as a noble cause for justice for the supposedly "subjugated" Shi'a population in Bahrain, the actions, if true, can create a very volatile situation in the region. To Saudi Arabia, Qatar's support of the Shi'as population, and that too with the support of Iran, their arch enemy, is simply not acceptable. To some observers of the geopolitical dynamics in the Persian Gulf, the situation reeks of the pull towards hegemony in the region between Saudi Arabia and Qatar. To the credit of the United States, it is heartening to note that it has played a conciliatory role between the opposing parties, seeking dialogue with the two parties in an effort at diffusing the tensions in the region.

This difference in Qatari's ideology vis-à-vis the others has come to the forefront in the reassembling of regional order after the Arab Spring when Qatar openly sided with the Brotherhood in its victory in Egypt.[36] Furthermore, James Dorsey states that Qatar, even though its native population is largely made of Wahhabis, believes that it does not have to follow in the footsteps of Saudi Arabia, which practices a rather repressive and restrictive form of Wahhabism.[37]

So far, the Qataris had played second fiddle to the powerful Saudis in terms of Saudi Arabia's puritan interpretation of

Islam. However, according to the "new" view from the Qataris, Wahhabism can be somewhat forward- and outward-looking. In this context, Qatar, which so far played a subversive role with respect to Saudi Arabia, has now challenged its much larger neighbor for its own identity in the region. This challenge, according to Dorsey, is rooted in historical tensions that stems from long-standing differences in religious interpretations that are likely results of "Qatar's geography, patterns of trade and history; and a failure to groom a class of popular Muslim legal scholars of its own."[38]

Qatar has thus formulated a soft power strategy designed to reduce its dependence on the Saudi umbrella of defense, prompted by a perception that Saudi Arabia may not be able to effectively protect it or expand its own interests in the region. While the differences in social, foreign, and security policies between the two countries cannot be denied, Qatar, which hosts the largest American military base in the Middle East, proceeded, as explained by Dorsey, with a modicum of good neighborly relations and cooperation, but with clearly defined, albeit unspoken red lines to "outright proxy confrontation with Saudi Arabia."[39]

Saudi Arabian influence in Washington. In the quest for dominance in the Persian Gulf region, it seems that most Arab countries have concluded that to position themselves ahead of their rivals in the region, they would have to "buy" influence in Washington. To this end, as stated in the Preface, oil-rich kingdoms have made large donations to think tanks and academic institutions, keeping in mind that Washington's policy decisions are often based on opinions and research undertaken by the various prestigious think tanks in the United States.

However, according to Max Fisher's investigations, the belief of Washington "insiders" is that the United States' favoritism of

Saudis would exist even in the absence of their funding. Their money only amplifies a belief in America's pro-Saudi conventional bias, which has long been the Washington consensus. All that the Saudi money has done is solidified this belief, even as the situation in the Middle East changes dramatically.

Although the common "interests" of the United States and its allies have gradually widened since the Arab Spring, Washington's pro-Persian Gulf consensus has proven strangely resilient with respect to Arab countries. While there is no definitive answer as to whether money has had an impact in the strengthening of the status quo between Saudi Arabia and the United States, or if the status quo exists independently of the funding, most experts, like Fisher, believe the two are working in conjunction. In other words, money reinforces Washington's preexisting preference for status quo bias.[40]

Besides pouring money into think tanks and undertaking conferences to strengthen or sway the United States' opinion, the Persian Gulf states have always worked on building personal relationships in Washington. In recent years, such activities have taken the form of splashy parties and media appearances, although Saudi Arabia still prefers to build its relationship on past methods of direct involvement with American policymakers or using lobbyists, rather than depending on more flashy methods.

The Relationship Between Turkey and the United States

Aside from the relationship between the United States and the Persian Gulf countries, subtle problems plague the relationship between Turkey and the United States. In 2002, the Turkey Justice and Development Party (AKP), because of its prospect of becoming a member of the EU, passed a series of consequential democratic reforms, which included a revision of the penal code, easing restrictions on freedom of expression, reining in the power of the military, and expanding the rights of the country's Kurdish minority. However, when negotiations with the EU faltered, the AKP government seemingly lost interest in democratization, and increasingly adopted illiberal and undemocratic practices.

After participating with UN' forces in the Korean War, Turkey joined NATO in 1952. However, its relationship with the United States has been strained since 2003, primarily because of the United States' war with Iraq. Turkey viewed the war as a significant threat to its security because Northern Iraq acts as a haven for the outlawed Kurdistan Workers Party (PKK), which is hated by Turkey for its demands to form an independent Kurdish state within the country. According to Turkey, the destabilization of Iraq and Syria could act as a possible impetus for Kurds to claim their independence from Syria, Turkey, Iraq, and other Middle Eastern countries that have significant Kurdish populations. A further strain in relations between the United States and Turkey is attributed to disagreements over the indirect American support of the Kurdish Popular Defense Unit, known as the YPG/J (where YPG is the male unit and the YPJ is female), which is believed to be an offshoot of the PYD (Kurdish Democratic Union Party).

The complexities of the relationship between Turkey and the United States reached a pinnacle of distrust after the arrival of Daesh in Syria. Political analysis by *Washington Institute's* Soner Cagaptay and James F. Jeffrey explains the different motivations of the two countries in the war in Syria. Until very recently, in 2017, when a rash of Daesh-related incidents occurred in Turkey, Ankara's priority was to bring down the Syrian regime of Bashar al-Assad, which it views as a threat to its border security, while Washington has, for the present, limited its objectives to fighting Daesh. In addition, there are tensions regarding how much American leadership, Ankara can stomach, and how much Washington values Turkey as a partner after the failed *coup d'état* attempted against Turkey's state institutions and the government of President Recep Tayyip Erdoğan on July 15, 2016.[41] Erdoğan believes the coup was the work of Fethullah Gulen, a Muslim Imam who lives in exile in the United States, through his followers in Turkey. Ankara's pressure on Washington to extradite Gulen, fueled speculation that the Incirlik Air Base in southern Turkey, a key launch pad for American fighter planes entering Syria, Iraq, and beyond, would be blocked from American access.

Michael O'Hanlon, a senior fellow in foreign policy at the Brookings Institution in America, states that ex-United States' secretary of state, John Kerry, warned Turkey that it could run afoul of NATO's "requirement with respect to democracy," if it failed to uphold the rule of law in the wake of the attempted coup. According to some experts, this warning from Kerry could be the result of Erdoğan's rather autocratic behavior after the coup, whereby more than fifty thousand people, including soldiers, police, judges, teachers, government staff, clerics, and intelligence officials were taken into custody or fired from their jobs.[42]

Once again, it should be noted that the relationship between Turkey and the United States, like that between the United States and Saudi Arabia, is symbiotic. However, the relationship may not be as "balanced" as it seems to imply. Ankara, for example, knows that the United States, besides Russia, is the only major player with teeth to destroy the Islamists. Though Ankara needs the Americans in fighting Daesh, it fears the Kurds will come knocking on its doors with the United States' blessing while it is involved in getting rid of Daesh. For the United States, Turkey is a major crossroad between the Middle East and Europe, but while the prospect of being denied access to the Incirlik Air Base in southern Turkey could cause the United States some hardships, according to some experts in the field, it could still control its operations in Syria from its bases in Qatar and Bahrain, if necessary. However, as O'Hanlon muses, "it's way beyond Incirlik, it's the entire US-NATO-Turkey relationship, the entire collaboration in Syria"that is at stake.[43]

Whether such dire predictions would ever come to fruition is doubtful, given the great strides made by the coalition forces in driving out Daesh from the region, and the internal political problems Erdoğan has to attend to, in addition to the war taking place on the Syrian side of its borders. In the final analysis, it should be noted that the rather tenuous relationship between Washington and Ankara, is more of a problem for Turkey that the United States. Ankara needs America's help to provide a decorum of stability within the region, given that Russia has sided with Assad in Syria. According to Shadi Hamid, Turkey, like Qatar, is tied to the United States militarily and strategically. However, it has so far been able and willing to establish itself as an "independent, assertive regional power, despite occasional (or increasingly frequent) American grumbling," which under President Trump may be less pronounced.[44]

United States' Venture in Afghanistan

Among the various problems created because of America's indecisiveness in the formulation of an action-based policy, and its hesitancy in interfering with "matters overseas," is the issue of the Taliban in Afghanistan. Due to ever-changing geopolitical conditions, and some major faux pas on the part of the Americans, the Taliban have been a perpetual problem not only for the Afghanis, but for all those who desire democratic rule in the country.

While some academics and journalists have argued that Al-Qaeda and the Taliban are results of American policy gone amok, senior lecturer at the Naval Postgraduate School, and a resident scholar at the American Enterprise Institute, Michael Rubin, argues that neither Osama bin Laden's Al-Qaeda, nor Mullah Umar, the spiritual head of the Taliban, were direct products of the United States' CIA. The Afghanistan problem, according to him, started as a competition between the Americans and the Soviets for a stake in the area during the 1950s. Initially, when the Soviets flexed their muscles in the area, Pakistan (Afghanistan's neighbor to the north) looked with suspicion at the growing New Delhi-Moscow-Kabul alliance, in which the Shah of Iran tried to play a meditative role in May 1963. After the Soviet invasion of Afghanistan in 1979, resistance groups known as the Mujahedin grew exponentially in influence and size as they gathered force, becoming the only viable opposition movement in the region. Within two weeks of the Soviet invasion, the United States, under the Carter administration, with Saudi Arabia and several other countries, joined together to provide financial aid to the Mujahedin. This aid to the Mujahedin grew substantially, both in terms of finances and direct arms assistance, during the Regan administration in 1986.[45]

However, while the United States, through the CIA, coordinated the purchase of weapons and training for the Mujahedin, they left the distribution of arms in the war zone to Pakistan's Inter-Services Intelligence (PISI). The ultraconservative PISI refused aid to non-religious groups, but gained disproportionate influence with religious groups in the region through aid distribution. The United States not only failed to control the PISI in its religiously biased practices, but they provided no help to the Mujahedin, only a year after the departure of the Soviet Union from the country. In the meantime, Saudi and Kuwaiti aid poured into Afghanistan, mostly distributed to Wahhabi resistance-movements and other ultra-conservative religious commanders in Afghanistan.[46]

According to Ed Girardet, a journalist and Afghan expert, "the United States really blew it" by removing itself from the country. Other experts also echo Girardet's sentiments, and criticize the United States for walking away from Afghanistan once the Soviets withdrew from the country. Eventually, internal local fighters, such as Hikmaytar, were fed up with the restrictions on aid provided by Saudi Arabia and Kuwait. Instead, they found new patrons in Iran, Libya, Iraq, and from Muslim fighters living in Central Asia and the Middle East, who came to them from the Muslim Brotherhood or other conservative Islamic organizations to fight in Afghanistan.[47]

In this context, because of the Americans' shift in focus to the Iraqi troop invasion of Kuwait in 1990, and the fact that it delegated the responsibility of arms distribution to the repressive, religiously-based PISI, it likely created an environment in which Islamism could flourish. The chaos in Afghanistan, with many warlords overlooking many different fiefdoms, provided the climate for the rise of the Taliban, a group of fundamentalist Sunni Muslim militants, mostly living near the border between Afghanistan and Pakistan. Many members of the Taliban as stated in Chapter 5, are ethnic Pashtuns who came from the madrassas that teach the Deobandi theology in Pakistan, while others rose from the ranks of the Mujahedin.

In 1996, the only barrier to Taliban rule was the Mujahedin leader, Ahmad Shah Masood, whose army proved difficult to dislodge because of its superiority on the battlefield. In the same year, a gift was received by the Taliban in the form of Osama bin Laden, who relocated from Sudan to Afghanistan with some two thousand devoted and well-trained men ready for terrorism abroad, and who assisted the Taliban in its fight against Masood.[48] However, Israeli author Yacov Ben Efrat cautions that the intimate relationship between Bin Laden and the Taliban was not a result of Osama's interest in the welfare of the Afghanis, but instead was a key piece to the megalomaniac strategy bent on turning Afghanistan into a major base for Islamists in Osama's quest for spreading terrorism abroad.[49]

According to Phillip Knightley of *The Guardian*, Ahmed Rashid, a leading author and expert on Afghan affairs, states that during the earlier part of Taliban governance, the United States encouraged Saudi Arabia and Pakistan to support the Taliban because of the stability brought about by their governance. This stability was very important to the Americans, who, during that time, led a consortium that included the California-based UNOCAL Corporation (on whose board ex-President Bush sat as a member), the Saudi-based Delta Oil, and Pakistan's Crescent Group, among others, to build a $4.5 billion 1,040-mile oil and gas pipeline across war-ravaged Afghanistan; from Uzbekistan and Kazakhstan to the Indian Ocean. In addition to tapping new energy resources, Knightley notes that it was also an endeavor to help the United States isolate its nemeses, Iran and Russia, and stifle a "frequently-mooted rival pipeline project backed by Tehran."[50]

British diplomat Craig Murray strongly believes that the Afghani war initially had no relationship to the current fight against terrorism. Instead, Murray believes that the chief cause of the war was oil.[51] There may be some credibility to Mr. Murray's opinions, based largely on the fact that Caspian oil is a prized commodity for South East Asia and some Western countries, especially for those who depend on Russia and the war-torn Middle Eastern countries for their oil.

In a sense, one could identify terrorism and pipeline-building as parts of the same mold, with pipelines being dependent on the stability within a region. One could also conclude that a mix of different interests were responsible for the invasion of Afghanistan, justifiable in the eyes of the United States and the United Kingdom, with each interest being a compelling reason for their actions. However, whatever the reasons were for the United States to invade Afghanistan, the pipeline scheme with UNOCAL was eventually forfeited because the then-Taliban government was not fully recognized internationally as the legitimate government, and therefore the project "could not receive funding from international financial institutions like the World Bank." UNOCAL could also have pulled out as a result of the continual conflict raging in Afghanistan between various groups in search for hegemony in the region.[52] Besides financial and safety concerns in Afghanistan, there were political pressures applied by Hillary Clinton, and former U.S. Secretary of State Madeline Albright to stop investments in Afghanistan due to their poor treatment of the Afghani women. In this respect, it is likely that campaigns by Feminist Majority and other women's rights groups appealed to the conscience of the United States, and were instrumental in helping defeat "the energy company UNOCAL's efforts to construct an oil pipeline across Afghanistan that would have supplied the Taliban with over $100 million and dramatically increased their control in the region."[53]

Mr. Murray's assertions about the importance of oil are further exemplified by the current interest of South East Asian and Western countries in pipe-building in the region — especially for those countries who depend on Russia and the

Middle East for their oil. While the original UNOCAL scheme collapsed in 1998, other pipelines are in the offing or have been completed in the area by different consortiums, reflecting the continued interest in the region by the United States and various other countries in the world. For example, ex-United States President Bill Clinton, supported the approximately $3.6 billion, 1,000-mile pipeline that was opened in 2005 to carry oil from Azerbaijan through Georgia to Ceyhan in Turkey, bypassing the turbulence in Afghanistan. Similarly, a $700 million, 597-mile pipeline has been constructed between the China National Petroleum Corporation and the Kaz Munai Gaz Company of Kazakhstan. Furthermore, China and Pakistan have agreed, in principle, to build a Trans-Karakoram pipeline, which, once constructed, would set the stage for landlocked oil to reach world oil markets, particularly the rapidly growing economies in Asia, by bypassing conflict-prone and politically problematic countries like Afghanistan, Iran, Russia, Armenia, Chechnya, and Georgia.[54]

Even though the United States withdrew major support for Afghanistan, the Taliban continued to govern the country from 1996 to 2001, with military support from Osama's Al-Qaeda, the PISI, and financial support from Saudi Arabia, until it was overthrown by an American-led coalition in the later part of 2001. It should be noted that formal diplomatic recognition of the Taliban during its rule was acknowledged by only three nations: Pakistan, Saudi Arabia, and the UAE.[55]

While the ideology of the Taliban is extremely cruel and misogynistic to most people around the world, the group did bring relative stability to Afghanistan during its reign. Pakistanis viewed the Taliban favorably because the stability it provided in Afghanistan stopped the flow of refugees into Pakistan. Furthermore, the Taliban provided vital help to Pakistan in its confrontation with

India, particularly in the disputed region of Kashmir. The group, however, was disbanded after 9/11, and supposedly lost all support from its sponsors, including from PISI and the Saudis. However, the group later arose as an insurgency movement to fight the American-backed Karzai administration and the NATO-led International Security Assistance Force (ISAF).

Although Afghanistan is sometimes likened to "hell on earth," with blame thrown around as to who was responsible for such horrendous conditions in the country, the United States has had some major successes in the region, the foremost of which was the killing of Osama bin Laden. Additionally, the Americans also killed Mullah Akhtar Mansour, the leader of the Taliban, in a May 2016 drone strike. While such progress in eliminating the Taliban is well worth applauding, one cannot forget the fact that the United States and its allies were partly responsible for its insurgency in the first place.

American policies in the Middle East are propelled by history and the reluctance of the United States to alter the status quo. However, there is reason to believe that cognizance of dynamism as it pertains to the "happenings" in the Middle East, may provide the initiative needed to disturb America's inflexibility in its relationship with the Islamic world.

Chapter 9

The Iranian Factor

According to the West, Iran is a hostile, violent country; but this view is contested by some non-Muslims and Muslims who see Iran as being unfairly treated. For example, award-winning foreign correspondent Stephen Kinzer states:

> Many people in the world, however, see Iran quite differently: as just another struggling country with valuable resources, no more or less threatening than any other, ruled by a regime that, while thuggish, wins grudging admiration for standing up to powerful bullies.[1]

Even as recently as May 2017, Robert Fisk, a celebrated English writer and journalist, commented on President Trump's denouncement of Iran as a terrorist state on his trip to Saudi Arabia, by stating that it is not Iran but Saudi Arabia that "is the fountainhead of the very Wahhabi Salafist extremism whose 'terrorists' murder 'innocent people.'" According to Fisk, it was incredible that instead of blaming Daesh, Trump blamed Iran for secular violence in the region, demanding further isolation of the world's largest Shi'ite Muslim country in the Middle East, only a day after the Iranians had overwhelmingly re-elected the liberal reformer Hassan Rouhani as their president..."[2]

Although some critics of the Iranian regime may consider the election in Iran to be non-democratic, given the power of the country's theocratic supreme leader and its security and its military institution – the Islamic Revolutionary Guard Corps – it is fascinating to note that even these supposedly hardcore religious conservatives allowed the re-election of a moderate liberal Hassan Rouhani who had been vocal in his non-support of the Iranian "morality police," known as the Gasht-e Ershad (Persian for Guidance Patrols). These morality police – men and women – impose strict Islamic law of conduct such as ensuring the observance of hijab for women and discouraging the use of cosmetics in public; although men may also be chastised for sporting, say, "Western" hairstyle. Even though President Rouhani has expressed opposition to the Gasht-e Ershad, considering them as a menace on urban women's desire to partake in international dress styles, Iran's constitution gives him little sway over the country's security forces.[3]

However, under the new reform movement, many of the powers of the morality police, such as admonishing the offenders, fining, and arresting them, are to be removed. Instead offenses will be reported to the police who *may* decide to take action. The elections in Iran, according to Ishaan Tharoor from the *Washington Post*, are a large improvement in comparison to Arabian countries, such as the Saudi Arabian governing system, which is essentially a "strict monarchy where women's rights are curtailed much more severely, and where one large royal family controls the levers of power."[4]

United States' Relationship with Iran – in the Context of Saudi Arabia

In light of Iran's current standing with the West, it is difficult to come up with a well-planned action for long-term solutions to the issues surrounding Iran, especially since there are, according to the West, many worthwhile reasons for continuing hostility against it. As it stands, there are no formal diplomatic relations between the United States and the Islamic Republic of Iran, although there is an "interest" section set up in the Pakistan Embassy in Washington D.C. by the Iranians, and a corresponding section set up by the United States at the Swiss Embassy in Tehran.

Initially, the United States was perceived by Iran as a more trustworthy ally than many other nations it had ties with. Even after the coup (orchestrated and later acknowledged by the CIA), leading to the overthrowing of democratically elected nationalist, Prime Minister Mohammad Mossadegh, in 1953, a very close alliance and friendship remained between Shah Mohammad Reza Pahlavi's regime and the American government. The shah's regime lasted from 1941 to 1979. According to BBC News and various other internet sources, the reason for Mossadegh's ousting as prime minister of Iran was because "the secular leader had sought to nationalize Iran's oil industry," run by the British, which did not sit well with the pro-Western elite in Iran.[5] Later, the CIA feared that Mossadegh had communist leanings and would move Iran into the Soviet orbit if allowed to stay in power. After the British Intelligence Agency (MI6) backed out, the CIA helped the shah regain his autocratic position by assisting in the overthrowing of Mossadegh from power on August 19, 1953. The shah thanked the United States by signing over 40 percent of Iran's oil fields to American companies.[6] During the time of the Shah, Iran was one of the United States' closest allies.

While most people chalk this off as "past news," it portrays the powerplay that takes place in international politics, which is not always what appears on the surface. In fact, there are instances when the hypocrisy of a country is evident when it touts one aspect of its policy, only to secretly act in complete contradiction to its officially stated political or moral stance. To rehash this point with respect to Iran, in 1986, contrary to American law and policy, the United States administration sold arms to Iran to sustain its lengthy war with Iraq. In exchange for the arms, Iran was to use its influence to help gain the release of Americans, held hostage by Hezbollah in Lebanon. According to an article in *The Washington Post* by Larry Sabato, the arms purchased by Iran were at high prices, and the excess profits were diverted by the United States to fund the Contras, who were fighting the Sandinista government in Nicaragua.[7]

The Iran-Contra Affair, as the incidence is popularly known, helped free three American hostages held by Hezbollah in Lebanon. The incidence, however, highlights how country rules are manipulated, disregarded, or broken, to satisfy a self-serving political agenda. "It was a grand scheme that violated American law and policy all around. Arms sales to Iran were prohibited; the U.S. government had long forbidden ransom of any sort for hostages; and it was illegal to fund the Contras above the limits set by Congress."[8]

What constituted the fallout in the relationship between the United States and Iran is debatable, but the dramatic reversal and disagreement between the two, commenced after the 1979 Iranian Islamic Revolution, when the shah, who was hated by most Iranians, fled to the United States. Ayatollah Ruhollah Khomeini, meanwhile, returned from exile, and following a referendum, established the Islamic Republic of Iran on April 1, 1979. For the United States, the seizing of American hostages on November 4, 1979 by student militants, who demanded the return of Shah Mohammad Reza Pahlavi to Iran for trial in exchange for the release of the captives, could be the turning point in its relationship with Iran. According to some Iranians, on the other hand, the breakup in the relationship between the two countries was a natural and unavoidable conflict between what the common Iranian perceived was America's desire for global domination, and the Islamic Revolution's desire to set-up a religiously based state.

After the overthrow of Mohammad Reza Pahlavi, the relationship between the two countries deteriorated quickly. However, according to Karim Sadjadpour, Iran's centrality to urgent U.S. and European foreign policy challenges, such as terrorism, Arab-Israeli peace, and the issue of Afghanistan, makes it unwise for the West to refrain from communicating with Tehran.[9] In fact, the United States seemed to have come to this realization as they, together with Germany, France, China, Russia, and Britain, lifted the long-standing trade embargo against Iran, sanctioned in 2015, after successful negotiations with the country to dismantle its nuclear program. Although the agreement has been signed, there is concern among many Americans, the Israelis, and the Saudis, that Iranians may not live up to their promise in the future. While such concerns are understandable, it seems that it was a chance the West needed to take, because sanctions applied against the country provided no respite regarding the lingering question of "what Iran was up to" with respect to its nuclear power.

On the other side of the coin, however, it is important to note that, although siding with one's allies is the name of the game in the international arena, it becomes a bit hypocritical when the United States, as stated above by Robert Fisk, denounces Iran for its terrorist activities and human rights violations, when the same, if not worse activities are undertaken by some of its Arab allies. For example, the Saudis were involved as recently as 2016 in the horrendous activity of stamping out dissent in their country through mass executions, to which the United States paid no attention. While the gravity of executing 47 people in a single day in Saudi Arabia may not be completely apparent, it can be quite distressing to know that the mass executions, according to Sarah Leah Whitson of *Human Rights Watch*, took place only a year after Saudi Arabia boasted one of the highest execution rates in its recent history.[10]

The dogmatic "attachment" between Washington and Riyadh gives the Saudis a lot of leeway to counter Washington's wishes, which would likely not be tolerated of other countries in the region by the Americans, except for Israel. In preserving the relationship between the two countries, there is an expectation of predictability and stability in the region, even though the recent turmoil in the Middle East, does not seem to be even vaguely associated with a quid pro quo relationship that Washington likely desires with Riyadh. However, according to Seyed Hossein Mousavian, because the United States is bent on preserving the status quo in its relationship with Saudi Arabia, it deems any country who undermines this status quo, a hostile enemy of Washington.[11]

This is particularly true with regard to the United States' relationship with Iran. According to Max Fisher's investigative report, there is a practice in Washington whereby "bad behavior" of other Middle Eastern countries, particularly Iran, receives heavy attention and debate, but Persian Gulf countries' opposition to democracy movements, human rights abuses, and foreign policy actions that undercut the United States' officially stated interests, receive very little, if any attention.[12]

Due to the turmoil in the Middle East after the Arab Spring, and the issue of Islamists, Saudi Arabia and other Middle Eastern countries, prior to President Trump's visit to Saudi Arabia in May 2017, were probably plagued with lingering doubts about the United States' resolve in "containing" the Iranians. Their doubts, perhaps, were specifically exasperated by the signing of the non-nuclear proliferation agreement with Iran, and the fact that the West, much to the chagrin of Saudi Arabia and other Arab nations, was rooting for the success of the Arab Spring in bringing democracy to the Arab world. According to Seyed Hossein Mousavian, former head of Iran's Foreign Relations Committee, Saudi Arabia was enraged at the United States for trying to change its broader strategy in the region. This change in approach was spurred in large part by America's decreased dependence on Persian Gulf hydrocarbons and its failed interventions in Afghanistan and Iraq.[13]

Because there is no formal treaty between Arab countries and the United States, the Saudis could have had qualms about how much the United States was willing to intervene with respect to their fear of Iranian activities, that could shift the balance of power for regional hegemony. To substantiate Saudi Arabia's fear of Iran's dominance in the region, it should be remembered that both the Israelis and Saudis did not want the nuclear agreement with their longtime enemy, Iran. Such a move on the part of Washington had likely conjured a feeling that America was gradually moving away from the Arabs and opening its doors to "other" agreements with the Ayatollahs in Iran. However, as stated in Chapter 8, the Americans seemed to have somewhat pacified the Saudi rulers by, among other things, turning a blind-eye to their bombing of civilian Houthi targets in Yemen, and signing a massive armament deal with the Saudis on President Trump's visit to Saudi Arabia.

Whatever the expectations are between the Persian Gulf countries and the United States, one thing is clear: Iran is a major player in the Middle East, solidified by the fact that it is deemed to be so by Saudi Arabia, who fears its intentions for hegemony in the region. However, distrust between Iran and Saudi Arabia also underlines the fact that Washington's status quo stance is not easing the stability problem in the region by excluding Iran from the picture or ranting about Iran being a terrorist nation in the Arab world. As Christopher Dickey succinctly points out, the issue of American credibility in providing stability within the region may hinge on many issues, "but Iran figures in all of them."[14]

From the point of view of the Iranians, there could be a confusion regarding the United States' behavior towards them. They are faced with a hostile culture in Washington, which punishes aberration to any action that is in support of Saudi Arabia. As Max Fisher points out:

> Because the old order was so aligned with Saudi interests, Washington's status quo bias is expressed as a pro-Saudi bias. When the foreign policy community calls for maintaining the old alliance structure, isolating Iran, and staving off Islamist movements, these are all core Saudi interests.[15]

It could be frustrating for the Iranians to admit that such a pro-Saudi culture in Washington is not easy to overcome. This is true especially since there seems to be a concentrated effort by the Saudis and some other Persian Gulf countries to make sure the United States remains hostile towards Iran on the grounds of their longstanding status quo. When this status quo is backed by money (as stated in Chapter 8), it further cements Arab influence in the United States' capital. The continued presence of Arab representatives in Washington leads to a familiar and comfortable relationship between them and United States' officials, and builds empathy toward their worldview and policy goals. In such an environment, American officials are more apt to humanize and empathize with the Saudi cause than the Iranians, whom they have presumably, seldom or never met.[16]

As stated earlier in Chapter 5, the Iranians and Arabs have always had problems in the Middle East, personified by their strained relationship for hegemony in the Persian Gulf area. For a while, things seemed to progress well between the Arabs (especially the United Arab Emirates) and the Iranians. Iran's government, led by moderate President Hassan Rouhani, has promised to work on improving ties with nearby Arab countries. In that respect, Iran's foreign minister, Javed Zarif, had made overt gestures reaching out to his Arab neighbors through reciprocal travels between the United Arab Emirates and Iran in 2013. On a more concrete level, the July 4, 2016 bombings in Saudi Arabia, exemplified an interesting aspect of the rather uneasy geopolitical situation in the region by the force of circumstances. Following the Medina blast near the Prophet's mosque (the second most revered holy place in the Muslim world), which killed four security officers and wounded five others, Muslims from every faction of the Islamic faith expressed their outrage. For example, *Al Jazeera Newspaper* quoted tweets of Iran's foreign minister, Javed Zarif, and those of the crown prince of Abu Dhabi, Muhammad bin Zayed Al Nahyan, both asking for all Muslims (Shi'as and Sunnis) to come together to save Islam.[17]

While such anecdotes may seem "trivial" and non-consequential in geopolitical affairs, it is not so for the people of the East, where "saving face" and respect are synonymous with the preservation of their pride. In any negotiations with Iran, it may be worthwhile to consider the differential behavioral attitudes of the Saudi and Iranian governments, keeping in mind that the masses in Iran are much more accepting of Western norms than those in Saudi Arabia, whose citizens are governed by the principles of an ultra-conservative form of Islam. By the same token, religion is very important in the Middle East, and the Iranians are not likely to give up on Saudi "hospitality" in visiting two of the most sacred places in Islam — Mecca and Medina — keeping in mind that the pilgrimage to Mecca to perform Hajj, as stated in Chapter 5, is obligatory for *all* Muslims who are physically and financially able.

The importance of a symbiotic relationship between the United States and the Arab countries of the Persian Gulf cannot be denied. But while the proverbial "burying the head in the sand" seems to rule the United States' status quo policies with respect to Saudi Arabia, the undertaking of long-term, sustained stability in the region would likely be a wiser move. In this context, while the consistency of America's intervention on behalf of its Arab allies might be seen by some as reliable, its validity in preserving stability in regions where it intervenes, is yet to be established. Such validity may perhaps be only be possible if the United States is willing to deviate slightly from its "written-in-stone," symbiotic relationship with the Saudis. To this end, a working relationship with Iran might not only fit the bill, but it would also help dissuade it from activities that could upset the rather tenuous stability in the region. Furthermore, incorporating Iran's perspective in order to enhance long-term stability in the region may be a worthwhile action to take, keeping in mind that the nuclear agreement signed with Iran is set to last for ten years, and it is in the United States' interest to increase the terms of the agreement indefinitely after their expiration.

However, for the present, the United States seems to believes that the only way to deal with Iran is through the use of sanctions rather than through diplomacy. In this context, MSNBC TV News in the United States stated on July 18, 2017, that the United States government agrees in Iran's compliancy with the nuclear agreement it has signed, but it was not acting in the "spirit of the accord" and was creating tensions in the region. While there could be truth in such a statement, the scenario unfolding in the Middle East has to be observed from a bird's eye view, rather than at a microscopic level that may be too narrow in its evaluation. Iran's activities in the Persian Gulf are no more sinister than others in the region. However, because of Saudi Arabia's hegemonous status, the base-line for stability in the region is based entirely on its dictates which are accepted by other Sunni monarchs in the region – partly because some autocrats are in agreement with its agenda (UAE, as an example), are too dependent on Saudi Arabia for its internal stability (for example, Bahrain) or, as in the case of Qatar, has towed the Saudi Arabian line - up until recently – in deference to its formidable position as guardians of Islam's holiest cities and its military prowess. However, Shi'ite Iran has its own aspirations that are different from the agenda set by its Arab neighbors – an Arab/Sunni agenda in which it would have to play second fiddle to its Sunni-Arab nations. Iran's reaction is tantamount to, say, the expectations that Russia would play a passive role for the sanctions applied against it (and rightfully so) by the United States and its allies. Simply put: Iran with its large Persian-Shi'a population wants to play a significant role in the geopolitics of the Persian Gulf, which in turn can only happen when Saudi Arabia and it can respect each other's role in the Islamic factions and the ethnicities they represent – through diplomacy and negotiations.

Iran is the world's largest Shi'a Muslim country. It strives for a position in the region which is dominated by Sunni Arabs, many of whom believe Shi'as to be apostates – if not outwardly, at least in some conservative Sunni Muslim hearts. While Iran has been declared a rogue nation for a reason, it has not committed any terrorist acts on United States soil, nor is it any more "roguish" than its Arab neighbors.

However, some of Iran's behavior in the international arena is likely to foster a belief that the Iranians support interests that are controversial to the interests of the West. While there is much truth in such a statement – considering Iran's anti-Israel stance and its support for the Assad regime – it should be kept in mind that accusations of Iran being a terrorist state come from some nations who themselves could be accused of similar atrocities against others, as well as their own people. When a country is surrounded by supposedly hostile countries who have a very different ideology and agenda, it is likely to gyrate towards that which is common and familiar to its people. In the case of Iran, while there may be no justification for it siding with Assad, there is an undeniable reason for it — Shi'ite Iran's instinctive pull away from its perceived hostile Arab neighbors to side with non-Sunnis, particularly those, like the Alawites, who share the same religious beliefs as them (albeit with syncretistic elements).

The establishment of a relationship between Arab countries and Iran may not be the panacea for all problems in the Middle East, but it is likely a very important step towards "real" stability in the region. However, because of the age-long hatred between Arabs and Iranians, an overnight turnaround is not expected, especially after the many long years of distrust between the two parties, particularly as it pertains to Iran's relationship with Saudi Arabia. An "understanding" between the Saudis and the Iranians may be a shot in the dark, but one could start with small steps, first appealing to other Arab countries in the region (Abu Dhabi and Dubai, for example) that may be more receptive to efforts toward amicable relations.

Mousavian attended a workshop in Doha, Qatar, in which he stated that Saudi Arabia was "doing everything [it could] to prevent a reduction of hostilities between Iran and the United States and an improvement in Iran's relations with the West."

However, while all GCC countries expressed concern about Iran's regional clout, which, according to them, stretches from Iran to Syria, Lebanon, and Yemen, only Bahrain yielded to Saudi Arabia's demands to sever relationship with Iran.[18]

While Iran's acceptance in the region by Saudi Arabia may seem a daunting task, it is certainly doable, keeping in mind that both countries had "pursued détente in the 1990s after the Iran-Iraq War and Saddam Hussein's invasion of Kuwait, culminating in the signing of a security pact in 2001."[19] Reestablishing a modicum of a relationship with Iran may be worthwhile attempting, because starting an arms race in the region, or adding to the distrust that already exists between the Arabs and the Persians, is in no way conducive to long-term stability in the region.

The complexity of starting a dialogue with Iran, however, comes with the realization that a fundamental shift in Iranian domestic and foreign policy may be unlikely if the current Islamic leader, Ayatollah Khamenei, remains Iran's supreme leader. According to Sadjadpour, even though Khamenei has been amenable to an evolution in Iranian foreign policy toward its Arab neighbors and Europe, it would be extremely hard for him to adopt "a conciliatory approach toward the United States and a nonbelligerent approach toward Israel." Sadjadpour also brings attention to the fact that Khamenei's rationale is not purely ideological. His writings and speeches suggest he believes that if Iran were to start a relationship with the United States, it would spur major cultural, political, and economic reform in Iran which may not entirely be to his advantage. While Sadjadpour stated in 2009 that a relationship between the United States and Iran "could be a long time in coming," it seems that the nuclear agreement signed between the two countries in 2015 suggests that the "long time" has now arrived for the beginnings of a relationship based on diplomacy between the two countries[20]

But, prior to contemplating a resourceful way to unite the Arabs and Iranians, the United States must recondition itself away from its fixation on distrust and hatred for Iran. Part of the difficulty in achieving this goal can be largely attributed to the mindset of the American people, who tend to show disdain towards the country, but has no understanding for the reasons of their hatred for it. According to a BBC World Service Poll based on 2013 data, most Americans expressed a negative view of Iran. On the other hand, the polls showed that most Iranians have positive attitudes toward American people, though not toward its government.[21]

The United States' relationship with Iran is also subject to the ideology of the government in power in the United States at a particular time. During President Obama's presidency, communication with the Iranians was opened by the United States on two fronts. In the first place, as stated earlier, the non-nuclear proliferation agreement was signed with Iran. Despite all the disgruntlement professed by Saudi Arabia and Israel, nothing untoward has happened (so far) in the relationship between these countries and Iran. Secondly, in an interview with Jeffrey Goldberg, writing for *The Atlantic*, President Obama seemed to scoff at Saudi leadership and its influence in Washington. Aside from referring to European and Arab allies as "free riders," he criticized the treatment of women in Saudi Arabia, and its practice of promoting fundamentalism abroad. In the context of Iran, Obama suggested that "Saudi Arabia would have to learn to 'share' the Middle East with its adversary, Iran."[22]

On the other hand, however, the new administration in Washington, under President Trump, does not seem to hold the same view as the previous administration. In this respect, the United States seem to believe that isolating Iran, even as the nation gingerly attempts to move beyond conservatism that has governed its population in the past, is the best way to preserve stability in the region. However, some opinion writers are likely to agree that it is not the question of the Iranians having committed terrorist activities and human rights violations, but that they have only acted in a manner similar, if not better, to America's pre-existing Arab allies.

For the West, it is important to note that the hatred between Riyadh and Tehran is likely to continue unless Washington takes a decisive role in trying to end the stalemate. While Iran may not break the nuclear treaty, it has shopped for weapons from other countries, and is successfully building a defense system with Russian help at a cost of $800 million dollars. In this context, it should be noted that this is a defensive initiative that was agreed between the Iranians and Russians in 2007. The agreement was frozen because of sanctions imposed on Iran. Elizabeth Trudeau, a spokeswoman for the United States' State Department, said that the United States objected to the sale of such sophisticated equipment as the S-300, but such weaponry does not violate either the nuclear deal or U.N. Security Council resolutions.[23]

While there is some worry at this development in the United States, it should be noted that the building of non-nuclear defensive and offensive weaponry in Iran is likely what most countries in a similar situation would do; situated as Iran is in the heart of the volatile Middle East. There is no doubt that arms build-up in the region is very dangerous, but one can understand Iran shopping for such weapons when its arch enemy, Saudi Arabia, is being provided increasingly more sophisticated weapons by the United States.

A "working relationship" between Saudi Arabia and Iran may seem an idealist's dream. However, it should be noted that the Iranians are not going anywhere, and the faster they are made to play a "role" of some importance, the faster the possibility of "real" peace in the region will become an actuality. Most importantly, the United States should keep in mind that the Iranians too have been attacked in Tehran by Daesh operatives, and Iran's citizens do not clandestinely support Daesh or Al-Qaeda, unlike some of its allies who supported Daesh at one time.

The Israeli-Iranian Problem

However, a more severe problem for the Americans in bringing the Arabs and the Persians to the negotiating table, is that such a move could jeopardize Israel's reliance on its Muslim neighbors in the formation of a coalition that is unified in its hatred of Iran. In this context, the relationship with Iran would have to be built in small steps, first and foremost requiring the nation to give up its hostile attitude towards Israel.

There is no doubt that Iran has uttered ridiculous statements against Israel in the past. However, the view among some civilian Shi'as, and even some non-Muslims, is that Iran is doing what is typically done in many parts of the Middle East — talking big, but doing little. It is trying to assert its own stamp — an identity that separates it from Arab countries who may share the same bias in the Israeli-Palestinian conflict, but don't dare utter it openly. Its bombastic statement in the past that "the holocaust never happened," according to some, is not so much a true translation of beliefs, as it is an attention-grabbing tactic — a statement meant to denounce its Sunni neighbors for selling off their Palestinian brethren's hopes in order to curry favor from the Americans; or a juvenile cry at being left out of an issue in which it would like to be involved.

Iran, as should be noted, is no saint, promoting an agenda that has often been violent in its activation. However, Stephen Kinzer, in a comparative analysis of Iran with Israel, provides a report that outlines the rather aggressive and defiant stance taken by Israel, which includes the pursuance of its active nuclear weapons program, conducted in secrecy without any hindrance of Western pressure. More importantly, however, Israelis, who are supposed to be the bastion of logic and reason in their political dealings, now have their political process, "hijacked by religious fundamentalists who believe they are doing God's will."[24]

According to Juan Cole, a history professor at the University of Michigan (one of the few Americans who has visited both Iran and Israel), since most Jews are secular-minded, the Jewish response to the European genocide against them was not immediately religious. However, over time, religion has come to play a bigger and bigger part in Israeli life.[25] In the context of Israel exerting its power in the region, the country is seen to be impervious to pressure, and often seems to turn a blind eye to reason. Many people around the world visualize Israel as brazenly flaunting its reckless behavior, such as building Israeli settlements on Palestinian lands, thus adding fuel to fire in one of the world's most volatile regions. As Kinzer states:

> American attitudes toward the two countries is striking. Toward Israel the attitude is: You may be rascals sometimes, but whatever pranks you pull, you're our friend and we'll forgive you. Toward Iran, it's the opposite: You are our implacable enemy, so nothing you do short of abject surrender will satisfy us.

Iran is the Middle East region's outcast — yet the region will never stabilize until it is brought back out of the geopolitical cold. As Kinzer cautions, rather than stoking Iranian hostility, it would be better for the United States to reduce tensions between Iran and Israel.[26] By the same token, while many Americans may justify Israeli behavior as part of "security necessity," Juan Cole states that "the searing honesty and high ethics of the Israeli thinkers"he has talked to, is very different from the vociferous and almost cult-like cheers from the right-wing Jewish Americans on their view of Israel.

In fact, Cole found some similarities as well as some disconcerting differences between Israel and Iran that is worthwhile exploring. To underline the similarities, Cole draws parallels between the histories of the two countries. In a sense, both countries have been affected by European nationalism and imperialism. Obviously, there are few horrendous acts in the world that would come close to the systemic killing of six million Jews during the period of Nazi genocide. But, according to Cole, Iran, too, has suffered some indignities by "outside" interference with respect to loss of property and human life. For example, in the nineteenth century, Russia annexed substantial Iranian territory. Furthermore, the British and the Russians opposed the Constitutional Revolution of 1905–1911, and prevented Iranians from liberty and a rule of law. Besides many such atrocities, Britain also backed the rise of the Pahlavi dictatorship in the 1920s, and as stated earlier in this chapter, the United States, as late as 1953, helped overthrow the elected government of Mossadegh from Iran.[27]

In concurring with Cole, it is natural that Westerners should find Israel's behavior more to their liking than Iran's, given the close alliance between Israel and the United States, and Iran's antipathy towards the West. However, Cole, implementing a qualifier that he does not agree with the Iranian government on anything — most of which is "dictatorial and puritanical" — states several compelling reasons that might compel the West to rethink its perception of Iran. For example, Iran does not have a nuclear bomb and has signed the non-nuclear proliferation agreement. Israel, on the other hand, as stated in Chapter 8, has not signed a nuclear non-proliferation treaty, and has constructed nuclear weapons secretly, "including through acts of espionage and smuggling in the United States, and against the wishes of Presidents Kennedy and Johnson." Most importantly, although Israel has stated that it will not be the first to use nuclear weapons in the region, according to Cole, ex-Prime Minister Ariel Sharon OF Israel alarmed United States President George W. Bush when he intimated that he'd nuke Baghdad if Saddam tried to send SCUD missiles tipped with gas to Israel.[28]

It should be noted that modern Iran has never occupied the territory of its neighbors. Even in the 1980s, after the hostilities between Iraq and Iran ended, both countries did not hold on to each other's territories, which is in compliance with the UN Charter of 1945 that forbids countries to annex the land of their neighbors through warfare. In contrast, it could be argued that Israel controls the fate of 4 million stateless Palestinians, who are treated as any subjugated, colonized population would be.[29] Even now, as late as 2017, after a 20-year hiatus, Israel announced its plans to build 5,500 settlements on West Bank Palestinian lands.[30]

Furthermore, on the topic of how countries treat their governed population, all Iranians living in Iran can vote in national elections. While Iranian elections are tempered by the religious authority of the Ayatollahs in its adherence to Islamic laws, even Iranian Jews have a representative in Iranian parliament. In contrast, as Cole points out, "of the 12 million people ruled by Israel, 4 million of them have no vote in Israeli politics, which is the politics that actually rules them."

As outlined above, some Iranian policies can be seen to be in line with the expectations of any "good-willed" country in the world. However, for most Westerners, Israel is easier to identify with and accept, because it has a more distinct rule of law that awards and allows more personal liberties to its citizens. On the other hand, "Iran is a very complex society, with an opaque and Byzantine political system," and a convoluted interaction with the outside world.[31]

Defining Modifications of the Status Quo in the Middle East

As it stands, there is a great battle under way for the soul of the Muslim world. It is essentially a battle among Muslims, between the Khomeini and Atatürk (former president of Turkey) dispositions; among the Persians, the Kurds, and the Arabs; between the Shi'as and the Sunnis, and the different sub-factions within the major factions of Islam. However, it is interesting to observe that the lively new ideas in Kemalist (Atatürkist) Turkey under President Erdoğan are reverting more towards religion, whereas the lively new ideas in Iran are those of a secular nature. In Turkey, the coup attempt on July 16, 2016 underlines the population's desire for a change from President Erdoğan's governance, who in 1999 spent four months in jail for religious incitement. According to BBC News, he had publicly read a nationalist poem that included lines such as: "the mosques are our barracks, the domes our helmets, the minarets our bayonets and the faithful our soldiers." While the "reformed" Erdoğan has denied the imposition of Islamic values, saying he is committed to secularism, he supports the Turks' right to express their Islamic beliefs more openly, and in October 2013, lifted rules banning women from wearing headscarves in the country's state institutions, ending a decades-old restriction.[32] In the meantime, Erdoğan has become increasingly autocratic by narrowly winning a referendum on April 16, 2017, that, according to Patrick Kingsley of *The New York Times*, allows him vast powers to change the constitution, allowing the winner of the presidential election to assume full control of the government, and end the current parliamentary political system. However, the ramifications, as Kingsley states, are immediate.

> The 'yes' vote in the referendum is a validation of the current leadership style of Mr. Erdoğan, who has been acting as a de facto head of government since his election in 2014 despite having no constitutional right to wield such power. The office of Turkey's president was meant to be an impartial role without full executive authority.

> The result tightens Mr. Erdoğan's grip on the country, which is one of the leading external actors in the Syrian civil war, a major way station along the migration routes to Europe and a crucial Middle Eastern partner of the United States and Russia."[33]

On the other hand, in Iran, Pejman Abdolmohammadi, writing in the *Gingko Library*, defines a radical change that he calls the "Iranian Renaissance." The Iranian Islamic Republic is facing a time of important domestic generational change which is likely to alter its political future in the next two decades. Among the burgeoning younger generation (approximately 66 percent of its population), a significant portion is critical, or even opposed, to the current political system. This younger generation has elaborated on and adopted ideas such as secularism and nationalism, trying to achieve political goals that are consistent with democracy and freedom. The young people are the new Iranian Opposition Group. They are divided into two parts that call for: (a) the creation of a secular democracy in Iran, or (b) the creation of an Islamic democracy. Nevertheless, both sub-groups would like to defunct the current Islamic Republic and create the institution of a "true" democratic state. Most importantly, according to Abdolmohammadi, they would like to promote laws apart from religious demands, allow freedom of expression, and instill laws for the protection of all minorities.[34] In this context, the election of the moderate, Hassan Rouhani in 2017, is in line with the author's predictions of the direction in which Iran is heading.

In such an environment, it would behoove the United States to make "controlled" gestures toward Iran in hopes of a future relationship that could help in the establishment of permanent stability in the Middle East. But, despite the suggestion that some changes should be made to the United States' relationship with Iran, it is not meant to imply that the United States should halt its preferential relationships with the Arab nations and Israel. Israel has been an ally of the United States for a long time, and the relationship between these two countries not only has geopolitical aspirations, but it has deep-rooted emotional ties with each other. Saudi Arabia, too, in spite of all the setbacks with United States, has been an important ally that may not have the same emotional aspect in its relations with the United States as does Israel (there are many more Jews than Wahhabis and Salafist in America), but its symbiotic relationship with the United States is important not only because it is "symbiotic," but for the simple fact that it is the guardian of the Islam's' holiest lands, and therefore very important to *all* Muslims.

In this context, some top-most analysts of the Middle East region at the Saban Center for Middle East Policy at the Brookings Institute, provide an analysis on strategies to be used in dealing with Iran. The basic tenets of their paper hinge on a policy of persuasion, followed up by attempts at engagement. The authors outline a wide variety of options that include sanction, airstrikes, boots-on-the ground, and some sort of a regime change. There is also a general understanding that successful persuasion can only happen over time.[35]

The options outlined by the authors in the persuasion and containment phases (containing the country from doing anything drastic while the persuasion phase is going on) were written in 2009, mainly to deter the Iranian nuclear program. Since then, Iran's nuclear program has, as stated earlier, been shelved under the nuclear agreement signed with Western countries. This signing of the nuclear agreement was the by-passing of a phase whereby Washington was willing to start with an engagement approach – using diplomacy - even when the threat of military persuasion, according to the researchers at the Saban Center, was always on President Obama's mind.[36]

In the context of different persuasion strategies, it should be noted that regime change as a part of the persuasion strategy, according to the experts at the Saban Center, would, as expected, not sit well with the clerical regime in Iran, or with the government of any other country in the world. As an example, according to the analysis paper, from 1994 to 1996, when Tehran believed that Washington was forming its covert action plan against the Islamic regime, "the Iranians showed no willingness to compromise." On the contrary, Tehran "lashed out at the United States" in whatever way it could. The authors believe that the 1996 Khobar Tower attack in Saudi Arabia, which killed 19 Americans, was the work of the Iranians. Once Tehran believed that the United States had a regime change in mind, it conducted aggressive surveillance of American diplomatic mission and military installations in the Middle East. It also instigated attacks through Hamas and Hezbollah against Israel to subvert the peace process.[37] While such actions by Iran may seem terrorist-minded (and they were), it behooves the West to understand the predicament of any ruling party who believed that they were about to be ousted.

As the authors have stated in their paper, establishing a new policy toward Iran "is a complicated and an uncertain challenge."[38] However, the fundamentals of the engagement policy have already worked well with Iran in persuading them to sign the nuclear agreement. Perhaps it can also be used to further prevent Iranian terrorism and help instill stability within the region. The recent partnership between Iran and Russia in Syria, further justifies the need for negotiations with the country before it turns entirely to Russia, and becomes a greater headache then it is perceived to be at the present.

Chapter 10

The Dynamics of the Many Facets at Play in the Middle East (Beyond the Obvious)

At the fast pace in which the world's geopolitical dynamics are changing, the days when past events were used to predict the future no longer exist. In this respect, the West needs begin with a blank slate, realizing that past solutions that may have worked well for it, may now require modifications or drastic changes, not only as it pertains to its relationships with its allies, but also with its enemies. For example, the West must contend with Russia, which has abducted a part of the sovereign nation of Ukraine, sided with Assad in Syria, and interfered in the West's political system.[1] It also has to contend with North Korea, which is attempting to extend its nuclear program in a determined show of military strength against South Korea and the United States. And then there is China, which has staked maritime claims in the international waters of the South China Sea, where the United States conducts "freedom of navigation" operations.

But, besides these world-wide geopolitical problems the United States faces, there are Islamists who have now become a household word for the danger they pose to masses around the world, not only through their direct confrontations in Libya, Iraq, Syria, and Afghanistan, but also through their violent acts of terror all over the world. While diplomacy is naturally preferred over military actions, such is easier said than done in the case of the Islamists who have already pursued their own violent agenda. This agenda is not only polar opposite to the beliefs and values of the world, but its actions directly impact Middle Eastern citizens through violent terrorism and refugee problems it espouses.

America's Faux Pas in Building a Relationship With al-Nusra

Although Daesh commands most of the attention from the general public and politicians in the West, Al-Qaeda is not too far behind in its recognition as a terrorist organization by the Western public. For example, one of Al-Qaeda's strongest affiliates, Jabhat al-Nusra, is known to be fighting in Syria with the explicit purpose of overthrowing Assad. However, to concentrate its efforts in fighting Syrian government forces and other rebel groups without any apparent terror agendas, al-Jolani, the head of Jabhat al-Nusra, had the blessings of al-Zawahiri to sever Nusra's affiliation with the Al-Qaeda group. Furthermore, to better reflect the group's purpose in the region (liberating Syria from Assad), al-Jolani changed his group's name from Jabhat al-Nusra to Jabhat Fath al-Sham, translated as "The Front for Liberation of al-Sham."[2] However, the United States, together with the UN Security Council, has refused to acknowledge the new name chosen by al-Nusra, and still considers the group a terrorist organization because of its history as an affiliate of Al-Qaeda.

On the other hand, Farah al-Atassi, a spokeswoman for the Syrian Opposition's main negotiating bloc, welcomed al-Nusra's disassociation from Al-Qaeda because it was the Syrian Opposition Party's hope that its non-affiliation status with Al-Qaeda would remove it from the international terrorist list. This

208

would, according to al-Atassi, give no excuse for the United States to bomb al-Nusra's positions, and would likely allow the Syrian Opposition Party and Nusra to join forces in fighting their common foe, Assad — the same latent objective that has been for the West.[3]

The scenario outlined above could have played to the West's advantage in the sense that al-Nusra would be fighting against the hated Assad, but the real issue is whether such a reversal in the stance of Jabhat al-Nusra can be trusted. After the supposed separation of al-Nusra from Al-Qaeda, United States' White House spokesman, Josh Earnest, stated that, "there continues to be increasing concern about Nusra Front's growing capacity for external operations that could threaten both the United States and Europe."[4]

Eric Schmitt, writing for *The New York Times*, states that partly because Al-Qaeda has suffered badly in Pakistan from fighting with the Americans, it has now sent some of its top fighters to expand its niche in Syria with its former affiliate, al-Nusra back at its side. Such a move "most likely foreshadows an escalation of the group's bloody rivalry" with Daesh, since, as stated in Chapter 6, there is no love lost between the two Islamist groups. A Syrian-based Al-Qaeda, however, would not only be within closer striking distance to Europe, but would also hold the benefit of recruiting and obtaining logistical support of fighters from Iraq, Turkey, Jordan, and Lebanon. According to Schmitt, some Nusra leaders, however, opposed the timing of such a move, and have, therefore, not yet taken that step.[5] Charles, Lister, a senior fellow at the Middle East Institute, states that the combination of an Al-Qaeda emirate and a revitalized central leadership for the group in northern Syria would likely boost Al-Qaeda's confidence. The group could then project itself as the smart, methodical, and persistent violent jihadi movement that, in contrast to Daesh, would try to adopt a strategy more aligned with everyday Sunni Muslims.[6]

However, in spite of Al-Qaeda's aspirations in the region, the war in Syria appears to being fought by the United States and its allies mainly against Daesh. Anne Barnard, Michael R. Gordon, and Eric Schmitt announced in *The New York Times* that the United States and Turkey were to plan a "safe zone" free of Daesh.[7] However, according to Bloomberg's Josh Rogin, the safe zone plan, announced on July 23, 2015, was a complete fallacy. According to him, "in fact, there is really no 'zone,' and there is no plan to keep the area 'safe.'" Indeed, Rogin said, three "senior administration officials" from the United States had taken part in a conference call to assure reporters that there were no plans "for a safe zone, a no-fly zone, an air-exclusionary zone, a humanitarian buffer zone, or any other protected zone of any kind."[8] The purpose of the no-fly zone that Turkey and the United States may or may not have wished to establish was, in reporter Daniel Lazare's opinion, a free-hand to Turkey to bomb the Kurds if they tried to get to the Turkish side of the fence, and for the United States an opportunity to engage in joint operations with Al-Qaeda's affiliate, al-Nusra, in fighting Daesh.[9]

The announcement by Lazare, if true, can be a real game-changer for the United States and its allies. Such an action means that the United States, in fact, is actively involved in "regime change," in Syria even though its official position has been to only fight Daesh. Furthermore, its strategy in Syria "amounts to a de facto alliance with Al-Qaeda's Nusra Front [considered as a terrorist organization] which is driving toward a possible victory with direct and indirect aid from Saudi Arabia, Turkey and Israel."[10]

However, the strategy seems to have backfired. A front-page article by Eric Schmitt in *The New York Times*, on August 1, 2015, reported that an American-trained rebel unit, "known as

Division 30," which had been sent into Syria to combat Daesh, came "under intense attack on Friday from a different hardline Islamist faction ... the Nusra Front, which is affiliated with Al Qaeda."[11] Anne Bernard and Eric Schmitt also reported in *The New York Times* that American military trainers did not anticipate an assault from the Nusra Front. In fact, United States' officials said they expected the Nusra Front to welcome Division 30 as an ally in its fight against Daesh. "'This wasn't supposed to happen like this,' said one former senior American official." In other words, the United States' Defense Department officials expected al-Nusra to see Division 30 as allies, and were perplexed when it didn't. The Americans "had no known plans to fight the Nusra Front," the authors went on, adding that, while "allied with Al Qaeda," Nusra "is seen by many insurgents in Syria as preferable to Daesh, and it sometimes cooperates with other less radical groups against both Daesh and Syrian government forces."[12]

While the United States is reluctant to be directly involved in toppling Assad from power, the use of chemical weapons by Assad against its Sunni population, *may* tilt the scale when it comes to the United States' "necessary" level of involvement in the Syrian civil war.[13] While the use of Sarin gas against Syrian civilians (mainly the Sunnis) in the Iblid region of Syria likely increased common American citizens' angst on morality grounds, the fate of Assad does not seem to be in jeopardy. As U.S. ambassador to the U.N. Nikki Haley said just days before the incident, America's "priority is no longer to sit and focus on getting Assad out."[14]

Different Parties – Different Agendas

Despite disparity in handling conflicts based on religion, ethnicities, and hegemony in the Middle East and North Africa, a silver lining has appeared in the form of a common enemy in the Islamists, providing a semblance of unity among the various groups fighting in Syria. However, while there could be some solace for the Shi'as in having attention diverted to the common purpose of defeating Daesh, the strange alliance between the two major denominations of Islam and the various ethnicities currently fighting Daesh is extremely tenuous and not without bitter mistrust. Thus, while the two factional groups, the Shi'as and the Sunnis, acted together for the recapture of Tikrit, Iraq (Sunnis sided with the Iranian Shi'a militia to help prevent Daesh's insurgency), they have different alliances in their respective responses to the crises in Yemen and in Syria. Fortunately, the West has finally come to understand the ingrained hatred among factions in the Middle East. In the reclaiming of Ramadi in Iraq, the Shi'a-Sunni Iraqi army, together with the Kurds, under the cover of United States' aerial bombings, recaptured the town from Daesh, but only the Sunnis partook in the temporary governance and control of Ramadi, due to Ramadi's major population being Sunnis.[15]

For the sake of stability in the region, it is understandable that allegiance to a particular religious denomination or ethnicity is often used as a tool to manipulate or soothe the religiously-devout parts of the population, such as in Iran, Saudi Arabia, and parts of Pakistan. In Iran, as stated in Chapter 9, there seems to be a distinct demarcation between Ayatollah Ali Khamenei's promulgation of religious dictates via his favored interpretation of the Sharia law, and the Iranian population with a large number of young, progressive Muslims. The same is also partially true for a country like Pakistan, even though it is a pluralistic society, containing many different factions of Islam. On the other hand, in Saudi Arabia, there seems to be a tenuous line between the religious fanatics and the ruling party's political aspirations. For example, in 1979, the Grand Mosque in Mecca was seized by extremist insurgents in an effort to overthrow the ruling party (the House of Saud). Their purpose was to instate Mahdi, the redeemer of Islam, who had arrived in the form of Muhammad Abdullah al-Qahtani, the supposed leader of all Muslims across the world.[16] Although the Saudi Royal Family were successful in ending the "seize" after two weeks, according to some internet sources, they had to implement a stricter enforcement of Sharia law, to appease the followers of the insurgents.[17]

According to Bruce Rubin from CNN iReport, and various other sources, Abdul Rahman al-Sudais, the current imam of the Grand Mosque in Mecca, Saudi Arabia, has spoken disparagingly against non-Muslims such as Hindus (whom he calls idol-worshippers) and Christians (cross-worshippers), and has prayed to God for the termination of Jews in his sermons.[18] In addition, while he preaches Islam's opposition to terrorism and proposes a peaceful interfaith dialogue, he has, on the other hand, called for an all-out war against the Shi'as. Al-Sudais has also been very vocal in his sermons in the condemnation of Israel for what he believes is Israel's poor treatment of Palestinians and asking for more aid in the form of food and medicine to be sent to Palestine. Furthermore, al-Sudais singled out women as he recited a catalogue of sins responsible for a drought the kingdom was experiencing. Their sins, he said, included "unveiling, mingling with men, and being indifferent to the hijab." Evidently, the imam placed partial blame on women's "un-Islamic" behavior for the 2006 winter drought in Saudi Arabia.[19] Such statements shed light on the interpretative aspects of Islam and the hostility many Saudi Muslims have towards the Jews and the Shi'a Muslims. Due to al-Sudais's rather controversial beliefs, he has been barred from religious conferences in America. He has also been refused entry into Canada, the United Kingdom, and Australia.[20] However, the volatile nature of al-Sudais' preachment brings forth an understanding of the rather shaky hold the Saudi ruling party has in balancing the expectations of its populace with its own political agenda of promoting its alliance with the United States and other countries of the West. For example, in Ruben's article, he talks of Adel al-Jubeir, the foreign policy adviser to the Saudi crown prince's interview with NBC's Tim Russet in May 2003, where the prince agreed that al-Sudais' statements were "clearly not right," and stated that while he was reprimanded, he was still allowed to preach, [presumably because of the demands of the Saudi population].[21]

But aside from the Arab-Iranian/Sunni-Shi'a conflict in the region, there are also other parties involved, with their own particular conflicts in the Middle East. For example, there are the Kurds, who are disliked by the Arabs (both Shi'a and Sunnis). The Kurds are an ethnic group like the Persians and the Arabs, but they are not a separate religious group. On the contrary, they have diverse religious origins that include Sunni, Shi'a, Sufi, Christian, and Jewish members. In Iraq, the Kurds, according to some internet sources, make up 16 percent of the total Iraqi population, of which 78 percent are Arabs (62 percent Shi'a and 30 percent Sunni). According to the Pew Research Center (2014 estimate), about 98 percent of Kurds in Iraq are of the Sunni sect.[21] These Kurds reside in a semi-autonomous region known as Iraqi Kurdistan, although its status as an autonomous region is not quite clear under the new democratically elected government in Iraq. In Syria, they mostly reside in Rojava in Syrian Kurdistan. However, the Syrian government of Assad does not consider Rojava independent.

Kurds in Iran are Iranians of Kurdish ethnicity who speak Kurdish as their first language. In Iran, they are the third largest ethnic minority after the Persians and Iranian Azerbaijanis, comprising more than 10 percent of the country's population, and are split about evenly between Sunnis and Shi'as. Many Kurds also live in Turkey, mostly in the southeastern and eastern parts of the Anatolia area, commonly referred to as Northern Kurdistan. According to the World Factbook published by the CIA, Kurdish people make up 19 percent of Turkey's population (about 15 million, out of 77.8 million people).[22]

While the large population of Kurds in the Middle East are, to some extent, culturally different from the Arabs, Persians, and others in the Middle East region, they do not have an independent state of their own. According to some accounts, the anti-Kurd sentiments of other Muslims could be due to the Kurds' desire for independence (especially in Turkey and Syria), their pro-West stance, their fiercely territorial attitudes, and their less restrictive approach to religious practices. This behavior has never sat well with the Arabs, some of whom see the Iraqi Kurds as "polyethnic," and thus as non-Arabs. Similarly, the Iranians and Turks have never accepted Kurds in their countries as equals, partly because of their cultural and lingual differences.

It should be noted that many Kurds have been stripped of their citizenship rights in Syria since 1962. As a gesture to placate the country's restive minority, Syrian President Bashar Assad announced in April 2011 that he would recognize some of the rights demanded by the Kurds and allow them to register as citizens. However, for Kurds, the offering was too little, too late. They rejected the concessions, instead siding against Assad in a bid to overthrow him from power. As the war dragged on in Syria, Kurdish groups have taken the opportunity to gain more power, and in November 2013, the Kurdish Democratic Union Party (PYD) declared self-administration in the Kurdish region of Syria.[23]

The United States' Role in the Region – Between the Devil and the Deep Sea.

The balancing act that the United States plays in the Middle East, particularly in signing the non-nuclear treaty with Iran, seems to be giving further credence to the Islamists' hatred for the West, which perhaps is second only to its hatred for Shi'as. While one can understand the complex decisions, the United States needs to make in playing a leadership role in the Middle East, the uneasy trust of the Islamic world toward Americans may be hard for readers to fully grasp, especially when many Americans believe that their country is in the business of promulgating "goodness" around the world. However, it would be worthwhile to consider that in the interest of truly propagating the spread of "American goodness," it is imperative to consider the old cliché, "one man's food could be someone else's poison."

It is due to the specific needs of different cultures and religions, that the United States' aspirations of spreading democracy (nation-building), should be examined under the axiom that such commitments require much more than providing ballots for free elections. Elections are a capstone to a deep, often long-term process of change that ideally includes "fair" governance, and an effective rule of law based on the consensus of society, without overriding the right of the minorities. While creation of laws based on the United States' Bill of Rights, for example, would be desirable from an American point of view, one cannot have the same "Western" expectations of countries that have no concept of democratic rule. In this context, while equalizing aspects of governance for the minorities are an expectation in Western style democracies, such a democratic outcome would likely never be successful in a largely homogeneous population that exists in certain Arab countries like Saudi Arabia, Kuwait, and Qatar.

By the same reasoning, in singular homogeneous societies, overthrowing a monarchy is not likely to greatly alter the expectations of the population, which, in ultra-conservative Islamic countries, is entirely dictated by their common belief in religious laws. Even in Islamic states that are not ruled by monarchies and dictators, an impartial constitutional law *may* never happen because of the nature of Islamic principles, which, in the extreme are very specific about running the state on religious dictates. Pragmatically, this would imply that the governance of the country based on the beliefs of the majority faction of Islam, is the only viable option of law in the country.

To hold unprepared premature elections, as happened in the off-the-cuff democratic "set-up" immediately after the ouster of Saddam Hussein from Iraq, often leaves the country worse off than it was originally, especially during the short-term period of change. The same is also true in the case of Libya, where according to a presentation by David Gartenstein-Ross at the hearing before the Committee on Oversight and Government Reform in the United States, Daesh has infiltrated the country, causing violence and chaos after the quick departure of the United States and other NATO forces once Qaddafi was overthrown.[24]

While it is easy to assert that advance planning is a necessary condition for United States' political and military involvement in foreign affairs, such planning is not as easy in practice, mainly because the changing dynamics in the region make it impossible to predict and execute a well-planned solution. For example, besides the internal power-play within the Middle East, a greater worry remains as to who would govern Iraq after freeing it from Daesh's control. The re-captured territories in Iraq may inadvertently revert to the democratic set-up in place at present, or the Iraqis may have to accept the possibility of a factional solution, as acknowledged by former Vice President Biden of the

United States on MSNBC News' Morning Joe.[25] The factional
solution would likely separate the three major parties in Iraq into
semi-autonomous states as a permanent solution after the defeat
of Daesh. The frightening aspect of such a solution, however, is
that the Kurds, the Shi'as and the Sunnis, might take it upon
themselves to carve out choice pieces of land (the oil wells and
refineries) for their individual "nations", thereby creating further
infighting among themselves. An alternative solution, being
talked by some experts, is to have the three factions rule their
respective areas separately but have a common agreement in
sharing the "riches" of the nation.

While there is every hope that the present democratic set-
up, based on representation of Shi'as, Sunnis, and Kurds will
hold, this issue may need revisiting now that Daesh is almost
incapacitated in Iraq, and a semblance of stability has been
achieved in the country, or when the next elections take place.

In Syria, somewhat similar problems might occur between
the Kurds, the Shi'as (including the Alawites) and the Sunni
population, but it hinges on various factors, including Russia's
involvement and the potential outcomes of the civil war. The
United States has been very reluctant in entering the Syrian
civil war, and has agreed that they, together with the Russians,
would not get directly involved in the civil war. However, it has,
according to some sources, jumped into the fray in a very limited
role, clandestinely helping its allies fight Assad, without having
concrete answers as to what may happen during or after the war.

Since the United States' presence in Syria is only for the purpose
of defeating the Islamists, it could do nothing but stand and watch
while the opposition party was annihilated by Assad's forces in
the fight for Aleppo. Russia *eventually* provided safe passage for
the civilians in Aleppo, who had been, according to various media
sources, indiscriminately slaughtered by Assad's forces.[26]

Chapter 11

Islamophobia in the West

Unfortunately, due to the balancing act America must play in world politics and in the preservation of its interests across the globe, the United States Constitution has been subject to various interpretive analyses regarding security concerns. For example, "fairness" in the guise of constitutional rights takes a secondary or interpretative role in cases of espionage against American citizens without a court order. According to a report by Appalachian State University in the United States, the law could possibly tilt the scales so far in favor of law enforcement and intelligence agencies that the civil liberties of Americans may be sacrificed.[1] By the same token, Andrea Peterson, reporting in the on its own people.[2] In the case of fighting terrorism, the national security doctrine of the Patriot Act could raise its head against Muslims (not Islamists). However, the pros and cons of balancing security with personal rights of citizens are not easy to determine. There is always the fear that constitutional rights may become unimportant in cases where terrorist attacks are seen as stoppable with prior information, clandestinely obtained. By the same token, public outcry against such "snoop tactics" is likely to be more popular during calm periods, void of terrorist attacks or threats.

While the debate on safety versus personal rights will likely continue, it should be noted that global terrorist acts, while much more common in Europe, are unique for the United States, which had not faced such large-scale international terrorism on innocent people on its own soil prior to 9/11. In fact, internal domestic terroristic attacks, such as the killing of Black Africans in the Emanuel African Methodist Episcopal Church in Charleston, South Carolina, on June 17, 2015, and the murders of children at Columbine High on April 20, 1999, have been far more common than acts of international terrorism in the United States. Despite this, the anti-Muslim movement is so strong, that Americans do not seem to care that there were, as per a study reported by The New America Foundation in the *Huffington Post*, twice as many White Supremacist attacks in the 14 years after 9/11 as those by self-identified jihadists.[3] Similarly, according to the think tank *New America's* 2016 article, attacks motivated by ethnic, racial, and religious hatred, and anti-government views, have killed 48 people, while attacks by individuals linked to or inspired by foreign terrorist groups have claimed 26 lives.[4]

Fareed Zakaria gives a plausible explanation for why *all* Muslims are perceived by some as violent in the Western world, when in fact only a negligible fraction of Muslims advocate hatred towards the West. According to Zakaria, since the large majority of Westerners are Christians, an environment of interaction and awareness exists, wherein through personal experiences, individuals learn that all Christians simply cannot be placed into the same tightly-defined group. On the other hand, most Westerners, particularly those living in the hierarchical social structure of Europe, have little to no contact with minority groups who practice alternative religions.[5] For example, National Public Radio (NPR) in the United States reported that a Syrian woman, who has been living in Amsterdam for three years, has no Dutch friends. In fact, since many Westerners have relatively little contact with minorities, particularly those whose percentages are rather low with respect to the total population, there is very little understanding of their cultures, especially in rural areas where recent minorities in America, generally do not reside. Many Muslims, along with other minorities in the West, live and work within their own small communities, with very little cognizance of the local population, and vice versa.

The intermingling of communities is initially often restricted to job or school-related activities rather than as an outcome of friendship. However, as expected, the older generation of immigrants, with their set ways toward life, are less likely to mix with the local population than those who are younger, who go or have gone to Western schools, or who work in professional fields. In such a scenario, where only about one percent of the total population of the United States is Muslim, the West is likely to judge *all* followers of Islam in their country by the actions of the few, their suspicions personified, often prejudicially, by Muslims' "alienating" features, such as long beards and head scarves.

In today's world, Muslims are also often blamed for the financial crises in some Western countries. There are some in Europe who assert partial blame for their economic woes on the influx of Muslim refugees into their countries, and on the increased resources necessary to secure civilians against terrorism. The influx of refugees and the consequent effect of likely terrorist activities that is often wrongfully associated with all refugees was, for example, one of the main reasons cited by voters who elected for Britain to leave the EU in 2016. In fact, one may be tempted to conclude that now-a-days, blame for financial doldrums, cyber hacking, and the enactment of anti-constitutional laws are all scrutinized under the banner of "national security." International terrorism, which is a large part of national security, has now become a household word (particularly in Europe), whereby rationality has assumed the shape of senseless accusations and inhumane acts against those with "suspicious-sounding" names, and perceivably unacceptable "Muslim" features, or personas, that have no proven correlation with their being Islamists.

This type of Western behavior is reminiscent of the interpretative Biblical meaning used by the Dutch Reformed Church when enforcing their policy of apartheid in South Africa. In a case study from the 1990s, the white-dominated Dutch Reformist Movement Church supported apartheid, arguing that in Genesis 11, God deliberately divided people into different races. Since Church leaders were generally more committed to apartheid than many of their followers in the 1970s and 1980s in South Africa, the church became a direct impediment to political reform.[6]

Assimilation and/or Integration of Muslims in the West

One of the criteria proposed by psychologists for promoting harmonious relationships among members of a population is to address the question of how well the minority population is assimilated within the framework of majority acceptance. In cognitive development theory, the process by which new information is taken into the previously existing schema is known as assimilation. Generally speaking, in the context of immigrants, assimilation is defined as adopting the ways of another culture and fully becoming part of a different society. Immigrants who are assimilated accept the ways of their host and thus become a full part of the community. Assimilation, according to Matt O'Brien, "implies that immigrants, through education and experience, can earn their way into the host culture and be seamlessly accepted as full members of their new community."[7] While the basic premise of assimilation is for immigrants to accept the "ways of their host," a more pragmatic aspect arises when we perceive it as a two-way street where amalgamation occurs in a manner such that some of the new experiences and knowledge of the immigrants are reinterpreted, and then included to fit in with existing information.

However, when new experiences brought in by an immigrant population are "markedly" different from the existing schema of familiarity of the indigenous population then, according to Piaget, acceptance may have to take the form of accommodation instead of assimilation, in which case, existing schemas are *changed* or even *replaced* based on new information.[8] Assimilation, therefore, can be intuitively appealing when there are similar ideas and concepts, while accommodation may be appropriate when there are different concepts and ideas.

Expectations of accommodation as a strategy for harmony between different groups of the population is often not incorporated in societies across the world, mainly because ideas from two different cultures can often be conflicting with each other. The Refugee Resettlement Fact Sheet, produced by *Refugee Resettlement Watch* (*RRW*), reports that assimilation in the United States is no longer a part of the government's lexicon, and, therefore, is no longer a goal in refugee resettlement, whether through a government agency or a private contractor. Instead, the term "integration" is in vogue, with its clear intent being the maintenance of ethnic identity and preservation of diversity.[9]

Integration is typically defined as incorporating individuals from different groups into society as equals. In this respect, integration can be seen as being similar to accommodation with one difference: the existing schema existing within the country is neither reinterpreted, modified or replaced, but it allows the new ideas and concepts to coexist with emphasis on equality, within the existing schema. In fact, integration "forces" accommodation, even if it conflicts with the existing schema in a society. The concept of integration suggests drawing boundaries among different peoples, but its definition within the framework of equality indicates that a host is obligated to embrace foreign cultures as equal, irrespective of whether they conflict with the values and traditions of the host.[10] Contrary to assimilation, which is generally defined as being included as part of a different society through the adaptation of their culture, integration is typically defined as incorporating individuals from different cultures into a society as equals.

Integration is laudable because it is built on the principle of equality, which in turn fosters the much-touted belief in diversity. However, while it provides an easier path for migrants to simply continue their previous way of life away from their home countries, within the framework of the law in the new country, it seems to place the burden of integration entirely on the indigenous population. This can become very problematic, especially when new ideas and information are fundamentally different, to the point of being contradictory to the existing schemas within a country. Besides the obviously conflicting ideas that must be overcome (however subliminal or minor they are), there could be a likelihood of a push-back from the indigenous population when they must compete with non-assimilated "outsiders" for scarce resources. Such push-backs could also occur from minorities and the immigrants when the indigenous population is perceived as taking part in "manipulated" justice resulting in unequal treatment. In this context, it is likely that assimilation may be seen as the greater alternative to integration by the local population for people who enter their country, either as refugees or legal immigrants.

However, a quid pro quo situation arises when immigrants enter the country as "professionals," contributing their unique talent to the community in return for the betterment of their lives. In such a situation, integration, rather than assimilation, would likely be their preferred choice, especially in abiding by the benefits of diversity that is likely to be much more readily acceptable by the indigenous population when it is displayed by immigrants who are professionals. Immigrants who bring in a trade or expertise not available, or only available in limited quantities in their host countries (such as the shortage of nurses in the United States at one time), can be the best example of easily workable integration. It should be noted that with respect to "fitting in" with the local population, even in a country as widely accommodating as the United States, it has taken a very long time to integrate the minority Native American, Mexican-American, and African-American populations. Yet, according to some people, the integration process is not yet completed, whereby there are still examples of unfair treatment dished out in discordance with the wishes of minority populations.

In this context, Christopher Browning's theory on people's desire to conform to a group (see Chapter 7), can also apply to diverse heterogeneous societies in the West, in which many people find security and comfort within their ethnic or cultural groups. On the basis of this theory, people are likely to restrict their social interactions with those from their familiar ethnicity, culture, or religion. It should be noted, however, that when it comes to a group succumbing to expectations beyond their level of customary comfort, the pull of "like-mindedness" often becomes secondary to the immediate gratification provided by the lure of physical, religious and cultural identifiers. For

SHANBREEN

example, even though some people (like-minded folk) may have a low opinion of their party leader, they still vote for that leader based on party loyalty.

However, even though the onus for integration or assimilation appears to lie entirely on the shoulders of the indigenous population, in reality, as alluded earlier, it is a two-way street. While the indigenous population need to make an effort at integrating or assimilating the immigrant population, a corresponding effort should be made by immigrants in carving out a mainstream niche for themselves. In this context, the demands of extra effort put on minority immigrant populations are understandable when viewed within the framework that they are, after all, being granted permission to live in someone else's land. However, this does not provide blanket justification for the indigenous population to impose their will on the assimilating or the integrating population. There is a code of ethical and moral conduct that needs to be honored. If not, the West would be no more morally superior than a country that imposes its will on minorities, even at the risk of trampling their basic beliefs and customs. Such disregard for basic rights would be no different than ethnic cleansing, for which the United States and NATO, in 1999, bombed the Federal Republic of Yugoslavia (FRY) forces in Kosovo, a region in Serbia, under the accusation of "ethnic cleansing" of the Albanians.

Due to the increase in Islamist activities in Europe and lone-wolf activities in the United States, Islamophobia in the West is now becoming progressively worse. The phobia, however, is not only a result of regulatory policies that are being implemented to control the migration of Muslims from certain Islamic countries, but because there are no "real" counter-proposals or communications to the public from policy-makers, which would at least control the spread of bigotry and hatred for Muslim

226

citizens living in the West. Besides, even in controlling the migration of Muslims from so-called "terrorist-prone countries," Washington fails to include countries like Saudi Arabia, that are historically linked to the production of terrorists. In this context, it seems that those traveling from Muslim countries are not evaluated based on their likelihood of committing acts of terror, but instead on Washington's relationship with their home countries.

In the United States, the Muslim population is relatively better integrated than in Europe, partly because many of the Muslim immigrants initially came to the United States for education or as professionals. However, now that Islamophobia has raised its ugly head, every act of an Islamist in the country can be evaluated in terms of how well Muslims are integrated in America. Often, this integration is measured by whether the Islamists' or lone-wolves' families, religious heads, and friends provide information prior to the terrorist activity. In other words, there is an expectation of Muslims who belong to the same community as the Islamist, to know of the possibility of such activities and inform the authorities prior to its commitment. While informing the authorities of "questionable behavior" is a given, it is important to remember that law-abiding Muslim communities face the same difficulties of identifying prospective Islamists as others do in identifying a domestic terrorist.

As it stands, it often seems that integration of Muslims in the West seems to rest largely on how many potential terrorists are apprehended with the help of Muslims. However, this evaluation method has flaws, especially considering the likelihood of potential terrorists taking extra effort (just like some domestic terrorists) at hiding their thoughts and actions from everyone around them, including their loved ones. Ironically, however, even when law-abiding Muslim citizens bring information about a potential terrorist to the authorities, sometime nothing gets done. For example, the British Security Service MI5 had been tipped off by family and friends of the Islamist (Salman Abedi) living in Manchester England, but missed five_opportunities to stop him. "What more can a law-abiding Muslim do?" asked an exasperated British radio host. As Muddassar Ahmed, chair of Forum for Change, a British think tank, states:

> Let it not be said that Muslims didn't cooperate with the authorities to report Abedi. Abedi flew a black Jihadi flag out of his window in Manchester. He was banned from his mosque. His Imam reported him. His family reported him. His friends reported him. He wasn't a lone wolf — he was a known wolf.[11]

Although there may be some justification for MI5 not following-up on Abedi due to lack of funding, one wonders if some of the defense funding, could not be diverted to monitoring potential terrorists for internal security purposes. Even if such a course of actions is not financially or logistically practical, one certainly cannot justify ordinary Muslim as wrong-doers in such cases. But the issue of unrealistic expectations become all the more relevant when one considers that Islamists like Abedi cannot even be considered Muslims, based on their unacceptable ideological belief in Islamism (not Islam).

Equity as a Function of Diversity

Americans have always believed in individual rights. These rights have so far been examined under the "normal" conditions of their lives, which occasionally includes fighting conventional wars. The truth of their convictions, however, come under scrutiny in the current war with Islamists, which is unlike any other war they have encountered. While Americans seem to be desensitized to domestic terrorist activities, their pent-up frustration at the number of senseless killings in recent history has led to the full weight of blame being placed on "international" terrorist activities, which, as stated earlier in this chapter, account for only about half the number of people who are murdered via domestic terrorist activities. While even a single murder, for whatever reason, should not be acceptable in a civilized society, many Americans seem resigned to the policemen and innocent people being killed on their streets, and yet find inflated morale in making scapegoats out of people who are culturally and physically different from them. This misdirected hate toward Muslims, particularly on those who can be identified through common "Islamic" features and behavior, alienates the Muslims from the majority population, even if they have no cause for suspicion other than, say, the alienated groups' Islamic faith. In other words, for Islamophobes, logic and reason can take second place to fear and hysteria in identifying the true enemy — the Islamists.

Since most recent *international* terrorism activities have been committed by self-identified Muslims, one can perhaps make an effort at understanding (not condone) the generalization of fear for *all* Muslims, even though such crimes are committed by only a minute fraction of those who claim to be Muslims. This is an understandable behavior of the population in any country where assimilation or integration of the minority has not completely occurred, particularly if the minority group is easily identifiable by its habits, attire, or other physical or ideological differences. While some may argue that it was because of the Japanese attack on Pearl Harbor in the United States that had Japanese-Americans placed in concentration camp during World War II, there are others who believe that it was subtle racism, based on alienating features and culture differences that placed them, and not the Germans and Italians, in camps.

Social awareness of the effects that targeted actions have on innocent people dragged into the fray, need to be evaluated not only in terms of what is right or wrong, but also on its physical and psychological impact on the targeted population. However, awareness of the effects of governmental policy on innocent minority populations in terms of its moral and equity impact has seldom, if ever, been well thought out, and this unfortunate oversight has been the hallmark of knee-jerk governmental targeting in most countries around the world.

The main argumentative point is that few people would raise an eyebrow if, during times of *emergency*, people were identified based on their religion, nationality, or possible affiliation with suspect groups, and scrutinized under appropriate laws. The problem, however, arises when actions are arrogantly applied out of bigotry, or for the purpose of pacifying panicked populations, rather than due to an application of logic and justice that lacks bias against any one party.

It should be noted that bigotry exposed in the application of justice, seldom accounts for the contribution of diversity in the country. Literature is rife with the benefits of diversity, especially as it pertains to the United States, which is seen across the world as a hub of diverse cultures. However, for diversity to work, cultures, ethnicities, and religions need to be integrated (not assimilated) with the indigenous population of the country. But, in considering integration in the increasingly heterogeneous societies of the West, the role of diversity may be at cross-purposes with the basic requirements of equality. This conflict between diversity and integration stems mainly because assimilation is taken out of the equation. As an oxymoron, the degree to which assimilation occurs, therefore, can often dictate the success of "pragmatic" integration of diverse groups. In other words, some can argue that both assimilation and integration are necessary as a conduit for a progressive and unbiased society. This type of an assimilation-integration mix, not only creates an acceptance between groups that are demarcated on the basis of their inherent diversities – even if such diversities are in conflict (the integration process) – but it helps both parties to incorporate part of the non-conflicting customs into their lives (the assimilation process), if they so desire. The incorporation of migrants into a community can then be seen as dependent on both the indigenous as well as the immigrant population.

As can be understood from the discussions above, not only is assimilation hard to achieve but so is integration with its burden of promoting diversity, which may cause some to question the usefulness of diversity in their country. Diversity, while philosophically and even psychologically is greatly beneficial for the foundation of pluralism in a democracy, it does have some setbacks when it comes to creating homogenous rules that are fair for all parties concerned. As alluded to earlier, the more the diversity is physically noticeable (cultural behavior, for example) the more difficult is the assimilation, and perhaps to a certain degree, even integration. It is in this context, that assimilation or integration of immigrant populations (unless it is a quid pro situation discussed above) with identical or similarly defined indigenous populations (based on say, physical appearance, religion, or culture) is likely to occur much more quickly and easily than assimilation between two very different groups. In Kerala, India, for example, Hindus, Christians and Muslims live in harmony, perhaps because they are well integrated as well as assimilated based on the similarity of their physical characteristics and their culture, which allows them the freedom to achieve the integration-assimilation mix without stepping on one another's toes — some even partaking in each other's religious festivities. The benefits of diversity, in his context, far outweigh its setbacks, particularly when the "best" features of immigrants are adopted by the indigenous population, and vice versa. In such an assimilation-integration mix, diversity may seem not to exist, but it does, nurtured under the differences attributed to a single population – not to different groups within the population.

But, while incorporating the beneficial traits of a migrant group is generally a gradual, long-term undertaking, sometimes it is not easy to put into practice when the extreme belief in the "greatness" of one's own culture lessens everything else the immigrant has to offer. Even in cases where integration without assimilation is the name of the game, external variables, such as the fear of immigrants "taking away" jobs that are perceived to "belong" to the indigenous population, can be a major setback in the integration or the assimilation process. However, as a general rule, integration can be seen as less threatening to the indigenous population than is assimilation because integration is presumed to accommodate new skills and cultural aspects that are acceptable to the indigenous population. Since there is no force of assimilation in the equation, diversity is allowed to exist on the other side of their fences, if the indigenous population decide not to partake in it. In this sense, integration can also be seen as a faster process than assimilation.

As a corollary to the discussions above, it should also be noted that indigenous people's preconceived "perception" of the minority population is a great factor in a successful integration cum assimilation process. In the context of Muslim integration or assimilation, the poor attributes assigned by the indigenous population to Muslims need to be changed. An aspect of change in creating a positive attitude towards Muslims in the West, can be intimated by those who are genuine converts to Islam (not Islamism). These converts, generally speaking, are already assimilated, and therefore, can be catalysts in helping new-comers establish themselves into the Western world. While there is a risk of these people, themselves, being considered outcasts in their communities because of their affiliation to the "new" religion, they certainly have the wherewithal to function in western societies, and therefore, can prove very helpful in integrating new-comers into their own home communities, of which they are indigenous members.

Besheer Mohammed's 2016 research for the Pew Research Center, however, states that based on new estimates of the Muslim population in the United States, there has been "little net change in the size of the American Muslim population in recent years due to conversion." While there may not be a substantial change in the number of converts to Islam, it is important to realize that a substantial proportion of Muslims — about one-fifth of the Muslim population in the United States — did not previously belong to a religious faith, or were from a different religious faith.[12]

Type of Muslim Immigrants in the United States

While identifying successful integration and assimilation strategies can best be left to psychologists and social scientists, the type of immigrants who live in the West may provide some helpful hints for developing integration or assimilation strategies for future immigrants. In this respect, the following ten identifiers listed below, outlining the type of Muslim immigrants who live in the West (particularly in the United States), can be useful.

1. Those who have climbed the financial ladder *outside* their own communities, such as Dr. Oz, a well-known successful Turkish immigrant who discusses health issues on American TV, and Sadiq Khan, the Muslim mayor of London, England. These are, generally speaking, educated, professional people, many of whom have integrated very well within the non-Muslim world.

2. Those who have climbed the financial ladder serving their *own* communities, such as running ethnic grocery stores and restaurants, and selling their distinctive style of clothing. In short, they provide the immigrant population with a "taste" of their home. These people, generally speaking, are likely to remain within their own little enclaves made up of people from the same ethnic background for cultural strength, in much the same way as the early settlers from Europe did in the United States.

3. Those who are poor, uneducated, and have no tools to climb the ladder of Western financial success, which perhaps was the reason for their migration. These people work hard at menial jobs to make a living, but tend to spend most of the little spare time they have, in their own communities, clinging to their religious and cultural beliefs (not Islamism).

4. Those Muslim youths who are young and restless, perhaps even mentally unstable, because of the conflicting behavioral expectations of them by their families' cultural values, and the demands of peer pressure at school. These students often do not subscribe to the regular lifestyle of American students. They, like some of their indigenous but

"displaced" non-Muslim brethren, may try to expel their restlessness by joining gangs, committing acts of brutality on their own, or withdrawing into seclusion. These youths are susceptible to the "call" of the Islamists.

5. Those who are very conservative in their religious and cultural beliefs, and have no interest in assimilation or integration. They only live in the West because it provides them financial security, and a relatively safe haven for them to practice their religion (again Islam, not Islamism).

6. Those "born-again" Muslims who are disenchanted with their lives in the West, and suddenly find light in the religion of their fathers and forefathers.

7. Those who were radicalized in their respective countries and come to the West with the purpose of creating havoc in the West (presumably more in Europe than in the United States), as was the case with the terrorists in Paris, France; Brussels in Belgium; and Manchester and London in England.

8. Those who are refugees who fled their homes because of wars or violence due to terrorist groups or government atrocities.

9. Those Muslim students who have assimilated into the school system, but may now find themselves ridiculed and segregated because of the prevalent anti-Muslim rhetoric (Islamophobia) advocated by some politicians and/or through a few xenophobic media. The same may also be true of those who are not students.

10. Those adults who may make a decent living but do not have the emotional satisfaction of belonging

(family problems, no friends, no expectations of anything better). These people often want to integrate or assimilate but do not know how to do it. Some of them may have tried, but have had bad experiences in their efforts at being accepted. These people are all the more susceptible to the Islamists' call if they have a traumatic experience (death in the family), losing a job, or some other equally horrible setback that may trigger a violent mental reaction, perhaps arising from self-pity.

Except for categories 1, 2, 3, and 5 mentioned above, the rest could be worrisome results of non-integration or assimilation. In today's economy, the harsh reality of functioning in the West without education, and without much knowledge of the local language, can be very difficult. Some immigrants may find their life of relative poverty in their home country better than the one they lead in their new country, because at least their previous life lacked the isolating cultural burden subconsciously imposed on them in the West.

Many people are likely to overlook the fact that there is a difference between the emotional burden borne by disenchanted Muslim youth and their disenchanted non-Muslim counterparts in the West (category 4, above). Western youth, who themselves may be isolated from their societies, find some consolation in forming groups with like-mined youths, while Muslim youth may not find the consolation of cultural ties with like-minded Westerners. These disenchanted Muslim youths seldom find emotional solace in joining Western street gangs, and are often not accepted even if they try to gain their favor. Since these students do not have the advantage of numbers, they have no means with which to establish their own gangs, thus furthering their departure for adventure in recognizable, understandable, and inviting forms of familiarity, espoused through religion and culture by their first-generation parents or the subconsciously enshrined lives of their forefathers. These youths are primary targets for the Islamists, who could easily manipulate their "need to belong." While this type of recruitment effort is mainly directed at Muslim youth by the Islamists, the open-armed acceptance of groups like Daesh could also prove enticing for non-Muslim youths attempting to fill a void in their supposedly "mundane" lives, or increasing the thrill of excitement through dangerous adventures. By the same token, category 9 can be problematic because it alienates students from their adopted culture, which in turn could have a mental impact on those who were otherwise happy with their lives, and appreciative of their friends and acquaintances at school or the workplace.

On the other hand, it is quite possible that those who are religiously and culturally conservative, and who have no interest in assimilating in the West, are likely not dangerous. They may be ultra-conservative (akin to, say, the Hasidic Jews in the United States) but they, generally speaking, are not harmful to others. These Muslims are quite content being isolated from Western society. Their children, on the other hand, could fall under category 4, above, and face the consequences of conflicting lives at home and in school. Because of the easy escape social media provides from their confusing lifestyles, these kids may have a higher possibility of falling for terrorist demands and recruitment efforts via the internet, in comparison to other Muslim kids.

Peter Bergen's mix of factors that can cause an individual to convert to Islamism, presented in Chapter 7, can be extremely telling, especially when paired with a personal disappointment, like the loss of a job. As Bergen points out, "for many, joining a jihadist group or carrying out an attack allowed them to become heroes of their own story." However, the complexity in identifying a precise motive increases because of the large number of various "other" influential factors (such as receiving false information), that may also be instrumental in the motivational process. Bergen justifies such a theory by providing the example of the non-practicing Muslim, Tamerlan Tsarnaev, the older of the two brothers who carried out the Boston Marathon bombing in 2013. Tamerlan became an Islamist at a time when he was unemployed and his dreams of becoming an Olympic boxer had faded. His younger brother, Dzhokhar, drank alcohol, smoked marijuana, chased girls, and never seemed to embrace Islam, let alone Islamism. "Dzhokhar Tsarnaev's motivations for the bombings were instead largely molded by his older brother, whom he admired and feared, and by his own half-baked opposition to American foreign policy."[13]

It is perhaps obvious that the "born-again Muslims" (see category 6 above) who are disenchanted with their lives in the West and suddenly find light in the religion of their fathers and forefathers are similar to born-again Christians in the United States. However, for Muslims, the question is not whether they believe in Islam in their hearts, but what *form* of the religion they have committed themselves to: Islam or Islamism? They are of no harm to society if they follow Islam. These people, like those in category 5, are likely to live their lives with like-minded people, with little to no assimilation within Western population. However, those who were already radicalized in their respective countries, come to the West with one purpose — to create havoc in the West, or any other Islamist-targeted country in the world.

Islamophobes and Their Perception of Islam

While the lack of integration or assimilation of Muslims in the West can be seen as one reason for the growth of Islamophobia, it is not the primary reason for its occurrence, keeping in mind that the same problem also exists in varying degrees for other ethnic groups in the West. With this in mind, it should be noted that while integration and assimilation may compound the problem for Islamophobes, the real reason for their fear of Muslims is the problem of the way Islam is perceived in the West. Among the first things that likely come to mind about Islam for most Islamophobes, is that the religion preaches intolerance against those of different faiths. To emphasize the fact that Islamism (not Islam) is intolerant towards other religions, Dr. Ahmed H. Sakr, a Muslim scholar and president of the Foundation for Islamic Knowledge in the United States, depicts the Prophet's acceptance of Christianity via a letter Muhammad addressed to his Emissary with respect to the protection of religious leaders of Saint Catherine's Church. Muhammad specifically emphasized that Christians were his citizens and no one was to destroy a house of their religion, damage it, or carry anything from it to the Muslims' houses. Furthermore, no one was to force them to travel or to oblige them to fight. On the contrary, the Muslims were to fight for them. By the same token, a Christian female could not be married to a Muslim by force, nor was she to be prevented from visiting her church to pray.[14]

The Prophet also selected a non–Muslim, Amr ibn Umayyah al-Damri, as the ambassador he sent to Negus, the King of Ethiopia. It is worthwhile noting that according to the Quran, the Jews and Christians are "people of the book," who worship the same Allah (another word for God, used also by many Christian Arabs). Recognition for the rights of other religions, and for an individuals' right to choose the path they believe to be true is explicitly stated in the Quran (Surah 2:256): "…There is no compulsion in religion…"[15]

It is quite possible that this selected surah from the Quran could be contradicted by meanings from other surahs; however, it should be reiterated that it is the differential or selective understanding of religious texts that has led to the disagreement among and within different factions within most of the religions of the world today. For example, it is the variant understanding of the scriptures, or the process used in following the "words of God," that is responsible for religious factions along Orthodox, Reform, and Conservative lines in Judaism, and has created the rise of various schools of thought within Sunni, Shi'a, and Sufi Islam. Similarly, it was Martin Luther's separation movement from the Roman Catholic Church that divided the religion into Protestants on one side, and Catholics on the other. Even one of the oldest religions in the world, Hinduism, has Saivism, Shaktism, Vaishnavism, and Smartism, all as sub-factions within the religion. But aside from how different meanings are argued for and against any religious dogmas, what matters eventually in the context of identifying a particular belief associated with a religion is what is practiced by the majority of its followers. In this case, it goes without saying that the majority of Muslims do not accept Islamism.

In the context of the expectations of Muslims to live harmoniously in modern society, Pew Research Center highlights some key differences emerging between American Muslims and Muslims in other countries. "In general, American Muslims are more at ease in the contemporary world." About 63 percent of the Muslims living in the United States believe there is no tension between being religiously devout and living in a modern society, compared with a median of 54 percent of Muslims worldwide. American Muslims also are more likely than Muslims in other parts of the world to say that many religions, other than Islam, can lead to eternal salvation (56 percent versus a global median of only 18 percent). Additionally, American Muslims are much more likely than Muslims worldwide to say that all or most of their close friends are non-Muslim (48 percent versus a global median of 5 percent).

American Muslims are even more likely than Muslims in other countries to firmly reject violence in the name of Islam. In the United States, about 81 percent of Muslims say that suicide bombing and similar acts targeting civilians are *never* justified. Across the globe, a median of roughly seven-in-ten Muslims agree. These statistics, while specific to Americans, are likely true in varying degrees in Western Europe and other Christian countries as well.

In the context of the Islamists, it is their "interpretative" understanding of the scriptures in the justification of their political agenda that causes their belief in Islamism and not Islam. However, proponents of anti-Islam in the West have so clouded some Western minds with their rhetoric that sometimes there is very little truth to what is understood. While there is no doubt that Christians are persecuted in the Middle East, it should be noted that according to the *United States Counter Terrorism Guide*, responsible for national and international counterterrorism efforts, "in cases where the religious affiliation of terrorism casualties could be determined, Muslims suffered between 82 percent and 97 percent of terrorism-related fatalities over the past five years." In fact, Christians are persecuted no more than the Shi'a Muslims, the Kurds (both Shi'a and Sunnis), the Jews, the Yazidis who practice a syncretic religion influenced by pre-Islamic Assyrian traditions, the Sufi faction of Islam, Nestorian Christians, the Zoroastrians, and others who live in the region.[16] This type of non-factual understanding of what is happening in the war against the Islamists discredits those who advocate hostility towards Muslims mainly because of the belief that Daesh persecutes Christians.

The irony of this dilemma for Muslims is that the use of religion as a discriminatory tool is not only utilized by the misinformed Islamophobes, but is also used diligently by politicians in swaying majority religious groups in the country to their side. Some politicians in the United States, for example, identify terrorists through religious affiliations, thus inciting the masses to harbor ill-feelings against *all* Muslims, when most of them are not terrorists and have the same fear of Islamists as do the Christians, Jews, and other religious ethnicities living in the West and in the Middle East.

It should also be kept in mind that this is precisely what the Islamists want from the West — to make the war into a religiously ornamented confrontation. Notwithstanding the possibility of no help or very little help from Muslims in fighting the Islamists (which the West badly requires), such anti-Muslim rhetoric should also be examined under the scrutiny of how the action affects the Islamophobes and the Muslims living in the West. In this respect, it is incumbent upon politicians and the media to weigh their words carefully, with the understanding that "words" uttered in the context of a political win could have far-reaching implications for the population that may not be immediately evident. "Harmful" words, even if used with explanations as to their legitimacy or later retracted as misunderstood, often underline the latent thoughts of politicians, and could be indicative of their own prejudices. While some of these politicians may deliberately provoke crises through hateful words, there are others who re-track their words as an afterthought, not realizing the harm they have already caused in susceptible hearts and minds.

However, other than the perception of Muslims being intolerant of other cultures and faiths, a point of contention for Islamophobes, is associated with the perception of misogyny in Islam. Most Muslims, even those who are relatively progressive, have a somewhat different attitude on "gender equality" than Westerners. While the West has fought for many years to bring women's rights to the forefront, it remains an on-going battle involving issues such as equal pay for women in the United States. For Muslims, however, gender roles are well-defined and based largely on their cultures, which are steeped in religious beliefs. These gender differences are well exemplified by renowned advocate for the Muslim Reform Movement, Asra Nomani, a professor of journalism at Georgetown University in the United States.[17]

As discussed in Chapter 2, all religions have started with women playing a secondary role to men. Over the years, however, the scriptures, with respect to women, have been interpreted to reflect the changing times, or have simply been ignored by the scholars and the clergy. For Muslims, on the other hand, the degree of changes has been somewhat limited, with some, such as the Wahhabis, and the Salafists, clutching to their perception or interpretation of the religion's historic past, partly because of the bleeding of culturally driven state laws into religion, as explained in Chapter 4.

There is no doubt that to many Westerners, Muslim women are treated unfairly by their communities. In popular and even not-so-popular media, particularly the internet, cases are made against Muslim women's supposedly "poor" treatment, sometimes enforcing their personal biases, and, in some cases, basing their claims on non-scientific research. It is, therefore, hard to comment on the reality of the actual situation. In this context, other than the research done by the Pew Research Center, published in 2013, most other aspects of these discussions are based on my observations and personal realizations through contacts with Muslims and non-Muslims — leaving the digestion of such information to the reader in forming an opinion.

The perception of Muslim women being treated "badly" from a Western point of view, should not be seen as a case of Muslim women being persecuted, as long as the women have themselves accepted such rules propagated by their communities. In light of the Pew report, it becomes evident that while the understanding of Muslim behavior may be associated with religion, it is equally a cultural aspect, molded by the Muslims' geographical region. It is also the Muslims' personal interpretation of what moral, cultural, and religious beliefs are acceptable, particularly in syncing the progression of the world around them with their own particular beliefs (religious or otherwise).

While a comprehensive study on the topic of women's rights in Islam would be hard to tackle fully in this book, certain indicators, as studied by the Pew Research Center, can provide cognizance of the functioning of Muslim women in Muslim societies. In this respect, attitudes toward women's rights defer on such topics as the right to wear a veil, and whether women need to obey their husbands (an archaic concept in most Western societies). From the findings in the Pew Report, which did not include Western Europe and the Americas, just a little above half the population of Muslims living in South Asia and the Middle East-North Africa region were agreeable to women having a choice in whether or not to wear a veil.[18] On the other hand, seven-in-ten or more, take this view in Southern and Eastern Europe, and Southeast and Central Asia. The only region where the right of women to choose to wear a veil fell below the 50 percent median was in Sub-Saharan Africa.

On the other hand, while many Muslims "endorse a woman's right to choose how she appears in public, overwhelming majorities in most of the six regions surveyed, say a wife should always obey her husband."[19] In this context, more than eight-in-ten Muslims in Southeast Asia, South Asia, and the Middle East-North African region believed that women were required to obey their husband. "Even in Central Asia, a region characterized by relatively low levels of religious observance and [relatively] strong support for a woman's right to decide whether to wear a veil, seven-in-ten Muslims agree that a wife should carry out her husband's wishes."[20]

The survey finds that most Muslims agree (more than three-quarters of the people from 23 countries out of the 36 researched) that certain behaviors, such as pre- and extra-marital sex, are morally wrong. However, significant minorities of Muslims in some countries consider such behaviors morally acceptable, or say they are not a moral issue. As expected, "Muslims are even more emphatic that prostitution is morally wrong. More than seven-in-ten, in each country surveyed, say it is immoral."[21]

Some aspects of the survey are further evaluated in terms of the composition of the population. For example, older and more devout Muslims are more likely to say that Western entertainment negatively affects morality and is harmful to their society than those who are younger than 35, or those who are not devout in the practice of their religion.

Interestingly, despite the prevalence of Islamophobes in western countries, Muslims in most of the regions surveyed believe that being religious is compatible with life in modern society. Even Muslims who are extremely religious do not believe that the practice of Islam and "modernity" are in conflict.

Generally speaking, Muslims living in Southern and Eastern Europe (except for those living in Russia) were among the least impacted by women's rights issues, Western pop culture, and other issues discussed above.[22] Women's rights issues, however, bring forth the additional question of female genital mutilation (FGM), which according to most health experts is a traumatic experience and a major health and human rights issue.[23]

While the traditional cultural practice of FGM started way before the birth of Islam and Christianity, there is a prevalent belief in the West that FGM is a Muslim issue. However, the U.S. Department of Health and Human Services, according to El-Damanhoury's research, published in the *African Journal of Urology*, states that FGM is actually practiced by some Muslims, Christians, and an extremely small minority of Jews.[24] A 2013 UNICEF report quotes American anthropologist Ellen Gruenbaum, who emphasizes that followers of all the three major monotheistic religions "have at times practiced female circumcision and consider their practices sanctioned, or at least not prohibited, by God."[25] While Gruenbaum's research is enlightening, it should be noted that FGM is more prevalent in Muslim societies, perhaps because non-Muslims seem to be slowly weaning themselves away from such practices through a force of religious condemnation, leaving it entirely as a cultural issue. Muslim clergy, on the other hand, do not outright denounce FGM. Even though many now agree that it is not religiously-authorized, most Islamic clergy do not condemn its practice, instead providing a subtle layer of desirability for its practice.

For Islamophobes, issues such as females' obedience to their husbands' wishes, and an over-emphatic expectation in preserving female modesty through the wearing of specific clothes, likely contribute to their view of female subjugation, and patriarchal dominance in Muslims countries. In this context, there is no doubt that societies in many Muslim countries strongly emphasize a distinct understanding of gender roles, and the expectation of specific behavior between males and females.

There are some Muslims who argue that separation of genders, as stated in Chapter 2, have created a society where sex crimes (not including those committed by the Islamists) are limited. Without delving into proof of whether gender separation is the cause of low sex-crime statistics in Muslim countries, an alternate argument suggests that the lack of such crimes in Muslim societies has less to do with reduced gender mixing, and instead is an outcome of the strict laws against sex crimes prevailing in some regions of the Muslim world. As an extreme case, countries like Saudi Arabia, stone citizens to death for sexual crimes.

While one reason for wearing a loose-fitting hijab in the Middle East (for both men and women) is that it serves the purpose of keeping cool from the heat of the desert sun, the black color of most women's hijab in that region, is questionable in such an argument. However, according to some scholars, the other reason for the loose covering is to promote an attire that does not outline the curvature of the human body, thereby avoiding the potentiality of undesirable "fantasies" from onlookers. This argument for male-female equality based on gender-specific clothing, however, is not, generally speaking, equally practiced by the males. While many men in Arab countries often wear Western clothing, especially when they visit Western countries, such freedom is more often than not, denied to women. In this respect, differences in gender-allowable behavior becomes a point of contention, alluding to the belief that men may be seen as predators who cannot keep their hands off of women. To counter the expectation of predatory behavior by men, women are subjugated to rules that do not allow them to deviate from "hiding" their bodies with loose coverings, such as a hijab, or the burqini while swimming, unless they are away from the prying eyes of unrelated males.

Some Muslim women living in the West, however, have given up such habits of modesty, perhaps because they do not have the force of religious or cultural laws dictating their behavior. It is interesting to note, however, that in controlling sexually unacceptable conduct, the onus is largely placed on women's behavior control rather than it being a joint responsibility of the sexes. As an example, a well-educated Muslim man stated that women are required to pray behind men or in a separate place away from men, because the women bending in prayer may be sexually arousing for men; confirming the oft stated belief that men are easily aroused, or implying that women do not have sexual urges. This is amply evident in extremely conservative Muslim societies, such as in Saudi Arabia, where women, as stated earlier, were not even allowed to drive. While the reasons for such a law is not entirely clear, one can guess that it could be for fear that a woman is either incapable of driving, or perhaps because she is likely to take advantage of her freedom in pursuit of a rendezvous with, God forbid, a man.

While restrictions on Muslim women's behavior in comparison to Muslim males may seem rather "belittling" for women through Western eyes, there is little likelihood that it plays a significant role in promoting Islamophobic attitudes in the West. However, when Muslim women are viewed through the ultra-conservative faction of Islam practiced in countries like Afghanistan, there is a great likelihood for Islamophobes to blame Islam as the cause of Muslim women's supposedly disparaging condition. The demeaning conditions of these women would be of little interest to Western society, sidelining it as something the Muslims do, if most Muslims across the world (men and women) agreed with the atrocities committed against women by, say, the Taliban in Afghanistan. On the plus side, however, there is some push-back from such stalwarts of women rights as Nobel Prize winner Malala Yousafzai, who was shot in the head by the Taliban for speaking against the preachment of girls not being allowed to go to school, and the successful demands of Saudi women for their right to drive.

Country-Based Islamophobia

It is important to note that because many countries in the Middle East either have the power of oil reserves on their side, or are strategically located with respect to Western interests, they have become one of the main focuses of Western attention. This interest has increased exponentially considering the current war between the Islamists and others in the region. The focus of the West on these countries brings their cultures and populations into the limelight, such that their rather small populations become the main source of identifiable Muslim faces in the West and in evaluating Muslim behavior. Other than Persian Gulf countries, many countries in North Africa and the Middle East are in close proximity to the United States' closest ally, the Israelis, and thus have also been on the radar of Muslim-watchers in the United States and Europe. One more country, Afghanistan, has likewise encountered its share of scrutiny, mainly because of the United States' prolonged war against Al-Qaeda in that region, especially after 9/11. Unfortunately, many of the Islamists, although minuscule in numbers compared to the total Middle Eastern Muslim population, reside in these countries, exhibiting the perception that all Muslims are violent.

While Westerners may be tempted to consider these Islamic countries' populations as representative of most Muslims in both thought and action, it is important to note that these countries' populations, according to the MENA Team's World Bank Report, are around 355 million, and that includes Israeli Jews, Christians, and people of other faiths living in the Middle East and North Africa.[26] According to this report, more than 75 percent of Muslims who are rather moderate or liberal in their practice of Islam, even when examined under the scrutiny of Western norms, do not live in this region. Under such an evaluation, one is hard pressed to understand some American commentators' perceptions of Islam being a violent religion. Many Muslims may be conservative in their practice of Islam, but they are not misogynistic and cruel as practiced by a minority of Muslims, most of whom belong to the Wahhabi, or Salafi movements of Sunni Islam, and the Deobandi movement practiced by the Taliban. These people live mainly in a small area in northern part of Pakistan, Afghanistan, and in some countries in the Middle East and North Africa.

In the context of geographical identification of Islamists, most of them do come from these countries. It is, therefore, commendable that the West has learnt to identify Islamists on the basis of country origin rather than on their religious affiliations. Such an action frees Muslims from the prejudicial classification that all of them are suspects under the umbrella of Islamists. However, while such an action may take away the burden of "proof" from all Muslims as not being terrorists to those entering the United States from certain suspect countries, it does not do away with the obligations of equality and morality under which the United States has functioned in the past. This travel ban, temporarily disallows entry into the United States for people from six Muslim countries (originally Iraq was also included as the seventh country): Iran, Libya, Somalia, Sudan, Syria and Yemen.

But aside from getting into the specifics of whether Muslims should be allowed to travel from suspect countries into the West, one needs to evaluate the reasons for such an action. If Islamophobia is what drives one to dislike or hate, then a further question is raised in deciphering the specific reasons for Islamophobia's existence. Is it the fear of civilians being killed by the Islamists that drives Islamophobia, or is it just a dislike for something that is alien and not entirely understood by the West? If the desire is to keep Muslims from war-torn countries at bay because of the perception that some of them might commit acts of terror, then not allowing Muslims from war-torn countries into the United States can be seen by some as a plausible course of action, although, as of this writing, it is not clears of its validity in terms of the constitution of the United States.

However, barring immigration from the countries stated above, reeks of prejudice, because it does not stop Saudi Arabians from entering the country, knowing full well that the largest terrorist activity in American history, on 9/11, was the action of individual Saudi Arabians from the Al-Qaeda group. As *The Daily Mail* online reporter questions, "And why are Pakistan and Saudi Arabia not on this list? There is not a lot of logic behind this but it's a lot of politicking."[27] This type of selective action against specific targeted countries makes one wonder whether such a move is based on political reasons or a sane evaluation regarding the fight against terrorism.

The refugee dilemma. In the interest of logic, the targets of the ban should be those who are travelling to the United States from countries where Islamists are universally known to reside. These countries include Libya, Afghanistan Iraq and Syria among others. However, while Iraqis are off the banned list -- perhaps because of their help in defeating Daesh in Iraq, -- travelers from Syria (except for those who fall under certain conditions, such as having the so-called "green-card," are recruited by American companies, or are related to an American citizen) will not be allowed entry into the United States, which raises the issue of morality in refusing entry to refugees, who basically are the people most in need of help from the West. The balancing act between national security and providing safe-havens in the West for those in need, at the risk of letting the odd violent jihadist fall through the security cracks, is a hard call for the West to make. If moral values are important to the West, then there is no easy way out of such a conundrum, other than keeping a watchful eye on those who enter the West from suspect countries.

Syrian President Assad's infamous chemical attacks on his own citizens in Syria, and Daesh's ruthless expansion in creating an Islamist community, has caused Syrian Sunnis, Kurds, and Yazidis to flee the country into next-door Turkey and to the West as refugees. According to some experts and politicians (such as Senator John McCain from the United States), the indecisiveness of the United States and its allies on the Syrian problem some four years back has led to a massive humanitarian crisis that is likely to sit heavy on the West's moral conscience in years to come. In this context, lack of Western leadership in the conflict could create crises of massive proportions in destabilizing countries such as Jordan, Lebanon, Turkey, and some of those in Europe through the exodus of refugees from Syria. This type of crisis will not only test world-resolve on moral grounds, but could also create cultural and geopolitical problems that could likely have an impact on world financial and security concerns.

Lone-Wolves as a Justification for Islamophobia

It is important to understand that disassociating religion from international terrorist activities is favorable for most Muslims living in the West (except for members of Daesh, Al-Qaeda, and other Islamist groups). However, there are Muslims who would prefer to place terrorism committed by mentally ill Muslims, or by Muslims who commit terrorism for personal reasons, under the definition of "domestic terrorism" rather than Muslim or international terrorists. In this context, many Muslims believe that the violent actions committed by some lone-wolves are no different than those committed by any other type of domestic terrorism. These actions, like those that fall under the umbrella of domestic terrorism, may be the products of twisted minds, which erupt not due to a political agenda or an ideology they support, but rather out of deep-seated hatred for the targeted victims, or psychological conditions that activate a mental trigger. In line with this type of reasoning, the horror committed by Omar Mateen in the United States, in killing 49 members of the Lesbian, Gay, Bisexual, Transgender, and Queer (LGBTQ) community on June 12, 2016, for example, is no different than that committed by Adam Lanza, the Sandy Hook Elementary School shooter in Newtown, Connecticut — both terrorists were mentally ill. This type of "Islamist" labelling to what is basically domestic terrorist activities may seem inconsequential, but it might have helped curb the tide of Islamophobia in the country. Nowadays, such labelling is likely to make no difference, because any such terrorist activity committed by a Muslim, is perceived as an Islamist activity. However, for those who examine the activities of all Muslims through Islamophobic lenses, these lone-wolf activities only add to their fear of Muslims, even if the perpetrator is proven to have little understanding of Islamism, and even less of Islam.

To emphasize Islamophobes' false impressions when associating religion with all activities committed on behalf of Islamist organizations, it's important to note that Mateen's murder of LGBTQ community members highlights the fact that some of these lone-wolves are locally generated, with no meaningful links to Islamists or their ideology. According to a press briefing by the then Federal Bureau of Investigation (FBI) Director James Comey, Mateen swore his allegiance not only to Daesh but also to Daesh's hated enemy, Hezbollah, which is backed by Shi'ite Iranians.[28] This type of a mix-up would never be made or accepted by a true Daesh affiliate. Such a comment is a clear evidence of the ignorance of Mateen in terms of his allegiance to Daesh or any other Islamist group, and casts doubt on whether his actions were truly an act of international terrorism.

To elaborate the point, the massacre of LGBTQ community members may have been activated by the suppression of Mateen's own derogatory feelings of being gay, likely exacerbated by his Islamic beliefs, which are common to that of other religions, such as Christianity and Judaism. While such diagnoses are outside the realm of non-professionals, one can be forgiven for inferring that it was perhaps the teachings of Mateen's Muslim clergy that further enhanced whatever pre-existing hateful feelings he had against the LGBTQ community. However, the relentless violence projected by Daesh on social media may have been the trigger that graduated Mateen's misguided thoughts from "dislike" and "hate" to violence.

It should be noted that while some Muslims in the West are radicalized by Islamists through interpretations of scripture, there are others who, as stated earlier, embrace the Islamists' ideology with the illusion of partaking in a fabulous adventure, without any interest or an understanding of the ideology. When detained for their violent actions, many of these terrorists display no understanding of Islamism, as is exemplified by the case of Edward Archer, the non-Muslim man who shot Officer Hartnett in the name of Islam as he sat in his car in Philadelphia.[29] Similarly, Mateen, although vaguely familiar with the terrorist groups based on what he learned from the media, had no idea which group's ideology actually inspired him. He was so misguided that he probably invoked whatever international Muslim terrorist group's name came to mind — Al-Qaeda, Daesh, or the Shi'a Hezbollah group based in Lebanon — sustaining a false sense of belonging and purpose in his misguided view of "taking one for the team" in which he had yet to belong. These groups, as discussed earlier, are not allies, and have disdain and even hatred for one another. The influence of religion in Mateen's life, other than its value as reinforcement for his twisted mind, is doubtful.

According to Adam Taylor, correspondent for the *Washington Post*, Mateen's family stated that he preferred "working out" instead of studying religion.[30]

However, Simon Cottee does not discount the role of Islamism in such radicalization. He points out that Mateen needed the justification to commit murder, and when that permit was given with the supposedly implied reward for martyrdom (as is commonly advocated by the Islamists) through the preachment of Islamism, it provided him with the resolve he needed to commit the act. According to Dr. Cottee, Omar Mateen, aside from his personal reasons for committing an act of horrendous violence, needed the license provided by his shaky interpretative understanding of "combative Islamic martyrdom" to justify his act of suicidal mass slaughter. As the author states, this understanding of Islamism may not have given him the command to kill, but it "gave him the moral license, however hallucinatory, to do it, and thus directly facilitated his murderous plan." Therefore, any attempt to fathom the conundrum of jihadist violence, with respect to personal and political motives, must include an examination of ideological-religious motifs.[31]

While some may claim that such acts fall within the realm of international terrorism, it is likely this may not actually be the case, especially since no political or even religious motives are attached to such actions. Simply stated, Mateen's action in a country where he was not mentally assimilated or integrated could have been the result of clutching to something familiar that provided justification for his actions. The justification could have come from any other source in the absence of Daesh and Al-Qaeda. In fact, some could argue that if Mateen had not had access to the Islamists' message of violence on social media, other aspects, such as watching a series of violent movies that struck association with his own life, or listening to rhetoric by an anti-

LGBTQ hate group, could have provided him the justification for his actions.

The above discussions are merely philosophical annotations that apply only to lone-wolves (mostly in the United Sates), with the understanding that identification of the reasons leading to terrorist activities may lessen the burden of proof on the claim that Islamist ideology is the only reason for the perpetuation of such crimes. By the same token, some lone-wolves (mainly in Europe) may indeed be radicalized abroad or through active contact with Islamists' through online messages, and could, therefore, be acting on their instructions when carrying out a political agenda that promoted killing Westerners. Terrorist activities by such people give understandable stimulus to Islamophobia in the West, and in other non-Muslim as well as Islamic countries around the world.

The lone-wolf recruits, and the Islamists having cells in some Western countries, have contributed to rising Islamophobia in the West, giving foreign observers the impression that the Islamists' violent methods are sanctioned by Islamic theology, however radicalized it may be. Ironically, this is what Daesh seems to appreciate, because calling Muslims to arms in the name of Islam, probably helps its agenda of uniting all Sunni Muslims against the "others" who stand in its way as it tries to march towards its ideological goals.

Remedying Islamophobia

In attempting to change Islamophobes' perceptions of Muslims, it is important for Muslims to understand the power of speech and articulation in the West. For example, instead of having a clergy speak on their behalf in broken and heavily accented English, a less intimidating representation could be helpful. According to some research, there is a link between content knowledge and language proficiency. While Xuan Jiang's findings, published in *The Qualitative Report,* are specifically targeted at Chinese teaching assistants' training requirements, and may not have direct scientific backing when generalized across the entire population, it could be hypothesized that content knowledge and language competency are both important for meaningful communication of knowledge to the public at large.[32] In light of this awareness, it is likely that an Islamic cleric who lacks language proficiency could be erroneously assumed to be lacking Islamic knowledge. Besides, it is also likely that such a cleric could mistakenly articulate a different message from the one he intended, or that his manner of communication could infer a different meaning than the one he meant to relate.

These types of psychological projections and statements are important if one considers the power of an "appealing personality" in getting a message across. It was for this very reason that some people in the United States were riled up when the Boston Marathon bomber, Dzhokhar Tsarnaev's youthful "Americanized" image was displayed on magazine covers. His picture, according to some people, projected a "likable" face of terror. Although, as most are likely to agree, no amount of "beautification" can forgive an act of terror, or change the mind of those who subscribe to xenophobic views.

In the context of improving Muslim image, United States President Barrack Obama mentioned in an interview on CNN that it is important for Muslims to make an effort in helping spread the word that "ungodly" activities committed by Islamists have no place in Islam. In a sense, there is an inducement for the Muslim community in the West to do just that because it is to their benefit not to further arouse the indigenous population's wrath against them. In this respect, it is important for the Muslim clergy to make themselves accessible and heard, directly fighting the Islamists' perception with the explanation of scholarly, religious interpretations of the text, and providing counter verses from the Quran to negate the distorted views preached by the Islamists.

However, any efforts by Muslims to placate and educate Islamophobes are futile unless such "efforts" are well publicized. In this respect, the West's unfairness in its portrayal of Muslim characteristics is evident with respect to the rather lackadaisical coverage of United States' media concerning atrocities committed against Muslims, and acts of heroism and goodwill displayed by them. While the United States' government has been relatively fair within the framework of its governing laws, such as prohibiting the identification of individuals based on their religion in job applications, the same cannot be said of media coverage in helping to alleviate Islamophobia in the country. Most media outlets, other than a few, such as NPR in the United States, seem to prioritize ratings over the imparting of "relevant" information. While keeping a close eye on the bottom-line is nothing new for media or profit-based businesses in general, it is one aspect of reporting that comes off as prejudicial to those who are the "underdogs," and thus the victims of it. For example, except for a few reporters, such as Annie Gowen from the *Washington Post*, there was a lack of coverage in Western media when the hate speeches by the ultra-nationalist Buddhist monks in Myanmar, known as the Ma Ba Tha, fomented the murder of more than two hundred people and displaced a quarter-million people, most of whom were the stateless Rohingya Muslims.[33] Almost half of these Muslims were stripped of their voting rights, and now live as virtual prisoners in fetid camps, ostensibly for their own safety. By the same token, other than a small remark in *The New York Times* by Laurie Goodstein, hardly any attention was directed by the media when eleven Muslim imams and scholars living in the West were targeted as apostates by Daesh for waging a theological battle against them. According to Goodstein, "it is a religious rumble·that barely makes headlines in the secular West since it is carried out at mosques and Islamic conferences and over social media."[34]

To stress the point of bias in media reporting, Assistant Attorney General John P. Carlin of the United States, cites the example of Khalid Ali-M Aldawsari, a Saudi citizen and Texas resident, who in 2011 was accused of plotting to build a bomb and researching potential killing targets that included former president George W. Bush. Around the same time, according to Carlin, Kevin William Harpham, with ties to a neo-Nazi group, planted a pipe bomb along the route of a Martin Luther King Jr. Day parade in Washington state. Fortunately, a parade worker spotted the bomb and law enforcement officials were able to defuse it without any harm to the public.[35] While the two incidents, one in the planning stage and the other in the execution state, were both extremely diabolical in nature, Carlin, who was at that time, senior counsel to FBI Director Robert S. Mueller, was struck by the difference in the attention the two different terrorist acts received by the public (and the media). According to him, the Aldawsari case got a lot more public attention, while the Harpham case, which also had Mueller's attention and required full use of the agency's arsenal of resources, including hundreds of FBI agents and local law enforcement officers, was barely covered by the media.[36]

The American media's selective reporting practices have the inherent consequence of unconsciously promoting Islamophobia. For example, the American and French bombings in Syria prove this point. In a report by Spencer Ackerman, writing for the British newspaper *The Guardian*, the United States committed its bloodiest error in the two-year-old war in the village of Toukhan Al-Kubra, near the Turkish-Syrian border and the city of Manbij in Syria, killing women, children, and the elderly.[37] Sayed Mansur Hashim, assistant editor of *The Daily Star*, confirms Ackerman's reporting, stating that the French and United States airstrikes targeted the village, presumably for suspected Islamists in the area, and killed approximately 140 civilians. However, what seems to have upset Hashim is the way such tragedies are reported in the West. According to him, civilian deaths by the Syrian army are reported as deliberate onslaught on innocent people, but these types of deaths by Western coalition forces are seen as "collateral damage" and ignored by the media. Amnesty International and Human Rights Body, according to Hashim, agreed with the Syrian government, that the disaster was a "bloody massacre," even though most of the Western press, other than a few, such as *The Guardian* and *The Telegraph*, gave the tragedy little to no attention in their reporting.[38]

One would be inclined to agree with the idea that without proper explanation of the incident and acknowledgement of the deep-seated regrets of the Western forces by the media, hatred for the West quietly festers amongst millions of non-combatant Muslims around the world. Furthermore, it does nothing to alter the minds of Islamophobes, who are likely to believe that Manbij-type incidents seldom, if ever, take place by Western forces. Sayed Hashim succinctly points out that, "selective news coverage is unhelpful in the information age where a large portion of the world populace is connected and news in one form or another reach them." Such reporting plays "into the hands of radical forces that can and do argue that the West is there to occupy the lands of Arabs for the purposes of controlling resources."[39]

The assistant editor of the *Daily Star* chastises the media for not reporting on the issue and calls out Western forces for not taking public responsibility for their actions. Such actions, he argues, not only create hatred for the West by Muslims, but also play a significant role in Daesh's recruitment efforts. Hashim entreats his fellow journalists to practice their trade with the honesty it deserves, and to abandon selective reporting as an extension of foreign policy.[40]

While there is a certain appreciation for Hashim's concerns for the media's downplaying and ignoring such events, the true implications of such selective reporting are not clear as they pertain to Muslims around the world and Islamophobes in the West. If the West was to accept responsibility for its mistakes, such reporting could likely evoke empathy for Muslims from some Westerners, and may even touch the heart of certain Islamophobes, who could learn that their hate should really be directed at Islamists, not Muslims.

On the other hand, while most Muslims would likely appreciate an acknowledgement of the mistakes made by the United States, it is doubtful that such a public apology would help change the minds of those Muslims who are already radicalized and uneducated. Furthermore, recognition of the significance of collateral damage by the United States through an apology may be misconstrued to mean that similar future damage would be acceptable when post-marked with an apology, inciting a free-for-all, especially for the Russians, to bomb civilians in their efforts to win the war.

In the end, the significant benefits to reviewing and reforming media coverage strategies — including diffusing Muslim anger and frustration and reversing the current misconceptions of Islamophobes — has to be evaluated by the media in terms of how helpful such information is vis-à-vis the negative aspects discussed above for such reporting. There is simply no easy way to determine what should be reported or passed over by the media. However, while there may be occasion for discretion in selective reporting (perhaps as a construed extension of citizenship responsibility), the significance of Western media in playing an informative role through "honest" coverage of war, and in advertising the comments and activities of progressive Muslims, cannot be understated.

In this respect, the portrayal of the Pakistani-American Muslim man, Khizr Khan, and his wife Ghazala, eulogizing the death of their son Humayun, who sacrificed his life for the country he loved, further exemplifies the power of the media in fighting Islamophobia. In this context, the absence of Islamophobia would not only develop more meaningful and enduring relationships between Muslims (particularly those living in the West) and other Westerners in fighting the Islamists, but would also render much of Al-Qaeda's assertions about the mistreatment of Muslims by the West meaningless.

Chapter 12

The New War without Rules

In today's world, where wars are fought with highly technological weapons of mass destruction, collateral damage is an inevitable outcome. If terror is caused by an unknown suicide-bomber blowing up buses, trains, and malls, terror is also caused by a massive launch of F-15s or F-16s on selected targets — an attack which, despite best intentions, can and does result in collateral damage of innocent lives.

Historically, collateral damage has always been accepted as an outcome of war. As Raymond Seitz, the principle American negotiator for the provision of additional United States' funds to the Contras in their campaign against the state of Nicaragua, replied to Father John Metcalf's portrayal of the brutal atrocities committed by the Contras in the late 1980s: "in war, innocent people always suffer."[1] However, there is one major difference between the actions of violent jihadists and that of Western militaries: while the West generally speaking, tries its best to lessen collateral damage, Islamists intentionally set out to kill as many "non-believers" and innocent bystanders as possible — in their view, the more killed, the better.

Unlike the Assad regime, which does not appear to care about the destruction of its own citizens, or the Islamists, whose main purpose is to deliberately cause civilian damage by using its own people as frontline defense, the West is credited for trying to diminish collateral damage in the pursuance of its political imperatives. In this context, the West seems to be burdened with a conscious. If, as argued by some Muslims abroad, the West deliberately targets Islamist strongholds irrespective of how many civilians it kills, why would Islamists use civilians as shields to *deter* attacks by the West?

The war in Iraq and Syria against Daesh has worldwide repercussions, and involves countries in the Middle East, including Iran and Turkey; countries in Europe and North Africa, such as Egypt and Libya; Australia; North America; Asian countries, such as Pakistan, Afghanistan, and India; and Russia, all of whom are fighting the Islamists in some form or another. It should be noted that many of these countries may not be directly involved in fighting the Islamists in Iraq and Syria, but are likely involved in fighting Al-Qaeda and/or Daesh in their own countries. However, contrary to the belief that these wars are like any other wars fought by the West in the past, these wars are not as conventional as some might like to believe.

In this context, the primary factor that makes this war so different is the apocalyptic view of the Islamists, who glorify martyrdom to enrich their eternal lives, and have no moral obligations against slaughtering thousands of innocent civilians in the process. According to Emma Glanfield, writing for the *Daily Mail*, Daesh's belief in a 1,300-year-old apocalyptic prophecy is romanticized by the group's militants. The prophecy "warns of a battle between an Islamic army and an 'infidel horde' in Syria which will herald the destruction of the world." This little-known hadith, almost certainly classified as weak or fabricated (most Muslims have not even heard of it), refers to a "horde" flying eighty banners as they attack a Muslim army in the Syrian town of Dabiq. "It warns of a 'malahim' — the equivalent to Armageddon in Christian teachings — in which the Muslims ultimately prevail."[2]

The prophecy is said to be central to Daesh's ideology, and is used to fuel recruitment of military jihadists "who believe they are on the 'cusp of history.'" Many Daesh supporters on social media, according to Glanfield, "have compared developments in Syria to the prophecy, amid warnings that the malahim is coming." The terrorist group is said to have increasingly drawn on the prophecy since conquering Dabiq in August 2014, and "the town's name has become a byword for the struggle against the West. Daesh has even named its official magazine 'Dabiq,' in which it pushes its extremist views and reports victories."[3]

According to some people, the apocalyptic aspect of Daesh's ideology may play in its favor with respect to "hopeless" Muslims who are culturally and financially destitute. In some of these Muslim's mind, sacrificing their lives to rid the world of the supposed perpetrators of their plight (identified as non-believers via the rhetoric of Daesh) can be appealing as it provides means to assert some control over their lives. The thought of attaining both purpose and meaning in their life through the following of Daesh's ideology is likely uplifting for them, however twisted such a view may seem to outsiders. For these Sunnis, Islamism can become an incentive to join Daesh and attain martyrdom.

However, in the fight against the Islamists, there seems to be a confusion as to whether the West is fighting Daesh as well as Al-Qaeda in Syria and Iraq, or whether it is focusing its attention entirely on annihilating Daesh. As was discussed earlier in Chapter 6, these two groups have different forms of *modus operandi* for their slightly different goals and objectives. In this respect, the West's military engagement in Iraq and Syria has, according to some sources, the prioritized goal of removing

Daesh, and the casualties inflicted on Al-Qaeda are simply seen as a side-benefit.

American political scientist (specializing in United States foreign policy), Ian Bremmer, writing in *Time Magazine*, opines that it makes things increasingly difficult for the West when players in Syria seem to change every few weeks, and when each newcomer has his own list of allies and enemies.[4] On the other hand, Patrick Cockburn, reporting in the British paper, the *Independent*, states that there are some political and military sources in the United States who believe that the West is very slowly but surely on its way to defeating Daesh in the Middle East.[5] In light of the recapture of Mosul, Iraq, in July 2017, and the almost certainty of recapturing Raqqa, the military demise of Daesh in Iraq and Syria, and its dream of procuring a caliphate in the Middle East, is assured.

The "leading-frombehind" strategy of the United States in fighting the Islamists has proven beneficial for the West because it has not had as many casualties as would likely have happened in sending an army of ground troops to Iraq and Syria. In the context of saving human lives, most people would likely agree that military actions should be secondary to diplomatic negotiations, and should be only used if the negotiations fail, and all other deterrent methods such as the involvement of a third party/s in pacifying the aggressor and/or the applications of sanctions, are exhausted. However, there are instances when the only answer against an aggressive enemy is to take military action, as is the case in the West's fight against the Islamists.

The War in Iraq

As noted above, to counter the concern over prolonging or losing the war by not placing its own soldiers on foreign soil, the

United States, according to Army Colonel Steve Warren, the United States has American-trained Iraqi boots (Shi'a, Sunni, and Kurds) on the ground, under the cover of its air-power. The number of American troops involved in the war differs largely, depending on who is doing the reporting. According to Erik Ortiz, reporting on September 28, 2016, for example, the number was to climb to a little more than 5,000.[6] These troops are mostly supposed to be engaged as non-combative advisors; deployed in training, advising, and assisting capacity to help local militias directly engage Daesh. With American help, Iraqi soldiers have now proven that they are ground-forces to be reckoned with, as indicated by the recapture of Ramadi in Iraq, and their victory in recapturing Mosul (Iraq' second largest city), thereby clearing most of Daesh out from its strongholds in Iraq.

In the West's fight against Daesh in Iraq, the United States' understanding of the power-play between various parties involved has proven to be very helpful. As stated in Chapter 10, the liberation of Ramadi by the Kurds and the Iraqi army, for example, paved way for control to be given to the Sunni factions of the army for the governance of the Sunni town. In this context, Patrick Cockburn's provocative headline in the *Independent* — "ISIS Faces Likely Defeat in Battles across Iraq and Syria — But What Happens Next?"[7] — is a reminder of the importance of a peaceful plan for the country once Daesh is defeated.

One benefit to the strategies used to stabilize volatile areas in Iraq has been the United States' effort in ensuring that Iraqi Sunnis and Kurds are given a stake in Iraq's governance through political, military, and financial sharing of oil wealth and military resources in areas where the Shi'as, Sunnis, and Kurds reside. Because of the conscientious effort towards forming a governing party that suits all citizens living in the area, including the Kurds, the Shi'as, and the Sunnis, the current government in Iraq has

President Fuad Masum, a Kurd; Prime Minister Haider al-Abadi, a Shi'a; and Speaker of the Parliament, Salim al-Jabouri, who is a Sunni. It should be noted that al-Abadi heads a cabinet with Sunni and Kurdish support, something which the previous government lacked.

While there did not seem to be an immediate need to further equalize representation of all three major groups in Iraq, largely because of the country's priority in defeating Daesh, Joe Biden (ex-Vice President of the United States) has stated that after the defeat of Daesh, there may be a reason, as explained in Chapter 10, to separate the three major parties into semi-autonomous states for a permanent future solution in Iraq. However, it is hoped that the current system will carry on well with the Iraqi population in an effort to stop the hostile fragmentation of their country, and displacing families and resources in the bargain.

The following tongue-in-cheek proposals, based on some politicians' views in the United States, and conversations with a few lay people in different parts of the World, are sarcastically presented below as options for bringing a quick end to the war with Daesh. Such ridiculous proposals could evoke responses that could have global repercussions. However, examining them is important, if only because there are people who have expressed these options as plausible solutions. These methods have little to no possibility of ever coming to fruition, and would likely never be accepted by Westerners, not only because of their moral connotations but also because they almost certainly would conflict with the constitutions of most countries in the Western world.

One option to end the fight quickly would be for the West to carpet-bomb Daesh-held positions. This type of indiscriminate bombing would be unacceptable to most countries in the world because it would kill countless civilians, but it would likely be effective in bringing a quick end to the war. On the other hand, the West could grant Daesh's wish for a caliphate in the Middle East, but it would be detrimental to the interests of Israel and America's allies in the region, likely resulting in a bloodbath for thousands of innocent people in the region.

There are some who opine that the West should acknowledge terrorism as part of modern-day warfare and create its own terrorist cells. However, Westerners are unlikely to have the stomach for such immoral tactics, and it would prove nearly impossible to recruit a sizable number of suicide-bombers, because most Westerners are not susceptible to the magnetic lure of heavenly afterlife offered by Daesh to Islamist martyrs.

The War in Syria

The Syrians' story is not quite the same as that of the Iraqis. The Syrian war is actually two separate, distinct conflicts, although there are times when they seem to merge into one. The war started as a civil war between Assad's forces, and a haphazard coalition of Sunni opposition forces. It was not long before the Kurds in the country also took arms against the Assad regime. The situation becomes complicated, however, because some groups have multiple motives for being in the region, which are often in conflict with the priorities of their allies. While there is a common agenda between the Assad regime, the Russians, the Iranians, and the West in defeating Daesh, the other priority for Assad has been his fight against the Syrian Opposition Party and the Kurds, who are trying to unseat him from his throne in Damascus.

Broadly speaking, the key players in Syria can be split into those who are for or against Assad, and those who are fighting against Daesh. Overall, these parties can be consolidated into the following groups:

1. The Assad regime (Syrian Arab Republic) and its allies (Russians and Iranians)
2. The Syrian Opposition Party (a coalition of different Sunni groups) which wants to oust Assad
3. Daesh
4. Al-Qaeda affiliate, Jabhat al-Nusra
5. The Syrian Democratic Force (SDF), established in 2013, which has support of the United States in fighting Daesh
6. Others such as the Saudi Arabian forces, Turkish forces, and other Muslim and non-Muslim countries' involvement

The SDF comprises thousands of Kurdish fighters, as well as a mixture of religious and ethnic groups dominated by the original YPG/J, which descended from the PYD (see Chapter 8). The SDF receives some American military support exclusively for operations against Daesh, as did the YPG before it. Besides these different groups fighting in the region, Turkey, together with the Turkey-backed Sunni Arab Opposition, is also militarily involved in an ongoing cross-border operation in the region between the Euphrates River to the east and the rebel-held area around Azaz to the west.[8]

Nancy Youssef and Michael Weiss report that the United States does not have much confidence in the untrained Sunni Arabs holding areas recaptured from Daesh, while at the same time trying to advance toward Daesh's self-proclaimed caliphate, Raqqa, in Syria. On the other hand, according to Youseff and Weiss, there was a chance of ethnic cleansing occurring if the Kurds were given control over non-Kurdish populated areas.[9] The concerns of the authors could be based on Amnesty International's accusations of war crimes levied against the autonomous

Kurdish administration of the northern Syrian region known as Rojava.[10] Although allegations of ethnic cleansing surfaced during the period from July 21, 2016 to February 28, 2017, no evidence was found to substantiate claims that YPG or SDF forces ever targeted Arab communities on the basis of ethnicity, nor that YPG cantonal authorities systematically sought to change the demographic composition of territories under their control through the commission of violence directed against any particular ethnic group.[11] Furthermore, the UN Independent International Commission of Inquiry on the Syrian Arab Republic released a report that reputed allegations by Amnesty International and Turkey that the Kurds had been involved in ethnic cleansing in northern Syria.[12]

To complicate matters further, the American-backed SDF is considered a suspect by Turkey because of its hatred for Kurds, and its belief that there is a link between the PKK (see Chapter 8) and the SDF. In this respect, Kamal Sheikho, a correspondent for *Al Jazeera*, reports that in leading the battle to liberate Manbij (near Aleppo in northern Syria), the SDF was warned by Turkey about expanding their influence into areas under Turkish control.[13]

The SDF is very useful for the YPG, and indirectly for the PKK, not only because they're supplied with arms and other kinds of support from the Americans, but, as Aron Lund, editor of Carnegie Endowment's Syria in Crisis site, points out, it helps rehabilitate them politically and provides a platform from which to engage in public diplomacy. To this end, the Kurds have set up a political branch of the SDF, called the Democratic Syrian Assembly (DSA).[14]

It is ironic that the United States and some other Western countries classify the PKK as a terrorist organization even though the group has never committed acts of terror against the

West. This could likely be a case of appeasing Turkey, whose military and strategic location as a gateway to the Middle East is vital to the United States. For the present, the United States does not seem eager to press the issue, mainly because it deals directly with the SDF; although, according to Aron Lund, the SDF has provided an indirect template for United States-PKK cooperation, even if the United States professes to bypass the PKK.[15]

In the meantime, the Americans have the SDF train Sunni Arab militias who would be able to take over where Kurdish territory ends. These trained militia would be required to push deep into Daesh's heartland in the Sunni-Arab tribal region that connects Syria with Iraq. While the extremely capable SDF would be more advantageous in re-capturing territories from Daesh, relying entirely on the Kurds could create resentment among some Syrians and regional allies, and would risk sending locals into the arms of the Islamists. It may also be true, however, that the Kurds have no desire beyond securing their own population in Syria's Northern Kurdistan, and keeping Turkey out of the area. Besides fighting Daesh, their interest likely lies in confronting their rivals, the Turkey-backed Sunni Arab rebels north of Aleppo, and in linking Kurdish enclaves in Kobane and Efrin to their regions north of Aleppo. In these battles, the SDF does not receive support from the Americans because that would play against the expectations of the Turks who consider the SDF a terrorist group, even though, the United States likely considers both parties — the SDF and Turkey — its allies.

For Washington, what matters is the excellent job the SDF is doing against Daesh in Kurdish territory and on the fringes of it. No one has proven comparable to the SDF so far in fulfilling that job. It has established itself as an irreplaceable local ground troop component of the international coalition led by the United States Air Force. Seeing no other options, and very happy with results so far, American policymakers have taken a step in bypassing the desires and concerns of their ally, Turkey, and the coalition of Sunni anti-Assad forces in their relationship with the SDF.[16] In this context, President Trump, according to some reports, has now openly armed the Kurdish element of the PDF for the recapture of Raqqa in Syria, in spite of President Erdoğan's likely opposition to it.[17]

For the time being, the United States is left to play the only game it can under the circumstances — concentrate on destroying Daesh by leading from behind. The United States strategy in leading from the behind, also seems to resonate in the lower Persian Gulf countries, which too are very reluctant in committing ground troops, even in the protection of their own regional lands. While the level of involvement of Persian Gulf countries fighting against Daesh in Syria is not entirely known, countries such as the UAE, and Saudi Arabia, might be conflicted in prioritizing a plan as to which enemy to oust first with their bombing activities – Assad or Daesh. The various parties fighting independently in the area - Hezbollah, Assad's forces, Al-Nusra, Daesh, and others - likely makes the situation more complex than in just fighting a single enemy.

In this context, Turkey, may not be 100 percent in its commitment to destroy Daesh instead of Assad or the Kurds, mainly because of Erdoğan's hatred for the Syrian president and the uncertainties surrounding the Kurds' plans after the Islamists are defeated in Syria. In parts of the Turkish establishment, there is a fear that Kurdish success on one side of the border will carry over to the other. Richard Spencer from *The Telegraph* underlines the loathing Erdoğan has for Assad, stating that he really considers Daesh worthy of his support in its fight against

Assad, "or at least turn a blind eye" to Daesh's advances if it turns out to be the best means of bringing Bashar al-Assad down.[18]

Undoubtedly, there is some resentment in the Middle East over the "wishy-washy" attitude of the United States in entering the Syrian civil war and its indecisiveness in siding with the terrorist group, al-Nusra (if true). However, the potential for cause-effect damage, analyzed within the context of the United States' "non-direct" interference policy, reaches way beyond sparing American lives in the war. While the United States changed its mind in directly entering the Syrian conflict after drawing an "uncrossable red line," the consequence of its decision was the global perception that it had lost hegemony in the Middle East under President Obama. This world perception of the United States taking a backseat in terms of its position as a world leader, was also intensified by its lukewarm acceptance of NATO's role, and backing out of the Paris Climate Agreement under President Trump.

Complexities in the functioning of Russia and the United States in the Syrian wars. While negotiations have stalled between Russia and the United States regarding what should happen after Daesh is defeated, , it is heartening to note that the eradication of Daesh from Syria has progressed, however tenuously, without any serious stepping by the two countries on each other's toes.

While the West is not directly involved in the civil war currently tearing Syria apart, the United States had considered lending its support (including heavy military equipment) to the Syrian Opposition militia, but found the group's divisiveness, lack of common consensus on a leader, and no clear strategy for fighting the Assad regime, hard to reconcile. The most the Obama Administration could agree upon was to support the rebels with humanitarian aid and some military gear.[19]

Recently, according to Michael R. Gordon and Eric Schmitt, President Trump has "officially" decided to arm the YPG, the Kurdish militia fighting alongside Syrian Arab forces against Daesh. While this action, according to American military commanders, "is the fastest way to seize Raqqa, the capital of the militants' self-proclaimed caliphate," the decision, as expected, is vehemently objected by Turkey, a NATO ally. As Gordon and Schmitt explain, such an action raises "fears of a backlash that could prompt the Turks to curtail their cooperation with Washington in the struggle against the Islamic State."[20]

While there seemed to be an unwritten understanding between the United States and Russia that neither country would get involved in Syria's civil war, instead concentrating their efforts on fighting Daesh, the complexity of key players and agendas involved in Syria, has made it impossible to know who is fighting whom. It is due to the overlapping interests of these two military superpowers that various infractions have occurred, with each party pointing blame at the other.

However, to avoid such confrontations, the two super military powers have held discussions about avoiding cross-purposes with one another in their common goal of defeating Daesh in Syria. Such negotiations were primarily undertaken to identify each party's responsibilities, and to remain neutral and unengaged in the civil war taking place between Assad and the coalition of Sunni groups that make up the Syrian Opposition Party.

An important outcome of these negotiations was that the United States and Russia were willing to talk further about the future of Assad. As Russian Foreign Minister Sergey Lavrov stated in a news conference, "the truce created the necessary conditions for resumption of the political process, which has been stalling for a long time." However, on October 3, 2016, the United States suspended talks with Russia over the protracted conflict in Syria, accusing the Kremlin of having joined the Syrian Air Force in carrying out a brutal bombing campaign against the besieged city of Aleppo.[21]

While it is impossible to decipher which country was at fault for the breaching of agreed-upon conditions, Chris Martenson makes the audacious claim that the United States targeted the Assad regime presumably to appease its Middle Eastern allies, which included Saudi Arabia, Qatar, the United Arab Emirates, and Turkey, all of whom despise the Syrian president. In so doing, America inadvertently made a show of aggression against Russia, and even paved the way for Daesh to enter the conflict against Assad and the Russians.[22] In this context, the author asserts that in mid-September 2016, according to correspondents for *The New York Times*, Anne Barnard and Mark Mazzetti, the United States bombed a Syrian government position, killing anywhere from sixty to one hundred government troops that where garrisoning a surrounded position whose borders, according to the reporters, were well known to all parties. The Americans, it seems, dismissed the incident as a "targeting error."[23] However, according to Martenson, this was no accident, especially since the slower low-flying A-10s were also used for close-in support with high-flying F16s. He substantiates the claim that the United States' knowingly bombed Syrian government troops by pointing out that a coordinated Daesh attack followed minutes later on the same position, allowing the Islamists to make a key advance.[24] While the veracity of such an assertion is not entirely verifiable, it is very telling, not only in terms of what the United States' population is supposed to believe, but also in terms of the agreement between the United States and Russia in fighting Daesh.

The incident, if true, leads one to believe that the United States militarily attacked the Syrian government, and thereby broke the rules of engagement with Russia. In this context, Chris Martenson seems to further cast doubts about American intentions when he states that this was not a onetime deal. Such support was also previously provided to Daesh in 2014, "when 'errant' drops of pallets loaded with military gear … landed on Daesh's positions."[25] The United States, however, has, according to Richard Sisk, writing for *Military.com*, never denied that the airdropped pallet of weapons, ammunition, and medical supplies intended for the besieged Kurds of Kobani missed the drop zone (by mistake) to subsequently be taken by Daesh.[26]

While Chris Martenson and veteran Arab journalist, Nicola Nasser, stationed on the West Bank in Palestine, provide persuasive arguments regarding the disingenuous involvement of the United States in fighting Islamists, the claim by Martenson that Daesh was provided arms by the Americans, requires further scrutiny.[27] Even if the United States provided weaponry to Daesh in 2014 to fight the Assad regime, why did it take them almost two years before next assisting the group in 2016? On the other hand, why does the United States eliminate senior members of the Islamists if it needs the help of the terrorist groups to fight Assad?

Statements, such as that made by Martenson regarding the United States intentionally helping Daesh, would never have even been considered as a topic worth stating under normal circumstances. However, similar statements made by Anne Bernard and Eric Schmitt in *The New York Times* regarding the help the United States gave Al-Qaeda affiliate al-Nusra (stated in Chapter 10), may make some people accept the veracity of Martenson's statement. In this context, it is likely that while the United States *official* stance has always been to label al-Nusra, a terrorist organization, it had perhaps covertly changed its mind, and accepted al-Nusra's claim that it was only interested in fighting Assad, without supporting its "previous" benefactor, Al-Qaeda's worldwide terroristic ambitions.

On the other hand, there is a possibility that the United States could have "inadvertently" helped support Daesh in its bid to eliminate Assad's regime from the region. However, while Martenson's insinuation that the United States was *deliberately* (and directly) helping Daesh may be a bit farfetched, there may be some truth in the United States helping known terrorist groups in the area through the backdoor. In this context, as per United States Congress Representative Tusli Gabbard's interview by Jack Tapper on CNN News, the United States supported Islamists in Syria indirectly through monetary and "other" assistance to the coalition of Sunni groups in the Syrian Opposition Party and the United States' Arab allies, all of whom prioritize the ousting of Assad over defeating Daesh.[28] Also, as Lucas Tomlinson stated on Fox News, the United States limited its strikes against Daesh, hoping that the Islamists, together with the Syrian Opposition group, would overthrow Assad, as per the wishes of Turkey and its Arab allies.[29]

However, because Russia and the United States are fighting Daesh in the same geographical region where the Syrian civil war is being fought, there is still a strong potential for overlap and misunderstanding between the two parties. This is especially true when one considers that many of the parties fighting in Syria have hidden agendas and motives that are not openly known. For example, American-backed troops fighting in a certain region against Daesh, are likely to encounter Syrian Opposition parties fighting Assad. Such encounters in the war zone may be approached differentially by different parties, and highlight the need for continuous negotiations between the United States and Russia in fighting Daesh.

Negotiations, however, can be difficult when parties are untrusting of one another and have their own politically-motivated agendas, exacerbated by the might of their respective militaries to support them. It is under these circumstances that a "mistake" made on the battlefield by one party begins to look like a pre-planned effort to the opposition. The "talks" between Russia and the United States failed because, according to the Russians, the Americans did not hold up their end of the agreement, which called for them to separate the so-called moderate rebels from terrorists on the ground.[30] Besides, as former Russian diplomat Vyacheslav Matuzov told Sputnik News, a United States-led coalition bombed positions of the Syrian Army near Deir ez-Zo, killing 62 Syrian army personnel. According to Matuzov, this was "a blatant provocation aimed at undermining the political agreements."[31] In addition, in the opinion of Andranik Migranyan, a political science professor at the Moscow State Institute of International Relations, the United States did not want a binding agreement that held the potential to restrict its actions in the future.[32]

On the other hand, David Usborne, reporting for the *Independent*, stated that the United States blamed Russia for the agreement's demise, accusing it of being alongside the forces of Assad, and resuming the bombing of rebel-held parts of Aleppo, which was in direct violation of the agreement. In the outcome of these tensions between Russia and the United States, the only consoling factor, according to Usborne, has been a decorum of official cooperation between the two countries in avoiding any inadvertent clashes between them as they use military power to attack Daesh networks in Syria.[33]

However, there seems to be much greater involvement in the Syrian war against Daesh by the United States under President Trump. Civilian deaths in American airstrikes targeting Daesh in Iraq and Syria, according to journalist Zack Beauchamp, "have skyrocketed since Trump took office." Beauchamp explains that the president in 2017 has sent conventional ground troops to fight in Syria, and is considering the deployment of one thousand additional ground troops in the country to fight Daesh, which would triple the total number of American soldiers on the ground in Syria.[34]

With that in mind, it is hoped that the United States, the Russians, and "others," realize that while the necessity of military confrontation can never be taken off the table (as in the fight against the Islamists), building trust through negotiations are an important aspect of conflicts, whereby each party, whether it's the United States, Russia, Turkey, or Iran, has to "give in," even if there is no quid pro quo in the bargain. In some cases, however, sanctions may be the only available option, especially if an unforgiveable action has been committed – interfering in a country's elections, for example – and both parties have nuclear arsenals. This is particularly true since none of these countries have announced an apocalyptic ideology like the one espoused by Daesh.

Although the likelihood of Assad being removed from power seems very unlikely at the present, there are many people who doubt that the United States' has a tangible plan for the governance of Syria after Daesh is defeated militarily, or by some quirk of fate, the Russians agree through re-negotiations to remove Assad from power. This is perceived by some as a major problem, especially considering America's rather poor track record in the aftermath of the Iraqi and Libyan wars. But, unlike in Libya, Ken Dilanian and Courtney Kube state that the CIA in the United States believes there is a credible, moderate Syrian force, that has the potential to help run the country in a brokered agreement following Assad's ouster.[35]

However, such sentiments are not shared by Chris Martenson, who paints a very different picture of the rebels who make up the Syrian Opposition Party. According to him, the rebel parties would likely pose a major problem in the governance of Syria after Assad's ousting because they are some of the "dodgiest humans to ever walk the planet. The rebels backed by the US include nasty elements of al-Nusra Front, Al-Qaeda, Daesh and a host of really vile outfits."[36]

Conflicting factors at play in Syria. The complications of the web woven in Syria is further substantiated by the secretive role Israel plays in the conflict. Nicola Nasser, relates an account of Israeli air force and artillery intervening in the Syrian war to protect the UN Security Council's (UNSC's) designated terrorist group al-Nusra's locations against fire from the Syrian military.[37] These acts by Israel, verified by United Nation's Secretary General Ban Ki-moon, as stated in a report in *Foreign Policy* on June 14, 2014, and also by several reports by the UN' Disengagement Force (UNDOF) to the UNSC, are in complete contradiction to the West's fight against the Islamists. In the first place, it breaks the1974 ceasefire agreement between Syria and Israel.[38] Secondly, it lends credence to Representative Tusli Gabbard's assertions (stated earlier) that the United States *indirectly* helped al-Nusra, the very organization it deemed a terrorist group, by allowing Israel to commit such actions — perhaps to sustain the interest of its Arab allies and Turkey.

Although the United States should have found Israel's blatant disregard of UNSC's expectations disconcerting, it more likely welcomed its interference as a blessing in disguise. While there may be a belief that the actions by Israel were committed clandestinely with no outward portrayal of an association with the United States or its Arab allies, one can never be sure of that. Israel was doing the very thing that the United States was trying to do – discretely defeat Assad without any outward show of its intentions.

While the United States and its Arab allies (and Israel) would have preferred to oust Assad by an aggressive open war against him, the Americans are reluctant to pursue this course, especially after the active involvement of the Russians, leaving the mission of removing Assad to political venues – through the UN – rather than the militant takeover of his regime. Even on this count, the Russians, together with the Chinese, once again vetoed a resolution on February 28, 2017 to impose sanctions against Syria for using chemical weapons against its own people. By the same token, the recent comments by United States Secretary of State, Rex Tillerson, regarding letting Assad remain in power — a problem to be solved by the Kurds and the Syrian Opposition parties— further exemplifies the fact that not only is there any foresight regarding the fate of the Syrian people, but even worse, nobody seems to care what happens to them.

Israeli intervention in the Syrian war (if true) could be beneficial in one other respect — it is likely that such an action could lead to a favorable outcome between Israel and its Arab neighbors, who want to overthrow Assad. In an analysis published by the Saban Center at Brookings in November 2012, Itamar Rabinovich states that the Syrian conflict has the potential to unearth common ground between Turkey and Israel in seeking to foster a stable post-Assad government in Syria.[39]

The moral issue as an argument between the United States and Russia. Dr. Martenson justifies his belief in the "two-faced" role the United States plays against openly established American policies via a comparison of its military actions against those by Syria and Russia. For example, the Russians and Syrians are accused of bombing two hospitals in the rebel-held sector of Aleppo as part of an assault that threatened the lives of 250,000 more people. Similarly, the United States have also accused the Russians of air-striking a humanitarian convoy that killed 20 people, which, as expected, Russia and Syria have both denied.[40]

However, not many people in the United States may be aware that its drone program in Afghanistan, which killed 42 people at the MSF (*Medecins Sans Frontieres*) Trauma Center in Kunduz, was condemned by the UN, and most Humanitarian Groups.[41]The exact number of civilian casualties from the American drone program has had very little media coverage, except for an occasional passing remark from some commentators on American TV. As further indication of unreported American "mishaps," Martenson cites the example of more than four thousand dead civilians in Yemen, where, as stated earlier in Chapter 8, the United States turned a blind eye while the Saudis bombed hospitals and civilians in its fight against the Iranian-sponsored Houthi rebels.

Such comparisons by Martenson, based on the violation of human rights seems rather unfair, because it brings into question what the United States has done worldwide without according the same accusations for the atrocities Russia has done in Ukraine and elsewhere in the world. According to most experts and laypeople alike, it is Syrian atrocities with Russian awareness or help, that have caused humanitarian crises in Syria which in turn have created massive refugee problems in Europe and elsewhere.

On the other hand, while most Americans are likely to downplay assertions of American atrocities by Martenson as "unlikely truths" – collateral damages are likely to happen in a war – his statements do provoke one to question why a seeming hypocrisy exists in the promulgation of American moral values. Americans condemn the acts of other nations as inhumane and unjust, but under the umbrella of their own beliefs in national security, the same actions by their own country, are often dismissed as unfortunate but unavoidable fallouts of war.

However, while history may be able to show us countless examples of atrocities committed by the Americans on moral grounds, in the eyes of most countries around the world, the United States still seems to be on a much better moral standing than Russia (even though recently in 2017, America's credibility as spreading "goodness" has taken a massive fall). While the two countries can point fingers at one other for breaking the underlying expectations of their agreement, such a "game" can prove dangerous if it escalates. In such cases, rationality used in cogent evaluations of consequences is subsumed under irrational, emotional outbursts. Such outbursts can do irreparable damage, which is not always easy to undo. As Martenson wisely states, "while we can all hope this too blows over and cooler heads prevail, hope alone is a terrible strategy."[42]

There are some people in the United States, such as former Pentagon Deputy Assistant Secretary for Defense of Russia, Ukraine, and Eurasia, Dr. Evelyn Farkas, who believe that Russia is not to be trusted, even if negotiations were conducted between them and the United States. In her opinion, the best bet for success lies in what former United States Secretary of State, Hilary Clinton and Vice President, Mike Pence stated they ought to have done — create safe zones and no-fly zones, both for humanitarian reasons and to attain better control in the region. Although this is not a conclusive strategy for winning the war against Daesh or assisting civilians escape from war-torn regions, it would have been, according to Dr. Farkas, the first step in developing future strategies.[43]

However, these types of operations would prove complicated, especially with Russian aircrafts flying in the area. It should be remembered that engaging a major nuclear superpower with advanced hardware is different from ousting Qaddafi in Libya or Saddam in Iraq. It is possible that such no-fly zones, even in fighting the "common" enemy Daesh, would have greatly increased the risk of Russia following suit in certain areas where the United States and its allies could not fly, or, as opined by Senator Rand Paul on MSNBC TV, they could have initiated direct confrontation between the United States and Russia, potentially leading to World War III.[44]

The Libyan Assessment and the Yemeni War

It is important to note that an important aspect of Daniel Byman's testimony to the House Committee on Homeland Security also serves as caution for the West to employ far-sightedness in their undertakings against the Islamists.[45] While the West has concentrated most of its efforts on fighting militant jihadists on their turf in the Middle East, efforts to halt potential hot spots for violent jihadists' expansion, likely deserves attention. For example, due to the West's focus in Syria and Iraq, the strong foothold Daesh has obtained in Libya as a result of the overthrow of Qaddafi and the aftermath of the Arab Spring, has been somewhat overlooked. Daesh's desire for expansion should be carefully monitored lest it escalates to dangerous proportions like it did in Nigeria and Yemen, where the United States paid limited attention. As of August 1, 2016, at the request of the Libyan government, the United States has started bombing Daesh sites in Libya, which has now become one of the largest Daesh strongholds outside Iraq and Syria.[46]

A number of American special operations teams have also been deployed in northeast and western Libya, conducting patrols and advising local militias as part of the American-led campaign against Daesh. In addition, the United States and its allies have begun shipping weapons and equipment to Libya's fragile unity government to battle the Islamists' threat, despite a UN' arms embargo against the nation. The West has taken it upon themselves to overlook the UN embargo because, according to United States' Secretary of State John F. Kerry, "if you have a legitimate government and that legitimate government is fighting terrorism, that legitimate government should not be victimized" because of an embargo.[47]

According to Carlo Muñoz, despite the escalation of Daesh's activities in Libya, the Pentagon remains adamant that the United States will not fight with soldiers on the ground, even as the campaign to oust Daesh is well underway. The United States, however, is helping the NATO-accepted government militia in Libya with air-power in its fight against Daesh.[48]

While such a move in Libya may seem to be in the right direction in the United States' efforts toward defeating Daesh without major casualties, it only came to fruition because Libyan Premier Fayez al-Sarraj recognized that his country faced a major challenge and urged the international community to assist him against the Islamist group. Though Daniel Byman believes in the necessity of American intervention in seeking political reform in such countries, it seems the best the United States can do at the present, is exactly what it is doing now in Libya — actively offering its resources for advice, guidance, and military assistance in the form of bombing the terrorist group, and supplying arms to al-Sarraj, without a major risk of jeopardizing American lives.[49]

Besides the Libyan, Syrian, and Iraqi wars, the United States has been dragged into one other conflict, that started as an internal conflict in the country between those who were loyal to former president, Ali Abdullah Saleh (the Houthis supported by the Iranians) and the president operating from Aden, the capital of Yemen, Abdrabbuh Mansur Hadi, who is supported by the UAE and Saudi Arabia (see Chapter 8). Although at the onset it was an Arabian war against the Iranian supported Houthis, Al-Qaeda and Daesh soon found their way into the fray. The United States, therefore, is involved in fighting the Islamists in yet one more country in the Middle East.

Fighting Islamists in the West

Exercising caution against Muslims entering the West, particularly from war-torn countries, is a given. President Trump, of the United States, would like to refuse admittance to travelers from the previously mentioned six countries for ninety days. His executive order would also ban Syrian refugees indefinitely from coming to the United States, and all other refugees for 120 days. The concern that accompanies such policy, however, is based on political, financial, moral, and legal justification, rather than its obvious utility in restricting entry of would-be terrorists to the United States. While such an action, if legalized by the Supreme Court of the United States, is likely not to be appreciated by the minute number of Muslims living in the United States, adverse feelings in American Muslim hearts is less likely to percolate into violent actions as it could in Europe, which already seems to have been infiltrated by the Islamists, and its sympathizers. Aside from restricting travelers into the United States, however, the president has also spoken of extreme vetting of non-American Muslims entering the country or those American Muslims arriving back to their homeland from the list of banned countries. In this respect, it is important to note that to lessen the impact of agitating *all* travelers, a careful understanding of who needs thorough vetting is important. One obviously does not want to be extremely stringent in their evaluation of Muslims coming from

SHANBREEN

Malaysia, India, Morocco, and other such countries, regardless
of whether they are diplomats, businessmen, or tourists. In the
case of immigrants, particularly those who are refugees, it is
important to thoroughly vet them for obvious security reasons
(as is presumably already being done).

While there is no guarantee that the West would be
creating a safe haven for itself by the stringent vetting process,
such thorough vetting would most likely be a detriment to the
entry of Islamists in the country. However, it is important to
understand that most international terrorist activities in the
United States and Canada, unlike Europe — where movement
from one country to another is relatively easy — are carried
out by citizens of their own country (the so-called lone-wolves),
with most of them having no clue as to what Islam and Islamism
are about.

Fighting the Radicalization of Western Citizens

Aside from stopping international terrorists from entering the
West, the United States and its allies (mainly the Europeans
and countries in the Middle East) are also concerned about
their citizens becoming radicalized abroad and then returning
to create havoc in their home country. Then there are those who
are self-radicalized within their own countries, manipulated into
adopting the Islamists' goal of mayhem and murder remotely
(online), without any direct psychological persuasion from the
Islamists, or physical "linkage" to the central body of these
international terrorist groups.

The overseas recruitment of Western citizens by Daesh or
Al-Qaeda, as stated in Chapter 6, is not only reserved for the
discontented Sunni Muslims, but also for non-Muslim converts,
such as the woman known as "Betsy" from Holland, now living

288

in Syria; and former German rapper Denis Cuspert (also known by his Muslim name, Abu Talha al-Almani), who was killed in an American airstrike in Syria.[50] While there is every reason to believe that the West is trying its best to identify and control the activities of these people, some lone-wolf activities, as stated in Chapter 11, can be seen as results of pre-existing mental conditions, or some other cause that has no intrinsic or extrinsic link to Islamism. However, the Islamists' ideology proves useful for such disenfranchised people as an anchor for the justification of their violent actions.

It is also possible that the violence depicted ideology of the Islamists through the social media, boosts mentally sick lone-wolves to action much faster, awakening their disturbed minds with hatred that otherwise might have remained festering much longer with perhaps no actual path for an outlet. In this context, disfranchised Muslim are more susceptible to the Islamist message because they speak with a recognizable language of their parents and their forefathers, even if their family practices have no connection with the Islamist ideology.

As stated in Chapter 11, lone-wolves are very hard to detect, even if the West is ready to increase its "monitoring" resources by an astronomical amount. For the present, all the West can do is depend on their relationship with the local Muslim communities in the hope of an occasional hit in lone-wolf identification.

It should be noted that lone-wolf activity that gives credence to Daesh or Al-Qaeda, without any effort on the group's part, is not just a fringe benefit for the Islamists, but a very desirable part of the Islamist agenda. While such activities may not account for the same number of deaths as those that occur in direct wars, its value is immeasurable to Daesh because it instills fear in ordinary citizens, with the hopes of psychologically paralyzing them and permanently disrupting their lives.

While the Islamists have no control over the actions of self-radicalized lone-wolves, the use of social media to initiate disfranchised youths to travel to countries such as Iraq and Syria (mainly through Turkey) for training and membership into Daesh before returning to the West is a well-choreographed plan on the part of the Islamists. These recruits go abroad to be initiated into Islamism and either join Daesh's forces in the Middle East or return to the West to create havoc through terrorist activities. In such cases, the West can either protect the rights of all citizens with respect to their privacy, and process each terrorist act on an ad hoc basis, or it can forgo citizens' rights to privacy and monitor the activities of all who are deemed *potentially* dangerous. In many countries across the world, prioritizing the protection of basic rights of citizens over the elimination of all individual rights for the security of the nation is not even considered. In these countries, citizens' rights are always secondary to the protection and security of the nation.

The West, however, is cognizant that an across-the-board policy to eliminate some citizens' rights could ruin the lives and reputations if mistakenly identified, and would tear at the very fabric of equal rights for all citizens, which is held in high esteem in Western democracies. However, while such bills of rights may be the cornerstones of most democratically governed nations in the world, they too, often take a second seat when nations are at war, or their security is at stake. In France, for example, various Islamist websites have been blocked, prompting the opposition to accuse the government of using vague legislation to block websites that are seen as "condoning terrorism," which, according to Geoffrey King, a journalist and an advocate for equal rights, is tragic coming from the country that gave the world Voltaire, the champion of free speech and tolerance. The new laws in France, update a 1955 law, giving the government authority during a state of emergency, to block websites and social media accounts that encourage or condone terrorism. After the Paris attacks, many other European officials have also considered blocking Islamist websites. French and Belgian lawmakers have already established laws to silence online propaganda and hate speech by followers of the Islamists, restricting the groups' civil liberties in the name of national security.[51]

These types of emergency laws are not new. In the United States, for example, Congress quickly passed the Patriot Act after the 9/11 terrorist acts, which, according to Kaveh Waddell of *The Atlantic*, was "a bundle of heavy-handed national-security laws that included expanded authority for electronic surveillance." Historically, however, Americans are known to favor their First Amendment rights with respect to free speech over protecting at-risk groups — controlling hate-speech laws, for example, are unpopular among Americans. In this context, Europe's shift towards control over civil liberties is perhaps less likely to be mirrored in the United States.[52]

But, in the wake of the Paris attacks, even American lawmakers have pushed for the government to shut down internet sites that spread Daesh's propaganda. However, Waddell brings to light that many modern European hate-speech laws are a product of World War II, where protecting the persecution of a segment of the population meant taking down images of swastikas posted in public squares. However, the war against Islamists is a far cry from simply shutting down hateful websites in the name of national security. In this context, Estelle Massé, the lead EU policy analyst for a digital human rights group, *Access*, states that while the French government gave itself the power to take down websites after the *Charlie Hebdo* attacks, the effectiveness of restricting online speech to prevent terrorism is unproven.[53] In other words, restricting civil freedom not only infringes on individual civil liberties in the name of national security, but it does so without providing any proof that the change would actually make the country safer. According to Massé, the French law is a violation of free speech because it lacks oversight and checks and balances. Besides, because the law allows the removing of sites without requirement of a court order, there is potential for governmental overreach.[54]

In the United States, although chairman of the Federal Communications Commission (FCC) Tom Wheeler shot down suggestions that the agency should take down websites used by the Islamists, it was done for a slightly different reason than the one criticized by Estelle Massé in France. In responding to whether the FCC has the authority to block such websites and social media accounts, Wheeler told the panel that his commission does not have the authority to shut down terrorists' websites or social media accounts. The same argument was repeated by Mr. Wheeler when questioned about targeting the social media accounts of gang leaders in the United States (not international terrorists), who are contributing to urban violence.

Because the FCC itself has no jurisdiction over social sites like Facebook and Twitter, one specific action that the FCC could carry out without being affected by the requirements of law, could be the use of bully pulpits to press tech companies on these issues. In this context, shuttering Islamist social media accounts has met with some success.[55] For example, according to Tom Wheeler cited in Kaveh Waddell's report, by April 2015 Twitter suspended 10,000 accounts associated with Daesh, cutting out a chunk of the group's network, which was estimated to include between fifty thousand and ninety thousand accounts.[56] Besides social media companies, there are other companies fighting the Islamists in cyberspace as well. One such vigilante group, known as Anonymous, claimed to have taken down more than 20,000

Daesh-related accounts in 2015, as part of the operation dubbed #OpParis.[57]

However, Anthony Cuthbertson, writing for *Newsweek*, found that while Twitter's suspensions targeted the network's most influential users, which temporarily disrupted Daesh's online propaganda machine, it allowed the remaining supporters of the terrorist group to isolate themselves from outside voices.[58] In a sense, according to Cuthbertson, these Daesh supporters were more likely to be radicalized, and perhaps much faster than they would have been otherwise, because they now have the opportunity to converse with likeminded people through alternate communication channels.

Daesh, on its part, is quite aware of the blockades created by social media groups and vigilantes. According to British based researcher Charlie Winter, Daesh is now using cartoons to relay its message, because it is easier for cartoons to by-pass scrutiny and remain on social media platforms longer.[59]

While some people theorize that clandestine monitoring of all suspects' whereabouts and activities has already been actualized (creating terrorist watchlist, for example), the reality of such actions means the United States has crossed a line that *may* be a suspect with respect to its legality. As stated above, monitoring citizens who are considered likely targets may not comply with the Bill of Rights, keeping in mind that the real test of a country is not in its actions when the going is good, but how it reacts during difficult trials. If the United States behaves on an ad hoc basis, and acts in direct conflict with its basic laws and foundational values, then to some citizens, it may be no better than many third-rate countries who flip to dictatorship at any opportune moment, even if done under the guise of democracy.

It should be noted that in this context, Americans may have to prioritize their requirements. Should the United States curtail the rights of those who are *suspected* to be harmful, or let them continue without any clandestine monitoring of their lives, leaving their rights (as defined by their citizenship) untouched? If history is any indication, the number of people willing to give up their basic civil liberties is always higher immediately following a terror act than after time has lapsed. In addition, numbness and desensitization set in with each passing incident, to the point that the population is no longer drastically affected by terror-related violence, irrespective of whether it is domestic or international. It is also likely that more people would be willing to give up their rights if the damage was excessive versus that which is minimum – like the almost immediately forgotten case of Ahmad Khan Rahami, the September 2016 New York and New Jersey bomber in the United States, who, fortunately, did not manage to kill anyone.

For many people, it may be hard to understand why Ahmad Rahami was not on terror watch lists, even though he had visited Pakistan and Afghanistan several times, had a history of domestic violence, and was referred to by his own father as a terrorist. This is a classic case of someone who had family problems and lacked a sense of belonging even though he made a decent living (see category 10 in Chapter 11).

While the debate over monitoring potential suspects is a no-brainer according to some, there are still considerable arguments against restricting civil liberties on both sides of the Atlantic in the fight to safeguard the West. As most technology experts can confirm, the ease with which anyone can disseminate information on the internet makes it nearly impossible to silence a persistent online voice, be it a food blogger, Al-Qaeda or Daesh operating from Syria, especially for those Islamists who are technologically savvy and use the internet as a recruiting and propaganda tool. As an example,

Kaveh Waddell cites Europe's long-running campaign to shut down the Swedish-based site Pirate Bay — a massive online host that allows internet users to download pirated songs and movies. Over its nearly 12 years of existence, it has been shut down numerous times, always popping up again, often under a new domain name.[60]

Generally speaking, while the belief in abiding by the law in a democratic system of government is strong in the West, it is occasionally seen as a hindrance when the law seems to be in conflict with efforts to safeguard the country against security concerns and immediate threats. For example, according to Alan Fram, reporting on PBS News Hour, the FBI's Terrorist Screening Center, created in 2003 following the 9/11 attacks on the United States, maintains a terrorist watch database of people known or suspected of being involved in terrorist activities.[61] The list, according to testimony by the center's director, Christopher Piehota, given in September 2014 to a House subcommittee in the United States, includes a subset of the no-fly list that has around 64,000 people on it. However, when the FBI was asked why people on the terrorist watch list (which includes the small number of United States citizens on the no-fly list) could buy guns, Piehota replied that it was the law. According to a 2013 report by the nonpartisan Congressional Research Service, being on a terrorist watch list is not "in and of itself a disqualifying factor" for people who want to purchase firearms and explosives.[62]

However, most people in the United States would likely prefer weaponry to remain out of the hands of suspected terrorists, especially those who appear on the so-called "no-fly" list. While the merits of placing suspected terrorists on a no-fly list is not evaluated in these discussions, the fact remains that these are people are not allowed to travel by air, but can easily purchase a gun in America. The argument in favor of allowing these people the rights to own firearms is partly based on civil liberties and on due process grounds, and partly due to the potential for ethnic, religious, economic, political, or racial profiling and discrimination. In the case of identifying international terrorists, a problem could arise if people are mistakenly classified as suspects due to incorrect information or the unfortunate circumstance of having similar names as of those to known terrorists. However, it beguiles basic reasoning as to why due process suddenly becomes of unshakable importance when it is used for these peoples' right to purchase firearms, if it is not employed when they are placed on the no-fly list in the first place. By the same reasoning, if these people are already scrutinized within the context of due process requirements for their no-fly status, and are justifiably deemed potential terrorists, then, once again, there would be no reason for due process in prohibiting them from buying a gun.

Ironically, according to Harry Sarfo, the former Daesh fighter (quoted in Chapter 6), the importance of access to guns for Daesh in recruiting foreign nationals cannot be denied. For example, Daesh needs more jihadists in Germany and Britain because it is difficult for them to recruit people who have easy access to guns in these countries. Due to the belief that people with a criminal history are more likely to possess unauthorized guns or know where to obtain guns in European countries, those with a criminal history are likely candidates for recruitment. When questioned about the United States as a potential home for would-be terrorists, according to Sarfo, the Islamists indicated that recruiting warring jihadists in the United States would likely pose little problem since anyone in America can freely obtain a gun. It should be noted that such information provided by Sarfo has no basis of proof regarding the recruitment efforts of the Islamists in the United States.[63] Besides, after the lone-wolves' use of trucks in Nice (France), Berlin (Germany), and London (England), new methods may become a priority to be used in the future, although guns and suicide bombings would likely be the preferred choice for Daesh in carrying out acts of terror in the West.

Chapter 13

Some Peripheral Thoughts

Most powerful countries with well-equipped militaries fight wars with technologically enhanced weapons of mass destruction because that is what is available to them, and what is deemed "acceptable" by the global body, within the framework of fighting a "morally acceptable" war. In other words, most of these countries, generally speaking, do not deliberately set out to commit acts of terror on ordinary people, as is done by Daesh. In a manner of speaking, this articulation of fighting a "correct" war is no different than that which is prescribed by military jihad practiced under Sharia law. In fact, some may argue that the military jihad is very restrictive even in comparison to Western norms of fighting a "proper" war. While the Sharia does not allow the killing of civilians, children, or women, one can never be sure how it would hold up in today's world, where large arsenals of weapons of mass destruction exist. To the West's credit, other than some major history-changing "faux pas," such as the invasion of Iraq, the West has tried to follow the injunction of "morally correct" wars through such endeavors as the articles of the Geneva Convention. However, there will always be debate over whether laws involving warfare are only considered important to the country that is militarily favored, is winning, or has already won the war.

When innocent civilians are cornered, with no perceivable escape, the ugly war becomes uglier, especially if it is fought on the foundation of a twisted ideology. The world must realize that terrorist activities are tactics of war — very effective weapons, to say the least. There is no getting away from them. According to some in the Muslim world, the West has been a great help in fighting the Islamists, but it too is guilty of activities that harm civilians — for example, bombing areas where there is a great likelihood of collateral damage. In this context, it might be worthwhile pondering when morality and pre-established "allowances" in fighting a war takes second place to survival and protecting one's lives – or to put it bluntly – for the sake of the "greater good." Would the West not commit direct terrorist acts or use prohibited weapons if their people were deprived of fundamental rights, or were bullied into submission by the use of force? In other words, would a country not use extreme measures, unacceptable under the Geneva Convention, if it knew it was going to be conquered or destroyed, or knew that a country was planning to use extreme measures against it?

As it stands, the West is faced with a wide range of potential actions as it wades its way through the maze of conflicts existing in the Middle East. However, each individual "move" is not likely to be a panacea for winning, because each of the parties in the Middle East, as has been discussed in this book, has different reasons and agendas for fighting the war. Among the many tangled aspirations in the Middle East, common consensus supposedly exists on two fronts: (1) the Islamists are enemies of all parties concerned, although some Islamist groups' relationships, such as al-Nusra's with Turkey, the United States and some Arab countries, are not easy to decipher; and (2) the resolution of the Israel-Palestinian conflict is a major issue not only for those in the Middle East, but for most Muslims across the world.

In the current war with the Islamists, theology is used indiscriminately by Daesh, whereby it fuses its perverted ideology, Islamism, to realize political ambitions (the creation of a caliphate). But then perhaps, we give too much emphasis to Daesh's desire in acquiring a caliphate. When push comes to shove, perhaps, it too will phase out like Al-Qaeda and simply continue its horrible activities, even if it means that it has no chance for creating its caliphate. For the United States, on the other hand, its involvement in the Middle East can be seen as a means to assert its hegemony in the region and look after its own safety (from Islamists functioning in the West) — perhaps with a dose of moral turpitude in the case of refugees, toward whom some Westerners prefer a stance of "non-involvement."

There is no doubt that the war against Daesh took the West by surprise. To reiterate the point stated in the Preface, Major General Michael K. Nagata told *The New York Times* in December 2014, that President Obama's references to Daesh as a "JV" (junior varsity) team, reflected confusion about the Islamists, and may have "contributed to significant strategic errors."[1] Now that the war with the Islamists is well-entrenched, the West has some hard decisions to make - once Daesh in Syria is defeated, which is very likely to occur in the near future— what is to be the future of Syria? Would Russia be willing to come to the negotiating table now that extra sanctions are applied to it for its interference in the elections of the United States, or will it be more confrontational, and not abide by the sanctions put on Iran, for example?

Effects of Sanctions Applied Against the Russians

America's main problem – other than the one with North Korea – that is perhaps on par with defeating the Islamists, is its tussle with Russia. So far, it is commendable that the United States has let logic prevail and avoided flexing its military muscles with Russia, instead issuing sanctions against the country. In all cases, especially where quid pro quo is not on the table, punitive actions in the form of sanctions against "errant" countries are the best source of "punishment" used to modify the countries' behavior. Thus, it is very easy to levy sanctions against countries like Cuba and Iran because their power of retaliation, in any form, is not a significant issue for the sanctioning countries. However, the application of sanctions is not all that easy when the country against which they are imposed also has a part to play in the economic functioning of the country imposing them. Thus, it was due to Europe's large oil imports from Russia that sanctions against the Russians were stalled for a while immediately after they annexed Crimea.

But even after the sanctions imposed by the West, there have been mixed messages in the media as to the effects the sanctions have had on the Russian economy. An article in 2014 by Ivana Kottasova and Alanna Petroff, writing for *CNN Money*, states that, economically, things were going from bad to worse for the common Russian citizen, with "falling oil prices and sanctions imposed over Ukraine." This in turn has led to "rampant inflation, a plunging currency, a stagnant economy, and a loss of confidence among foreign investors."[2]

In 2016, however, Sergey Aleksashenko stated that even though President Obama rightfully mentioned in his State of the Union address on January 20, 2015 that "Russia is isolated with its economy in tatters," the Russian economy since then had proved surprisingly resilient to the sanctions and had stabilized by the middle of 2015.[3] This view was further substantiated by Andrey Movchan in *Politico*, who cautioned that although the sanctions imposed by the West have been a major cause of Russia's economic woes, they "might not actually be hurting Russia all that much if at all." In fact, Russians have imposed sanctions on European food products in retaliation for the sanctions imposed upon it.[4]

While sanctions against Russia seem to have had some effect in the short-term, their mid- and long-term effects are likely to be quite telling, especially now that new sanctions are imposed on Russia for its intervention in American politics. However, there are some of the opinion that Russian president Vladimir Putin is not really phased by sanctions imposed against his country, and would likely be unperturbed even if they were stronger than what they are at present. Part of the reason for this is that despite Russia's economy being in somewhat of a shamble, he is known to be very brutal with dissenters, focusing more on his political and military power, and in maintaining his and his colleagues' financial fortunes. But despite these rather dire views of some commentators, the general consensus among pundits in Western countries is that the sanctions are hurting Russia (especially as it applies to the finances of Putin and his cronies), and will hurt it even more with the passage of time, especially when stricter sanctions are imposed on it in light of its interference in the American political system.

The involvement of Russia, the issue with Assad, the Kurds and the coalition of the Syrian Opposition parties, is likely to remain a continued source of concern for the West, even after Daesh is defeated in Syria. It is highly unlikely that the government of Syria will change unless the SDF and opposition parties simply call it quits, or are destroyed by the Assad regime, or Russia agrees through some quirk of fate, to initiate a regime change.

Underlying Currents in the Syrian War

While forging three nations from Syria may seem an acceptable solution for some people, such would not be viable for others in the Middle East and also for those in the West. As stated earlier, members of the coalition that comprise the Syrian Opposition Party are, as opined by Martenson, incapable of fighting trained armies, let alone govern a country.[5] Besides, there may be a push-back from Turkey and a few other Arab countries, if the Kurds were given autonomy in the region. In such a situation, the repercussions of a three-way divide may prove more disastrous than successful. In the context of such dire predictions, the best alternative, as acknowledged by many countries around the world, is a regime change in the country. For the present, however, the only choice available seems to leave the status quo in place, and concentrate Western efforts in fighting Daesh. Perhaps at a slightly later stage, the United States can try and "rearrange" the status quo by starting renegotiations with the Russians regarding the post-Daesh period – which may require some quid pro quo depending on how much the new sanctions that are imposed upon Russia (for trying to disrupt the American political system) will hurt the Russians. To this end, the will of American allies to be on the same page can be beneficial.

In the context of the Syrian war, the United States' dilly-dallying about intervening in Syria is, according to some (like American Senator John McCann), one of the biggest mistakes made by the country in recent years – the others, according to many people, being the invasion of Iraq, and perhaps, to a lesser degree, the early withdrawal from Libya after Qaddafi's overthrow.

Perhaps there is some truth that the quick escalation of the Syrian war was the result of the West's refusal to enter the war at an opportune time. The hesitation of the West in helping the rebels who were fighting Assad not only made the United States seem vulnerable as a leader, but also gave Daesh time to increase its foothold in Syria. As reported in *Business Insider*, Fred Hof, a former special adviser for transition in Syria, believes Syria and Iraq would both be in better places now if the requisite assistance to arm and equip Syrian rebels in Jordan had started in 2012.[6] However, there are others who believe that the United States has no right to be fighting in a sovereign country without an invitation from the country's governing body. German politician Willy Wimmer, a veteran member of the Christian Democratic Union and ex-state secretary of the German Defense Ministry, states in an interview by Sputnik Deutschland on October 1, 2016, that the intervention by Americans and Europeans in Syria is a clear violation of international law because it was not authorized by the UN.[7]

While Mr. Wimmer's comment is valid in a strict sense of international laws, direct adherence to the law is complicated by the fact that Daesh, which has declared war against the West by sending insurgents into their countries, and by using social media to promulgate military jihad against it, operates from Syria, where al-Baghdadi resides. Since the war was started by Daesh, there was no alternative but to "go after them," wherever they were located. It would therefore seem justifiable for the West to go into Syria, irrespective of whether the West's military actions were pre-sanctioned by the UN, or they were invited by the government of the country to fight Daesh. In other words, the war with Daesh was not only a fight between Syria and Daesh but by the West and Daesh.

On the other hand, if the United States had interfered in the Syrian *civil* war without UN authorization, then one could understand Wimmer's call for non-interference. However, in this context, the 2017 American bombing of a Syrian airfield in response to Assad's use of chemical weapons comes into question. While most of the world seemed to appreciate the token gesture by the United States (and rightly so), it is a bit unnerving that countries with military strength often disregard laws set by the UN, when they were involved in creating such a body and its laws in the first place. Perhaps, because of the preponderance of world opinion, and the fact that other such chemical actions by the Syrian government might have been imminent, the actions undertaken by President Trump without waiting for UN' approval, were likely justified on moral grounds. While the definition of "moral" behavior is rather uniform across most part of the world, a problem often arises, if the concept of moral behavior is perceived differently by different nations – such as in some very conservative Muslim countries vis-à-vis moderate and progressive Islamic countries. The situation, becomes all the more complex, when the identity of a perpetrator of a "crime" is not recognized to be the same across decision-making parties. It is in this context, that a an important" country, such as the one belonging to the five permanent members of the UN who have veto power, may be inclined to change the course of a ruling through its veto power and or go on its own, if the ruling does not meet with its expectations – in a sense making the UN's function inconsequential.

In most American's opinion, the United States' policy of not putting boots on the ground can be appreciated, but the crux of the argument is often discussed on a cost-benefit ratio, and not on moral grounds. For the present, unless moral issues surrounding the plight of the Syrian refugees trump the rationale for leading from behind, preserving Western lives may remain paramount for the West in its war against the Islamists. In this case, it may be worthwhile to disturb our status quo with Arab allies by initiating consequences (lack of American military and/or diplomatic support, as an example) if their intentions fall short of the expectations of the United States, even if it is an internal fight between bickering nations in the region that may not be seen as having a direct effect outside the region, but could easily lead into one.

Israel's Dominance in the Middle East

A major impact in understanding Muslim psyche with respect to their attitude towards the West hangs, as alluded earlier, on the outcome of the Israeli-Palestinian conflict. In this context, the contrasting views and motivations of Israel regarding the preservation of its security in the Israeli-Palestinian conflict are expounded by George Friedman, a geopolitical forecaster and strategist on international affairs, who asserts that the Palestinians being a threat to the Israelis' security concerns is simply not true. For Israel, the Palestinians are merely an "irritant" whose missiles fall far outside the vicinity of the Israeli population, occasionally finding their mark through an insurgent attack on a small number of victims and their families.[8] At most, such activities may affect the morale of the Israeli population, but they cannot threaten the existence of the Israeli state or its core interests, irrespective of whether a political arrangement with the Palestinians comes into being or not.

As it stands, it is to the Israelis' advantage to have the many factions in Palestine (Hamas and Fatah, for example) in conflict with each other because, according to Friedman, it reduces the risk of a singular well-planned attack from the Palestinians (see Chapter 3). While an occasional attack may not be a major concern for Israel, the effect of such an occurrence could create a worrisome impact on the Israeli population's psyche, especially if the Palestinian attacks were to end in the deaths of Israeli civilians. It is in this respect that a central condition for the re-initiation of negotiations for Israelis would most likely be a guarantee from the Palestinians that terrorism would cease. However, as reflected by Friedman, the settlement for a Palestinian state remains gridlocked from the Israeli point of view, because the Palestinians cannot unanimously guarantee an end to hostility prior to negotiations, and therefore have no meaningful advantage for them.

Israel's current status. Despite the Palestinian conflict, the Israelis, contrary to what some may think, are not working in a vacuum with respect to Muslim countries in the Middle East. They have, for example, formal peace treaties with Jordan and Egypt. Jordan, which has never been sympathetic to the Palestinian cause, at least since 1970, when the Palestine Liberation Organization attempted to overthrow the Hashemite regime in Jordan, has effectively been an ally of Israel for a long time. In fact, Friedman states that the Jordanians regard the Israelis and Americans as guarantors of their national security. Even with Egypt, the Israelis' relationship is likely to publicly improve under Egyptian President Sisi, because Sisi hates Hamas for its association with the Muslim Brotherhood (see Chapter 3).[9]

The only countries in the region that pose some kind of confrontational threat to Israel are Syria and Iran. There are some who opine that the Syrians would never help the Palestinians to acquire a separate state because the Assad regime believes the Palestine region to be a greater part of Syria. If conflict had escalated in the area prior to the civil war, Syria might have aimed its hostility towards Israel, not to help the Palestinians, but for its own stake in claiming the region as a part of Syria. According to Aaron David Miller. former adviser to several United States administrations on Israeli-Palestinian negotiations, for Israel, the expected fallout of the Syrian war is that it will make the Syrian regime so weak it will no longer be able to live up to its historical support for the anti-Israel occupation movement.[10]

But aside from Syria, there is also Iran, a nation that is, based on its rhetoric, prepared to face annihilation if it means destroying Israel. However, as George Friedman points out, given that the Iranians have signed a nuclear disarmament treaty, they are far from having a deliverable weapon of mass destruction, and since rhetoric in the Middle East is seldom taken too seriously, the Iranian threat is not one the Israelis are compelled to deal with for the present.[11]

However, Israel's position in the Muslim world, even beyond the so-called confrontational states, is much more secure than either it or its allies would like to admit. Israel has close, formal strategic relations with Turkey, as well as with Morocco. Turkey and Egypt are the giants in the region, and alignment with them provides Israel with a foundation of regional security. Although Lebanon, like Palestine, is too divided to come to a state-to-state agreement with Israel, the Israelis have had "understandings" with different Lebanese factions in the region at different times, and likely has close relations with some of the Christian factions in the country.[12]

But Israel, besides its tacit understanding with some Lebanese groups and its alliance with some Middle Eastern countries, also has excellent relations with countries where formal relations do not exist, particularly in the Persian Gulf area. Israeli intelligence provides monarchies in the area with information that has often prevented assassinations or uprisings.[13] Saudi Arabia, for example, has never, in recent years, engaged in anti-Israeli activities beyond the usual rhetoric to appease its ultra-conservative population, as well as Muslims around the world, to whom it acts as a guardian of some of Islam's holiest places. In fact, according to Friedman, the Saudis forged a close clandestine relationship with the Israelis in the aftermath of the 2006 Israeli-Hezbollah conflict to indirectly counter Iran, their common foe.[14]

As Friedman points out, Israel does extensive business with the Arab states in the Persian Gulf, particularly in the area of defense, working formally through American or European subsidiaries. These actions are never publicized because governments of both Israel and the Persian Gulf countries would have internal political problems with their populations if they were.

Israel is also doing extremely well in the broader world, especially regarding its need for weapons and technology. Its first two patrons were the Soviet Union, which hoped to gain a foothold in the Middle East, and later on, France, which saw Israel as an ally in Algeria against Egypt. Nowadays, Israel's biggest benefactor is the United States. Contrary to some people's belief, the United States started its relationship with Israel in 1967, not as a quid pro quo with the Jewish lobbyist groups in the country, but for its own political reasons. Washington, it seems, saw Syria as a threat to Turkey from the south, at a time when the Soviets were threatening Turkey from the north. To stop the aggression by Syria and Egypt, which were aligned with the Soviet Union, the United States aligned itself with Israel, although a close working relationship between the two countries came to fruition much later.[15]

Israel's apprehension of Russia. In retrospect, one can see that it is not so much Syria and Iran that could be a concern for Israel, but the effect of Russia's role in the region. Russia is a major military power that has the potential to intervene overtly or covertly in the region for its own interests, and in the course of so doing, redefine the regional threat to Israel. In hindsight, Israel's fundamental fear may not be Iran as it is today, but a nuclear, motivated, and hostile Iran, and Syria with its cache of chemical weapons – both countries operating under the umbrella of protection from Russia.

While the Russians on their part, may not be particularly interested in Israel, they have, according to some people's opinion, already intervened in the region by supplying arms to Hezbollah (presumably) and the Assad regime. So far, the Israelis have played their cards close to their chest. They can live with weapons in Hezbollah's hands a lot more easily than they can live with nuclear weapons in the hands of Iran, or an anti-Israel coup in Egypt (that had, according to some, the potential of happening when the elected Muslim Brotherhood were in power). As Friedman points out, "one is a nuisance; the other is an existential threat" for Israel.[16]

Israel's efforts at preserving its security are understandable. It is due to the same security concerns that the country opted to back off from the United States' and Europe's attempt to prevent Russia's re-emergence as a great power during the Russo-Georgian war in August 2008, when Israel was not militarily and diplomatically as powerful as it seems to be today. As soon as the Israelis got wind of an impending clash between the Russians and Georgians in South Ossetia, they, unlike the United States, switched policies dramatically. Whereas the United States increased its hostility towards Russia, the Israelis ended weapons sales to Georgia before the war. According to Friedman, it seemed that the Israelis knew what was coming and wanted no part in it. Afterwards, unlike the Americans, the Israelis did everything they could to placate the Russians, including having Israeli Prime Minister Ehud Olmert travel to Moscow to offer reassurances. Whatever the Israelis were doing in Georgia, it is clear that they did not want a confrontation with the Russians.[17]

For the United States, Israel is its partner on many fronts such as tactical information sharing, technology and military arsenal production, and much more – tethered within the context of their respective country's public sentiments However, persuading the Israelis and the Palestinians to come to a resolution would likely be a major factor for the United States' global stability policy. A settlement of the Israel-Palestine conflict would placate Muslims around the world (not only their governments) and would probably help curtail the rise of further terror groups created on the platform of hatred for the Israelis – like Al-Qaeda. In this context, even though the Israelis have recently increased their settlement activities, President Trump of the United States seems to have done the right thing in trying to restart negotiations between the Palestinians and the Israelis.

Defining the Israel-Palestine conflict in the context of Hamas and the involvement of the United States. As is common knowledge, every country's self-interests, including those of the United States, will always trump outsiders needing help, if that help becomes contradictory to the country's political aspirations or agenda. Helping a nation, unless it is a quid pro quo situation, requires the nation seeking assistance to be in complete compliance with the wishes of the donating nation. The issue, therefore, is not that the United States, like most other nations, is doing something that is in the best interest of its own agenda in the Middle East; but in order to preserve its own "greatness" (so to speak), it has, as discussed in this book, often worked at cross-purposes with potential allies in its role as a leader of the free world.

If the United States is serious about carving a futuristic path that would accommodate the changes occurring in the world, it must step out of its comfort zone and make hard choices, which would likely include changes to its status quo with respect to countries in the Middle East. With this in mind, United States' relationship with Israel may have to be reevaluated. For example, while it is important for Israel and the United States to keep their favored relationship intact (with only an occasional exaggerated rebuke at each other when an action by one party goes against the other's wishes – such as signing the nuclear agreement with Iran), Israel's rather deliberate provocation in continuing to build Jewish settlements on Palestine lands must be addressed.

Although, as stated earlier, a solution to the Israeli-Palestinian conflict may not be of great help to the Israelis, it is an issue that inspires feelings of hate toward the United States and Israel by civilians in the Middle East. Even the governments of the Middle East, who have cordial relationships with the Israelis, have an underlying wish of statehood for the Palestinians, which they hold dear to their hearts. While there are Islamic countries in the Middle East that have maintained a rather non-committal attitude toward the Palestinian-Israeli conflict, this is likely done to please Washington in order to preserve their security, and due to their hatred of the Iranians; not as an act of sympathy or as security concerns for Israel.

For the West and the Middle East, the democratic election of Hamas, a designated terrorist group, may not have been a favorable indication of what the Palestinian people ought to achieve. However, in unearthing the reasons for Hamas' success — the social welfare programs it provides to the Palestinians, the hope it provides to the people of Palestine for a separate state, substantiated by the occasional military clashes it has in the region with Israel — brings to light the obvious reasons for its popularity.

According to a 2014 BBC News, Hamas was militarily degraded after the 2008 and 2012 conflicts with Israel, but it emerged with renewed support among Palestinians in Gaza and the West Bank for having confronted Israel and survived. In April 2014, Hamas agreed to a reconciliation deal with Fatah that led to the formation of a national unity government (see

Chapter 3), mainly because it became increasingly isolated under the joint blockade imposed on Gaza by Israel and Egypt, and the falling out with regional powers in the wake of the Arab Spring in July 2013 that overthrew Egyptian President Mohammed Morsi, a key ally of Hamas.[18]

Now that there is a semblance of unity in Fatah's and Hamas' acceptance of each other's "importance," a viable single policy can be presented to Israel for a possible outcome. In such a case, Arab nations will simply have to overlook their biases and acknowledge the two-state solution to appease their populations, even if they are not happy with Hamas' involvement. Israel and the West may also have to give in to the reality of the situation. Hamas is the choice of the Palestinian people and, therefore, hard to ignore. Besides, Hamas is militarily weakened with the Brotherhood's future on the downward slide. Its occasional acclamations of bravado are mere verbal incantations, keeping in mind that, as alluded earlier, in the Middle East, "machismo" is often displayed through verbal threats and chants that have no foundation in reality.

In this context, there are many, especially in Europe, who, according to George Friedman, believe that if Israel were to withdraw from the occupied territories and allow the creation of an independent Palestinian state, then perceptions of Israel in the Islamic world would shift. While the statehood for the Palestinians may not greatly alter current relationships between Israel and the Muslim world, it would be a great success in placating the general civilian Muslim population around the world, especially with respect to their view of Israel and the United States.[19] Besides, it may have some substance in defuncting Al-Qaeda's legitimacy for its ideology, whose one major cause for hostility, (as stated in Chapter 3) is the unsettlement of the Palestinian-Israeli conflict.

Israel's covert military actions against Syria. While Israel, like all other countries, evaluates events in the Middle East within the context of its own strategic interests, it is likely that these interests may not be in sync — or may even be at cross-purposes — with those of the United States in its role as the policeman of the free world. For example, Nicola Nasser explains that the Israelis, who are the strongest military power in the Middle East, were not asked by the United States to join a broad coalition of international forces to fight Daesh because such an "official invite" would not sit well with the populations of the enlisted Muslim allies in the coalition. Covertly, however, Israel is a player in the region with an interest in neutralizing the Syrian military, which has so far eluded yielding to the terms dictated by the American-backed Israeli regional force for making peace with the Hebrew state.[20]

In its effort at neutralizing the Syrian military force, Israel, as stated in Chapter 12, may have supported al-Nusra and the Syrian resistance forces through provision of military, medical, and other humanitarian help in its fight against the Assad regime. According to Nicola Nasser, Israel's aggression against Syria is further enforced by several unprovoked bombings of Syrian defenses by Israel.[21]

If Nasser's accusations are true, then Israel is violating the UN sponsored ceasefire agreement, and the UNSC' anti-terror resolutions between Syria and Israel. Moreover, if there is a collapse of the UN peacekeeping mission on Syrian Golan Heights, it would provide Israel with a pretext not to withdraw Israeli Occupational Forces (IOF) from the Golan, thereby undermining the UNDOF's mandate for removal of Israeli forces from the Israeli-occupied Golan Heights in Syria. While the return of the Golan back to Syria is a thorny issue for both sides – a strategic location for Israel, and the unacceptability of foreign occupancy of their land for the Syrians – it may be a long time until Tel Aviv can revisit the prospect of giving the Golan back to Damascus.[22]

In the context of the Syrian war, it is interesting to note the way Israel plays the part of a chameleon — supporting al-Nusra (if true) in its efforts to overthrow the Assad regime, and using the war as a pretext to avoid making peace with the Palestinians. In this context, Israeli Prime Minister Netanyahu has argued against setting a timeframe for withdrawal from the Israeli-occupied Palestinian territories because, according to him, the rise of the Islamists will bring them to the suburbs of Tel Aviv and to the heart of Jerusalem.[23] Under the cloud of such dire predictions, the Israelis have, without any known recent provocation by the Palestinians, furthered their 2017 provision of continuing to settle Israelis in Palestinian territories.[24]

The above discourse highlights the self-interested goals of the key players in Syria, prior to the active involvement of the Russians. However, now that the Russians are an active participant, it is unclear whether Israel has actively continued supporting al-Nusra and the Syrian Opposition Party to dislodge Assad, or whether it has withdrawn support so as not to openly confront Russia.

It should be noted that although a lot has changed since George Friedman's analyses and forecasts way back in 2008, many of his articulations remain quite relevant in 2017. While the veracity of some of the author's statements have not been cross-referenced or empirically verified, especially with respect to the business Israeli does with the countries of the Persian Gulf, they do provide a verifiable logical understanding of the affairs as they existed in the Middle East prior to the arrival of Islamists on the scene. For the Israelis, however, even after the Arab Spring and the arrival of Islamist groups, nothing much has changed. Israel is still in control of Palestinians and their land, and its relations with countries along its borders are about the same as they were prior to the Arab Spring. The impression of the general population of Islamic countries that Israel is an American stooge and a tyrant also remains the same. However, there has been one big change in the region that may have, as stated earlier, made the Israelis nervous — the buildup of Russian military in the area, and the knowledge that Assad still possesses chemical weapons. Although the Russians have been in Syria for many years, their current activities and the outcome of the war may not sit well in the context of Israeli security concerns.

The "Not So Well-Defined" American Policies in the Middle East

Aside from the Israeli-Palestinian conflict, the United States' reputation as a war-weary nation that is hesitant to get involved in other countries' affairs, with respect to direct involvement (either in terms of supplying arms or putting boots on the ground), is seen differently, at different times, by different people.

Shadi Hamid, as stated in Chapter 8, emphasizes that based on the United States' history of regime-building, it may now be too late for it to back out.[25] On the other hand, a stronger American presence in the region may be in sharp contrast with the desires of the Arab peoples, who in turn may perceive or "imagine" an American hand in their autocrats' heavy-handed rule. The simmering discontent among the people in many Middle East countries may once again erupt, and could likely culminate in many more Arab Springs in the future. It is perhaps in this context that, as stated earlier, perhaps a diplomatic strategy that builds confidence in the United States through investments, would likely be a better strategy than the military strategy (arming the allies) that is in practice at the present.

As Hamid theorizes, the lack of cohesive Western policies when promoting democracy in Arab countries is a model in vogue for the West, whereby Arab governments are expected to do the West's bidding in return for their overlooking the suppression of dissent in their countries. These policies can be directly linked to the lack of stability in the region, reinforced by the aftermaths of the December 2010 Arab Spring. As the author states, "regimes that once seemed resilient crumbled more quickly than anyone could have imagined." Hamid argues that if there was a lesson to be learned, it was that human rights and democratic reforms need once again to be prioritized and not deemphasized, as has been done by the United States over the last few years.[26]

However, the unwillingness or inability of the United States to use leverage to pressure Arab governments, including those with Islamist leanings, came at a cost. It is likely that the American *laissez-faire* attitude indirectly pushed the Muslim Brotherhood to veer right and overreach. Empowered by its conservative Salafist base, the Brotherhood alienated old and new allies, thus creating devastating effects on the course of Egypt's democratic transition.

In such situations, the United States could provide a credible threat of sanctions, as it did with Iran. However, such punitive approaches could backfire, given that the United States needs a friendly Egypt towards Israel, Egypt is geopolitically quite powerful, is closely entwined with Saudi Arabia, and receives substantial funding from oil rich sheikdoms. Besides, there is a unified sensitivity to the interference of foreign powers in any regional country's business by the Middle East populations. Hamid, instead, suggests positive conditioning by the United States through investment in diplomatic, political, economic (through financial investments), and humanitarian efforts to meet explicit, measurable benchmarks on democratic reform, and not by [selling sophisticated military armaments], and expanding military bases in the region.[27]

David Vine concurs with Hamid in stating that expanding the infrastructure of military bases in the Greater Middle East (see Chapter 8) will perpetuate a "militarized foreign policy," premised on assumptions about the efficacy of war, which unfortunately will only increase turmoil in the area. In this context, it seems beyond irony that the target of Pentagon's outwardly stated reason is the annihilation of Daesh, whose very existence and growth is partly due to the invasion of Iraq and the dismantling of Iraqi armed forces by the United States and Britain.[28]

The Shady Nature of American Policies

As an extension of the discussions above, it would help if the United States "adopted" some awareness of what is expected of it in its role as a leader of the free world, and what are its policies in attaining such expectations. For example, America must understand that any admonishments with respect to human rights violations should be evaluated in terms that are suitable for the country in question. While it certainly is morally satisfying to carve out definitions of human rights that meet with the West's understanding of uprightness and dignity for the "foreign" populace, one simply cannot invoke a universally accepted baseline of what is acceptable and what is not for everyone else to follow. In other words, while internal rules in the governance of the population within a Muslim country may seem misogynistic and even cruel, it is important to remember that people in these countries may not have the same appreciation of fairness and cruelty as those in Western countries. Even among Western countries, while the death-penalty is considered unusually cruel bymany European nations, it is not so in some states within America. In this respect, while chopping off a hand for stealing would be considered barbaric to us in the West, it has a culturally based justification for people in countries like Saudi Arabia and some tribal areas of Afghanistan; even though such rules, while on their books, seldom require enforcement.

While unjustifiable violence is seldom, if ever, acceptable by most people in the world (of any religious denomination) – within or outside their own countries – the crux of differential argument occurs in the definition of what is "unjustifiable." In this context, the West's involvement, supposedly "to make things right," should be taken with caution. A pre-decided, supposedly well-charted, one-size-fits-all approach by the United States, may not quite work out as expected. Azadeh Shahshahani's and Corinna Mullin's research study indicates that it is impossible to prepare for or adequately respond to all contingencies that could occur, and then be ready to control the outcomes of various processes once the activities and events in the international arena are set in motion.[29]

However, even when the West decides to intervene based on "moral" grounds, it often seems that it lets "subjectivity" dictate its actions, which are essentially determined, more often than not, by the country's relationship with the West. For example, in 1988, the West paid mere lip-service to the atrocities committed during the Iraq-Iran war, particularly by Iraq's use of chemical weapons as an arsenal of war. As stated by Shane Harris and Matthew M. Aid (who based their reporting on CIA files obtained by them), the United States blamed Iran for using chemical weapons, when it knew Iraq was the culprit.[30] In these chemical attacks, besides the Iranians, thousands of Kurds were also killed in what is known as the Halabja massacre — one of the largest acts of genocide, committed by Saddam Hussein's Ba'ath regime against the Kurdish people in northern Iraq.[31] Dr. Jean Pascal Zanders (project leader for chemical and biological warfare at the Stockholm International Peace Research Institute), referencing a two-year study by Dr. Joost Hiltermann, who was the principal researcher for the Human Rights Watch between 1992 and 1994, states that the United States was fully aware of Iraq being the culprit for the deployment of chemical weapons but still accused the Iranians of the crime.[32]

But a more sinister view is provided by Rob Cooper (among others) writing in the *Daily Mail*, who states that the United States knew prior to the deployment of the Mustard and Sarine gas, what Iraq was going to do, but did nothing to stop its occurrence. According to retired United States Air Force Colonel, Rick Francona, who was working in Baghdad in 1988, "the Iraqis never told us that they intended to use nerve gas. They didn't have to. We already knew." On the contrary, the American's actually helped the Iraqis with their plan. It was only when foreign journalist got wind of what had happened and provided evidence as to what had been done by the Iraqis, that the United States down-played the role Iraq had played, instead cautioning *both* parties not to use chemical weapons.[33]

Hardly any actions, punitive or otherwise, were imposed on Iraq by the West for these horrific atrocities. It was not until the late 1990s when, according to Harris and Aid, the CIA, in an unclassified analysis of the war, altered its position radically, and frequently cited the Halabja massacre in justifying the possession of weapons of mass destruction by Iraq prior to the 2003 invasion of the country.[34]

Notwithstanding the time it took for the CIA to publicly point fingers in the right direction, the situation demands pause from those who require an understanding of American actions in the context of the war against the Islamists. While the United States knew of Iraq's plan to use chemical weapons (forbidden by international law), it not only did not do anything about it, but it placed the blame on Iran. By the same token, it would now like to remove Assad from his perch in Syria (which is what it should do on moral grounds), for reasons that are similar to those committed by Saddam. Could this type of reaction from the United States, although acceptable to most decent people in the world, be based not on what is morally or politically justifiable, but because it is willing to succumb to the to the wishes of its allies – Israel and the Arab states – just like it did in blaming Iran for what Iraq had done?

This kind of behavior reasserts the fact that the West does not care which direction the wind blows as long as it blows towards the fulfillment of its own political aspirations. While the manipulation of reasons for a particular task is the name of the game in geopolitics, such situations would be a bit less problematic if the United States does not blatantly accuse a country of an act committed by some other country, as it did with Iran.

Perhaps the United States, without being too morally ambitious, should do just what it has often done in the past — cough out an obscure grunt and then turn a blind eye to any country's internal violations - with one stipulation: it must be done as one identical grunt for all countries involved, including its allies, which are morally lacking. Ideally, Americans should not even bother with the "grunting" because it has no effect, unless of course, there is a quid pro quo situation that could be used as a part of an American-based solution. By the same token, it may not be in the United States' interest to police every country's human rights violations, particularly when the

West, for example, is often seen as a violator of its own civil laws with respect to minority populations. As an example, Sophia McClennen, professor of international affairs and comparative literature at the Pennsylvania State University, asserts that the construction of the Dakota Access Pipeline, which has been a cause of great concern for the Lakota Nation Native Americans, has racial overtones.[35] Irrespective of whether one agrees with McClennen or not, such opinions, rightly or wrongly, are also directed at the United States by other countries, just as the United States does to others around the world.

The Iranian Issue

The United States' relationship with Iran, as discussed in Chapter 9, needs to be re-assessed, with an eye towards the non-nuclear agreement as a guideline in evaluating its behavior over the years. In this context, it should be noted that such an action may not sit well with most Islamic countries, which are Sunni – and of course, Israel – but it may be a small price to pay in the long run to have a foundation of diplomacy in the region instead of a threat of military war or terrorist activities perpetuated against one another.

Iran's relationship with Saudi Arabia. For the sake of stability in the region, bringing Iran to the table in future discussions – as alluded earlier – especially in areas of Iranian interest, is likely an important cause-effect solution that could provide some obvious benefits. In the first place, it would appease millions of Shi'as around the world, many of whom look to Iran as one of the very few recognizable Shi'a countries, where most of the Twelvers sect of Shi'a Muslims live. Such a gesture would also likely invite the younger, increasingly pro-Western generation in Iran to look favorably upon the United

States when they come into power; hopefully in the not-too-distant future. Furthermore, trying to bring the Arabs and the Iranians together (even if only for communication purposes) may become, over the years, a useful tool for attaining peace and stability in the region.

Stifling communication with Iran, on the other hand, would beg an important question: What are the United States' reasons for not communicating with Iran?

One of the biggest sticking points for the Saudis has been the strength of the Lebanese Hezbollah movement (an Iranian ally), which was declared a "terrorist" organization in March 2016 by the 22 states of the Arab League. In this context, while Hezbollah was formed with assistance from Iran as a group to resist Israel's invasion and occupation of Lebanon in the early 1980s, it has now, according to Arab states, taken to terrorist activities in Yemen, where the Saudis and the Emiratis are fighting the Houthis; and has been assisting Assad in Syria.[36] It is ironic, but the same acts of terrorism, as stated in Chapter 8, are also levied against the Saudis in fighting the Houthis in Yemen.

According to Mousavian, Iran, on its part, needs to "acknowledge and take steps to alleviate the legitimate security concerns of the GCC states." He reminds the Iranians that the alternative to House of Saud in Saudi Arabia will be the "House Wahhab." On the other hand, Iran seems to have "been turned into a convenient scapegoat to distract Arab nations from the domestic factors that have been plaguing their lives." As Mousavian states:

> The people of Iran and the GCC states are condemned by geography to be neighbors forever. They would both benefit from living side by side in peace and harmony as opposed to viewing one another in a zero-sum manner.[37]

To this end, Mousavian provides a broad spectrum for cooperation and security in the Persian Gulf, which includes, among other things:

- Arms control
- Promotion of non-proliferation
- Establishment of a zone free from weapons of mass destruction
- Eventual conclusion of a non-aggression pact
- Undertaking a number of joint task forces on security, economic, cultural, scientific, environmental, and humanitarian cooperation

While the list Mousavian provides may seem overly ambitious, and would likely take a long time to achieve (even if all parties agree to arrive at the table), "this framework will allow Iran, Iraq and the GCC states to regularly engage in sincere dialogue to address their concerns and work with each other."[38]

From the West's point of view, it must be realized that if the Iranians are striving for hegemony in the region, so are the Arab states. If the Iranians are labelled as terrorists, there are reasons to believe that some Arab states are nothing short of promoting terrorism on their own as well as in conjunction with other countries. If history is what propels the United States in dealing with Iran, it should be noted that there may be some legitimacy, outlined earlier, as to why the Iranian Ayatollahs behave the way they do toward Americans. Besides, while Iran has been punished through sanctions, the errant behavior of countries like Saudi Arabia, Bahrain, and Kuwait is tolerated by the United States under the protection of their being "American allies."

While it may not be easy to facilitate negotiations between Saudi Arabia and Iran, it is important to note that every major political development of the post-Arab Spring period belies the belief that foreign powers can do little to respond to the conflicts and historical grudges in the region.[39] Iran may be a proud nation, but at the present it is also without any serious military hardware. However, just like Saddam Hussein, Iran is not likely to roll over and abide by whatever is dictated to it by the West. The time is now for the West to make some overtures of diplomacy with Iran. In this context, it may be worthwhile for the United States to gradually roll out a campaign in Washington to change policymaker views regarding the Iranians, and give them a chance to enter the capital's diplomatic scene.

The isolation of Iran is in no way helpful in achieving stability in the region, especially now that it is likely to have other military sponsors that would include Russia and perhaps even China (at a later stage). In the end, the situation rests on whether we need another North Korea, or have a more cordial if not a very friendly nation in the Middle East. If Iran fails to cooperate, the sanctions that worked well can be reapplied, although this time around, it may not be followed by all parties concerned, particularly those who are in direct confrontation with the United States, such as the Russians.

While President Trump's visit to Saudi Arabia has solidified the United States' relationship with its Arab allies, it has, in no way, diluted the volatile undercurrents in the region – the Qatar situation, is an example. Diplomacy and negotiations can be the real source for stability in the region because it does not create a burden of hatred for its people to carry, when force is used to promote an acceptation of behavior - especially in an era where terrorist activities have become a true arsenal of war. Such negotiations, however, would require, as stated in Chapters 8 and 9, a change in the status quo between the United States with its

Arab allies and Iran, and perhaps with Israel, and in working diligently towards an end to the Israeli-Palestinian conflict.

In this context, the United States' hegemonic control of the Persian Gulf area is riding high with President Trump's assurances of the Americans "being on their side." The American relationship with Saudi Arabia that once seemed to be teetering, is now far from toppling, despite the likelihood of Saudis' dogmatic behavior in sometimes having gone against the wishes of the United States. However, Martenson questions such a relationship between Saudi Arabia and the United States on moral grounds by asking where the sense of responsibility lies in the United States being the primary arms dealer to the Saudis.[40] It seems that the main driving objective for the United States in its relationship with the Arab countries is to keep the Saudis happy, with the understanding that political aspirations are more important than innocent lives -- such as in Yemen. But the question then becomes why innocent deaths in Syria are based on a moral imperative, but in Yemen it becomes strictly a political issue? If the United States can use a somewhat placating policy especially designed for the Muslims in the Persian Gulf (including Iran), its relationship with Arab countries may be a bit turbulent in the short-term, but in the long-run it may be just what it needs to do in creating a more peaceful world environment, and win back its slightly "shaken" worldwide goodwill. As it stands, most of the Middle Eastern autocrats are siding with the United States, but it would be to our benefit if we could win over their people, too. Not everyone can be pacified, but it sure would help if the United States kept an eye in that direction. As Shadi Hamid and David Vine have argued, economy building, instead of enforcing a military policy, may be a better solution to achieving peace in the Middle East.[41] In this context, a lesson can be learnt from the Chinese who are investing heavily in Africa and South America, although they do not have the burden of outwardly providing peace in the region in which they operate, as does the United States.

An evaluation of Iranian and Saudi behavior. While it is understandable why Iran may be playing a role in Bahrain that is generally reserved for the United States and the West – trying to right an internal injustice - Iran must realize that such problems are country-based, and instigating a civil war in any country is likely to have adverse consequences against it. There is nothing Iran can do about what it perceives to be atrocities against its Shi'a brethren because it simply does not have the military power for such activities (unlike the Russians in their hostile takeover in Ukraine). Besides its need for Saudi Arabia as a place of pilgrimage is much more important than Saudi's need for Iran. At the most, it can resort to terroristic activities, and exist as a depressed economy within the sanctions that are applied against it, but a more beneficial activity would be to gain the trust of the United States and Europe and then bring up the subject of violation of minority rights once such trust is well established. This, however, is not an overnight process. It will take a long time to attain, but it is doable if Iran indeed has plans for a prosperous future for its citizens, and the West deals with it with a decorum of civility and respect.

On the other side of the coin, one can understand the dilemma the Saudi government faces in dealing with Iran. Saudi Arabia has an extremely conservative population, and as a guardian of Islam's holiest places, it has to be very careful in how it manages the wishes of it population, especially the restless Egyptian Salafist population in the country, many of whom are associated with the Muslim Brotherhood. While it may be a bit disconcerting for Westerners and the Shi'a Muslim population that Abdul Rahman al-Sudais was allowed to practice as an imam after only being reprimanded for his remarks against the Jews, the Shi'as and other non-Sunnis (see Chapter 10), it is important to note that it is all what the ruling party could do to avoid a civil conflict in the country. In this respect, the ruling party is likely better off in subduing descent from the smaller Shi'a population in the country, than in riling up the ultra-conservative majority Sunni Muslims. It is this balancing act that the ruling party has to undertake – partly a result of their own preferences – that restricts its hand in dealing with its neighbors. Therefore, it is not so much that one expects them to throw their arms around the Iranians in friendship, but to start a dialogue with them in the interest of stability in the region. Such an outcome for long-term stability can only happen if the United States changes its attitude toward Iran and promotes a diplomatic policy in the region rather than a culture of military strength.

However, in the context of friendly relationship between the countries, it does not mean that Iran should surrender its need for an important role among the Persian Gulf countries as the largest Shi'a nation in the world, but it, as well as Saudi Arabia, need to understand that pre-learned hostility against each other is to no one's advantage. Simply using military force against Iran is not workable because Iran has more stomach to use terrorism in the region that could become a major problem for the Arabs. Besides, any kind of military undertaking between these countries could mobilize a "Persian Gulf Spring" that may not work well for all parties concerned. From Western point of view, it would be to its advantage to encourage both Iran and Saudi Arabia to let diplomacy play a role. By the same token, if there are any expectations by the West of Iran crawling on its knees to be reiterated within the community of the Middle East, it is likely not to happen.

The Effects of Colonialism in the Middle East

Aside from the distrust between the Shi'as and the Sunnis, the Arabs and the Persians, the Arabs against Qatar, the Muslim Brotherhood against some countries, and the populations against the autocrats, part of the problem in the Middle East can be related to history that has affected Eastern beliefs through Western colonization (except for the United States). According to Sandra Marker, "intractable conflict is found in many areas that were once colonized or controlled by Western European or Soviet powers (e.g., Africa, the Balkans, Southeast Asia, the Middle East, South America). The source of many of these protracted conflicts, in large part, lies in past colonial or Soviet policies" that promoted cultural, ethnic, moral, and political practices based on the inherent belief that Westerners were superior to the peoples of the East.[42] Among the most damaging of these policies were those regarding "territorial boundaries, the treatment of indigenous populations, the privileging of some groups over others, the uneven distribution of wealth, local governmental infrastructures," and the acknowledgment or formation of non-democratic or non-participatory governmental systems that helped the colonists' agenda.[43]

In the context of the Middle East specifically, Mohammed Abu-Nimer, a professor at the American University whose specialty is in peace and conflict resolution at the School of International Service, states that one needs to understand the history of colonialism and occupation that characterizes and affects, to some extent, the peace-building and conflict resolution in the region. According to Abu-Nimer, due to the historical memory of foreign occupancy, people are more suspicion of the motivation behind peace-building efforts if the effort comes from the Western hemisphere. People in the Middle East will always balance the cost of allowing foreign "help" in terms of what the *real* benefit would be for them. Based on the history of colonization, people in the region have doubts about the purpose for the help – as a tool to have the locals adapt to Western culture through a change in "their religious and cultural identity."[44]

Abu-Nimer also points out that because of the wars in the Middle East and the nature of the foreign policy of the United States in the region, concerns have been raised among Muslims as to who is funding "this type of work," and whether American policy in the Middle East is merely a biased extension of its policy with Israel. In such a scenario, the professor cautions that it is always important for Middle Easterners to identify the type of funding and its source.[45] If the funding, for example, is given through autocrats or dictators, it may never be dispersed to the common people, or perhaps dispersed under conditions that are specifically dictated by the donor to further the autocrat's and the donor's own agenda.

There are people in the West who cannot understand the in-fighting among Muslim nations in the Middle East, comparing their expectations of order in the region to that in Europe. But as Hamid points out, unlike the EU which has the ability to embed the individual concerns of European countries within a "thick regional order," there is no such comparable mechanism that exists in the Arab world. At the same time, however, he argues that the United States could have enveloped struggling democracies within a mutually beneficial regional order under the assumption provided by growing academic literature, which has pointed to the importance of international actors in bringing down autocrats elsewhere in the world.[46] The author substantiates his arguments by referencing the work of political scientists Steven Levitsky and Lucan Way, who, through extensive empirical support, explain that "it was an externally driven shift in the cost of suppression, not changes in domestic conditions, that contributed most centrally to the demise of authoritarianism in the 1980s and 1990s." In this context, Levitsky and Way find that countries' vulnerability to Western democratizing pressure was often quite decisive.[47]

A Summary Evaluation of the Middle East

In analyzing the situation in the Middle East, there are two aspects that should be considered: (1) the policies of the autocrats to preserve their rule and/or flaunt their oil-inflated importance in the world; and (2) cognizance of the sentiments of the population in the region. Because many pluralistic countries in the region are not constitutional democracies, and the governance of these and other Muslim countries (including most of those based in Asia) is based on Sharia law, they, as stated earlier, allow religion to dictate state policies. While the expectations of the rulers of some of these countries, such as Saudi Arabia, *may* be to keep the two aspects of their rule separated, religion often dictates foreign policy, partly because of the rulers' own religious beliefs, but also because of possible expectations of their people. However, even though many of these rulers' and dictators' fates are tied to the expectations of their people, the will of the people has, and will always be, secondary to the ruler's staying in power. Sometimes, for example, it is important for the autocrats to play a geopolitical game that may not be entirely in the interest of their people, often going beyond the demands of religion to preserve their rule. Unfortunately, this mishmash of contradictions in preserving their rule is likely one reason that riled the Islamists (especially Al-Qaeda) to confront their rulers and demand freedom from the West's influence in the region.

By the same token, there are other opinions that discourage the West's "interference" in the governing "affairs" of other countries, particularly related to regime-building. Harold Pinter in his acceptance speech for the Nobel Prize in 2005, criticized the United States as brutal, scornful, and ruthless in its dealings with the rest of the world. According to Mr. Pinter, Americans engendered every right-wing military dictatorship in the world after the Second World War, including Brazil, Paraguay, Haiti, Turkey, the Philippines, Guatemala, El Salvador, and Chile.[48] Notwithstanding the possibility of some stretching of truth in Mr. Pinter's assertions, the fact remains that the United States has a badly muddled foreign policy that has backfired on it on more than one occasion. It is perhaps with some guilt that the West should realize the folly of the United States in arming the Taliban in the Soviet-Afghan conflict and supplying arms to Saddam Hussein after Iraq was removed from a list of state sponsors of terrorism in 1982. Similarly, it was with the help of the United States' CIA and Israel's Mossad that the feared SAVAK (secret police) was set up in Iran under Mohammed Reza Shah Pahlavi (1957-1979) for internal security in preserving the rule of the Shah.[49]

Even in the immediate past, not accounting for the overthrow of Saddam Hussein from power, the ousting of Qaddafi, without making provisions for Libya's governance after his demise, was yet one more hotbed created in the Middle East by the West. The irony, however, is that instead of the United States and the West trying to placate the Muslim world for what in some cases have been their mistakes, there is an outflowing of rhetoric from some Westerners as to how badly the Muslims behave and how they should be punished for their violence and destabilization of the world.

Without passing judgment on the way the United States fights terrorism and orchestrates regime-building, one thing remains clear — the West has learnt nothing from past mistakes. It simply makes additions or assigns different interpretations to its laws when it is faced with a problem, without seemingly any consideration of its actions' long-term consequences, both at home and abroad. In this context, it is easy for a country to create a mass acceptance of the changes in its policies with carefully choreographed verbal usage, such as all actions committed in the *"interest"* of the public, or for the *"security"* of the people. The tactic is not new. Many countries in the East and the West have used it. Indira Gandhi's government declared the Emergency Act in India during its war with Pakistan, which provided a postponement of elections for, of course, "the good of the country."

Osama bin Laden and al-Baghdadi have used similar methods, such as employing an ideology (Islamism) in riling public support for the attacks on their perceived enemies, and to encourage acceptance of their actions. This tactic has worked well for them, especially among the non-educated, who have no understanding of their religion other than what is related to them by the Islamists. In the words of a sage old cabby in Toronto: "This is ingenious. Osama did not have a country to rally support for his cause, so he used religion. Religion is his nation and it encompasses so many different countries." Make no mistake, however, that the last word so far belongs to the terrorists. Americans may have killed Osama bin Laden, but he changed the way we had lived without fear in our adequately protected, flimsy veneer of national security, and the negligible economic burden associated with it.

From the point of view of some lay Muslims, it is often felt that every move of the United States is in its own interest, although in the case of many countries in the Middle East, the United States' relationship, as stated in Chapter 8, is symbiotic.

However, there are places in northeast Africa and the Middle East where Western countries, acting alone or through NATO, have provided different experiences. For example, Nicola Nasser, in a 2007 report for the *Asian Tribune*, states that the United States created a violent hotbed in the Horn of Africa by promoting an Ethiopian invasion of Somalia in 2006, which projected a clear American message that no "Arab or Muslim metropolitan has impunity" unless it falls into line with the United States' vital regional interest.[50] While such a statement (although written by a veteran journalist) *may* lean towards a personal opinion or bias, it does reflect the underlying discontent with the United States in parts of Africa and the Middle East.

Dealing with the Islamists

The United States, as it stands, is faced with a wide variety of turbulent conflicts around the world, which may make it difficult for it to concentrate on its geopolitical plans; but nonetheless it is important for the Americans to do just that. This is even more important for the United States in retaining its hegemony status in the world, considering the emergence of China as a massive economic power (spreading goodwill through investments), and Russia's nuclear capacity. However, as stated earlier, the United States has one basic advantage over the Russians and the Chinese: except for some Muslims residing in the Middle East (not their rulers), the world still likes Americans much more than either the Chinese or the Russians. Therein lies the United States' greatest advantage. In all such cases, it should be remembered that America is not perfect, but it scores points over others in a comparative sense, based on how much the other two countries are *not* globally trusted.

For the time being, it is with some sadness that one realizes the impact caused by the Islamists in turning our world upside down. In this context, it is sometimes very hard to preserve the ideologies on which America was built, because the rule-of-law seems to have been outpaced by the necessity for our survival. As mentioned in Chapter 11, the expectation of Muslims in a community to turn fellow Muslims on the foreknowledge of their plans to commit terrorism is an idealistic endeavor, just as it is for domestic terrorists to be apprehended via the information provided by its community members prior to their acts of terrorism. However, this does not negate the importance of providing information arising from a *suspicion* of potential terroristic activities to the authorities. This should always be foremost on Muslim minds, even if at times, the wrong person is profiled as a result of misinformation.

To stretch the point further, while every effort should be made to help reinstate or relocate (with compensation) those who are wrongfully identified back into the community, the real problem arises when parts of a community not only supports Islamist activities, but they even help radicalize regular Muslims in the West to Islamism. This is a serious problem, because it indicates that Islamists cells exist in the West for the purpose of recruitment and causing serious damage in the West and other countries. In fact, this is tantamount to creating an emirate within the West to nurture future Islamists and spread Islamism, just like it is now being done in Libya.

Such activity, for the time being, is less a problem for the United States than it is for Europe, where assimilation or integration of Muslims has never been actualized, and there is easier movement for Islamists from one EU country to another. In most such cases, debates persist with respect to human rights laws for the country's citizens, or bending rules in order to control the perceived possibility of a breach in the nation's security. For all our grandiose plans in abiding by our principles and the rule of law, there may be a breaking point, based on the number of Islamist attacks in the West and the number of people killed by them, when rules of equity and fairness *may* be trampled upon, taking second place to the rights of Muslim citizens in the West. There is little doubt that Daesh will eventually be defeated on the ground in Iraq and Syria, although the demise of Al-Qaeda may take longer, because it follows a less-centralized management policy than Daesh. Al-Qaeda activities from its headquarters in Pakistan or Afghanistan are hard to monitor, despite many drone successes in the region. It is not quite clear how thin the United States can spread itself in drone and air force activities to drive the Islamists out of Syria and Libya, although it has had major successes, such as driving Daesh out of Iraq, and being on the verge of retaking Daesh's caliphate, Raqqa, in Syria. It has also ramped up air-strikes against the Islamists in Yemen, and "drone-killed" a second-ranking Al-Qaeda official, Abu al-Khayr al-Masri (after Ayman al-Zawahiri) in Syria. *The New York Times* reports that according to Charles Lister, a senior fellow at the Brookings' Middle East Institute, the death of Mr. Masri was the most significant blow to Al-Qaeda's global network since the killing of its number two official, Nasir al-Wuhayshi, in June 2015.[51]

But aside from successful military activities, it is the political game being played that often prevents a positive outcome. For example, if there is truth to Turkey siding with al-Nusra (and perhaps Daesh) in attacking the Kurds and Assad (as stated in Chapter 12), then it may have the adverse effects of inadvertently providing room for Al-Qaeda to expand its base from Syria into Europe and Africa. On the other hand, al-Nusra may have modified its "objectives" and is only interested in driving out Assad from the region, although it is officially considered a terrorist by the United States and its Western allies.

In the final analysis, killing Al-Qaeda and Daesh leaders, and reclaiming lost territories will be a definite demoralizing factor for the Islamists. At the same time, the issue of what happens to Syria after Daesh is driven out of Raqqa, hangs heavy on Western minds. In this context, negotiations between the United States and Russia will have to ensue to determine the governing policies in Syria, particularly in "American-zone" areas where the Syrian Opposition Party and/or the Kurds are likely to dominate.

By the same token, it is important to understand that while defeating the Islamists militarily is likely to occur in the near future, defeating the "idea" propagated by the Islamists will not be that easy. Some may argue that al-Baghdadi's death will end the desire of a caliphate by Daesh followers. While there is certainty of driving Baghdadi out of Raqqa among most experts on the subject, there is a likelihood that "less-capable" leaders will rise to continue their ideological terrorist activities in the West. There is also a likelihood that many Daesh followers may join Al-Qaeda and continue with their sporadic attacks of terrorism across the world. But, with Daesh and Al-Qaeda leaders killed, and the physical ousting of its followers from their areas of control, international terrorism will likely fall back a step or two, and hopefully will become a case-by-case concern rather than a major world-wide issue. Also, an effort at winning over the people of the Middle East through diplomacy and investments will go a long way in defeating the "idea." Until that happens, our beliefs, reliant on our framework for abiding by a system of laws, may have to be balanced against the desire to preserve our way of life.

Appendix

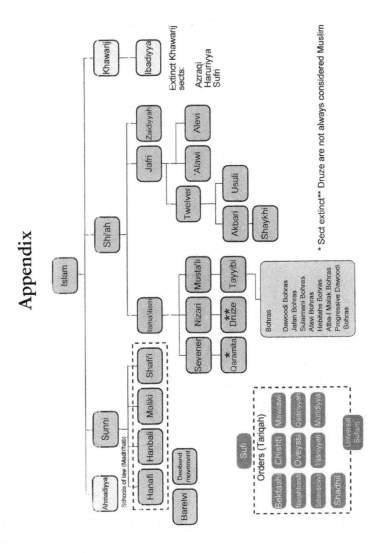

Figure 1. Different branches of Islam.[1]

339

Notes

Preface

1. Simon Cottee, "What's the Right Way to Think About Religion and ISIS?" *The Atlantic*, July 12, 2016, https://www.theatlantic.com/international/archive/2016/07/religion-isis-orlando/490958/.
2. Michael K. Nagata, in "In Battle to Defang ISIS, United States Targets Its Psychology," Eric Schmitt, *The New York Times*, December 28, 2014, http://www.nytimes.com/ 2014/12/29/us/politics//in-battle-to-defang-isis-us-targets-its-psychology-.html? _r=0.
3. Ibid
4. Chris Martenson, "About Chris Martenson," *PeakProsperity*, https://www.peakprosperity.com/about.
5. There are different names given to the area that includes Iran, Oman, the United Arab Emirates, Saudi Arabia, Qatar, Kuwait, and Iraq. The Arab countries prefer to call this area the "Arabian Gulf." However, in this book, "Persian Gulf," as an extension of the Arabian Sea, is used because the AP Stylebook (2000) dictates that "Persian Gulf" is the "long-established name" and, therefore, the best choice.

6. Eric Lipton, Brooke Williams and Nicholas Confessore, "Foreign Powers Buy Influence at Think Tanks," *The New York Times*, September 6, 2014, http://www.nytimes.com/2014/09/07/us/politics/foreign-powers-buy-influence-at-think-tanks.html?_r=0.

7. Amos Jones, in "Foreign Powers Buy Influence at Think Tanks," Eric Lipton, Brooke Williams et al., *The New York Times*, September 6, 2014, http://www.nytimes.com/2014/09/07/us/politics/foreign-powers-buy-influence-at-think-tanks.html?_r=0.

8. Saleem Ali, in "Foreign Powers Buy Influence at Think Tanks," Eric Lipton, Brooke Williams et al., *The New York Times*, September 6, 2014, http://www.nytimes.com/2014/09/07/us/politics/foreign-powers-buy-influence-at-think-tanks.html?_r=0.

9. Max Fisher, "How Saudi Arabia captured Washington." *Vox*. March 21, 2016. http://www.vox.com/2016/3/21/11275354/saudi-arabia-gulf-washington.

10. Terrence Cullen, "Trump Appointee Making Six Figures As Lobbyist For Saudi Arabia," *New York Daily News*, June 22, 2017, http://www.nydailynews.com/news/politics/trump-appointee-making-figures-lobbyist-saudi-arabia-article-1.3268751.

Introduction

1. The word "apostasy" comes from the Greek *apostasia*. Apostates, in a religious sense, are those who fall away from the "true" faith, abandoning what they formerly professed to believe.

Part I: Fundamental Knowledge for Understanding Islamism and Islamist Ideologies

Chapter 1: It's All in the Semantics

1. Faisal Irshaid, "Isis, Isil, IS or Daesh? One Group, Many Names," *BBC News: Middle East*, December 2, 2015, http://www.bbc.com/news/world-middle-east-27994277.

2. Alice Gutherie, "Decoding Daesh: Why Is the New Name for ISIS So Hard to Understand?" *Free Word*, February 19, 2015, https://www.freewordcentre.com/explore/daesh-isis-media-alice-guthrie.

3. Nicola Oakley and Suchandrika Chakrabarti, "What Does Daesh Mean? ISIS 'Threatens to Cut Out the Tongues' of Anyone Using this Word," *Mirror Online*, July 26, 2016, http://www.mirror.co.uk/news/world-news/what-daesh-mean-isis-threatens-6841468.

4. Mathew Weaver, "Syria Debate: The Linguistic Battle Over What to Call Islamic State," *The Guardian*, December 3, 2015, https://www.theguardian.com/world/2015/dec/02/syria-debate-the-linguistic-battle-over-what-to-call-islamic-state.

5. Ibn Warraq, "Virgins? What Virgins?" *The Guardian*, January 11, 2002, https://www.theguardian.com/books/2002/jan/12/books.guardianreview5.

6. Al-Ghazali and Al-Ash'ari, in *Encyclopedia of Islam (Third Edition): Middle East and Islamic Studies*, eds. Kate Fleet, Gudrun Krämer et al., *Brill Online Reference Works*, http://referenceworks.brillonline.com/search?s.f.s2_parent=s.f.book.encyclopaedia-of-islam-

3&s.q=Al-+Ghazali+and+Al-Ash%27ari+sensual+plea
sures+in+paradise.

7. N.J. Dawood, in "Virgins? What Virgins?" Ibn
    Warraq, *The Guardian*, January 11, 2002, https://
    www.theguardian.com/books/2002/jan/12/books.
    guardianreview5.

8. Ibid.

9. Christoph Luxenberg, transl., *The Syro-Aramaic
    Reading of the Koran: A Contribution to the Decoding of
    the Koran* (Berlin: Verlag Hans Schiller, 2007), 247–
    283, http://www.aramaic-dem.org/English/History/
    Christoph%20Luxenberg.pdf.

10. Ibn Warraq, "Virgins? What virgins?"

11. Interview with Qanta Ahmed, "'Rubbish' to Argue
    Saying 'Islamism' Tars All Muslims: Naming the
    Problem Legitimizes Anti-Islamist Muslims Like
    Me," *Kilmeade and Friends*, Fox News with Ian
    Hanchett, June 20, 2016, http://www.breitbart.com/
    video/2016/06/20/qanta-ahmed-rubbish-to-argue-
    saying-islamism-tars-all-muslims-naming-the-
    problem-legitimizes-anti-islamist-muslims-like-me/.

12. Daniel Pipes, "Distinguishing between Islam and
    Islamism," Center for Strategic and International
    Studies, *Middle East Forum*, June 30, 1998, *http://www.
    danielpipes.org/954/distinguishing-between-islam-and-
    islamism*.

13. Qanta Ahmed, in "Islamism Is Not Islam," *National
    News Review*, September 11, 2015, http://www.
    nationalreview.com/article/423866.

14. The exclusion of Iran, and its infamous Revolutionary
    Guard and their associates (e.g. Hezbollah in
    Lebanon) from being in the same league as the

Islamists, requires an explanation. Iran is not included in the definition of "Islamists" because it does not have expectations of the spread of a religious ideology, and is not directly at war with the West. For example, while the Americans bomb Al-Qaeda in Afghanistan/Pakistan, and Daesh in Syria, Iraq, and Libya, it takes part in no such aggression against Iran. In Syria, there may be a problem regarding the Iranians siding with Russia against Assad, and the Houthis in Yemen against Saudi Arabia, but Iranians have also fought alongside the United States in fighting Daesh in Iraq. By the same token, no direct terroristic activities have been recorded in recent years by Iran against the West.

While Iran, under hardliner President Mahmoud Ahmadinejad, was determinedly anti-American, the policies in Iran under the new president, Hassan Rouhani, are quite different, as specified by Jim Muir in "How Iran fell out with the West," *BBC News: Middle East*, July 17, 2015, http://www.bbc.com/news/world-middle-east-33552911. As Muir points out, though the nuclear deal is strictly confined to that issue, both sides seem to think that it will provide the basis for a gradual warming of United States-Iranian ties, and the eventual co-operation on stabilizing the region's many conflicts where Iran is a key player (directly or by proxy), including those in Iraq, Syria, Lebanon, and Yemen. In Lebanon, for example, Western diplomats have, for several years, made no secret of the fact that they see Iranian-backed Hezbollah as a stabilizing factor, given the deadlier threat they perceive from radical Sunni Islam, especially the self-professed Islamic state, Daesh.

Chapter 2: Comparing Religious Scriptures, and Sharia Law

1. Pipes, "Distinguishing between Islam and Islamism."
2. Rori Donaghy and Mary Atkinson, "Crime and Punishment, Islamic State vs. Saudi Arabia," *Middle East Eye*, October 13, 2015, http://www.middleeasteye. net/news/crime-and-punishment-islamic-state-vs-saudi-arabia-1588245666.
3. Religion and Public Life, "The World's Muslims: Religion, Politics and Society," *Pew Research Center*, April 30, 2013, http://www.pewforum.org/2013/04/30/the-worlds-muslims-religion-politics-society-overview/.
4. Nicholas Kristof, "How Well Do You Know religion?" *The New York Times: Sunday Review*, December 12, 2015, http://www.nytimes.com/interactive/2015/12/13/ opinion/sunday/13kristof-how-well-do-you-know-religion.html?_r=0.5. D. M. Murdock, "What does the Koran say about Women?" *Freethought Nation*, August 16, 2011. http://freethoughtnation.com/what-does-the-koran-say-about-women/.
6. Kevin Abdullah Karim, "Does Islam really allow wife beating," *Nour*, http://www.nour-dv.org.uk/tafseer-surah-434-does-islam-really-allow-wife-beating/.
7. This quote and the subsequent explanation about Saint Bernard and his beliefs regarding heretics ("Cathars and Cathar Beliefs in the Languedoc: Who's Who in the Languedoc during the Cathar Period," http:// www.cathar.info/cathar_whoswho.htm#bernard) is horrifically similar to Daesh's current rhetoric about the glorification by God for one dies while killing heretics.

Bernard of Clairvaux belonged to a religious group, the Cathars, who appeared in Europe in the eleventh century. Records from the Roman Catholic Church mention them under various_names and in various places. Regarding heretics, Barnard held that "it would without doubt be better that they should be coerced by the sword than that they should be allowed to draw away many other persons into their error" (Serm. lxvi. on Canticles ii. 15). Killing god's enemies was not merely permitted, but glorious. He asserted in a letter to the Templars: "The Christian who slays the unbeliever in the Holy War is sure of his reward, the more sure if he himself is slain. The Christian glories in the death of the pagan, because Christ is thereby glorified." He also pointed out that anyone who kills an unbeliever does not commit homicide but malicide (St Bernard, *De Laude Novae Militiae*, III [De Militibus Christi)]). For him, all infidels were creatures of Satan.

After questioned about how heretics could bear the agony of the fire not only with patience but even joy, Bernard answered in a sermon that he ascribed the steadfastness of heretical "dogs" in facing death to the power of the devil (Serm. lxvi. on Canticles ii. 15).

Bernard's comments justifying the killing of God's supposed enemies are echoed in the massacres carried out by a later famous Cistercian abbot and military commander, Arnaud Amaury, the Abbot of Citeaux, who at Béziers is credited with the immortal command "Kill Them All, God will know his own."

While Catholic theologians have debated for centuries whether Cathars were Christian or Christian heretics, Bernard was canonized in 1174 and declared a Doctor of the Roman Catholic Church in 1830. The question is apparently still open. Roman Catholics still refer to the Cathar belief as "the Great Heresy," though the official Catholic position is that Catharism is not Christian at all — just as the vast majority of Muslims do not regard the Islamists as Muslims.

8. Hasan Al-Banna, *15 Misquotes from the Quran (Part 2)*, http://www.aboutjihad.com/ terrorism/quran_misquote_part_2.php.

9. Gregory M. Davis, "Islam 101," *Jihad Watch*, https://www.jihadwatch.org/islam-101

10. Al-Banna, *15 Misquotes from the Quran (Part 2)*.

11. Muhammad Hisham Kabbani and Seraj Hendricks, "Jihad: A Misunderstood Concept from Islam — What Jihad is, and is Not," *The Islamic Supreme Council of America*, http://islamicsupremecouncil.org/understanding-islam/legal-rulings/5-jihad-a-misunderstood-concept-from-islam.html?start=9.

Scriptures of most religions (including Islam, Christianity, and Judaism) are faced with the problem of "contradictory" statements being interpreted differentially to espouse one meaning over the other. The importance of the definition of a word becomes a "following" when it is defined by an authoritative body to which the majority in the group subscribe. Those who do not follow what is generally accepted by a population then become an "aberrant" group, who are basically defined by a different identity. These aberrant groups become a recognizable force by the propensity of numbers they present — for example, the Protestants separating from the Catholics.

In Islam, the Islamists, as portrayed in this book, are also defined differently. Their ideology is completely unacceptable to the clear majority of Muslims. In fact, following the Islamism is done by such a minute fraction of the Muslim population that they should likely be relegated to the same status as, for example, the Dutch Reform movement in Christianity that considered the Africans as inferior to the white race. The movement never become a Christian issue because most Christians did not accept it. Similarly, most Muslims, whether Sunnis, Shi'as, or Sufis, do not believe in the concept of military jihad as is understood and enforced by the Islamists, and, therefore, consider the group a separate entity that has no meaningful link to Muslims or the principles of Islam.

12. Imam Safi'i, in "Jihad: A Misunderstood Concept from Islam — What Jihad is, and is not: Footnotes," Muhammad Hisham Kabbani and Seraj Hendricks, *The Islamic Supreme Council of America*, http://islamicsupremecouncil.org/understanding-islam/legal-rulings/5-jihad-a-misunderstood-concept-from-islam.html?start=9.

13. Kabbani and Hendricks, in "Jihad: A Misunderstood Concept from Islam — What Jihad Is, and Is Not."

14. Jamal Badawi, in *15 Misquotes from the Quran (Part 2)*, Hasan Al-Banna, http://www.aboutjihad.com/terrorism/quran_misquote_part_2.php.

15. David Radier, in "Koran a Book of Peace, Not War, Scholars Say," Peter Standring, *National Geographic Today*, September 25, 2001, http://news.nationalgeographic.com/news/2001/09/0925_TVkoran.html.

16. Sulayman S. Nyang, in "Koran a Book of Peace, Not War, Scholars Say," Peter Standring, *National Geographic Today*, September 25, 2001, http://news.nationalgeographic.com/news/   2001/09/0925_TVkoran.html.

17. Michael G. Knapp, in "The Concept and Practice of Jihad in Islam," *Parameters*, (2003): 82–94, http://ssi.armywarcollege.edu/pubs/parameters/articles/03spring/knapp.htm.

18. Dawood, "Virgins? What virgins?"

19. Scott B. Rae, "Views of Wealth in the Bible and the Ancient World,"*Action Institute: Religion and Liberty*, 12 (2010), https://acton.org/pub/religion-liberty/volume-12-number-6/views-wealth-bible-and-ancient-world;

20. Farhad Shafti, "Sunnah vs. Hadith," *Exploring Islam: The Path of Devotion to the Truth*, February 2013, http://www.exploring-islam.com/difference-between-sunnah-and-hadith.html.

21. "An Introduction to the Science Of Hadith: The Classification Of Hadith: According to the Reliability and Memory of Reporters," *Islamic Awareness*, http://www.islamic-awareness.org/Hadith/Ulum/asb7.html.

22. Jan Michiel Otto's quote from a research paper on twelve Muslim countries commissioned by the Netherlands Ministry of Foreign Affairs, part of which are incorporated in *Saudi Arabia: Criminal Laws, Regulations and Procedures Handbook* (Washington: International Business Publications, 2016), 65–73.

23. Pipes, "Distinguishing between Islam and Islamism."

24. Marshall Breger, "Marshall Breger: Why Jews Can't Criticize Sharia Law," *Moment*, May 10, 2017, https://

www.momentmag.com/why-jews-cant-criticize-sharia-law/.

25. Rabbi Jon Hausman, in Marshall Breger, "Marshall Breger: Why Jews Can't Criticize Sharia Law," *Moment*, May 10, 2017, https://www.momentmag.com/why-jews-cant-criticize-sharia-law/.

26. Breger, "Marshall Breger: Why Jews Can't Criticize Sharia Law."

27. David Yerushalmi, in Marshall Breger, "Marshall Breger: Why Jews Can't Criticize Sharia Law," *Moment*, May 10, 2017, https://www.momentmag.com/why-jews-cant-criticize-sharia-law/.

28. Breger, "Marshall Breger: Why Jews Can't Criticize Sharia Law."

29. Imam Youssoupha Sarr, "A Jihad Against Pollution in Senegal," Robyn Purchia, *Planet Save*, August 11, 2015, http://planetsave.com/2015/08/11/a-jihad-against-pollution-in-senegal/.

30. Ahmad Shafaat, "The Punishment of Apostasy in Islam," *Islamic Perspectives*, February 2006, http://www.islamicperspectives.com/apostasy1.htm.

Chapter 3: An Eastern Mind Shaped by Western Policies

1. Religion and Public Life, "The World's Muslims: Religion, Politics and Society."

2. Bruce Riedel, in *Israeli-Palestinian Peace: What Is the United States National Security Interest? How Can It Be Achieved?*; Bruce Riedel, Frank Anderson, Philip Wilcox, and Brian Katulis, *Middle East Policy Council*, January 20, 2011, Edited transcript of Capitol Hill

conference with Thomas R. Mattair moderating, http://
www.mepc.org/journal/middle-east-policy-archives/
israeli-palestinian-peace-what-us-national-security-
interest?print.

3. Ibid.
4. Ibid.
5. Christopher Dickey, "Through the Looking Glass:
    This Is Why the U.S. Still Backs Saudi Arabia," *The
    Daily Beast World News*, April 22, 2016, http://www.
    thedailybeast.com/articles/2016/04/22/through-the-
    looking-glass-this-is-why-the-u-s-still-backs-saudi-
    arabia.html.
6. Riedel, *Israeli-Palestinian Peace: What Is the United States
    National Security Interest? How Can It Be Achieved?*
7. Khaled Abu Toameh, "Egyptians Hoping Israel Will
    Destroy Hamas," *Gatestone Institute: International Policy
    Council*, July 13, 2014, https://www.gatestoneinstitute.
    org/4401/egypt-israel-hamas.
8. Dieter Bednarz and Klaus Brinkbäumer Bednarz,
    "Interview with Egyptian President Sisi: 'Extremists
    Offend the Image of God,'" *Spiegel Online International*,
    February 9, 2015, http://www.spiegel.de/international/
    world/islamic-state-egyptian-president-sisi-calls-for-
    help-in-is-fight-a-1017434.html.
9. Toameh, "Egyptians Hoping Israel Will Destroy
    Hamas."
10. Robert Baer, "Why Saudi Arabia is Helping Crush the
    Muslim Brotherhood," *New Republic*, August 26, 2013,
    https://newrepublic.com/article/114468/why-saudi-
    arabia-helping-crush-muslim-brotherhood.

In the explanation of the *Ulama*, it should be
noted that this religious body serves a unique role by

providing religious legitimacy for Saudi rule. According to Global Security.org (http://www.globalsecurity.org/military/world/gulf/sa-ulama.htm), the kingdom's Ulama includes religious scholars, qadis (judges), lawyers, seminary teachers, and the prayer leaders (imams) of the mosques. From these representatives, prominent clergy are selected to constitute the members of the Council of Senior Ulama, an official body created by King Faisal in 1971 to serve as a forum for regular consultation between the monarch and the religious establishment.

11. Baer, "Why Saudi Arabia is Helping Crush the Muslim Brotherhood."

12. Peter Baker, "White House Weighs Terrorist Designation for Muslim Brotherhood," *The New York Times*, February 7, 2017, https://www.nytimes.com/2017/02/07/world/middleeast/muslim-brotherhood-terrorism-trump.html?_r=0.

13. Graham Usher, "The Democratic Resistance: Hamas, Fatah, and the Palestinian Elections," *Journal of Palestine Studies*, 35 (2006):20–26, doi:10.15625/jps.2006.35.3.20.

14. Jeroen Gunning, *Hamas in Politics: Democracy, Religion, Violence* (London: Hurst & Company, 2009), 203.

15. Ibid.

16. Samantha Borders, "Hamas's Role in the Future of the Israeli-Palestinian Conflict," *E-International Relations*, July 21, 2013, http://www.e-ir.info/2013/07/21/hamass-role-in-the-future-of-the-israeli-palestinian-conflict.

17. Ahmed Melhem, in "New Palestinian Initiative Outlines Fatah-Hamas Reconciliation," Trans. Pascale

Menassa, *Al Monitor: Palestinian Pulse*, August 25, 2106, http://www.al-monitor.com/pulse/originals/2016/08/committee-initiative-palestinian-reconciliation-hamas-fatah.html#ixzz4IqxrUsYB.

18. Tala'al Zahran, in "Shiite, Sunni, Wahhabi and the Israel-Gaza conflict," Howraa Zakery, *Communities Digital News* (CDN), July 31, 2014, http://www.commdiginews.com/world-news/shiite-sunni-wahhabi-and-the-israel-gaza-conflict-22803.

19. Yashwant Raj, *The Trump Presidency: US Ready to Shed Policy on Israel, Palestine, The Hindustan Times: htworld* (Mumbai), February 17, 2017, 14.

20. Hassan Yassim, in "Through the Looking Glass: This Is Why the U.S. Still Backs Saudi Arabia," Christopher Dickey, *The Daily Beast World News*, April 22, 2016, http://www.thedailybeast.com/articles/2016/04/22/through-the-looking-glass-this-is-why-the-u-s-still-backs-saudi-arabia.html.

21. Ehab Zahriveh, "Who Owns Jerusalem?" *Al Jazeera*, October 30, 2014, http://america.aljazeera.com/articles/2014/10/30/jerusalem-statusinternationalregime.html.

22. Ibid.

23. Oakland Ross, "How Israelis, Islamists Dehumanize Each Other," *Toronto Star*, March 21, 2009, https://www.thestar.com/news/2009/03/21/how_israelis_islamists_dehumanize_each_other.html.

24. Yossi Alpher, in "How Israelis, Islamists Dehumanize Each Other," Oakland Ross, *Toronto Star*, March 21, 2009, https://www.thestar.com/news/2009/03/21/how_israelis_islamists_dehumanize_each_other.html.

25. Yehuda Shaul, in "How Israelis, Islamists Dehumanize Each Other," Oakland Ross, *Toronto Star*, March 21, 2009, https://www.thestar.com/news/2009/03/21/how_israelis_islamists_dehumanize_each_other.html.

26. Gabriel Ben-Dor, in "How Israelis, Islamists Dehumanize Each Other," Oakland Ross, *Toronto Star*, March 21, 2009, https://www.thestar.com/news/2009/03/21/how_israelis_islamists_dehumanize_each_other.html.

27. Benjamin Weinthal, "Hamas Site Encourages Europe Attacks," *Jerusalem Post*, posted by Sacha Stawski, November 25, 2009, http://www.think-israel.org/nov09bloged.html.

28. Ahmed Abu Tawahina, in "How Israelis, Islamists Dehumanize Each Other," Oakland Ross, *Toronto Star*, March 21, 2009, https://www.thestar.com/news/2009/03/21/how_israelis_islamists_dehumanize_each_other.html.

29. "Abdel Fattah el Sisi," in *Alchetron: The Free Social Encyclopedia*, http://alchetron.com/Abdel-Fattah-el-Sisi-422541-W.

30. "Israel and the Arab World: The Enemy of My Enemies," *The Economist*, July 23, 2016, http://www.economist.com/news/middle-east-and-africa/21702476-arab-states-warm-israel-palestinians-feel-neglected-enemy-my.

31. Dickey, "Through the Looking Glass: This Is Why the U.S. Still Backs Saudi Arabia."

32. Hussein Rashid, in "Why Images of Mohammed Offend Muslims," Daniel Burke and CNN Staff, *CNN News*, May 4, 2015, http://www.cnn.com/2015/05/04/living/islam-prophet-images.

33. Sheikh Yasir Qadhi, in "Why Images of Mohammed Offend Muslims," Daniel Burke and CNN Staff, *CNN News*, May 4, 2015, http://www.cnn.com/2015/05/04/living/islam-prophet-images.

34. Rashid, "Why Images of Mohammed Offend Muslims."

35. Daniel Burke and CNN Staff, "Why Images of Mohammed Offend Muslims," *CNN News*, May 4, 2015, http://www.cnn.com/2015/05/04/living/islam-prophet-images.

36. Aurelien Hamelle, in "What Does French Law Really Say About Free Speech," *RFI: The World and All Its Voices*, January 23, 2015, http://en.rfi.fr/culture/20150114-what-does-french-law-really-say-about-free-speech/; Audio tape on French free speech laws in the context of *Charlie Hebdo* and Dieudonne: What is the scope (and limits) of French free speech?

37. Robert Mackey, in "Paris Mayor Plans to Sue Fox Over False Reports of 'No-Go Zones,'" *The New York Times*, January 20, 2015, https://www.nytimes.com/2015/01/21/world/europe/paris-mayor-plans-to-sue-over-news-of-no-go-zones.html?_r=0.

38. Anne K. Ruane, in "Freedom of Speech and Press: Exceptions to the First Amendment," *Congressional Research Service*, Prepared for Members of Committees of Congress, September 8, 2014, https://www.fas.org/sgp/crs/misc/95-815.pdf.

39. Hamelle, in "What Does French Law Really Say About Free Speech."

40. "Gaston v. Sun Services, LLC," March 26, 2014, 2–3, uploaded to *Scribd* by Dan Schwartz, https://www.scribd.com/document/225772159/Gaston-v-Sun-Services-LLC.

41. Hamelle, in "What Does French Law Really Say About Free Speech."

42. Ali Abunimah, in "France Begins Jailing People for Ironic Comments," *The Electronic Intifada*, January 2015, https://electronicintifada.net/blogs/ali-abunimah/france-begins-jailing-people-ironic-comments.

43. Omid Safi, in "Why Islam Forbids Images of Muhammad, Daniel Burke, Nick Thompson, et al., *CNN News*, January 8, 2015, http://www.cnn.com/2015/01/07/living/islam-prophet-images.

44. Akbar Ahmed, in "Why Islam Forbids Images of Muhammad, Daniel Burke, Nick Thompson, et al., *CNN News*, January 8, 2015, http://www.cnn.com/2015/01/07/living/islam-prophet-images.

45. Sayed Abul Ala Maududi, in "Isra and Miraj: The Miraculous Night Journey," *Islamicity*, May 4, 2016, http://www.islamicity.org/5843/isra-and -miraj-the-miraculous-night-journey/.

46. Javad Zarif, in "Iran Frees U.S. Sailors with Start of Nuclear Deal in Sight," Bozorgmehr Sharafedin and Phil Stewart, *Reuters*, January 14, 2016, http://www.reuters.com/article/us-usa-iran-boat-comment-idUSKCN0UR0K120160114.

Chapter 4: The Marriage of Religion and State Laws

1. To some Westerners, the word "madrassa" may conjure up images of children being initiated to a diabolical hatred of the West and preparation for a violent jihad. The negative connotation of the word "madrassa," as it is understood by some common English-speaking Westerners is, according to Pierre Tristam,

in "Glossary: Madrassa or Madrasa — A Quick Glimpse into Islamic Schools," *ThoughtCo*, March 29, 2017, https://www.thoughtco.com/glossary-madrassa-or-madrasa-2352961, evocative of a place where "fundamentalist, Islamic instruction is combined with anti-Western vocations, or in the extreme, as a place where terrorists are formed ideologically."

However, the truth of it is that "madrassa" is simply an Arabic word for school, and in the Arabic and Islamic world refers to any place of learning, in the same sense that the word "school" is used in the United States for various different learning institutions — similar to the word "school," "madrassa" can be used to refer to secular, vocational, religious or technical schools.

That being said, when a madrassa is funded or run by a religious body, the madrassa is likened to the model of Catholic schools in America, where subjects like math, history, and social sciences are often taught with an underlying adherence to religious and cultural belief. For example, the Saudi government's funding of madrassas would likely result in a school run on the basis of the ultra-conservative Wahhabi faith. However, even then, generally speaking, the extremely conservative madrassas do not preach violence against others.

Tristam, however, does state that the number of religious Islamic schools, particularly those dominated by the more fundamentalist strain of Islam, such as the Deobandi, Wahhabi, and Salafi strains, have been rising. Pakistan, for example, reported that religiously based madrassas increased from 245 to 6,870 between 1947 and 2001.

More importantly, however, the author reports that a few of these madrassas have produced militants, especially in Pakistan, where the government, in the 1980s, actively supported the formation of Islamic militias to fight in Kashmir and Afghanistan. Such deliberate efforts by a government some 25 years ago in creating a religious militia is a product of the region, and is no longer viewed as deliberately sanctioned by governments in the Middle East. As Tristam states, "overwhelmingly, madrassas are apolitical and provide instruction and boarding to the poorer segments of society — segments generally neglected by the state."

But, while Middle Eastern governments may not be promoting schools for the purpose of producing terrorists, the madrassas run by the Islamists *do* teach hatred and destruction of others who do not share the same ideology as them. It is in this context that "radical" or "radicalized" madrassas will be used in this book to demarcate the madrassas' association with the Islamists.

2. Pastor Rick Scarborough, in *Glaad*, https://www.glaad.org/cap/rick-scarborough.

3. Pipes, "Distinguishing between Islam and Islamism."

4. Nawaf E. Obaid, in "The Power of Saudi Arabia's Islamic Leaders," *Middle East Quarterly*, (1999): 51–58; "Islam in Saudi Arabia," *Revolvy*, https://www.revolvy.com/topic/Islam%20in%20Saudi%20Arabia&item_type=topic.

Part II: The Rise and Spread of Islamists

Chapter 5: Prominent Islamic Factions in the Middle East

1. Stephen Schwartz and Irfan Al-Alawi, "Fatwa Fanatics — The Deobandi-Wahhabi Lust for Control Over Personal Life," *Millat Times*, March 11, 2013, http://www.islamicpluralism.org/2206/fatwa-fanatics-the-deobandi-wahhabi-lust-for.

2. James M. Dorsey, "Wahhabism vs. Wahhabism: Qatar Challenges Saudi Arabia," *Middle East Online*, August 9, 2013, http://www.middle-east-online.com/english/?id=61189.

3. Michael Lipka, "Muslims and Islam: Key Findings in the United States and Around the World," *Pew research Centre Fact Tank: News in the Numbers*, July 22, 2016, http://www.pewresearch.org/fact-tank/2016/07/22/muslims-and-islam-key-findings-in-the-u-s-and-around-the-world.

4. Bruce Livesey, "The Salafist Movement: An Examination of the Ideology that Has Inspired the Global Jihad and the Emergence of Its Most Dangerous Incarnation," *FrontLine*, http://www.pbs.org/wgbh/pages/frontline/shows/front/special/sala.html.

5. Trevor Stanley, "Understanding the Origins of Wahhabism and Salafism," *Terrorism Monitor: In-depth Analysis of War on Terror*, 3, http://www.jamestown.org/programs/tm/single/?tx_ttnews%5Btt_news%5D=528#.V7y7_zFTHIU.

6. Christopher M. Blanchard, "The Islamic Traditions of Wahhabism and Salfiyya," *CRS Report for Congress*,

January 25, 2006, http://www.investigativeproject.org/documents/testimony/47.pdf.

7. Mark Durie, "Salafis and the Muslim Brotherhood: What is the Difference?" *Middle East Forum*, June 6, 2013, http://www.meforum.org/3541/salafis-muslim-brotherhood.

8. American Foreign Policy Council, "Muslim Brotherhood," *World Almanac of Islamism*, From Quick Facts Courtesy of The Clarion Project Special Report on The Muslim Brotherhood (2015), http://almanac.afpc.org/muslim-brotherhood#.

9. Mohammad Ma'mun El-Hudaibi, "The Principles of The Muslim Brotherhood," Ikhwanweb, http://www.ikhwanweb.com/article.php?ID=813&LevelID=2&SectionID=116.

10. Peter Baker, "White House Weighs Terrorist Designation for Muslim Brotherhood."

11. Schwartz and Al-Alawi, "Fatwa Fanatics — The Deobandi-Wahhabi Lust for Control Over Personal Life."

12. "Deoband First: A Fatwa Against Terror," Report, *The Times of India*, June 1, 2008, http://timesofindia.indiatimes.com/india/Deoband-first-A-fatwa-against-terror/articleshow/3089161.cms.

13. Schwartz and Al-Alawi, "Fatwa Fanatics — The Deobandi-Wahhabi Lust for Control Over Personal Life."

14. Ibid.

15. Andrew G. Bostom, in "Sufi Jihad?" *American Thinker*, May 15, 2005, http://www.americanthinker.com/2005/05/sufi_jihad.html#ixzz4cd4T7Ix7.

16. Michael G. Knapp, in "The Concept and Practice of Jihad in Islam."

17. The entire section on Sufism is taken from Annemarie Schimmel, in "Sufism: Islam," *Encyclopaedia Britannica*, January 24, 2017, https://www.britannica.com/topic/Sufism.

18. Sadek Zibakalam, in "Hatred of Arabs Deeply Rooted in Persians, Says Iranian intellectual," Saud Al-Zahed, *Al Arabiya News*, October 9, 2011, http://www.alarabiya.net/articles/2011/10/09/170927.html.

19. Saud Al-Zahed, "Hatred of Arabs deeply rooted in Persians, says Iranian intellectual." *Al Arabiya News*. October 9, 2011. http://www.alarabiya.net/articles/2011/10/09/170927.html.

20. Sadek Zibakalam, in "Hatred of Arabs Deeply Rooted in Persians, Says Iranian intellectual."

21. The Arab Spring was the name given to major insurgencies in Syria, Libya, Turkey, and Yemen, along with civil uprisings in Bahrain and Egypt, and large street demonstrations in Kuwait, Algeria, Morocco, Iraq, Jordan, and Oman, with minor protests elsewhere. The crux of the 2010 Arab Spring revolutionary wave of demonstrations, protests, riots, and civil wars can be summed up in the protestors' slogan: *"Ash-sha`b yurid isqat an-nizam,"* which means "the people want to bring down the regime," quoted on various internet sites, such as *Alchetron*, 2017, https://alchetron.com/Ash-shab-yurid-isqat-an-nizam-1764310-W.

22. Bahrain Watch in "The military intervention that the world forgot: Saudi and Emirati forces continue to police Bahrain," Amy Austin Homes, *Al Jazeera News*. March 29, 2014. http://america.aljazeera.com/opinions/2014/3/bahrain.

23. Amy Austin Holmes, "The Military Intervention that the World Forgot: Saudi and Emirati Forces Continue to Police Bahrain," *Al Jazeera News*, March 29, 2014, http://america.aljazeera.com/opinions/2014/3/bahrain.

24. "The Iraq-Iran War," *Encyclopedia Britannica*, https://www.britannica.com/event/Iran-Iraq-War.

Chapter 6: The Rise of Islamists

1. Geraldine Bedell, "Sands of Time," *The Guardian*, December 13, 2003, https://www.theguardian.com/theobserver/2003/dec/14/features.magazine37.

2. World Report, "Bahrain: Events of 2016," Human Rights Watch (2017), https://www.hrw.org/world-report/2017/country-chapters/bahrain.

3. Fareed Zakaria, "Why They Hate Us?" *CNN TV Channel (US) and CNN (International)*, June 20, 2016, http://www.cnn.com/videos/tv/2016/05/20/exp-sayyid-qutb-why-they-hate-us.cnn/video/playlists/why-they-hate-us/.

4. David Vine, "The United States Has an Empire of Bases in the Middle East — and It's Not Making Anyone Safer," *Foreign Policy in Focus*, January 20, 2016, http://fpif.org/u-s-empire-bases-middle-east-not-making-anyone-safer/.

5. Michael W.S. Ryan, "The Islamic State: What Victory Means," The Jamestown Foundation, *Terrorism Monitor*, 12 (2014), http://www.refworld.org/docid/54aa6cd84.html.

6. Ahmed Saleh Hashim, "The Islamic State: from Al-Qaeda Affiliate to Caliphate," *Middle East Policy*

Council, 21 (2014), http://www.mepc.org/journal/
middle-east-policy-archives/islamic-state-al-qaeda-
affiliate-caliphate?print.

7. Ryan, "The Islamic State: What Victory Means."
8. Daniel Byman, "Comparing Al-Qaeda and ISIS:
    Different Goals, Different targets," Prepared testimony
    before the Subcommittee on Counterterrorism and
    Intelligence of the House Committee on Homeland
    Security, *Brookings Institute*, April 29, 2015, https://
    www.brookings.edu/testimonies/comparing-al-qaeda-
    and-isis-different-goals-different-targets.
9. Ryan, "The Islamic State: What Victory Means."
10. Nancy A. Youssef and Michael Weiss, "Big Win
    Over ISIS Could Mean A New War," *The Daily
    Beast*, June 6, 2016, http://www.thedailybeast.com/
    articles/2016/06/01/big-win-over-isis-could-mean-a-
    new-war.html.
11. Harry Sarfo, in "How A Secretive Branch of ISIS Built
    A Global Network of Killers," Rukmini Callimachi,
    The New York Times, August 3, 2016, http://www.
    nytimes.com/2016/08/04/world/middleeast/isis-
    german-recruit-interview.html?_r=0.
12. Ibid.
13. Ryan, "The Islamic State: What Victory Means."
14. Ibid.
15. Micah Zenko, "When Regan Cut and Run: The
    Forgotten History of When America Boldly
    Abandoned Ship in the Middle East," *Foreign
    Policy Guide*, February 7, 2014, http://foreignpolicy.
    com/2014/02/07/when-reagan-cut-and-run/.
16. Byman, "Comparing Al-Qaeda and ISIS: Different
    Goals, Different Targets."

17. Ryan, "The Islamic State: What Victory Means."
18. "Dua" (ex-member of The Khansaa Brigade), in "ISIS Women and Enforcers in Syria Recount Collaboration, Anguish and Escape," Azadeh Moaveni, *The New York Times*, November 21, 2015, http://www.nytimes.com/2015/11/22/world/middleeast/isis-wives-and-enforcers-in-syria-recount-collaboration-anguish-and-escape.html?_r=0;

     In an anecdote related by Dua, the cruelty and complete disregard for the Islamic Sharia law is exemplified by Daesh's perverted ideology. The Brigade, according to her, is Daesh's all-female run unit that controls women's moral behavior in public places, such as the wearing of mandatory *abayas* (flowing black robes) and face-concealing *niqabs*. Dua recalls an episode in which some of her friends were whipped for wearing tight-fitting *abayas*. When the officers removed their face-concealing niqabs, her friends were also found to be wearing makeup. They received twenty lashes for the abaya offense, five for the makeup, and another five for not being meek enough when detained.
19. Azadeh Moaveni, "ISIS Women and Enforcers in Syria Recount Collaboration, Anguish and Escape," *The New York Times*, November 21, 2015, http://www.nytimes.com/2015/11/22/world/middleeast/isis-wives-and-enforcers-in-syria-recount-collaboration-anguish-and-escape.html?_r=0.
20. Riz Ahmed, in "Riz Ahmed Tells Parliament That British TV's Lack of Diversity Might Inspire People to Join ISIS," Winston Cook-Wilson, *Spin*, March 3, 2017, http://www.spin.com/2017/03/riz-ahmed-parliament-diversity-isis/.

21. Paula Newton, "Son Died Fighting for ISIS, Mom Wants to Fight Propaganda," *CNN World*, February 20, 2015, http://www.cnn.com/2015/02/19/world/canada-isis-fighter-mother/.

22. Eric Schmitt, "Al Qaeda Turns to Syria, with a Plan to Challenge ISIS," *The New York Times*, May 15, 2016, https://www.nytimes.com/2016/05/16/world/middleeast/al-qaeda-turns-to-syria-with-a-plan-to-challenge-isis.html.

23. Bruce Riedel, "The Foreign Policy Essay: Where is Al Qaeda Leader Ayman al-Zawahiri?" *Lawfare*, May 17, 2015, https://lawfareblog.com/foreign-policy-essay-where-al-qaeda-leader-ayman-al-zawahiri.

24. Janine D. Giovanni, Leah McGrath Goodman, and Damien Sharkov, "How Does ISIS Fund Its Reign of Terror?" *Newsweek*, November 6, 2014, http://www.newsweek.com/2014/11/14/how-does-isis-fund-its-reign-terror-282607.html.

25. Ibid.

26. Matthew Levitt, "Terrorist Financing and the Islamic State," *The Washington Institute for Near East Policy*, Testimony submitted to the House Committee on Financial Services, November 13, 2014, https://www.washingtoninstitute.org/uploads/Documents/testimony/LevittTestimony20141113.pdf.

27. Daniel Wagner, and Alex Stout, "Why There Is No Stopping the Funding of the Islamic State," *HuffPost*, http://www.huffingtonpost.com/daniel-wagner/why-there-is-no-stopping-_b_7518012.html.

28. Janine D. Giovanni, Leah McGrath Goodman, and Damien Sharkov, "How Does ISIS Fund Its Reign of Terror?"

29. Ibid.

30. Lizzie Dearden, "Isis' 'Business Model' failing As Group Haemorrhages Millions while Losing Territory Across Syria and Iraq," *Independent*, February 18, 2017, http://www.independent.co.uk/news/world/middle-east/isis-islamic-state-daesh-funding-iraq-syria-territory-losses-oil-air-strikes-icsr-report-antiquities-a7586936.html.

31. Janine D. Giovanni, Leah McGrath Goodman, and Damien Sharkov, "How Does ISIS Fund Its Reign of Terror?"

32. Lizzie Dearden, "Isis' 'Business Model' failing As Group Haemorrhages Millions while Losing Territory Across Syria and Iraq."

33. Ibid.

34. Peter Neumann in Lizzie Dearden, "Isis' 'Business Model' failing As Group Haemorrhages Millions while Losing Territory Across Syria and Iraq, *Independent*, February 18, 2017, http://www.independent.co.uk/news/world/middle-east/isis-islamic-state-daesh-funding-iraq-syria-territory-losses-oil-air-strikes-icsr-report-antiquities-a7586936.html.

35. Paul Cruickshank, "Algeria Gas Facility Attack Fuels Jihadist Rivalry," *CNN: Security Clearance*, January 30, 2013, http://security.blogs.cnn.com/tag/cnn-terrorism-analyst-paul-cruickshank/page/2/.

36. Kouchi Brother, in "AQAP vs ISIS: Who Was Really Behind the Charlie Hebdo Attacks?" Charlie Winter, *Middle East Eye*, January 15, 2015, http://www.middleeasteye.net/columns/aqap-vs-isis-who-was-really-behind-charles-hebdo-692115745.

37. Nasr Ibn Ali Al-Ansi, in "AQAP vs ISIS: Who Was Really Behind the Charlie Hebdo Attacks?" Charlie Winter, *Middle East Eye*, January 15, 2015, http://www.middleeasteye.net/columns/aqap-vs-isis-who-was-really-behind-charles-hebdo-692115745.

38. Adam Withnall, in "Were Paris Attacks the First Case of Al-Qaeda and Isis Working Together? Six questions raised in aftermath of France shootings," *Independent*, January 13, 2015, http://www.independent.co.uk/news/world/europe/were-paris-attacks-the-first-case-of-al-qaeda-and-isis-working-together-six-questions-raised-in-9975349.html.

39. Winter, "AQAP vs ISIS: Who Was Really Behind the Charlie Hebdo Attacks?"

40. Ibid.

41. Ryan, "The Islamic State: What Victory Means."

42. Byman, "Comparing Al-Qaeda and ISIS: Different Goals, Different Targets."

43. Ibid.

44. Ibid.

45. Zaina Konbaz, "After Fatal Attack on Shi'as, Saudi Arabia Gets Tough on Terrorism," *Terror Monitor*, The Jamestown Foundation: Global Research & Analysis, 12 (2014), https://jamestown.org/program/after-fatal-attack-on-shias-saudi-arabia-gets-tough-on-terrorism.

46. Ryan, "The Islamic State: What Victory Means."

47. Ibid.

48. "Only One Caliph?" *Global Security: Military: Islam: Caliphate*, http://www.globalsecurity.org/military/intro/islam-caliphate-one.htm.

49. Ryan, "The Islamic State: What Victory Means."

50. "Only One Caliph?"

51. Alessandria Masi, "If ISIS Leader Abu Bakr al-Baghdadi Is Killed, Who Is Caliph of the Islamic State Group?" *International Business Times*, November 10, 2014, http://www.ibtimes.com/if-isis-leader-abu-bakr-al-baghdadi-killed-who-caliph-islamic-state-group-1721638.

52. Ryan, "The Islamic State: What Victory Means."

53. Byman, "Comparing Al-Qaeda and ISIS: Different Goals, Different Targets."

54. Patrick B. Johnston and Anoop K. Sarbahi, "The Impact of U. S. Drone Strikes on Terrorism in Pakistan," Research paper, April 21, 2015, http://patrickjohnston.info/materials/drones.pdf; Earlier versions of this article were presented at the 2011 Annual Meetings of the American Political Science Association, the Belfer Center for Science and International Affairs at Harvard University's Kennedy School of Government, and the New America Foundation.

55. New America Foundation, in "Drone War Pakistan: Analyses," November 13, 2016, http://securitydata.newamerica.net/drones/pakistan-analysis.html.

56. Johnston and Sarbahi, "The Impact of U. S. Drone Strikes on Terrorism in Pakistan."

57. Ibid.

58. Winter, "AQAP vs ISIS: Who Was Really Behind the Charlie Hebdo Attacks?"

59. Byman, "Comparing Al-Qaeda and ISIS: Different Goals, Different Targets."

Chapter 7: The Spread of Islamism

1. Cottee, "What's the Right Way to Think About Religion and ISIS?"

2. Sir Lewis Namier, in "What's the Right Way to Think About Religion and ISIS?" Simon Cottee, *The Atlantic*, July 12, 2016, https://www.theatlantic.com/international/archive/2016/07/religion-isis-orlando/490958/.

3. Christopher Browning, in "What's the Right Way to Think About Religion and ISIS?" Simon Cottee, *The Atlantic*, July 12, 2016, https://www.theatlantic.com/international/archive/2016/07/religion-isis-orlando/490958/.

4. Mehdi Hasan, in "What's the Right Way to Think About Religion and ISIS?" Simon Cottee, *The Atlantic*, July 12, 2016, https://www.theatlantic.com/international/archive/2016/07/religion-isis-orlando/490958/.

5. Ishaan Tharoor, in "What's the Right Way to Think About Religion and ISIS?" Simon Cottee, *The Atlantic*, July 12, 2016,https://www.theatlantic.com/international/archive/2016/07/religion-isis-orlando/490958/.

6. Ayaan Hirsi Ali, "Why Islam Needs A Reformation," *The Washington Post*, March 20, 2015, http://www.wsj.com/articles/a-reformation-for-islam-1426859626.

7. Professors Scheherazade S. Rehman's and Hossein Askari, "How Islamic Are Islamic Countries? *Global Economy Journal*, Berkley Electronic Press, 10 (2010),

http://hossein-askari.com/wordpress/wp-content/
uploads/islamicity-index.pdf.

8. Ibid.

9. Cottee, "What's the Right Way to Think About Religion and ISIS?"

10. Peter Bergen, "Why Do Terrorists Commit Terrorism?" *The New York Times: The Opinion Pages*, June 14, 2016, http://www.nytimes.com/2016/06/15/ opinion/why-do-terrorists-commit-terrorism. html?_r=0.

11. Quentin Skinner, "What's the Right Way to Think About Religion and ISIS?" in Simon Cottee, *The Atlantic*, July 12, 2016, https://www.theatlantic. com/international/archive/2016/07/religion-isis-orlando/490958/.

12. Browning, in "What's the Right Way to Think About Religion and ISIS?"

13. Ojibwa, "Religious Racism: South African Apartheid," *Daily Kos*, June 19, 2010, http://www.dailykos.com/ story/2010/6/19/877658/-.

14. Azadeh Moaveni, "ISIS Women and Enforcers in Syria Recount Collaboration, Anguish and Escape."

15. Jeff Ranklin, "Peoples Temple Cult — Jim Jones," *Yuku*, March 18, 2009, http://cultbustersgalactica.yuku. com/topic/121/PEOPLES-TEMPLE-CULT-JIM-JONES#.WRCkn-XyvDc.

16. Paul Bentley, "Warren Jeffs Sentenced to Life Plus 20 Years in Prison as Picture Emerges of 50 Brides, Bred to Worship the Polygamous 'Prophet'," *Daily Mail*, August 9, 2011, http://www.dailymail.co.uk/news/ article-2024150/Warren-Jeffs-trial-Paedophile-gets-life-sentence-50-brides-photo-emerges.html.

Part III: Current Challenges and Strategies for the Future

Chapter 8: United States' Uncharted Policies in the Muslim World

1. Vine, "The United States Has an Empire of Bases in the Middle East — and It's Not Making Anyone Safer."
2. Ibid.
3. Ibid
4. David Vine, "The Pentagon's New Base Plan Will Achieve the Exact Opposite of Its Goal," *The Nation*, January 14, 2016, https://www.thenation.com/article/the-pentagons-new-base-plan-will-achieve-the-exact-opposite-of-its-goal/.
5. Vine, "The United States Has an Empire of Bases in the Middle East — and It's Not Making Anyone Safer."
6. Bradley Bowman, in "The United States Has An Empire of Bases in the Middle East — and It's Not Making Anyone Safer," David Vine, *Foreign Policy in Focus*, January 20, 2016, http://fpif.org/u-s-empire-bases-middle-east-not-making-anyone-safer/.
7. Army's Military Review, in "The United States Has An Empire of Bases in the Middle East — and It's Not Making Anyone Safer," David Vine, *Foreign Policy in Focus*, January 20, 2016, http://fpif.org/u-s-empire-bases-middle-east-not-making-anyone-safer/.
8. Shadi Hamid, "Islamism, the Arab Spring, and the Failure of America's Do-nothing Policy in the Middle East," *The Atlantic*, October 9, 2015, http://www.

theatlantic.com/international/archive/2015/10/middle-east-egypt-us-policy/409537; This article has been adapted from Shadi Hamid's book *Temptations of Power: Islamists and Illiberal Democracy in a New Middle East*, which was selected by Foreign Affairs as one of the "Best International Relations Books of 2014," and named one of Foreign Policy Association's "Ten Most Important Books of the Year." The book is also featured in the Wall Street Journal's "10 Must-Read Books on the Evolution of Terrorism in the Middle East."

9. It should be remembered that the Russians have been an ally of the Syrians for quite some time. They have always had their bases in Syria, but their official involvement in fighting Daesh happened after Russia's commercial flight, Metrojet Flight 9268, was believed to have been bombed by Daesh on October 31, 2015, killing all 224 people on board.

10. Hamid, "Islamism, the Arab Spring, and the Failure of America's Do-nothing Policy in the Middle East."

11. Ibid.

12. Ibid.

13. Mahdi Akef, in "Islamism, the Arab Spring, and the Failure of America's Do-nothing Policy in the Middle East," Shadi Hamid, *The Atlantic*, October 9, 2015, http://www.theatlantic.com/international/archive/2015/10/middle-east-egypt-us-policy/409537.

14. Hamid, "Islamism, the Arab Spring, and the Failure of America's Do-nothing Policy in the Middle East."

15. Nina Hachigian and David Shorr, "The Responsibility Doctrine," *Centre for Strategic and International Studies*, December 18, 2012, https://csis-prod.s3.amazonaws.

com/s3fs-public/legacy_files/files/publication/ TWQ_13Winter_HachigianShorr.pdf.

16. Robert Baer, "Why Saudi Arabia is Helping Crush the Muslim Brotherhood."

17. Max Fisher, "How Saudi Arabia Captured Washington," *Vox*, March 21, 2016, http://www. vox.com/2016/3/21/11275354/saudi-arabia-gulf-washington.

18. Chris Martenson, "Do We Really Want War with Russia?" *PeakProsperity*, October 7, 2016, https://www. peakprosperity.com/blog/102294/do-we-really-want-war-russia.

19. Ibid.

20. Lilit Marcus, "Bahamas, Bahrain, and U.A.E. Issue Warnings About Travel to United States," *Condo Naste Traveler*, July 11, 2016, http://www.cntraveler.com/ stories/2016-07-11/bahamas-bahrain-and-uae-issue-warnings-about-travel-to-us.

21. Kelsey Davenport, "Nuclear Weapons: Who Has What at A Glance," *Facts Sheet and Briefs*. August 19, 2016, Information obtained from Arms Control Association, Federation of American Scientists, International Panel on Fissile Materials, U.S. Department of Defense, and U.S. Department of State, updated January 2017, https://www. armscontrol.org/print/2566.

22. Martenson, "Do We Really Want War with Russia?"

23. Craig Murray, in "Why They Invaded," Duncan Thomas (Interviewer), *Jacobin*, August 18, 2016, https://www.jacobinmag.com/2016/08/chilcot-report-iraq-war-blair-cameron-wmd/.

24. Dexter Filkins, "Did George W. Bush Create ISIS?", The New Yorker, May 15, 2015. http://www.newyorker. com/news/news-desk/did-george-w-bush-create-isis.

25. Christopher Hill, interview with Chris Hayes, All In, *MSNBC News*, September 8, 2016, http://www.msnbc. com/transcripts/all-in/2016-09-08.

26. Seyed Hossein Mousavian, "Saudi Arabia Is Iran's New National Security Threat," *Huffington Post* in partnership with *The Berggruen Institute*, http://www.huffingtonpost.com/seyed-hossein-mousavian/saudi-arabia-iran-threat_b_10282296. html.

27. Maria Abi-Habib and Adam Entous, "United States Widens Role in Saudi-led Campaign Against Houthi Rebels in Yemen: Washington Has Concerns About Riyadh's Goals in the Conflict," *The Wall Street Journal*, April 12, 2015, http://www.wsj.com/articles/u-s-widens-role-in-saudi-led-campaign-against-yemen-rebels-1428882967.

28. Fisher, "How Saudi Arabia Captured Washington."

29. "America Is Complicit in the Carnage in Yemen," *The New York Times: Opinion Page*, August 17, 2016, http://www.nytimes.com/2016/08/17/opinion/stop-saudi-arms-sales-until-carnage-in-yemen-ends. html?_r=0.

30. Fisher, "How Saudi Arabia Captured Washington."

31. Binyamin Applebaum, "Saudi Threat to Sell United States Assets Could Hurt, but Mostly the Saudis," *The New York Times*, April 19, 2016, http://www.nytimes. com/2016/04/20/business/international/saudi-threat-to-sell-us-assetscould-hurt-but-mostly-the-saudis. html?_r=0.

32. Fisher, "How Saudi Arabia Captured Washington."
33. Ibid.
34. Patrick Wintour, "Gulf Plunged Into Diplomatic Crisis As Countries Cut Ties With Qatar," *The Guardian*, June 5, 2017, https://www.theguardian.com/world/2017/jun/05/saudi-arabia-and-bahrain-break-diplomatic-ties-with-qatar-over-terrorism.
35. "Qatar-Iran Ties: Sharing the World's Largest Gas Field," *Al Jazeera*, June 15, 2017.http://www.aljazeera.com/indepth/interactive/2017/06/qatar-north-dome-iran-south-pars-glance-lng-gas-field-170614131849685.html.
36. Eric Lipton, Brooke Williams, and Nicholas Confessore, "Foreign Powers Buy Influence at Think Tanks," *The New York Times*, September 6, 2014, http://www.nytimes.com/2014/09/07/us/politics/foreign-powers-buy-influence-at-think-tanks.html?_r=0.
37. Dorsey, "Wahhabism vs. Wahhabism: Qatar Challenges Saudi Arabia."
38. Ibid.
39. Ibid.
40. Fisher, "How Saudi Arabia Captured Washington."
41 Soner Cagaptay and James F. Jeffrey, "Inside Turkey's Failed Coup: What Happened? Why? What Next?" *Washington Institute*, July 22, 2016, http://www.washingtoninstitute.org/policy-analysis/view/inside-turkeys-failed-coup-what-happened-why-what-next.
42 Michael O'Hanlon, in "Analysts Predict Rifts in US-Turkey Relationship," Joe Gould and Aaron Mehta, *Defense News*, July 20, 2016, http://www.defensenews.com/story/war-in-syria/2016/07/20/analysts-predict-rifts-uk-turkey-relationship/87351754.

43. Ibid.
44. Hamid, "Islamism, the Arab Spring, and the Failure of America's Do-nothing Policy in the Middle East."
45. Michael Rubin, "Who Is Responsible for the Taliban?" *Middle East Review*, The Washington Institute, March 2002, http://www.washingtoninstitute.org/policy-analysis/view/who-is-responsible-for-the-taliban.
46. Ibid.
47. Ed Girardet, in "Who Is Responsible for the Taliban?" Michael Rubin, *Middle East Review*, The Washington Institute, March 2002, http://www.washingtoninstitute.org/policy-analysis/view/who-is-responsible-for-the-taliban.
48. Rubin, "Who Is Responsible for the Taliban?"
49. Yaco Ben Efrat, "Afghanistan: How the US Put Taliban in Power," Trans. Stephen Langfur, *Green Left Weekly*, November 21, 2001, https://www.greenleft.org.au/content/afghanistan-how-us-put-taliban-power.
50. Phillip Knightley, "US Gave Silent Backing to Taliban Rise to Power," *The Guardian*, August 8, 2001, http://www.rense.com/general14/rise.htm.
51. Murray, "Why They Invaded."
52. Andrew Gavin Marshall, "Empire, Energy and Al-Qaeda: The Anglo-American Terror Network: The Imperial Anatomy of al-Qaeda, Part II," *Global Research*, September 8, 2010, http://www.globalresearch.ca/empire-energy-and-al-qaeda-the-anglo-american-terror-network/20944.
53. "Wars of Feminist Aggression: Feminism, Foreign Policy, and the Taliban," *KHarblog*, March 12, 2005, http://kwharbaugh.blogspot.com/2005/03/wars-of-feminist-aggression.html; The women's rights issue in this blog

has quotations from Steve Coll's 2005 Pulitzer Prize-winning book, *Ghost Wars: The Secret History of the CIA, Afghanistan, and Bin Laden, from the Soviet Invasion to September 10, 2001* (Penguin Press, 2004), 351–352, 362–363, and The Feminist Majority's 2000 Annual Report.

54. Murray, "Why They Invaded."

55. Laura Hayes, Borgna Brunner, and Beth Rowen, "Who Are the Taliban: Their History and Their Resurgence," *Infoplease*, http://www.infoplease.com/spot/taliban.html.

Chapter 9: The Iranian Factor

1. Stephen Kinzer, "Treat Israel Like Iran," *The Daily Beast*, February 6, 2010, http://www.thedailybeast.com/articles/2010/06/02/israel-iran-twin-pariahs.html.

2. Robert Fisk, "Saudi Arabia, Not Iran, Is the 'Fountainhead' of Terrorism: Fisk," *Press TV*, May 22, 2017, http://217.218.67.231/Detail/2017/05/22/522804/Saudi-Arabia-not-Iran-is-the-fountainhead-of-terrorism-Robert-Fisk.

3. BBC Monitoring, "Who are Islamic 'Morality Police'?" *BBC News*, April 22, 2016, http://www.bbc.com/news/world-middle-east-36101150.

4. Ishaan Tharoor, "Trump Embraces the Saudi Vision For the Middle East," *The Washington Post*, May 22, 2017, https://www.washingtonpost.com/news/worldviews/wp/2017/05/22/trump-embraces-the-saudi-vision-for-the-middle-east/?utm_term=.f0b07b82ec25.

5. "US-Iran Relations: A Brief Guide," *BBC News*, November 24, 2014, http://www.bbc.com/news/world-middle-east-24316661.

6. "August 19, 1953: CIA-Assisted Coup Overthrows Government of Iran," *This Day in History*, http://www.history.com/this-day-in-history/cia-assisted-coup-overthrows-government-of-iran.

7. Larry J. Sabato, "The Iran-Contra Affair — 1986–1987," *The Washington Post*, http://www.washingtonpost.com/wp-srv/politics/special/clinton/frenzy/iran.htm.

8. Ibid.

9. Karim Sadjadpour, *Reading Khamenei: The World View of Iran's Most Powerful Leader.* (Washington: Carnegie Endowment for International Peace, 2009), 29–31, http://carnegieendowment.org/files/sadjadpour_iran_final2.pdf.

10. Sarah Leah Whitson, "Saudi Arabia: Mass Execution Largest Since 1980," *Human Rights Watch*, January 4, 2016, https://www.hrw.org/news/2016/01/04/saudi-arabia-mass-execution-largest-1980.

11. Fisher, "How Saudi Arabia Captured Washington."

12. Ibid.

13. Mousavian, "Saudi Arabia Is Iran's New National Security Threat."

14. Dickey, "Through the Looking glass: This Is Why the U.S. Still Backs Saudi Arabia."

15. Fisher, "How Saudi Arabia Captured Washington."

16. Ibid.

17. "Iran's Zarif in UAE on Charm Offensive," *Al Jazeera News Agency*, December 4, 2013, http://www.aljazeera.com/news/middleeast/2013/12/iran-zarif-uae-charm-offensive-201312413194444573.html.

18. Mousavian, "Saudi Arabia Is Iran's New National Security Threat."

19. Ibid.

20. Sadjadpour, *Reading Khamenei: The World View of Iran's Most Powerful Leader*.

21. "Negative Views of Russia on the Rise: Global Poll," BBC World Service Poll, *BBC World Service*, June 3, 2014, https://downloads.bbc.co.uk/mediacentre/country-rating-poll.pdf.

22. Jeffrey Goldberg, "The Obama Doctrine," *The Atlantic*, April 2016, http://www.theatlantic.com/magazine/archive/2016/04/the-obama-doctrine/471525.

23. Elizabeth Trudeau, "Iran Announces Delivery of Russian S-300 Missile Defense System," Andrew Roth, *The Washington Post*, May 10, 2016, https://www.washingtonpost.com/world/iran-announces-delivery-of-russian-s-300-missile-defense-system/2016/05/10/944afa2e-16ae-11e6-971a-dadf9ab18869_story.html?utm_term=.0aa3c666b360.

24. Kinzer, "Treat Israel Like Iran."

25. Juan Cole, "5 Surprising Ways Iran Is Better than Israel," *Informed Comment: Thoughts on the Middle East, History and Religion*, February 27, 2015, https://www.juancole.com/2015/02/surprising-better-israel.html.

26. Kinzer, "Treat Israel Like Iran."

27. Cole, "5 Surprising Ways Iran Is Better than Israel."

28. Ibid.

29. Ibid.

30. Oren Liebermann and Euan McKirdy, "Israel to Build Entirely New Settlement in West Bank," CNN, February 1, 2017, http://www.cnn.com/2017/02/01/middleeast/israel-settlements-approved/.

31. Cole, "5 Surprising Ways Iran Is Better than Israel."

32. "Recep Tayyip Erdogan: Turkey's Dominant President," *BBC News*, July 21, 2016, http://www.bbc.com/news/world-europe-13746679.

33. Patrick Kingsley, in "Erdogan Claims Vast Powers in Turkey After Narrow Victory in Referendum," *The New York Times*, April 16, 2017,https://www.nytimes.com/2017/04/16/world/europe/turkey-referendum-polls-erdogan.html?_r=0.

34. Pejman Abdolmohammadi, "The Revival of Nationalism and Secularism in Modern Iran," *Gingko Library*, February 17, 2016, http://www.gingkolibrary.com/news/the-revival-of-nationalism-and-secularism/.

35. Kenneth M. Pollack, Daniel L. Byman, et al., *Which Path to Persia? Options for A New American Strategy Toward Iran*, Analysis Paper Number 20, (Washington D.C.: The Saban Center for Middle East Policy at the Brookings Institution, 2009), 145–155, https://www.brookings.edu/wp-content/uploads/2016/06/06_iran_strategy.pdf.

36. Ibid.
37. Ibid.
38. Ibid.

Chapter 10: The Dynamics of the Many Facets at Play in the Middle East (Beyond the Obvious)

1. At the writing of this book, there is a firm belief among American politicians, and some of the European nations, that Russia has interfered in Western politics through the internet. While this has been widely discussed in the media, the Federal Bureau of Investigation (FBI)

has acknowledged the involvement of the Russians in American politics and are doing their own in-depth analysis.

2.   Farah al-Atassi, "Al-Nusra Leader Jolani Announces Split from Al-Qaeda," *Al Jazeera*, July 29, 2016, http://www.aljazeera.com/news/2016/07/al-nusra-leader-jolani-announces-split-al-qaeda-160728163725624.html.

3.   Ibid.

4.   Josh Earnest, "White House Says Concerned About Nusra Front's Capacity to Attack West," *Reuters Canada*, July 28, 2016, http://ca.reuters.com/article/topNews/idCAKCN1082DI.3.

5.   Eric Schmitt, "Al Qaeda Turns to Syria, with a Plan to Challenge ISIS," *The New York Times*, May 15, 2016, https://www.nytimes.com/2016/05/16/world/middleeast/al-qaeda-turns-to-syria-with-a-plan-to-challenge-isis.html.

6.   Charles Lister, in "Al Qaeda Turns to Syria, with a Plan to Challenge ISIS," Eric Schmitt, *The New York Times*, May 15, 2016, https://www.nytimes.com/2016/05/16/world/middleeast/al-qaeda-turns-to-syria-with-a-plan-to-challenge-isis.html.

7.   Anne Barnard, Michael, R. Gordon, and Eric Schmitt, "Turkey and U.S. Plan to Create Syria 'Safe Zone' Free of ISIS," *The New York Times*, July 27, 2015, https://www.nytimes.com/2015/07/28/world/middleeast/turkey-and-us-agree-on-plan-to-clear-isis-from-strip-of-northern-syria.html?_r=0.

8.   Josh Rogin, in "How US Allies Aid Al Qaeda in Syria," Daniel Lazare, *Consortiumnews.com*, August 4, 2015, https://consortiumnews.com/2015/08/04/how-us-allies-aid-al-qaeda-in-syria/.

9.   Daniel Lazare, "How US Allies Aid Al Qaeda in Syria," *Consortiumnews.com*, August 4, 2015, https://consortiumnews.com/2015/08/04/how-us-allies-aid-al-qaeda-in-syria/.

10. Ibid.

11. Eric Schmitt, in "How US Allies Aid Al-Qaeda in Syria," Daniel Lazare,*Consortiumnews.com*, August 4, 2015, https://consortiumnews.com/2015/08/04/how-us-allies-aid-al-qaeda-in-syria/.

12. Anne Bernard and Eric Schmitt, in "How US Allies Aid Al-Qaeda in Syria," Daniel Lazare,*Consortiumnews. com*, August 4, 2015, https://consortiumnews.com/2015/08/04/how-us-allies-aid-al-qaeda-in-syria/.

13. Krishnadev Calamur, "How Is Syria Still Using Chemical Weapons?" *The Atlantic*, April 4, 2017, https://www.theatlantic.com/international/archive/2017/04/syria-chemical-weapons-attack/521883/.

14. Nikki Haley, "How Is Syria Still Using Chemical Weapons?" Krishnadev Calamur, *The Atlantic*, April 4, 2017, https://www.theatlantic.com/international/archive/2017/04/syria-chemical-weapons-attack/521883/.

15. Nancy A. Youssef and Shane Harris, "How ISIS Actually Lost Ramadi," *The Daily Beast*. December 30, 2015, http://www.thedailybeast.com/articles/2015/12/30/how-isis-actually-lost-ramadi.html.

16. The Khan, "The Mahdi" Islamic Board, October 25, 2008, https://www.islamicboard.com/clarifications-about-islam/134273395-mahdi-2.html; Maizoon-e Noor, "Imam Mahdi (A.S.) In the Eyes of Muslim Ascetics," Nematollahi Gonabadi, *Sufi News Agency*,

2006, https://www.majzooban.org/en/index.php/ articles/4234-imam-mahdi-a-s-in-the-eyes-of-muslim-ascetics.

The Mahdi, meaning the "Guided One," is professed to be a redeemer of Islam, who will remain on earth prior to the "Day of the Resurrection." Some Muslims believe the Mahdi, who will arrive alongside Jesus, will rid the world of non-Muslim thinking, injustice, and tyranny. The concept of the Mahdi is not explicitly mentioned in the Quran, nor are there any "reliable" hadith, such as Sahih Bukhari or Sahih Muslim, to substantiate the existence or the arrival of the Mahdi. Over the years, a few Muslims have claimed to be Mahdis. For the Sufis, the idea of the Mahdi is very important as it is for the Twelvers in the Shi'a sect who believe Muhammad ibn Hasan ibn Ali, the twelfth Imam of Twelver Shi'as, is the Mahdi in occultation — he is referred to as Muhammad al-Mahdi by them.

17. "When the Ka'ba Was Held Hostage — The Grand Mosque Seize," *IlmFeed*. http://ilmfeed.com/kaba-held-hostage/.

18. Bruce Rubin, "Abdul Rahman Al-Sudais Saudi Grand Imam of Mecca has Publicly Prayed to Allah for Genocide of Jews," *CNN iReport*, September 7, 2010, http://ireport.cnn.com/docs/DOC-489472.

19. John R. Bradely, in *Saudi Arabia Exposed: Inside a Kingdom in Crisis*, (Macmillan: 2006), 170.

20. "Abdul Rahman Al-Sudais," *Revolvy*, https://www.revolvy.com/topic/Abdul%20Rahman%20Al-Sudais&item_type=topic.

21. Adel al-Jubeir, in "Abdul Rahman Al-Sudais Saudi Grand Imam of Mecca has Publicly Prayed to Allah for Genocide of Jews," Bruce Ruben, *CNN iReport*, September 7, 2010, http://ireport.cnn.com/docs/DOC-489472.

22. Besheer Mohammed, "Who Are the Iraqi Kurds?" *Pew Research Center: FACTANK*, August 20, 2014, http://www.pewresearch.org/fact-tank/2014/08/20/who-are-the-iraqi-kurds/.

23. World Factbook: Middle East: Turkey, *Central Intelligence Agency (CIA)*, July, 2016, https://www.cia.gov/library/publications/resources/the-world-factbook/geos/tu.html.

24. Daveed Gartenstein-Ross, "Successes and Failures of the United States and NATO Intervention in Libya," May 1, 2014, Hearing Before the Committee on Oversight and Government Reform, *Foundation for Defense of Democracies*, (Washington: 2014), https://oversight.house.gov/wp-content/uploads/2014/05/Gartenstein-Ross-Statement-5-1-Benghazi-Libya.pdf.

25. Joe Biden, in "Joe Biden says the 'Democratic Party Overall Hasn't Spoken Enough to White Working-class Voters," *MSNBC News: Morning Joe*, July 27, 2016, http://info.msnbc.com/_news/2016/07/27/35882707-morning-joe-news-joe-biden-says-the-democratic-party-overall-hasnt-spoken-enough-to-white-working-class-voters?lite.

26. Asma Arjoudi, "Aleppo: 'People Want Safe Passage,'" *Al Jazeera*, December 13, 2016, http://www.aljazeera.com/indepth/features/2016/12/qa-aleppo-fall-161213053229455.html.

Chapter 11: Islamophobia in the West

1. Department of Government and Justice Studies, "The United States Patriot Act," *Appalachian State University*, 2016, http://gjs.appstate.edu/media-coverage-crime-and-criminal-justice/usa-patriot-act.

2. Andrea Peterson, "Why It's So Hard to Keep Up with How the United States Government Is Spying on Its Own People," *The Washington Post*, November 20, 2015, https://www.washingtonpost.com/news/the-switch/wp/2015/11/20/why-its-so-hard-to-keep-up-with-how-the-u-s-government-is-spying-on-its-own-people.

3. Julia Craven, "White Supremacists More Dangerous To America Than Foreign Terrorists, Study Says," *Huffington Post*, June 24, 2015, http://www.huffingtonpost.com/2015/06/24/domestic-terrorism-charleston_n_7654720.html.

4. "Drone Strikes: Pakistan," America's Counterterrorism Wars, *New America Foundation*, November 13, 2016, http://securitydata.newamerica.net/drones/pakistan-analysis.html.

5. Zakaria, "Why They Hate Us?"

6. ?Equest, "Case Study: Apartheid," http://request.org.uk/issues/social-issues/case-study-apartheid.

7. Matt O'Brien, "The Important Difference Between Assimilation and Integration," *Immigration Blog Posts Society*, September 29, 2016, http://immigrationreform.com/2016/09/29/the-important-difference-between-assimilation-and-integration/.

8. Saul McLeod, "Jean Piaget," *Simply Psychology*, 2015, https://www.simplypsychology.org/piaget.html.

9.   Ann Corcoran, ed., "Refugee Resettlement Fact Sheet," *Refugee Settlement Watch*, June 20, 2013, https://refugeeresettlementwatch.wordpress.com/refugee-resettlement-fact-sheets/.

10. O'Brien, "The Important Difference Between Assimilation and Integration."

11. Muddassar Ahmed, "Salman Abedi Wasn't a Lone Wolf – He Was a Known Wolf, and The Muslim Community Tried To Warn Us About Him," Independent, May 26 2017,

     http://www.independent.co.uk/voices/salman-abedi-manchester-attack-reported-family-imam-friends-did-nothing-a7757726.html.

12. Besheer Mohammed, in "A New Estimate of the U.S. Muslim Population," *Pew Research Center: FACTANK*, January 6, 2016, http://www.pewresearch.org/fact-tank/2016/01/06/a-new-estimate-of-the-u-s-muslim-population.

13. Bergen, "Why Do Terrorists Commit Terrorism?"

14. It should be noted that in the context of integration, the role of a convert to Islam in the West can be helpful. Many converts are already integrated in the societies they live in and their help could prove valuable in helping Muslims through the integration process.

     However, the recent population of Muslims, according to Besheer Mohammed's report for the *Pew Research Center: FACTANK*, January 6, 2016, is just about one percent of the total population in the United States, and just over half of the projected growth of the American Muslim population from 2010 to 2015 was based on immigration. The number of Muslim immigrants currently represents only about 10 percent of all legal immigrants arriving in the United States.

Besheer Mohammed also states that the other main cause of Islam's growth is "because American Muslims tend to have more children than Americans of other religious faiths. Besides, Muslims also tend to be younger than the general public, so a larger share of Muslims will soon be at the point in their lives when people begin having children."

On the other hand, according to Besheer Mohammed, there has been little net change in the size of the American Muslim population in recent years, due to conversion. About one-in-five American Muslim adults were raised in a different faith or none at all. At the same time, a similar number of people who were raised Muslim no longer identify with the faith. About as many Americans become Muslim as leave Islam.

An onsite article by the Christian Broadcasting Network (CBN) (http://www1.cbn.com/spirituallife/why-are-so-many-westerners-converting-to-islam) lists several reasons why conversion to Islam takes place in the United States. Islam's doctrine is simple and rational, where a great emphasis is placed on all believers being equal. It is, according to the article, a "practical" religion, and lacks a priesthood. The article gives an example of an American Muslim who gave the following reasons when asked why African-Americans are turning to Islam. First of all, Islam is attractive to African-Americans because it provides a way of rejecting the American culture that does not accept them, which they have endured all their lives. In sociological terms, according to the CBN article, "one of the reasons that many African-Americans who were Christians, go to Islam is that the people being prejudiced against them are also Christian. How often does one not hear it said, 'America is no more segregated than at eleven o'clock on Sunday mornings.'" The second reason that attracts not only African-Americans but Anglo-Americans as well, is that Islam offers "direction and discipline." The article states that, "our society is disintegrating for lack of discipline, especially in the city. Through its disciplined life-style, Islam, to some people seems to hold out the promise of helping them get their lives back in order again."

Finally, Islam offers a conversion experience and the opportunity to get one's life in order without needing to confess one's sin and need of salvation. "In fact, Islam makes quite a point of denying these truths. It tells people they do not need salvation; all they need is to follow the "guidance" of God's law, and they will make it to heaven. That, according to the article, is something the natural man likes to hear."

15. Ahmed H. Sakr, "Non-Muslims in Muslim History," *Islamic Research Foundation, Inc.*, http://www.irfi.org/articles/articles_301_350/nonmuslims_in_muslim_history.htm.
16. Ibid.
17. "Hamas," Counter Terrorism Guide, *National Counterterrorism Centre*, January 2014, https://www.nctc.gov/site/groups/hamas.html.
18. Asra Q. Nomani, "A Gender Jihad for Islam's Future," *The Washington Post*, November 6, 2015, http://www.washingtonpost.com/wp-dyn/content/article/2005/11/04/AR2005110402306.html.

SHANBREEN

19. Religion and Public Life, "The World's Muslims: Religion, Politics and Society."
20. Ibid.
21. Ibid.
22. Ibid.
23. Dr. Mohamed Moukhyer, "Female Genital Mutilation (FGM): Against Women's Health and Human Rights," Women and Health Learning Package developed by *The Network: TUFH Women and Health Taskforce*, Second edition, September 2006, http://www.the-networktufh.ys.be/sites/default/files/attachments/basic_pages/WHLP%20Female%20Genital%20Mutilation.pdf.
24. El-Damanhoury, "The Jewish and Christian View of Female Genital Mutilation," *African Journal of Urology*, 19 (2013), 127–129, http://www.sciencedirect.com/science/article/pii/S1110570413000258.
25. Ellen_Gruenbaum, in "Female Genital Mutilation/Cutting: A Statistical Overview and Exploration of the Dynamics of Change," UNICEF, July 2013, 69–71.
26. MENA Team, "Middle East and North Africa: World Bank Report," *The World Bank*, March 30, 2016, http://www.worldbank.org/en/region/mena.
27. Mail Online Reporter, "How terror attacks in Europe are connected to the seven countries Trump banned from the US: From home-grown killers to camps where fanatics were trained to slaughter," *The Daily Mail*, January 30, 2017, http://www.dailymail.co.uk/news/article-4171120/No-terror-links-FIVE-seven-targeted-countries.html.
28. James B. Comey, "Update on Orlando Terrorism Investigation," Press Briefing on Orlando Mass

390

Shooting, *FBI Headquarters*, Washington, D.C., June 13, 2016, https://www.fbi.gov/news/speeches/update-on-orlando-terrorism-investigation.

29. "Suspect Charged in Shooting of Philadelphia Policeman: Prosecutor," *Reuters — Edition: United States*, January 9, 2016, http://www.reuters.com/article/us-pennsylvania-police-idUSKBN0UM1L820160110.

30. Adam Taylor, "Omar Mateen May Not Have Understood the Difference between ISIS, Al-Qaeda and Hezbollah," *The Washington Post*, June 13, 2016, https://www.washingtonpost.com/news/worldviews/wp/2016/06/13/omar-mateen-may-not-have-understood-the-difference-between-isis-al-qaeda-and-hezbollah.

31. Simon Cottee, "What's the Right Way to Think About Religion and ISIS?" *The Atlantic*, July 12, 2016, https://www.theatlantic.com/international/archive/2016/07/religion-isis-orlando/490958/.

32. Xuan Jiang, X., "Chinese Biology Teaching Assistants' Perception of their English Proficiency: An Exploratory Case Study," *The Qualitative Report*, 19, 1–24, http://nsuworks.nova.edu/tqr/vol19/iss21/2.

33. Annie Gowen, "Muslims Are Dangerous: Myanmar Buddhist Monks Threaten Democracy with Support for Anti-Muslim Laws," *National Post*, November 7, 2015, http://news.nationalpost.com/news/world/muslims-are-dangerous-myanmar-buddhist-monks-threaten-democracy-with-support-for-anti-muslim-laws.

34. Laurie Goodstein, "Muslim Leaders Wage Theological Battle, Stoking ISIS' Anger," *The New York Times*, May 8, 2016, http://www.nytimes.com/2016/05/09/us/

isis-threatens-muslim-preachers-who-are-waging-
theological-battle-online.html?_r=0.

35. John P. Carlin, in "Assistant Attorney General John.
P. Carlin Delivers Remarks on Domestic Terrorism
at an Event Co-sponsored by the Southern Poverty
Law Center and the George Washington University
Center for Cyber and Homeland Security's Program
on extremism," *The United States Department of Justice*,
October 14, 2015, https://www.justice.gov/opa/speech/
assistant-attorney-general-john-p-carlin-delivers-
remarks-domestic-terrorism-event-co.

36. Ibid.

37. Spencer Ackerman, "US Military Says It May Have
Killed More Civilians in Latest Airstrike in Syria,"
The Guardian, July 28, 2016, https://www.theguardian.
com/us-news/2016/jul/28/us-airstrike-more-civilian-
casualties-manbij-syria.

38. Mansur S. Hashim, "What Happened at Manbij?" *The
Daily Star*, July 26, 2016, http://www.thedailystar.net/
op-ed/what-happened-manbij-1259290.

29. Ibid.

40. Ibid.

Chapter 12: The New War Without Rules

1. Raymond Seitz, in "Nobel Lecture: Art, Truth &
Politics," Harold Pinter, *Nobelprize.org*, Nobel Prize in
Literature: 2005, http://www.nobelprize.org/nobel_
prizes/literature/laureates/2005/pinter-lecture-e.
html.

2. Emma Glanfield, "The 1,300-year-old Apocalyptic
Prophecy that Predicted a War between an Islamic

Army and 'Infidel Horde' in Syria is Fuelling ISIS's Brutal Killers," *Daily Mail*, October 9, 2014, http://www.dailymail.co.uk/news/article-2786039/The-1-300-year-old-apocalyptic-prophecy-predicted-war-Islamic-army-infidel-horde-Syria-fuelling-ISIS-s-brutal-killers.html.

3. Ibid.
4. Ian Bremmer, in "Six Steps to Building an ISIS Strategy," *Time Magazine*, December 14, 2015.
5. Patrick Cockburn, "Isis Faces Likely Defeat in Battles Across Iraq and Syria — But What Happens Next?" *The Independent*, June 1, 2016, http://www.commondreams.org/views/2016/06/01/isis-faces-likely-defeat-battles-across-iraq-and-syria-what-happens-next.
6. Erik Ortiz, "Why the Number of U.S. Troops in Iraq's ISIS Fight Keeps Rising," *NBC News*, September 28, 2016, http://www.nbcnews.com/news/military/why-number-u-s-troops-iraq-s-isis-fight-keeps-n656111.
7. Cockburn, "Isis Faces Likely Defeat in Battles Across Iraq and Syria — But What Happens Next?"
8. Nancy Youssef and Michael Weiss, "Big Win Over ISIS Could Mean A New War," *The Daily Beast*, June 6, 2016, http://www.thedailybeast.com/articles/2016/06/01/big-win-over-isis-could-mean-a-new-war.htm.
9. Ibid.
10. Amberin Zaman, "Amnesty International Accuses Kurdish YPG of War Crimes," *Al Monitor*, October 13, 2015, http://www.al-monitor.com/pulse/originals/2015/10/syria-turkey-right-groups-accused-kurds-rojava-of-war-crimes.html.

11. Wladimir van Wilgenburg, "UN Says No Ethnic Cleansing by Kurds in Northern Syria," *ARA News*, March 15, 2017, tp://aranews.net/2017/03/un-says-no-ethnic-cleansing-by-kurds-in-northern-syria/.

12. "UN: YPG and SDF Have Not Committed Ethnic Cleansing,"*Rudaw Middle East*,March 14,2017,http://www.rudaw.net/english/middleeast/syria/14032017.

13. Kamal Sheikho, "Syria Pulse," *Al Monitor*, July 1, 2016, http://www.al-monitor.com/pulse/originals/2016/07/syria-kurdish-forces-liberate-manbij-turkey-border.html.

14. Aron Lund, "Origins of the Syrian Democratic Forces: A Primer," *News Deeply*, January 22, 2016, https://www.newsdeeply.com/syria/articles/2016/01/22/origins-of-the-syrian-democratic-forces-a-primer.

15. Ibid.

16. Ibid.

17. "US to Arm Kurdish fighters Against Daesh in Syria," *Gulf News: Syria*, May 25, 2017. http://gulfnews.com/news/mena/syria/us-to-arm-kurdish-fighters-against-daesh-in-syria-1.2024751.

18. Richard Spencer, "Does Erdogan's Hatred of Assad Run So Deep that he would court terrorists?", *The Telegraph*, June 25, 2015, http://www.telegraph.co.uk/news/worldnews/europe/turkey/11700040/Does-Erdogans-hatred-of-Assad-run-so-deep-that-he-would-court-terrorists.html.

19. Tara McKelvey, "Arming Syrian Rebels: Where the US Went Wrong," *BBC News*, October 10, 2015, http://www.bbc.com/news/magazine-33997408.

20. Michael R. Gordon and Eric Schmitt, "Trump to Arm Syrian Kurds, Even as Turkey Strongly Objects," *The*

New York Times, May 9, 2017, https://www.nytimes.
com/2017/05/09/us/politics/trump-kurds-syria-army.
html.

21. Sergey Lavrov, in "U.S., Russia clinch Syria deal, aim
for truce from Monday," David Brunnstrom and Tom
Miles, *Reuters*, September 10, 2016, http://af.reuters.
com/article/worldNews/idAFKCN11F2IK.

22. Martenson, "Do We Really Want War with Russia?"

23. Anne Barnard and Mark Mazzetti, "United States
Admits Airstrike in Syria, Meant to Hit ISIS, Killed
Syrian Troops," *The New York Times*, September 17,
2016, http://www.nytimes.com/2016/09/18/world/
middleeast/us-airstrike-syrian-troops-isis-russia.html?_
r=0.

24. Martenson, "Do We Really Want War with Russia?"

25. Ibid.

26. Richard Sisk, "Pentagon Admits Airdropped Weapons
Taken by ISIS," *Military.com*, October 23, 2014, http://
www.military.com/daily-news/2014/10/23/pentagon-
admits-airdropped-weapons-taken-by-isis.html.

27. Martenson, "Do We Really Want War with Russia?";
Nicola Nasser, "Israel's Role in Syrian Conflict
Brought into the Open: Direct Support to Al Qaeda
Terrorists," *Global Research*, December 17, 2014, http://
www.globalresearch.ca/israels-role-in-syrian-conflict-
brought-into-the-open-direct-support-to-al-qaeda-
terrorists/5420427.

28. Tusli Gabbard, "Rep. Gabbard: CIA Supporting
Terror-linked Groups in Syria," CNN New with Jack
Tapper, December 7, 2016, http://www.cnn.com/
videos/tv/2016/12/08/the-lead-trump-foreign-policy-
rep-tulsi-gabbard.cnn.

29. Lucas Tomlinson, "Russia Deploys Advanced Anti-Missile System to Syria for the First Time, US Officials Say," *Fox News World*, October 3, 2016, http://www.foxnews.com/world/2016/10/03/putin-suspends-nuclear-deal-with-us-citing-unfriendly-actions.html.

30. Sputnik News, "What's Behind the Failure of the Russia-US Ceasefire Agreement in Syria," *Sputnik International*, September 19, 2016, https://sputniknews.com/politics/201609191045481299-us-russia-syria-deal/.

31. Vyacheslav Matuzov, in Sputnik News, "What's Behind the Failure of the Russia-US Ceasefire Agreement in Syria," *Sputnik International*, September 19, 2016, https://sputniknews.com/politics/201609191045481299-us-russia-syria-deal/.

32. Andranik Migranyan, in Sputnik News, "What's Behind the Failure of the Russia-US Ceasefire Agreement in Syria," *Sputnik International*, September 19, 2016, https://sputniknews.com/politics/201609191045481299-us-russia-syria-deal/.

33. David Usborne, "US Suspends Talks with Russia on Ending Syria Conflict as White House Says 'Nothing More to Talk About,'" *Independent*, October 3, 2016,

34. Zack Beauchamp, "What Syria taught us About Donald Trump," *Vox*, April 13, 2017, http://www.vox.com/world/2017/4/13/15229246/syria-strike-trump-doctrine.

35. Dilanian and Kube, "Syria: White House Warns of 'Actions' if Russia Won't Negotiate."

36. Martenson, "Do We Really Want War with Russia?"

37. Nicola Nasser, "Israel's Role in Syrian Conflict Brought into the Open: Direct Support to Al Qaeda Terrorists," *Global Research*, December 17, 2014, http://www.globalresearch.ca/israels-role-in-syrian-conflict-brought-into-the-open-direct-support-to-al-qaeda-terrorists/5420427.

38. Ban Ki-moon, stated in UNDOF report at the UN, http://www.un.org/en/peacekeeping/missions/undof/background.shtml.

39. Itamar Rabinovich, "Israel's View of the Syrian Crises," *The Saban Center for Middle East Policy at Brookings*, Analysis Paper, Number 28, November 2012, https://www.brookings.edu/wp-content/uploads/2016/06/Rabinovich-web-final.pdf.

40. David Usborne, "US Suspends Talks with Russia on Ending Syria Conflict as White House Says 'Nothing More to Talk About,'" *Independent*, October 3, 2016, http://www.independent.co.uk/news/world/syria-conflict-peace-talks-us-russia-white-house-nothing-to-talk-about-a7343561.html.

41. Margherita Stancati, "U.S. Airstrike Kills 19 at Doctors Without Borders Hospital in Afghanistan," *The Wall Street Journal*, October 3, 2015, https://www.wsj.com/articles/airstrike-kills-doctors-without-borders-staff-in-afghanistan-1443851465.

42. Martenson, "Do We Really Want War with Russia?"

43. Evelyn N. Farkas, "It's Time: The US Should Create A No-Fly Zone, Deliver Aid — and save Syria," *Route Fifty*, August 26, 2016, http://www.defenseone.com/ideas/2016/08/save-syria-create-no-fly-zone-deliver-aid/131079/.

44. MSNBC News: Morning Joe, "Paul Considers National Security Possibles," *MSNBC News*, November 16, 2106, http://www.msnbc.com/morning-joe/watch/paul-considers-national-security-possibles-810287171767.

45. Byman, "Comparing Al-Qaeda and ISIS: Different Goals, Different Targets.

46. "U.S. Warplanes Launch Bombing Campaign on Islamic State in Libya," *Reuters*, August 1, 2016, http://www.reuters.com/article/us-libya-security-idUSKCN10C2NF.

47. John F. Kerry, in "Special Ops Teams Deployed to Libya in Campaign against Islamic State," Carlo Muñoz, *The Washington Times*, May 16, 2016, http://www.washingtontimes.com/news/2016/may/16/us-troops-deployed-to-libya-in-campaign-against-is/.

48. Carlo Muñoz, "Special Ops Teams Deployed to Libya in Campaign against Islamic State," *The Washington Times*, May 16, 2016, http://www.washingtontimes.com/news/2016/may/16/us-troops-deployed-to-libya-in-campaign-against-is.

49. Byman, "Comparing Al-Qaeda and ISIS: Different Goals, Different Targets.

50. Paul Cruickshank, "First on CNN: German Rapper Who Joined ISIS Killed in U.S. Strike, Official Says," *CNN Politics*, October 30, 2015, http://www.cnn.com/2015/10/29/politics/german-isis-rapper-killed-denis-cuspert/.

51. Geoffrey King, "In Blocking Websites, France Abandons Role as Guardian of Free Speech," *Ministere De L'Interieur*, March 24, 2015, http://mediashift.org/2015/03/in-blocking-websites-france-abandons-role-as-guardian-of-free-speech.

52. Kaveh Waddell, "Shutting Down Jihadist Websites Won't Stop Terrorism: Censoring the Web Isn't Just Illiberal — It's Bad Policy," *The Atlantic*, November 24, 2015, http://www.theatlantic.com/technology/archive/2015/11/free-speech-online-is-at-risk-after-paris-attacks/417411.

53. Estelle Massé, in "Shutting Down Jihadist Websites Won't Stop Terrorism: Censoring the Web Isn't Just Illiberal — It's Bad Policy," Kaveh Waddell, *The Atlantic*, November 24, 2015, http://www.theatlantic.com/technology/archive/2015/11/free-speech-online-is-at-risk-after-paris-attacks/417411.

54. Ibid.

55. Tom Wheeler, in "Shutting Down Jihadist Websites Won't Stop Terrorism: Censoring the Web Isn't Just Illiberal — It's Bad Policy," Kaveh Waddell, *The Atlantic*, November 24, 2015, http://www.theatlantic.com/technology/archive/2015/11/free-speech-online-is-at-risk-after-paris-attacks/417411.

56. Waddell, "Shutting Down Jihadist Websites Won't Stop Terrorism: Censoring the Web Isn't Just Illiberal — It's Bad Policy."

57. CBS This Morning, "Hacker Vigilante Group Anonymous Ramps Up Fight Against ISIS Online," *CBS News*, November 19, 2015, http://www.cbsnews.com/news/hacker-group-anonymous-ramps-up-cyber-attacks-on-isis-following-paris-attacks.

58. Anthony Cuthbertson, "Facebook Teams Up with Twitter, YouTube and Microsoft to Crackdown on Terrorist Content," *Newsweek*, December 6, 2016, http://www.newsweek.com/facebook-teams-twitter-crack-down-terrorist-content-528720.

59. Charlie Winter, on BBC News Radio (America), May 6, 2017.

60. Waddell, "Shutting Down Jihadist Websites Won't Stop Terrorism: Censoring the Web Isn't Just Illiberal — It's Bad Policy."

61. Alan Fram, "Why Can People on the Terrorist Watch List Buy Guns, and Other FAQs," *PBS News Hours*, June 14, 2016, http://www.pbs.org/newshour/rundown/why-can-people-on-the-terrorist-watch-list-buy-guns-and-other-faqs/.

62. Christopher Piehota, in "Why Can People on the Terrorist Watch List Buy Guns, and Other FAQs," Alan Fram, *PBS News Hours*, June 14, 2016, http://www.pbs.org/newshour/rundown/why-can-people-on-the-terrorist-watch-list-buy-guns-and-other-faqs/.

63. Sarfo, in "How A Secretive Branch of ISIS Built a Global Network of Killers."

Chapter 13: Some Peripheral Thoughts

1. Nagata, "In Battle to Defang ISIS, United States Targets Its Psychology."

2. Ivana Kottasova and Alanna Petroff, "5 Reasons Russia May Face Worse Times," *CNN Money*, November 10, 2014, http://money.cnn.com/2014/11/10/news/economy/russian-economy-putin/.

3. President Obama, quoted in "Is Russia's Economy Doomed to Collapse?", Sergey Aleksashenko, *The National Interest*, July 6, 2016, http://nationalinterest.org/feature/russias-economy-doomed-collapse-16821; Sergey Aleksashenko, "Is Russia's Economy Doomed to Collapse?", The National Interest, July 6, 2016, http://

nationalinterest.org/feature/russias-economy-doomed-collapse-16821.

4. Andrey Movchan, "How the Sanctions Are Helping Putin," *Politico Magazine*, March 28, 2017, http://www.politico.com/magazine/story/2017/03/how-the-sanctions-are-helping-putin-214963.

5. Martenson, "Do We Really Want War with Russia?"

6. Fred Hof, in "The Startlingly Simple Reason Obama Ignores Syria," Natasha Bertrand and Michael B. Kelley, *Military and Defense: Business Insider*, June 4, 2015, http://www.businessinsider.com/the-startlingly-simple-reason-obama-ignores-syria-2015-6.

7. Willey Wimmer, in "German Politician to Sputnik: 'US Pulling Us into Abyss of War in Middle East,'" *Sputnik International*, January 10, 2016,https://sputniknews.com/politics/201610011045900097-syrian-crisis-us-risks-pulling-europe-into-war/.

8. George Friedman, "The Stratfor Version of What Israel was Doing in Georgia," *The Vineyard of the Saker; A Bird's Eye View of the Vineyard*, September 10, 2008, http://vineyardsaker.blogspot.com/2008/09/stratfor-version-of-what-israel-was.html.

9. Ibid.

10. Aron David Miller, in "Miller: Five Things to Watch for in Israeli-Palestinian Peace process," OpEd, *Newsday*, July 22, 2013, https://fpgroup.foreignpolicy.com/fps-aaron-david-miller-in-newsday-on-israeli-palestinian-peace-talks/.

11. Friedman. "The Stratfor Version of What Israel was Doing in Georgia,"

12. Ibid.

13. Ibid.

14. Ibid.
15. Ibid.
16. Ibid.
17. Ibid.
18. "Profile: Hamas Palestinian movement," *BBC News: Middle East,* July 11, 2014, http://www.bbc.com/news/world-middle-east-13331522.
19. Friedman, "The Stratfor Version of What Israel was Doing in Georgia."
20. Nicola Nasser, "Israel's Role in Syrian Conflict Brought into the Open: Direct Support to Al Qaeda Terrorists," *Global Research,* December 17, 2014, http://www.globalresearch.ca/israels-role-in-syrian-conflict-brought-into-the-open-direct-support-to-al-qaeda-terrorists/5420427.
21. Ibid.
22. Ibid.
23. Netanyahu, in "Israel's Role in Syrian Conflict Brought into the Open: Direct Support to Al Qaeda Terrorists," Nicola Nasser, *Global Research,* December 17, 2014, http://www.globalresearch.ca/israels-role-in-syrian-conflict-brought-into-the-open-direct-support-to-al-qaeda-terrorists/5420427.
24. Peter Beaumont, "Israeli Guidelines Point to Largely Unconstrained Settlement Expansion," *The Guardian,* March 13, 2017. https://www.theguardian.com/world/2017/mar/30/israel-approves-west-bank-settlements-trump-administration.
25. Hamid, "Islamism, the Arab Spring, and the Failure of America's Do-nothing Policy in the Middle East."
26. Ibid.
27. Ibid.

28. Vine, "The United States Has an Empire of Bases in the Middle East — and It's Not Making Anyone Safer."

29. Azadeh Shahshahani and Corinna Mullin, "The Legacy of US Intervention and the Tunisian Revolution: Promises and Challenges One Year In," *Interface*, National University of Ireland Maynooth, 4 (2012): 67–101, http://www.interfacejournal.net/wordpress/wp-content/uploads/2012/05/Interface-4-1-Shahshahani-and-Mullin.pdf.

30. Shane Harris and Matthew M. Aid, "Exclusive: CIA Files Prove America Helped Saddam as He Gassed Iran," *Foreign Policy magazine*, August 26, 2013, http://foreignpolicy.com/2013/08/26/exclusive-cia-files-prove-america-helped-saddam-as-he-gassed-iran/.

31. Ibid.

32. Joost Hiltermann, in "Halabja Poison Gas Attack — Controversies — Allegations of Iranian involvement," Jean Pascal Zanders, http://www.liquisearch.com/halabja_poison_gas_attack/controversies/allegations_of_iranian_involvement.

33. Rob Cooper, "CIA 'helped Saddam Hussein Carry Out Chemical Weapons Attack on Iran' in 1988 Under Ronald Reagan," *Daily Mail.com*, August 26, 2013, http://www.dailymail.co.uk/news/article-2402174/CIA-helped-Saddam-Hussein-make-chemical-weapons-attack-Iran-1988-Ronald-Reagan.html.

34. Harris and Aid, "Exclusive: CIA Files Prove America Helped Saddam as He Gassed Iran."

35. Sophia A. McClennen, "Native Lives Matter: The Protests at Standing Rock Are Not Only About

Environmentalism, They're About Racism," *Salon*, November, 6, 2016, http://www.salon.com/2016/11/06/ nodapl-is-nativelivesmatter-the-protests-at-standing-rock-are-not-about-environmentalism-theyre-about-racism/.

36. Martenson, "Do We Really Want War with Russia?"
37. Mousavian, "Saudi Arabia Is Iran's New National Security Threat."
38. Ibid.
39. Hamid, "Islamism, the Arab Spring, and the Failure of America's Do-nothing Policy in the Middle East."
40. Martenson, "Do We Really Want War with Russia?"
41. Hamid, "Islamism, the Arab Spring, and the Failure of America's Do-nothing Policy in the Middle East"; Vine, "The United States Has an Empire of Bases in the Middle East — and It's Not Making Anyone Safer."
42. Sandra Marker, "Effects of Colonization," *Beyond Intractability*, November 2003, http://www. beyondintractability.org/essay/post-colonial.
43. Ibid.
44. Mohammed Abu-Nimer, "Suspicion of Outsider Interveners," *Beyond Intractability*, Interviewed by, Julian Portilla, 2003, ttp://www.beyondintractability. org/audiodisplay/abunimer-m-2-trust1.
45. Ibid.
46. Hamid, "Islamism, the Arab Spring, and the Failure of America's Do-nothing Policy in the Middle East."
47. Steven Levitsky and Lucan Way, in "Islamism, the Arab Spring, and the Failure of America's Do-nothing Policy in the Middle East," Shadi Hamid, *The*

Atlantic, October 9, 2015, http://www.theatlantic.com/
international/archive/2015/10/middle-east-egypt-us-
policy/40953

48. Pinter, "Nobel Lecture: Art, Truth & Politics."

49. *Iran: A Country Study*, (Washington, D.C. Library of
Congress Cataloging-in-Publication Data, /edited by
Glenn E. Curtis and Eric Hooglund. – 5th ed., 2008),
p. 276. http://www.loc.gov/rr/frd/cs/pdf/CS_Iran.
pdf.

50. Nicola Nasser, "Somalia: New Hotbed of Anti-
Americanism," *Asian Tribune*, March 1, 2007, http://
www.asiantribune.com/index.php?q=node/3958.

51. Charles Lister, in "Senior Qaeda leader is Killed in
Drone Strike," Michael R. Gordon and Eric Schmitt,
The New York Times, March 1, 2017, https://www.
nytimes.com/2017/03/01/world/middleeast/drone-
strike-kills-senior-al-qaeda-leader.html?_r=0.

Appendix

1. Angelpeream, January 31, 2011. "Tree showing the
    relationships among different branches of Islam,"
    Wikimedia Commons–File: Islam branches and schools.
    svg., https://commons.wikimedia.org/wiki/File:Islam_
    branches_and_schools.svg.

    Ahmadiyya, a faction started in India under
    Mirza Ghulam Ahmed, is not included in the chart,
    because many Muslims do not consider them to be
    Muslims.

Review Requested:

If you liked this book, would you please provide
a review at Amazon.com?

CPSIA information can be obtained
at www.ICGtesting.com
Printed in the USA
BVOW03s2306261017
498797BV00001B/6/P